DAILY LIFE IN

THE UNITED STATES, 1960-1990
DECADES OF DISCORD

Recent Titles in
The Greenwood Press "Daily Life Through History" Series

Daily Life in Elizabethan England
Jeffrey L. Singman

Daily Life in Chaucer's England
Jeffrey L. Singman and Will McLean

Daily Life in the Inca Empire
Michael A. Malpass

Daily Life in Maya Civilization
Robert J. Sharer

Daily Life in Victorian England
Sally Mitchell

DAILY LIFE IN

THE UNITED STATES, 1960-1990

DECADES OF DISCORD

MYRON A. MARTY

The Greenwood Press "Daily Life Through History" Series

GREENWOOD PRESS
Westport, Connecticut • London

Library of Congress Cataloging-in-Publication Data

Marty, Myron A.
    Daily life in the United States, 1960–1990 : decades of discord /
Myron A. Marty.
        p.   cm.—(The Greenwood Press "Daily life through history"
series, ISSN 1080–4749)
    Includes bibliographical references and index.
    ISBN 0–313–29554–9 (alk. paper)
        1. United States—Social life and customs—1971– 2. United
States—Social life and customs—1945–1970.   3. United States—
Social conditions—1960–1980.   4. United States—Social
conditions—1980– I. Title. II. Series.
    E169.02.M3547   1997
    973.92—DC21   96–53843

British Library Cataloguing in Publication Data is available.

Library of Congress Catalog Card Number: 96–53843
ISBN: 0–313–29554–9
ISSN: 1080–4749

First published in 1997

Greenwood Press, 88 Post Road West, Westport, CT 06881
An imprint of Greenwood Publishing Group, Inc.

Printed in the United States of America

∞

The paper used in this book complies with the
Permanent Paper Standard issued by the National
Information Standards Organization (Z39.48–1984).

10 9 8 7 6 5 4

FOR

Elizabeth, Jason, Miriam, and Timothy (1976)

Contents

Part III
Times of Adjustment: 1975–1980

Part IV
Crossing the Postmodern Divide: 1981–1990

Preface

Some books treat one subject in detail and depth. In contrast, a first impression of this book must be that it moves quickly through dozens of subjects. Separate books, even shelves of books, exist on almost every subject considered in these pages—as the bibliography bears witness. The purpose here is to give meaning to these subjects by relating them to changes experienced by the American people in their daily lives between 1960 and 1990. The changes both contributed to and reflected the American society's often-discordant transition from modern to postmodern times.

In concentrating on the social history of the 1960s, 1970s, and 1980s, we mark milestones in the nation's politics and economy only as they played a part in people's daily lives. For reference purposes, the framework that follows can be used to connect subjects treated in this book with important events of those decades:

1960	John F. Kennedy defeats Richard Nixon in the presidential election
1961	Bay of Pigs in Cuba is invaded with support by the United States
	Berlin Wall is constructed
1962	Cuban missile crisis occurs
1963	President Kennedy is assassinated; Lyndon Johnson becomes president
1964	First major civil rights bill is enacted

	War on Poverty is declared
	Gulf of Tonkin resolution is enacted
	Johnson is reelected, defeating Barry Goldwater
1965	U.S. involvement in Vietnam is expanded; protests begin
	Great Society legislation is enacted; voting rights bill is enacted
1968	Richard Nixon defeats Hubert Humphrey in the presidential election
	North Vietnam wages "Tet Offensive" in Vietnam
1970	United States invades Cambodia, widening the Vietnam War
	Students are shot at Kent State University and Jackson State University
1972	Nixon visits China, breaking years of hostile isolation
	Watergate break-in takes place
	Nixon is reelected, defeating George McGovern
1973	Cease-fire agreement in Vietnam is signed
	Arab oil embargo occurs
1974	Organization of Petroleum Exporting Countries (OPEC) raises prices sharply, affecting many aspects of American life
	Nixon resigns; Gerald Ford becomes president
	Ford pardons Nixon
1976	Jimmy Carter defeats Gerald Ford in the presidential election
1979–1981	Hostage crisis in Iran lasts for 14 months
1980	Ronald Reagan is elected president, defeating Carter
1981–1983	Tax cuts are enacted; deficit spending increases
1984	Reagan is reelected, defeating Walter Mondale
1988	George Bush is elected president, defeating Michael Dukakis
1989	Berlin Wall falls, symbolizing collapse of communism in Eastern Europe
	Union of Soviet Socialist Republics is dissolved

A work of this nature requires several cautionary comments. First, readers must recognize that this is "contemporary history." In fact, historians are still gathering and sorting evidence concerning the years it treats. But as H. Stuart Hughes has written in *History as Art and as Science,* "*Somebody* must interpret our era to our contemporaries. Somebody must stake out the broad lines of social change and cultural restatement, and he must not be afraid to make predictions or chagrined at being occasionally caught out on a limb."[1] In this book, I am one of those somebodies.

Second, as the historian E. H. Carr has written, historians are "both the product and the conscious or unconscious spokesmen of the society" to which they belong. "We sometimes speak of the course of history," Carr says, "as a 'moving procession.' " The metaphor is fair enough, he acknowledges, provided it does not tempt each historian "to think of himself as an eagle surveying the scene from a lonely crag or as a V.I.P. at the saluting base." Rather, each of us "is just another dim figure trudging along in another part of the procession." As the procession winds along, swerving right and left, sometimes doubling back, our perspectives change. Where we find ourselves in the procession shapes our perspectives on the past.[2] The perspectives I bring to this book reflect decades of work as a teacher and writer and a life of learning, but those perspectives may change as I learn more. Readers, of course, bring their own perspectives to the book's contents. If the book accomplishes its purposes, it will broaden and enrich those perspectives.

Third, the diversity of the people whose lives are portrayed in this book presents a particularly difficult challenge. Drive the length of Halsted Street in Chicago, or ride a subway in New York or Washington, D.C., or observe comings and goings in the Los Angeles airport, or stand on a street corner in any town in America, and you will gain a sense of the difficulty one faces in generalizing about "the American people" and how our daily lives have played out over the past three decades. I have been mindful of this difficulty throughout the book.

With these cautions in mind, I hope that you, the reader, will find a place for yourself in the book's narrative and that it will help you better understand the narratives of your own life.

ACKNOWLEDGMENTS

Most of the research for this book was done in Cowles Library at Drake University. I am grateful to staff members for accommodating my demands on the library's holdings and services and for procuring books and articles from other libraries. Their spirit of collegiality is admirable.

In the early stages, Diana Brodine, a Drake undergraduate, assisted with research. Later, John Facciola, a graduate student at Drake, provided invaluable research assistance. Drake University granted financial support for this assistance, for which I express my gratitude. A grant from Drake's Humanities Center supported acquisition of photographs and permission to publish them.

Critical comments offered by the following Drake colleagues on selected portions of the manuscript helped strengthen it: Dale Berry, Charisse Buising, John Canarina, Michael Cheney, Karen Conner, Philip Levine, Robert Lutz, Kenneth Miller, Michael Myszewski, Vibs Peterson, Richard Schwab, and Dan Spencer. Students in a Spring 1996 seminar on the 1960s, particularly Jerry Hoehle, offered useful ideas and perspectives.

Emily Michie Birch, my editor at Greenwood Press, read drafts of the manuscript at several stages and was always helpful in suggesting ways to improve it. Penny Sippel gave excellent guidance through the production process. My good friend and long-time collaborator, David Kyvig, Professor of History at the University of Akron, provided encouragement while the book was in progress and astute criticisms of the semifinal draft of the manuscript. Thomas Summerhill, a young historian on the faculty at Michigan State University, gave the entire manuscript a careful, perceptive reading and offered many ideas for improving it. Thomas Fischer, formerly dean at Grand View College, also read the manuscript and provided useful perspectives.

Although responsibility for this book is mine alone, it bears a family imprint. My brother, Martin Marty, a distinguished historian at the University of Chicago, who has always been generous in encouraging and supporting my work, was especially helpful in this endeavor. My sister and brother-in-law, Mildred Marty Burger and Gene Burger, elementary school teachers for more than four decades and now community volunteers in Fort Wayne, Indiana, provided many well-informed and insightful comments. Shirley Marty's patience and skill in editing the manuscript at successive stages represented only a small part of her contribution to this book. She continues to be an extraordinary partner in all aspects of my life.

Our children, who were born or came of age during the years treated in the book, all contributed in distinctive ways. Their comments on the manuscript reflected their perspectives on family life in changing times. On other matters, their insights were based on their professional expertise: Miriam is an English professor at Auburn University; Timothy teaches environmental policy at the University of Illinois; Elizabeth is a nurse and community activist; and Jason presently uses his academic background in rhetoric and communication as an entrepreneur in interactive technologies. To these four, who have done so much to enrich the lives of their parents and others, and who mean so much to me, I dedicate this book.

NOTES

1. H. Stuart Hughes, *History as Art and as Science: Twin Vistas on the Past* (New York: Harper & Row, 1964), 107.

2. Edward Hallet Carr, *What Is History?* (New York: Alfred A. Knopf, 1963), 42–43.

Introduction

To some, good times: Times of creativity, free spirits, and
human compassion. For pursuit of ideals, progress, and pros-   **The 1960s**
perity. Times marred, to be sure, by assassinations, cities
burning, and war—but on balance, good times. Times remembered for
improving the lot of the poor, rebuilding cities, battling for civil rights,
and opposing war.

To others, bad times: Times of excess, rebelliousness, destruction, and
despair. Times remembered for tramplings on American traditions and
ideals, loss of face in world affairs, and long-term damage to American
society.

To no one the best of times: Times remembered for war,
Watergate, OPEC, the oil crisis, Three Mile Island, inflation,   **The 1970s**
unemployment, and weakened families.

For some, nonetheless, a time to seek alternatives, keep ideals alive,
change attitudes on the environment, and create new possibilities.

To some, the best of times: Times for restyling the government, undoing damage done in the 1960s, championing free   **The 1980s**
enterprise, reducing inflation, cutting taxes, and building up
the military. Times to remember for the tumbling of the Berlin Wall and
the collapse of the Soviet Union.

To others, the worst of times: Times for ignoring the rights of minorities, assaulting the environment, forgetting the poor, wooing the privi-
leged, building a pie-in-the-sky defense system, and tripling the national
debt.

In 1960, things taken for granted in 1990 were unheard of—
Across the cable television, VCRs, and microwaves, for instance. Ster-
Decades eophonic sound and LP records had grown in popularity
since the 1940s, but audiocassette tapes did not arrive until
1966 and compact disks until 1983.

Huge, cumbersome computers entered the business world in the early
1950s; but not until the Apple II appeared in 1977 with 16K of memory
did personal computers capture attention. Used in schools, they replaced
clumsy mechanical gadgets called learning machines.

Medical practices seemed advanced in 1960, but yet to come were coronary bypass procedures and organ transplants. Gone or drastically reduced were many infectious diseases, but the incidence of sexually
transmitted diseases increased on a per capita basis by 50 percent. By
1990, a new and deadly disease known as AIDS afflicted nearly 200,000
persons.

In 1960, earnings of women across all occupational classes averaged
less than half the earnings of men. By 1990 they had risen to above 70
percent. In three decades, the percentage of women employed outside
the home increased from 31.9 to 58.4 percent.

In 1960, the middle class mused on economist John Kenneth Galbraith's provocative book, *The Affluent Society*, published two years earlier. As he saw it, affluence was not a vision for the future but a reality
of the present. By 1990, middle-class Americans wondered where the
affluence had gone, and growing numbers of have-nots in America wondered why affluence had eluded them.

Not that change was something new. In the three prior
Looking Back decades, the nation battled the Great Depression, fought
and won history's greatest war, and waged a "police ac-
tion" in Korea. The population grew from 123,202,624 in 1930 to
179,323,175 in 1960, a result of the "baby boom" that began in 1946.

Between 1930 and 1960, polio vaccines defeated a terrible scourge and
widespread use of antibiotics put bacterial infections on the defensive.
Television, room air-conditioners, and automatic washers and dryers
changed the way people lived. So did the arrival of jet aircraft, detergents, supermarkets, transistors, synthetic fabrics, and small imported
cars. For new homeowners, something so ordinary in today's world as
latex-based paint was a welcome innovation.

Although changes in the three decades before 1960–1990,
Meanings of and in earlier trios of decades, were notable too, there is
Change something about the character of the changes in more re-
cent times that captures our attention. The positions set
forth in two sharply contrasting books published in 1970 reflect the un-
certainties of the times treated in this book. At one extreme was Charles
Reich's naive but wildly popular *The Greening of America*. Bemoaning
America's plight, Reich described with dismay the destruction of the

environment, the artificiality of work and culture, and the absence of community in America. Submission to uncontrolled technology and reliance on a hypocritical "establishment" had made things worse. These forces were not evil by design, Reich said, but represented logic and science gone awry. In his view, the "counterculture," comprised largely of youth raised by "permissive" parents, would evolve naturally into a nonviolent, loving culture. "Consciousness III," as he called it, would reign in America as the corporate state and the surrounding evils crumbled and fell. Ugliness, competitiveness, and meanness would disappear from daily life. A new moral code stressing love, consideration, and the greening of the landscape would prevail.[1]

The Greening of America proved to be a romantic, mystical footnote on the 1960s rather than a forecast of things to come, but for a fleeting, sensational moment it captured the imagination of one segment of the population as much as it terrified another.

At the other extreme, but with far less immediate impact, political scientist Andrew Hacker raised concerns that anyone studying the decades treated in this book must take into account. In *The End of the American Era*, he contended that Americans in the coming decades would soon "no longer possess that spirit which transforms a people into a citizenry and turns a territory into a nation." We were at a point, he said, when "a preoccupation with private concerns deflects a population from public obligations" and when "the share of energy devoted to common concerns gradually diminishes."

America, Hacker continued, consisted of two classes. In the majority were "productive citizens who have attained respectable incomes and an honorable position in the social scheme of things." The minority were "superfluous people without steady employment or means of support, and looked upon with no small fear and disdain by those who have attained superior status." The majority would see their private lives get better and better, but they would never seem to have enough money for the enjoyments that enticed them. Meanwhile, the public lives of all would decline in quality as things decayed at an accelerating rate. "The list of discomforts," Hacker wrote, "is too familiar to warrant elaboration: overcrowded schools and understaffed hospitals, clogged highways leading to jammed recreation areas, growing slums producing a rising crime rate. When Americans set foot from their homes, they enter an environment that is physically dangerous, aesthetically repellent, and morally disquieting."[2]

Although critics at the time generally dismissed Hacker's thesis as overstated, it helps define this book's purpose. Its purpose is not to treat with unwarranted pessimism the evolution of society in these decades, nor to celebrate with false optimism the promise of times to come. Rather, it tries to make sense of these years by examining changes in the daily lives of the American people and the part the people played in causing these changes.

Four Themes   Given the differences of age, gender, race, education, social class, economic status, and geographical location of the people it treats, every generalization in this book has self-evident exceptions. Nonetheless, it is possible to strike four broad themes. These themes will be treated in each of the four parts in this book, although not necessarily in the same sequence.

The first theme deals with the dailiness of life in such things as family relationships, making a living, spending money, attending school, staying fit and fashionable, attending to daily routines, and being a member of various communities.

The second theme concerns changing patterns and relationships in the American population. In earlier times, despite occasional testings, rising resentments, and growing restlessness, dominant groups kept others in their place and ensured their own "domestic tranquillity." By the early 1960s, however, the civil rights movement assumed a new intensity. Court decisions and legislation enabled African Americans to claim rights long denied them, but they were not alone in getting "out of their place." Women, Native Americans, Hispanics, Asian Americans, members of white ethnic groups, senior citizens, students, homosexuals, persons with disabilities, and members of other groups engaged in activities designed to ensure their rights. Their struggles reflected discord in American society but also showed that discord can promote positive change.

The third theme considers changes wrought by technology in communication, transportation, medicine, food, schools, space exploration, business, and many other aspects of human concern. Technology affected livelihoods, personal routines, family life, politics, and the general shape of American society.

The fourth theme examines cultural transitions in the 1960s, 1970s, and 1980s. These resulted in a gradual displacement of the "modern" standards, temperaments, and behaviors prevailing at mid-century by new ones reflecting conditions gathered together loosely under the term *postmodern*. In modern times, the emphasis was on progress achieved through rational, coherent, single-minded processes. Commitment, predictability, and stability contributed to the progress that was sought and valued. In modern times, organizational structures tended to be centralized and hierarchical, and boundaries within them were clearly drawn. Government was seen as a positive force for change.

In Part IV we will see postmodern conditions expressed through decentralization in economic structures (in business organizations, for example) and fragmentation in social structures; skepticism over government's ability to act constructively for change; short-term rather than long-term commitments; swift changes in ways of doing things; and consumer-driven decision making in business, government, entertainment, and other aspects of life.

Part I considers 1960–1966 as years when modern times flourished and then quickly began to fade. Part II, treating **Organization** 1967–1974, describes challenges to the ideals and values of modern times and examines cultural transitions that began to remake America. Part III portrays 1975–1980 as years of uncertainty when cultural transitions became cultural standoffs and seeds of postmodern times took root. Part IV describes 1981–1990 as years when postmodern conditions broadened their influence. Because the dividing lines between these periods are in most instances artificial, we shall cross them occasionally to maintain the narrative.

NOTES

1. Charles A. Reich, *The Greening of America: How the Youth Revolution Is Trying to Make America Livable* (New York: Random House, 1970).

2. Andrew Hacker, *The End of the American Era* (New York: Atheneum, 1970), 7, 28.

DAILY LIFE IN

THE UNITED STATES, 1960-1990
DECADES OF DISCORD

Part I

Modern Times Flourish and Fade: 1960–1966

The 1960s, like all decades, was the product of the one that preceded it. In later years, the 1950s came to be regarded as an orderly, peaceful, almost languid decade—innocent, even boring. Scenes of the 1950s, mostly captured on black and white film, show neatly dressed men, women, and children enjoying the booming prosperity that followed World War II. Families grew happily and confidently. Prices and inflation remained relatively stable and jobs were plentiful. Persons in authority enjoyed respect, and hierarchical structures were largely free of challenge.

Appearances, however, are misleading. Having been drawn deeply into international affairs by World War II, the United States found itself in the Korean War in the decade's early years. In the middle years national leaders resisted the temptation to intervene in the struggle by the French to retain dominance in Indochina and a crisis surrounding the control of the Suez Canal. Throughout the decade the American people worried about the growing power of the Soviet Union, and fear of communism was a prevailing theme.

Nor was everything as tranquil as it might have seemed at home. Relations between races provide a glimpse of turmoil in the making. The Supreme Court ruled in the 1954 landmark case of Brown v. Board of Education that schools designed to be "separate but equal" were inherently unequal and therefore unconstitutional. The next year the Court said that segregated schools must be eliminated "with all deliberate speed." The South responded with massive resistance, and elsewhere in the country foot dragging on matters of racial justice was common.

The first dramatic civil-rights showdown to capture national attention occurred at Central High School in Little Rock, Arkansas, in the Fall of 1957. Resistance to court-ordered desegregation led by Governor Orville Faubus compelled President Eisenhower to send in paratroopers to escort the black students through the mob attempting to thwart their entry. The case for court orders and civil rights laws was powerful: Blacks were denied educational opportunities and were insecure in everything they did outside their communities. As producers and consumers in the marketplace they were almost always at a disadvantage. Discriminatory barriers kept them in their place socially. Denied voting rights, they were politically powerless. Only by suppressing their sense of moral outrage had they been able to survive, but outrage could not be suppressed forever.

In the 1960s, suppression failed. With the support of many whites, blacks challenged the laws designed to keep them in their place. So did other minority groups, women, and those who saw themselves as disadvantaged. Thus, even as economic progress and stable family life continued into the 1960s, sharper social and political discord emerged. America at the end of the 1960s stood in stark contrast to both the stereotypes and realities of the 1950s.

1

Family Life

Hoping and dreaming came naturally for young couples in
1960. They had begun their families in the "golden age of **Families in**
the American family," as historians call the 1950s. Historian **the 1960s**
Steven Mintz and anthropologist Susan Kellogg, in *Domestic
Revolutions*, treat this decade as a reference point for measuring changes
in family life. Young adults married in unprecedented numbers and at
younger ages than had earlier generations. By 1960, 70 percent of all
women were married by the age of 24, compared with 42 percent twenty
years earlier and around 50 percent thirty years later. They bore more
children at a faster rate. Between 1940 and 1957, the birthrate for third
children in a family doubled and for fourth children tripled.

Perhaps the start-early pattern of young families was a reaction to tales
told by their parents, whose marriages may have been delayed or childbearing limited by separations caused by war or the hardships of the
Great Depression. By the 1950s, Elaine Tyler May notes in *Homeward
Bound*, "childlessness was considered deviant, selfish, and pitiable."
Large families, on the other hand, were an indication of a man's potency
and ability to provide and a woman's success as a professional home-
maker. Popular magazines extolled the virtues of marriage and family
life, and movies and television programs portrayed them as romantic
ideals. Psychologists, educators, journalists, and religious leaders rein-
forced the idea that marriage was necessary for personal well-being. Failure to marry suggested some sort of personal deficiency. In the
prevailing view, according to Mintz and Kellogg, women's primary responsibility was to "manage the house and care for children."[1]

Mother, sister, and brother welcome the new baby's arrival. Snapshots like this one were common in family albums of the 1960s. © *Myron Marty.*

These circumstances, along with state laws limiting the grounds for divorce, explain why families in the baby-boom era stayed together to an extraordinary degree. The divorce rate between 1955 and 1963 fluctuated between 2.1 and 2.3 per 1,000 population. Not since 1940 had it been so low. It rose to 2.5 in 1966 and continued upward until reaching a peak around 5.3 in 1981 before declining gradually.

For many young couples, bringing a child into the world in 1960 was largely a matter of letting nature take its course. Family planning like that done in later years, when two-career marriages demanded it, was not commonly practiced—at least not until several children had already arrived. Besides, reliable means for preventing pregnancies were limited. In 1960, however, the Food and Drug Administration approved the use of the birth control pill—known simply as "the pill." The next year an intrauterine plastic contraceptive device known as the IUD came on the market, providing an alternative method for those wary of the medical side effects of the pill. Also in 1961, the National Council of Churches of Christ, a coalition of mainstream Protestant denominations, gave its blessing to the practice of birth control. Not coincidentally, these events occurred when the number of births had reached an all-time high: The

4,258,000 births in 1960 represented an increase of 80 percent over the 2,360,000 births in 1940.

If young couples *had* given their situation and the world around them an informed look, they could well have judged 1960 to be a good time to add to their family. The father's monthly paycheck may have been on the meager side, but his fringe benefits were probably good and his job was most likely secure. Both unemployment and the rate of inflation were relatively low.

Economist John Kenneth Galbraith was partly right in calling the America in which young families lived the "affluent society." Even with relatively low incomes, many of them managed to scrape together the down payment on a home. Sometimes that required a little help from parents and such things as loans drawn against life insurance policies.

For many families, adding another child in their modest home would leave them physically crowded for a while, but that was also the case for their friends and acquaintances. The typical family, according to the 1960 census, consisted of the father, mother, and three children. Many such families purchased homes in suburban developments, continuing the great migration of the 1950s. Suburbanites outnumbered city dwellers for the first time in 1960, and during the 1960s the margin of difference widened. "Starter" homes for many families were nearly identical to the other homes in their suburban neighborhoods, standing on small treeless lots and having one-car detached garages, but they were a sign of better things ahead.

Nonetheless, had young parents chosen to be uneasy about their families' prospects, they could have found rea-   **Uncertainties** sons for being so. Unreserved optimism about the future of the American economy was unwarranted, for the United States was on the brink of a transition to times in which a growing percentage of jobs would be in lower-paying service sectors. Labor unions, which claimed 35 percent of nonagricultural workers as members at the end of World War II, saw that figure drop to 28.4 percent in 1965 and to 17.5 percent in 1986. Although the number of work stoppages by unions attempting to enforce their demands for increased pay, improved fringe benefits, and better working conditions increased gradually throughout the 1960s, unions were slowly losing their power.

Another concern had to do with threats of nuclear war with Russia, portrayed by some political leaders as a real possibility if not a virtual certainty. Black and yellow signs in public buildings identifying fallout shelters—places to go during a nuclear attack—were reminders of the Soviet threat. So were articles like one in *Life* magazine showing how a family of five could survive in an 8'6" × 12' room equipped with food, a TV set, and exercise equipment. If war never came, the article explained, the children could use the shelter as a hideaway, the father for

poker games, and the mother as a guest room. Despite a "bunker men-
tality," however, most people lived as though prospects that the "cold
war"—the term used to characterize the hostile but peaceful relations
between the United States and the Soviet Union—would turn hot were
slight. Indeed, the Civil Defense Agency, troubled by the difficulty of
stirring interest in building backyard shelters, distributed a pamphlet
entitled *Family Fallout Shelter* to some 22 million homes, but most families
ignored it. Even when a crisis with the Soviet Union occurred in 1962
over placement of missiles in Cuba, the scare was short-lived. There is
evidence, however, of underlying fears in children, who may have taken
seriously the concerns their parents brushed aside. In *Baby Boomers*, for
example, political scientist Paul C. Light cites a 1961 survey of 3,000
elementary school children that showed that "even the youngest baby
boomers worried about the fate of the family and friends in the event of
a nuclear war." Although fears subsided in subsequent years, Light notes
that in a 1979 survey, 50 percent of the sample reported that "advances
in nuclear weaponry affected their thoughts about marriage and the future, and the majority said they were even affected in their daily
thoughts and feelings." This sense of "futurelessness," he muses, "may
haunt the baby boom through life, and may well be the most intense of
the generation's shared experiences."[2]

**The In-Between
Generation**

One can make a good case, as Elaine May does in
Homeward Bound, that the so-called "traditional family," romanticized in recent decades in discussions of
family values, was invented in the baby-boomers'
world. In many ways, May contends,

> the youths of the sixties resembled their grandparents, who came
> of age in the first decades of the twentieth century. Like many of
> their baby-boom grandchildren, the grandparents had challenged
> the sexual norms of their day, pushed the divorce rate up and the
> birthrate down, and created a unique youth culture, complete with
> music, dancing, movies, and other new forms of urban amuse-
> ments. They also behaved in similar ways politically, developing a
> powerful feminist movement, strong grass-roots activism on behalf
> of social justice, and a proliferation of radical movements to chal-
> lenge the status quo.[3]

In the "in-between generation," fathers went off to work in relatively
secure full-time jobs. To make ends meet, some moonlighted or worked
overtime. Wives were homemakers, enjoying conveniences that their
mothers could scarcely have imagined. Families with new babies especially appreciated the automatic washers and dryers introduced in the
1950s, because disposable diapers did not become widely available until

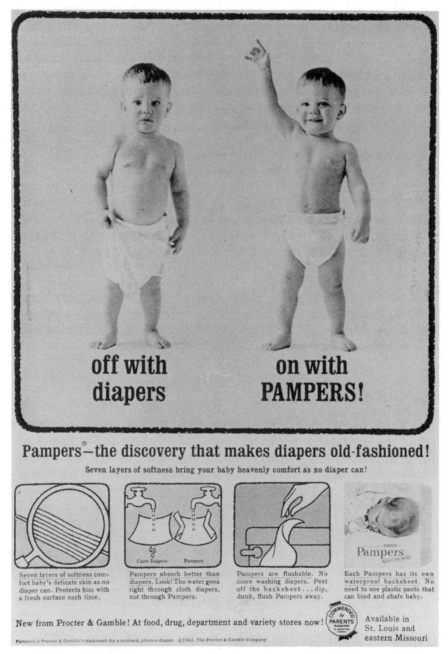

A 1962 advertisement for disposable diapers, then in the test-marketing stage. © *The Procter & Gamble Company. Used by permission.*

around 1970. At 10 cents each when they were test-marketed in 1961 they were too expensive. Diaper service by specialty laundries was also beyond the budget of many families.

By the early 1960s, changes in the patterns described here were already under way. The number of working women with children under age 17 increased from 40 million in 1950 to 58 million in 1960. Discontentment among women would soon encourage further changes; only 10 percent of the women who responded to a survey in 1962 said they wanted their daughters' lives to be the same as the ones they had lived.

Home Life   Neighborhoods teemed with children during out-of-school hours. To the playtime repertory of earlier years—swing sets, sandboxes, tricycles, bicycles, balls, and bats—parents added Frisbees, hula hoops, and Barbie dolls, plastic playthings introduced in 1957, 1958, and 1959. For many, playtime gave way to Brownies and Cub-pack meetings, Girl Scout or Boy Scout or 4-H activities, Little League (for boys), and after-school religious instruction and church choir practice. That meant lots of driving for mothers; in families with only one car, negotiating carpools and juggling schedules became an art.

The Place and Power of Television   Television's *Captain Kangaroo* and the characters around him, along with such programs as *Romper Room*, entertained and taught preschoolers during the morning hours, giving their mothers a chance to get the house in order for the day. In the evening, viewers from coast to coast watched such family shows as *Lassie*, *The Red Skelton Show*, *Andy Griffith*, and the *Beverly Hillbillies*, all of which portrayed what were intended to be wholesome (if somewhat zany) versions of the middle-class American dream. Later in the evening the parents might take in *Playhouse 90*, a weekly drama telecast live, or *The Untouchables*, a crime-solver starring Robert Stack. Maybe they also watched the most popular shows: *Gunsmoke*, *Have Gun Will Travel*, and *Rawhide*, all depicting the violence ingrained in romanticized views of the American West. At the end of the day the parents probably listened in on Jack Paar's conversations with his guests. His show was the forerunner of the less serious shows hosted later by Johnny Carson, Jay Leno, and David Letterman. Televised athletics contests, popular with broadcasters because of their low production costs, claimed weekend time, though not nearly so much as after the arrival of cable television.

Just as important in depicting American ideals and representing common concerns were the commercials that interrupted and paid for the programs. Knowing that nearly 90 percent of American households owned at least one TV set, advertising agencies saw television as an ideal medium for creating consumer needs. Advertising had been visible for many years on billboards and radios, and in magazines; but one could ignore printed advertisements, and radios were easy to tune out or turn off. Television, though, gave advertisers almost uninterrupted access to Americans of all ages, races, and social classes in all parts of the country. Thus it became the most powerful force in creating a national culture of consumerism, that is, a culture that catered to consumers' tastes.

In the 1960s, advertisers presented goods and services in idealized versions of family and community life. Using phrases like *new and improved*, they portrayed conveniences as necessities and wants as needs. Gratification deferred, advertising implied, is gratification denied. Encouraging this culture of consumerism while stressing the American values of hard work, discipline, patience, and responsibility, television sent mixed messages that contributed to intergenerational conflict later in the decade. As many older folks came to accept the culture of consumerism, the conflict became less severe.

The national culture transmitted by network television became part of the local culture the next day. Programs became the subject of conversations among friends, neighbors, and workers across the country. In 1950, with only 3 percent of farm families owning television sets, that was not the case; but by 1960 the figure had risen to 80 percent. Overall, 87 percent of homes in America had television sets by 1960. By 1962, *TV Guide* had become the nation's largest-selling weekly magazine, with its advertising revenue growing by millions of dollars each year.

Television's role in daily life was far-reaching. It influenced the way individuals and families spent their days. It determined how they arranged their schedules, thought about current issues, spent their money, found subjects for conversation, and chose books to read. It influenced the use of rooms in their homes and the arrangement of furniture. It diverted attention from other people in the room, stifling conversation, and it led to the invention of precooked TV dinners and TV trays for serving them.

Acknowledging in 1961 that television "possesses the most powerful voice in America," Newton Minow, chairman of the Federal Communications Commission, claimed that the television industry had "an inescapable duty to **Criticism of Television** make that voice ring with intelligence and leadership." What it offered, though, was a "vast wasteland." What did Americans see as they looked at their sets? "A procession of game shows, violence, audience participation shows, formula comedies about totally unbelievable families, blood and thunder, mayhem, violence, sadism, murder, Western badmen, Western good men, private eyes, gangsters, more violence and cartoons. And, endlessly, commercials—many screaming, cajoling, and offending. And most of all, boredom."[4]

In addition to watching television, families enjoyed popular
Other   and classical music on hi-fi records or FM radio in stereo-
Diversions   phonic sound, innovations of the 1950s. If they were lucky,
                     they might do so in the comfort of an air-conditioned room,
although the roar and rattle of the huge new unit in the window might
interfere with listening. Suburban homes provided fathers with basements or garages for workshops, possibly equipped with power tools. If
sewing and mending clothes consumed less time than in the past, knit-
ting and needlepoint remained outlets for women's creativity.

Not that families were lacking for things to do outside the home. So
busy were they that grabbing a bite to eat, on the run, was something
they *had* to do. Ray Kroc knew that when he began to open McDonald's
restaurants on busy thoroughfares in cities and towns everywhere. The
more than 100 stores in his chain in 1960 were but a sign of things to
come. They were a sign, too, that the accelerating pace and multiple
involvements of family members would shrink the number of families
who gathered around the table at mealtime. But family togetherness persisted. In the summer, many families made vacation travel affordable by
camping in tents or pop-up trailers, often in state and national parks.
National recreation areas in particular, gained new popularity: visits increased from 33 million in 1950 to 79 million in 1960 and 121 million by
1965, on their way to 258 million in 1990.

NOTES

1. Steven Mintz and Susan Kellogg, *Domestic Revolutions: A Social History of
American Family Life* (New York: Free Press, 1988), 179, 181; Elaine Tyler May,
Homeward Bound: American Families in the Cold War Era (New York: Basic Books,
1988), 139, 159.

2. Paul C. Light, *Baby Boomers* (New York: W. W. Norton, 1988), 140–43.

3. May, *Homeward Bound*, 9.

4. Newton Minow, Address to the National Association of Broadcasters, May
9, 1961; quoted in Diane Ravitch, ed., *The American Reader: Words That Moved a
Nation* (New York: HarperCollins, 1990), 318–20.

2

Changing Population Patterns

The daily lives of most Americans may not seem to have
been directly affected by what came to be known as the   Civil Rights
unrest of the 1960s, but the changes wrought by protests   for African
in those years rippled across America. The most striking   Americans
changes were the fruits of the civil rights movement, which
in its modern form traced its origins at least as far back as World War
II. At that time the cruel irony of asking African Americans to risk their
lives for a country that denied them constitutionally guaranteed rights
became glaringly obvious. Several Supreme Court decisions set prece-
dents for the 1954 landmark case of *Brown v. Board of Education.* In *Brown*
the Court ruled that schools designed to be "separate but equal" were
inherently unequal and therefore unconstitutional.

Armed with the conviction that the Supreme Court's decision outlawing "separate but equal" schools extended to other aspects of their lives,
and frustrated by resistance to calls for change, African American activists adopted a strategy that at first baffled those seeking to thwart them:
They defied laws that denied them rights but refused to defend
themselves against physical and verbal attacks. On February 1, 1960, four
students at North Carolina A&T College in Greeensboro took the first
nonviolent action of the 1960s. These students, the 66 who joined them
the next day, the 100 the next, and the 1,000 by the end of the week, sat
down at a "whites only" lunch counter in a Woolworth's store in Greensboro. The Greensboro "coffee party," which historian William Chafe says
"takes its place alongside the Boston Tea Party as an event symbolizing

The "sit-in" by Joseph McNeil, Franklin McCain, Billy Smith, and Clarence Henderson at the lunch counter of the Woolworth store in Greensboro, North Carolina, on February 1, 1960, launched a new phase in the nonviolent civil rights movement. *UPI/CORBIS-BETTMANN.*

a new revolutionary era," infuriated segregationists.[1] Television cameras captured the segregationists' resistance and broadcast it nationwide, thereby creating support for blacks who were ready to take further direct actions.

More Protests The practice of holding sit-ins spread, and before the end of the year an estimated 70,000 activists put pressure on white business leaders by challenging segregation laws and practices in more than 150 cities. In 1961 came Freedom Rides, organized by James Farmer of the Congress on Racial Equality (CORE). The Freedom Riders, small interracial groups who traveled by public buses into the Deep South to test whether federal court orders on integration of bus depots were being honored, encountered hostile and often brutal treatment. Again, television cameras brought the bloody scenes into homes throughout America. More important, the spreading outrage provoked by those scenes forced the federal government to take sides, and there was clearly only one side it could take.

In 1962 the nation watched the violence that erupted when James Meredith, a black Mississippian, enrolled at his state's university under a court order to admit him. The next year federal marshals led black students past Governor George Wallace as he attempted to block the entrance to the University of Alabama. Television carried that, too, across the nation. With each such incident, awareness of the civil rights movement reached into the lives of viewers. Children, particularly, seemed to be impressed by what they saw. "They can do what they want to," a former principal of a southern black elementary school remarked, "but millions of little eyes are watching, and they're making plans."[2]

Along with the Freedom Rides came protests and marches led by Martin Luther King, Jr., and the Southern Christian Leadership Conference in Birmingham and other cities in the South. Stressing nonviolence as essential in the practice of civil disobedience, efforts led by King laid the groundwork for the now-famous March on Washington in 1963. At that event, King spoke from the steps of the Lincoln Memorial to a crowd of 250,000. Carried by television to millions more—perhaps the first civil rights demonstration to capture the attention of the entire nation—Dr. King departed from his prepared text to speak of his "dream." "I have a dream," he said, "that one day this nation will rise up and live out the true meaning of its creed: 'We hold these truths to be self-evident; that all men are created equal.' " Rhythmically he intoned the next seven sentences with "I have a dream." Two sentences said simply: "I have a dream today." With the audience stirred by his eloquence and passion, King urged the nation to "let freedom ring." Eight times he repeated that line, concluding,

> When we let freedom ring, when we let it ring from every village and every hamlet, from every state and every city, we will be able to speed up that day when all of God's children, black men and white men, Jews and Gentiles, Protestants and Catholics, will be able to join hands and sing in the words of the old Negro spiritual, "Free at last! Free at last! Thank God almighty, we are free at last!"[3]

Just a month later, the Sunday-morning bombing of a church in Birmingham in which four black girls were killed was a sobering reminder that not everyone shared King's dream.

Despite the resistance that acts like the church bombing exemplified, modern America seemed ready for some of the changes demanded by civil rights leaders. In fact, the resistance helped build momentum for enactment of a civil rights law in 1964 that, among other things, prohibited racial discrimination in public accommodations in any business engaged in interstate commerce and in most employment situations. It soon became apparent that the Democratic Party's position on civil rights would cause it to lose its dominance in what had been known as the "Solid South" since the Civil War. Indeed, when Lyndon Johnson signed the 1964 Civil Rights Act he remarked to an aide: "I think we just delivered the

Ready for Change?

Surrounded by members of Congress, President Lyndon Johnson hands a pen to Martin Luther King, Jr. after signing the 1964 Civil Rights Act, July 2, 1964. Women benefited substantially from the act and played important roles in passing it, but none appears in the picture. *Cecil Stoughton, LBJ Library Collection.*

South to the Republican Party for a long time to come."[4] By the time of the presidential election that year, the phenomenon known as white backlash came into evidence not only in the South but in all quarters of America. Johnson's opponent, Senator Barry Goldwater of Arizona, had voted against the Civil Rights Act; although he lost the election, his followers adhered to his convictions on civil rights in rebuilding the Republican Party.

In 1965, responding to the leadership of President Johnson (himself a southerner), Congress passed the Voting Rights Act aimed at removing barriers that had long kept African Americans out of polling places, particularly in the South. For decades thereafter the new voters generally supported the Democratic Party, although not in sufficient numbers to offset the loss of white voters. Through their actions on racial matters, both parties prompted ordinary citizens to ask themselves where they stood on matters of race, access to jobs, housing, and social opportunity. As voters answered these questions, both parties gained and lost supporters in regions outside the South as well as in it, although party affiliation continued to rest on much more than one's position on racial issues.

Laws and court decisions were not alone in pushing and pulling the American people one way or another on racial matters. Two other things came into play: violent behavior and increasingly militant language by blacks. The most ex- **Growing Tensions** treme example of the former was the riot in Watts, a black ghetto in Los Angeles. Just five days after President Johnson signed the Voting Rights Act, on August 11, 1965, a confrontation between white police and a black man stopped for a traffic violation sparked a six-day riot. When it was over, 34 people were dead, 900 were injured, 4,000 were under arrest, and property damage amounted to more than $30 million. Despite the presence of 1,500 police officers and 14,000 national guardsmen, rioters destroyed entire city blocks. Seething black resentment of white police (in the 98 percent black Watts district, 200 of the 205 police officers were white) had set the stage for the riot, but the rioters lost whatever sympathies they might have inspired among whites, both in Watts and elsewhere, by chanting "Burn, baby, burn!" Riots in other cities, frequently sparked by confrontations between blacks and police, blurred the sense of progress that the court decisions and new laws had seemed to create.

The militant language of some black leaders dismayed many Americans, both white and black. Speeches by Malcolm X, a preacher formerly associated with the Nation of Islam, struck many as hateful and scornful of whites for the treatment of his people through the years. By stressing racial pride and dignity, he inspired his followers in ways whites had difficulty understanding. The assassination of Malcolm X by Black Muslims, followers of Elijah Mohammed, on February 21, 1965, did not silence his message.

Advocates of Black Power, led by Stokely Carmichael and the Student Nonviolent Coordinating Committee (SNCC, known as Snick), used language just as harsh. Working closely with the powerless and disadvantaged victims of discrimination, they understood the daily suffering of members of their race. As were the followers of Malcolm X, the activists in SNCC were driven by deep cynicism about the honesty and good faith of America's white leaders and the entire country's white population.

The division between Stokely Carmichael and those who stood with him on one side, and Martin Luther King, Jr. and his followers on the other, became starkly clear in June 1966. James Meredith was again a key figure in an event that once more drew Americans to their television sets. While he marched alone across Mississippi to give blacks the confidence to register and vote, a shotgun fired by an assassin from roadside bushes cut him down, planting sixty pellets in his body. With Meredith's consent, civil rights groups converged on the scene to complete the march.

At rallies along the way King continued to advocate nonviolence, but Carmichael spoke more militantly. Finally, in Canton, Mississippi, he exhorted: "the only way we are going to stop them from whuppin' us is to take over. We've been saying freedom for six years and we ain't got nothin'. . . . The time for running has come to an end. . . . Black Power. It's time we stand up and take over; move on over [Whitey] or we'll move on over you." "Black Power!" chanted the crowd. "Black Power! Black Power!"[5] The call for Black Power shattered the facade of unity among civil rights leaders and their followers. Martin Luther King, Jr. wanted yet to preserve a national coalition of blacks and whites committed to the cause of civil rights, but Stokely Carmichael refused to limit his efforts to stir black people to action.

Other Minority Groups

African Americans were not the only minority group seeking equal rights during the 1950s and 1960s. Puerto Ricans living in the United States, Mexican Americans, and others of Spanish descent had similar economic, political, social, and moral reasons to protest. However, their efforts to improve their condition during the 1950s had had little effect. The same was true of Native Americans, the poorest and probably the most ignored minority. During the 1960s, the civil rights movement made the plight of these minorities better known. Although their organizations attempted strategies similar to those used by African Americans, the results were meager. Only the work of Cesar Chavez, founder of the United Farm Workers, who gained support from Roman Catholics across the nation, drew much attention. Otherwise, the efforts of nonblack minorities were seen as peripheral to those of their black counterparts. Their protests gained attention locally, but because the national news media did not carry reports of their protests, their effect on ordinary Americans was less noticeable.

Women and the Civil Rights Movement

Women in the 1960s seeking to claim certain rights could trace the origins of their efforts as far back as the 1848 convention at Seneca Falls, New York, led by Elizabeth Cady Stanton. That convention had adopted a Declaration of Sentiments and Resolutions modeled on the nation's Declaration of Independence. "We hold these truths to be self-evident," they asserted, "that all men and women are created equal." It took more than seventy years for the sentiments to be translated into the right to vote, accomplished in 1920 with the adoption of the Nineteenth Amendment.

If women expected their votes to bring swift changes in their lives, they had few reasons to cheer. They benefited from employment opportunities caused by the impact of World War II, but most of those opportunities evaporated in the postwar years. After the war women were expected to step aside for returning veterans who wished to reclaim jobs; as a result, most women assumed roles that were just as restricted as before the war.

Two events in 1963 demonstrated women's plight and frustrations. First, a report on sex discrimination by the Presidential Commission on Women, appointed by President Kennedy in 1961, documented inequities women experienced in the workplace, and showed them to be similar to those suffered by minority groups. The Commission's findings revealed, among other things, that only 7 percent of the nation's doctors and fewer than 4 percent of its lawyers were women. While acknowledging the larger role married women played in the economy, the Commission nonetheless asserted that a woman's primary role was as mother and wife, and it recommended special training of young women for marriage and motherhood. It also expressed opposition to an equal rights amendment, maintaining that the Fourteenth Amendment sufficiently protected women's equality of opportunity. This Amendment provides that States may not "deprive any person of life, liberty, or property, without due process of law; nor deny an person within its jurisdiction the equal protection of the laws."

From today's perspective the Commission's recommendations seem unaccountably misdirected, but at least the federal government was looking more closely than before at the place of women in society. So were state governments. By 1967, all fifty states had set up commissions on the status of women. One tangible consequence of the Commission's recommendations was the enactment of the Equal Pay Act in 1963, prescribing that women must receive pay equal to that of men when they performed comparable work—the first federal legislation in American history to prohibit discrimination based on sex. Changes were slow in coming, however, for in 1995 the average pay of women remained 31 percent below that of men.

Commission reports and legislation are typically passionless, noticed by a few and then forgotten. But noticed by many and long remembered was the second event of 1963: publication of *The Feminine Mystique*, by Betty Friedan. The problem the book addressed, wrote Friedan,

The Feminine Mystique

> lay buried, unspoken, for many years in the minds of American women. It was a strange stirring, a sense of dissatisfaction, a yearning that women suffered in the middle of the twentieth century in the United States. Each suburban wife struggled with it alone. As she made the beds, shopped for groceries, matched slipcover material, ate peanut butter sandwiches with her children, chauffeured Cub Scouts and Brownies, lay beside her husband at night—she was afraid to ask even of herself the silent question—"Is this all?"[6]

According to notions of the times, healthy and educated women were supposed to find fulfillment in housekeeping presumed to be made drudgery-free by new household gadgetry, in childbirth considered to be danger-free, and in living only for their husbands and children. What more could women who had everything possibly yearn and struggle for? What could be their problem? It was a problem, Friedan said, that had no name but had clear symptoms: a sense of emptiness, frustration, dissatisfaction, resentment. Commercials featuring pretty housewives and magazine articles with upbeat essays on childbearing and childrearing could not conceal this problem, for it was too widely shared. The problem was not shared, of course, by working-class women who had been employed outside the home for years, but they were not the women at whom Friedan directed her message.

No doubt the biggest effect of *The Feminine Mystique* was that middle-class women discovered that they were not alone in feeling trapped. But what could they do? "When society asks so little of women," Friedan wrote, "every woman has to listen to her own inner voice to find her identity in this changing world. She must create, out of her own needs and abilities, a new life plan, fitting in the love and children and home that have defined femininity in the past with the work toward a greater purpose that shapes the future."[7]

It was the personal powerlessness of suburban domesticity that took its toll on the women for whom Friedan spoke so eloquently. Dealing with the problems that touched each woman who felt trapped required personal initiative more than political action, at least for a time. "If we continue to produce millions of young mothers who stop their growth and education short of identity, without a strong core of human values to pass on to their children, we are committing, quite simply, genocide, starting with the mass burial of American women and ending with the progressive dehumanization of their sons and daughters."[8]

The Feminine Mystique caused many women to examine their lot and discuss it with others. The fact that some men also found the book helpful in connecting the emerging concerns of women with those of racial minorities made it plausible to include women's rights in civil rights legislation. Simultaneously, the book opened a debate concerning parental responsibilities in childrearing and provision of day care for children of working mothers. The debate concerned concrete rather than abstract matters, since the numbers of married women and young mothers in the work force had been increasing for several decades, and there was no doubt that these trends would continue. Interestingly, even though Friedan was attacked by defenders of the status quo as a "women's libber," she did not explicitly call for equality, nor did she advocate anything called women's liberation or feminism.

Another boost to the women's movement occurred in a quirky way. Shortly before the bill leading to enactment of the 1964 Civil Rights Act went to the floor of the House of Representatives, Howard Smith, the 80-year-old chairman **Civil Rights for Women** of the powerful Rules Committee, surprised everyone: He proposed inserting the word sex into the list of grounds on which discrimination would be prohibited by the Act, thus making its provisions applicable to women. He thought this would kill the bill by making it unpalatable to a majority in the House. Emmanuel Celler, the 75-year-old chairman of the Judiciary Committee, reacted with outrage. He feared that granting women equal rights would deprive them of health and safety protections provided by other laws. He also believed the amendment would kill the bill. But pressure from women's groups and spirited work by a bipartisan coalition of congresswomen—three Republicans and two Democrats—caught Smith in his own trap. President Johnson had no choice but to offer his support for the amendment, and the kill-the-bill ploy failed. The result was a law that became the single most important force in guaranteeing women equal rights: the 1964 Civil Rights Act.

Recognizing that sensitivity to their plight and enactment of laws prohibiting discrimination were not enough to accomplish significant changes in their status, like- **National Organization for Women** minded women began in 1964 to organize for concerted action. Two years later they established the National Organization for Women (NOW), the first of a number of organizations to become increasingly vocal in the cause of equal rights for women. Not by any measure was NOW the most militant.

Despite new laws and new activism on behalf of women, the place of women in families remained much the same. **How Much Change?** The majority of married, middle-class women were full-time homemakers, and those who by necessity or choice were employed outside the home arranged their lives around their duties in the home. Women generally entered the work force at later ages than men, after fulfilling their primary childrearing roles, and fewer than half of those who worked outside the home held full-time, year-around jobs. Thus their jobs, often taken simply as a way of adding to their families' income, did little to increase their sense of autonomy within the family, and their opportunities for advancing in the workplace were limited.

Challenges to the status quo were many in the early 1960s: There was an uneasy sense, carried over from the **Context for Activism** 1950s, that America's national purpose was not clear. The civil rights movement was gaining in intensity. A "nation within a nation"—that is, the postwar baby boomers—represented a bulge in the population profile, with uncertain implications. The growing college-age population, and the increasing proportion of young men and women among them who were able to attend college, led to expansion of institutions across the nation. It is not surprising, therefore, that students along with racial minorities and women sought to establish for themselves a different place in the American mosaic. Moreover, folk and rock music, along with the use of drugs that helped shape the youth culture, reflected a sense of alienation that made it natural for many students to join in causes that challenged institutions judged to be part of an ill-defined "establishment."

Campus Protests   Students in colleges and universities, inspired by the strategies and tactics of the civil rights movement and stirred by opposition to U.S. engagement in the war in Vietnam, began to protest the direction in which they saw their colleges and universities moving. Restlessness had been growing since a handful of activists at the University of Michigan organized the Students for a Democratic Society (SDS) and set forth their ideology in *The Port Huron Statement* in 1962. The statement criticized racial injustice, cold war policies, grossly inequitable distribution of wealth, exploitation of natural resources, and the danger of nuclear war, among other things. Nonetheless, it conveyed optimism that the problems it identified could be corrected, given American ideals and the promise of democracy.

While mainstream media and the general public initially ignored the SDS, the debates that followed in the wake of the Society's *Statement* soon gained the attention of sufficient numbers of Americans, including college students, to force another look at the issues it raised, if not at the document itself. As ordinary folks mulled the issues inspiring the turmoil, divisions began to develop. On one side were those sympathetic to the concerns raised by the students. They might not have endorsed specific statements or actions, and they might have thought the students' strategies ill-advised, but they found themselves congenial to the students' goals. On the other side were many who attacked the *Statement* and those sympathetic to it by shouting, "America—Love it or Leave it" or, more likely, posting these words on their automobile bumpers. Some would characterize the growing national debate as a division between flag wavers and flag burners, although few flags were burned. Where SDS-inspired protests were laced with obscenities and accompanied by mob scenes and violence, the SDS itself became an issue.

The University of California at Berkeley became the first campus battleground. When the administration there attempted to placate conservative members of its Board of Regents by clamping down on political activism, the students insisted that their freedom of speech had been taken away. To protest the administration's decision to deny the use of a 26-foot strip of campus land that had long been a place for gathering signatures and funds for political and social causes, they organized a "free speech" demonstration. Disturbances that followed between September 1964 and January 1965 tore the Berkeley campus apart and established the pattern for turmoil on other campuses.

The sequence of events on campuses experiencing turmoil varied, but rallies, suspensions, demonstrations, arrests, sit-ins, and police intervention were regular occurrences that grew increasingly intense. Students protested large classes, classes taught by graduate assistants, the impersonality of relationships with professors, and the way bureaucratic machines seemed to control the institution as well as the issues beyond the campus that disturbed them. Despite occasional pushing, shoving, and name-calling, the student demonstrations remained nonviolent for a while; but that changed when concern over the war in Vietnam increased following the bombing raids on North Vietnam in 1965 and the sending of large numbers of troops into combat.

Several responses to campus disturbances had long-lasting effects. On the constructive side, institutions took a close look at their operations, particularly their curricula, and made them more responsive to student interests and concerns. At Berkeley, for example, a select committee chaired by Charles Muscatine, an English professor, went to work in March 1965 and in less than a year produced a final report with forty-two recommendations. Many of these recommendations reflected the judgment that student concerns were legitimate, and most were approved and implemented by the University. More problematic, governors, legislatures, and the citizenry took sides in the campus debates, spreading the issues across society. In California, the Berkeley events helped gain national prominence for Ronald Reagan, who won the governorship in 1966 by campaigning against the University. He called for a crackdown on radicals and questioned the concept of free tuition for students at state colleges and universities.

Who were these radicals? A study conducted by sociologist Richard Flacks, a scholar sympathetic to their cause, found that they frequently were intelligent children of highly educated parents. They had grown up in professional households and responded to pressures for success with high academic achievement. When they reached college, they readily assumed the roles of questioners and activists who were susceptible to the appeal of radicals.[9] Psychologist Kenneth Kenniston called the young rebels "psychological adults" but "sociological children." Coming from affluent families, they had the freedom and desire to postpone assuming the social roles they knew would be waiting for them. About careers they could worry later. Now their task was to change the world.[10] The nature of the war in Vietnam and the resistance faced by the civil rights movement challenged their ideals. They were not extraordinary Americans. Rather, they were ordinary Americans in extraordinary times

Mario Savio addresses supporters in the Free Speech Movement at Sproul Plaza at the University of California, Berkeley, October 1, 1964. *Lon Wilson, Bancroft Library. Used by permission.*

and places. The parents of many of these students were pulled in two directions. They may have understood where their kids "were coming from," to use a phrase of the day. But their own social and economic roles (possibly profitable ones in military or government service or in a defense-related industry) prevented these parents from offering support.

As the civil rights movement became more strident and protests on campuses increased in intensity, a new self- **Backlash** consciousness drew together members of ethnic groups— Poles, Czechs, and Italians, for example. As second- and third-generation Americans they had struggled to gain job security, own a home, and give their children educational opportunities. The impatience of blacks, who in their judgment wanted change to occur overnight, created uncertainty and fear, bringing about a sharp reversal in their attitudes toward blacks' quests for justice. In the mid-1960s, the number of white Americans who believed blacks were demanding too much too fast rose dramatically. This was a typical response to change by groups just one step higher on the economic and social ladder than those whom they resented.

Economic insecurity among "middle Americans"—that is, blue-collar workers, lower-level bureaucrats and professionals, and white-collar workers in nonmanagement positions—contributed to growing resentment against the civil rights movement, the women's movement, and student protests. The urban riots and student protests that middle Americans witnessed on television and read about in the newspapers convinced them that the foundations of America were under siege. The values, traditions, and personal security of their daily lives seemed in danger.

They were not the only ones scornful of the young radicals. Among intellectuals the radicals eventually drew such labels as "new barbarians" and "twentieth-century Luddites" (i.e., protesters against technological progress, after Ned Ludd, an English laborer who was supposed to have destroyed weaving equipment around 1780). By the 1970s, even those sympathetic with the radicals' goals charged them with being infatuated with "finding themselves," leading to a "culture of narcissism." Showdowns between the sides in the great national debate came later, but the seeds of discord were germinating before the end of 1966.

NOTES

1. William H. Chafe, *The Unfinished Journey: America since World War II*, 3d ed. (New York: Oxford University Press, 1995), 168.

2. Samuel Ethridge, quoted by Myron Marty in "Millions of Little Eyes Are Watching," *Concepts*, Spring 1975, 29.

3. Quoted in Diane Ravitch, ed., *The American Reader: Words That Moved a*

Nation (New York: HarperCollins, 1990), 333–34. The printed text differs slightly from the recorded version of the speech.

4. Quoted in David Farber, *The Age of Great Dreams: America in the 1960s* (New York: Hill and Wang, 1994), 98.

5. Chafe, *The Unfinished Journey*, 317–18.

6. Betty Friedan, *The Feminine Mystique* (New York: Norton, 1963), 15.

7. Ibid., 338.

8. Ibid., 364.

9. Quoted in Helen Lefkowitz Horowitz, *Campus Life* (New York: Alfred A. Knopf, 1987), 223, 226.

10. Cited in Norman L. Rosenberg and Emily S. Rosenberg, *In Our Times: America since World War II*, 5th ed. (Englewood Cliffs, N.J., 1995), 168–69.

3

Private and Public Lives

Individuals and families move freely between the private and the public spheres of life. What happens in the public sphere almost certainly affects conditions in the private sphere, and what one does in private shapes what goes on beyond it. Boundaries between the private and the public spheres of daily life are not readily visible or clearly fixed. Nevertheless, to understand changes in daily life it is useful to have a sense of the general character of both.

In their largely private lives, people establish and maintain family relationships, make a living, enjoy personal **Private Lives** security, strive for personal growth and advancement through education, have religious beliefs and practices, appreciate the arts, participate in recreational and cultural activities, maintain their health, buy goods and services, eat and drink at home and in restaurants and bars—among other things. Here people act with considerable autonomy and independence, although they are often limited by laws and customs.

For many people in the 1960s, their lives were private almost to the point of isolation. Even though they were surrounded by others, the others were strangers. Geographical mobility meant that many individuals lived apart from their extended families. Suburban developments did little to foster neighborliness or community spirit. As air conditioning became more common, people stayed indoors in the summertime, reducing over-the-fence socializing. Driving to work, typically alone, rather than taking public transportation deprived people of opportunities to build acquaintances with fellow commuters. Loneliness in a crowd was a common experience.

Public Lives   No matter how private individuals and families might wish their lives to be, involvement in public aspects of life was unavoidable. They lived under laws made in public spheres. By voting, they chose the men and women who made the laws, and special ballots allowed them to take sides and affect decisions on policy issues. They found employment and produced and bought goods in public arenas. They took advantage of opportunities offered by schools, churches, and a variety of other organizations. They responded to calls to public service, often in the military, participated actively or as spectators in recreational activities, and generally moved with the flow of public affairs in the larger world. The public mood affected their daily lives.

New Times   The inauguration of John F. Kennedy on a cold January day in 1961 meant, as the new president expressed it, that "the torch has been passed to a new generation." His address created a new public mood and gave the impression that the 1960s were new times for both public and private lives. Replacing the 70–year-old Dwight Eisenhower, President Kennedy at age 43 symbolized youth. For the first time in their lives, 45 million American citizens were older than their president. The most-remembered lines in Kennedy's inaugural address, "And so, my fellow Americans: ask not what your country can do for you—ask what you can do for your country," aroused the citizenry to think and talk about the nation's purpose. Opportunities for action followed. The creation of the Peace Corps in 1961, for example, gave thousands of young people the chance to volunteer for service in educational, agricultural, and technical assistance projects in places of need around the world. The Peace Corps displayed a sense of optimism, even as tensions of the cold war continued.

Although there were many critics of the Kennedy administration's record in economic, political, and diplomatic affairs, the assassination of John F. Kennedy in Dallas on Friday, November 22, 1963, was an unimaginable national trauma. Within an hour of the shooting, according to the University of Chicago's National Opinion Research Center, two-thirds of adult Americans knew about it. Six hours later, almost everyone had heard the news. More than half cried, and nearly as many had trouble getting to sleep that night. For three days the American people slumped before their television screens, hearing reports from the scene, witnessing the swearing in of a new president, and sharing the grief of the First Lady as she accompanied the body of her murdered husband back to Washington. They watched with relief when the alleged assassin, Lee Harvey Oswald, was apprehended. They shuddered when they saw him murdered on his way to the courtroom. Finally they participated, almost as if they were there, in the ceremonies laying John F. Kennedy to rest in Arlington National Cemetery. Perhaps never before had the American people, from all stations and walks of life, been brought together by a single event as they were at this time.

Despite this sense of national unity, Americans' personal lives took them in many different directions. **Personal Security** Much of their time was spent in quests for personal security—including good jobs with good incomes. Most fared modestly well in the early 1960s. From 1960 to 1964 the unemployment rate stayed at a relatively low 5.5 percent before dropping to 4.5 and 3.8 percent over the next two years. The median family income in 1960 was $5,620. By 1966 it rose to $7,436. (In 1990 dollars, the increase was roughly from $24,800 to $29,950.) The 1960 minimum wage of $1.00 per hour (about $4.40 in 1990 dollars), typically earned by young people working part time and by the unskilled, was about 50 percent of the gross hourly wage of production workers that year. By 1966 it had been raised to $1.25, with increases to $1.40 and $1.60 to occur in the next two years.

Crime also affected personal security. The national rate for violent crimes (murder, non-negligent manslaughter, rape, robbery, and aggravated assault) stood at 136 per 100,000 population in 1960; for property crimes (burglary, larceny, and auto theft) at 901 per 100,000. In 1950 these figures stood at 128 and 1,360, respectively; and in 1990 at 732 and 5,089. (In making comparisons, bear in mind that only *reported* crimes can be counted. Some observers believe that as police work has improved and crime rates have risen, there is a greater inclination to report crimes than in the past. Counting methods also change through the years.)

Teachers and parents had worried about discipline problems in schools for many years, but violence there was uncommon. A more important indicator of personal security is found in the fact that men, women, and children stood without fear on street corners, day and night, in most cities, waiting for buses and streetcars. Subways were presumed to be safe. Even so, citizens everywhere were concerned about crime rates in the larger society, although not until later in the decade did it become a controversial political issue.

Despite concerns over crime, Americans recalling the tragedies wrought by World War II and the cost **National Security** of the "police action" in Korea from 1950 to 1953 welcomed the peace that accompanied national prosperity. A series of incidents, however, served as sobering reminders that peace was fragile. The shooting down of an American spy plane by the Soviet Union in 1960 was one reminder. More troubling was the sponsorship by the United States in 1961 of a failed invasion of Cuba by Cubans living in the United States. Their purpose was to overthrow the dictatorship of Fidel Castro, who had installed a communist government in the island

President Lyndon Johnson reviews American troops in the rain at Fort Campbell, Kentucky, July 23, 1966. *Yoichi R. Okamoto, LBJ Library Collection.*

nation and established close ties with the Soviet Union. The building of the Berlin Wall by the Soviet Union in 1961, designed to prevent residents of East Germany from fleeing to West Germany by crossing from the East to the West sectors of Berlin, reminded everyone that peace could not be taken for granted. The 1962 crisis with the Soviet Union over missiles placed in Cuba—during which the American people heard President Kennedy tell them that American missiles, poised to be fired, were at "zero minus ten and holding"—revived fears of nuclear war.

Such incidents were disturbing and frightening, but the cold war with the Soviet Union hit ordinary Americans mainly in their pocketbooks. Spending for the military in 1960 accounted for more than half of the federal budget expenditures (compared to less than one-fourth in the early 1990s). Even so, most Americans did not protest defense expenditures as excessive, probably because they shared the cold war fears of the nation's leaders and supported policies designed to "contain" communism.

But war in Vietnam forced Americans to reconsider their commitment to containment of communism as the cost in lives as well as dollars became clear. By the end of 1962 the United States had sent 11,000 military and technical personnel to Vietnam to assist the Republic of Vietnam (South Vietnam) in its civil war with the National Liberation Front (known as the Viet Cong). Throughout 1963 and 1964 dissent regarding the U.S. involvement came principally from pacifist, religious, civil rights, and disarmament groups, with sprinklings of opposition evident on university campuses. Spotty uneasiness turned to widespread fear and dread in August 1964. On the basis of unconfirmed evidence of hostile actions by North Vietnamese warships, both houses of Congress passed the Gulf of Tonkin Resolution, authorizing "all necessary measures" to prevent "further aggression" by North Vietnam.

The next year President Johnson ordered bombing raids on North Vietnam in what he called "sustained reprisal." Those opposed to U.S. involvement in what they regarded as a distant civil war organized protests in more than forty cities, including Washington, D.C. For Johnson, though, there was no turning back, despite Secretary of Defense Robert McNamara's behind-the-scenes efforts to give him a way to do so. As time passed and involvement increased, those opposing the war gained more and more allies. Escalations of the war and of opposition to it ran in parallel.

Meanwhile, contests between the "hawks" and the "doves" became a staple of daily news reporting on television, accompanying the pictures showing the death and devastation in Vietnam caused by the war. **Growing Concern over Vietnam**
On March 24, 1965, students and faculty at the University of Michigan held the first "teach-in" to discuss issues surrounding the war. Initially, teach-ins were ridiculed. *Newsweek* called them "forensic marathons" designed to promote a softer line on Vietnam. Their "droning house of diatribes," said *Newsweek*, "fanned blazes of controversy on some 50 campuses."[1] Some institutions declared day-long "moratoriums." Instead of holding regular classes, they focused on matters of war and peace. Teach-ins and other campus protests may not have had an effect on the conduct of the war, but they helped make dissent respectable, as persons of prominence joined in. They also reflected the anxiety of the young over their vulnerability to be drafted into military service, called upon to fight a war they opposed.

On April 17, 1965, 15,000 people gathered on the grounds of the Washington Monument in the first national protest against the war, foreshadowing further unrest. By the end of 1966, President Johnson had brought troop levels in Vietnam to 320,000, putting their lives on the line and disrupting the lives of their families and communities. Many college students, who typically came from the more advantaged classes in American society, gained draft deferments, placing the burden of fighting the war on the less advantaged. This led to further antagonism between students and blue-collar workers.

If the personal security of the American people did not seem particularly threatened by crime, and if threats to peace mainly touched the disadvantaged or unlucky, there were other reminders that private lives might not be as secure as they appeared. A deteriorating and potentially dangerous environment was one cause for concern. In the early 1960s the federal government, led by Secretary of the Interior Stewart Udall, sought to show that protection against the "forces permanently altering the vital man to land relationship of the past" was in the national interest.[2]

At the household and family level, concern for the environment did not arise until hazards revealed their cumulative effects on personal health and well-being. In 1962 marine biologist Rachel Carson published a study in *The New Yorker* magazine on the damage done by pesticides, particularly DDT, used widely in agricultural production. Her book *Silent Spring*, published in the same year, made her case directly and ominously. "There once was a town in the heart of America where all life seemed to live in harmony with its surroundings," Carson began, and after describing the beauty and fullness of life there, she continued:

> [A] strange blight crept over the area and everything began to change. Some evil spell had settled on the community: mysterious maladies swept the flocks of chickens; the cattle and sheep sickened and died. Everywhere was a shadow of death. The farmers spoke of much illness among their families. In the town the doctors had become more and more puzzled by new kinds of sickness appearing among their patients. There had been several sudden and unexplained deaths, not only among adults but even among children, who would be stricken suddenly while at play and die within a few hours. . . . No witchcraft, no enemy action had silenced the rebirth of new life in this stricken world. The people had done it themselves.[3]

They had done it with insecticides. Carson did not contend that chemical insecticides should never be used. Rather, she protested that "we have put poisonous and biologically potent chemicals indiscriminately into the hands of persons largely or wholly ignorant of their potentials for harm. Future generations are unlikely to condone our lack of prudent concern for the integrity of the natural world that supports all life."[4]

Silent Spring met a hostile reception in many quarters. Fellow scientists accused Carson of overdramatizing the problem. Pesticide manufacturers waged a massive, $250,000 campaign to discredit her, calling her a hys-

Rachel Carson, author of *Silent Spring*—the book that inspired concern about chemical pollution and helped launch the environmental movement. *Library of Congress.*

terical fool. But Carson's scholarly credentials and the thorough documentation of her findings gave her work considerable credibility. Eventually her critics had to concede the accuracy of her case. Even though the use of DDT was banned in the United States in 1972 after fiercely fought battles in courts and in Congress, harmful residues remained in homegrown products for years.

Historical change can never be traced to a single source, but *Silent Spring* is regarded by some as the *Uncle Tom's Cabin* of the modern environmental movement. As that book by Harriet Beecher Stowe was regarded as an important cause of the Civil War, this one provided the impetus for enactment of the Water Quality Act of 1965, the Clean Waters Restoration Act of 1966, and in subsequent years a host of other measures to protect the environment. Because water and air are not contained by state boundaries, anti-pollution action at the national level was necessary. Just as the negative effects of the environmental hazards that the legislation sought to curb had been largely invisible, so were the positive effects of the new laws. The initial costs of implementing them, however, were not, and resistance to environmental protection laws continued.

Awareness of the extent of hazards to motorists arrived in American consciousness with the 1965 publication of Ralph Nader's *Unsafe at Any Speed*. Nader focused particularly on General Motors' Corvair, a rear-engine car he considered vulnerable to disastrous accidents. General Motors (GM) developed it

Consumer Security

to compete with the Volkswagen "Beetle," a car manufactured in Germany that had gained popularity in the United States after its introduction in 1949. Between 1955 and 1958, imported cars increased their share of the market from less than 0.5 percent to 8 percent, and the Beetle made up more than half of the total. But Nader did not limit his case against the automobile makers to the dangers he exposed in the Corvair. His larger case was unsparing:

> For over half a century the automobile has brought death, injury, and the most inestimable sorrow and deprivation to millions of people. With Medea-like intensity, this mass trauma began rising sharply four years ago reflecting new and unexpected ravages by the motor vehicle. A 1959 Department of Commerce report projected that 51,000 persons would be killed by automobiles in 1975. That figure will probably be reached in 1965, a decade ahead of schedule.[5]

In Nader's judgment, automobiles were unsafe by design, the result of manufacturers' greater concern for appearance, efficiency, and profits, and no one forced the automakers to change their priorities. Resenting and fearing Nader's criticism, GM placed him under surveillance, hoping to find something in his personal life to discredit him. Later its chairman, seated before a Senate investigating committee, was compelled to apologize. Nader, an attorney, took matters a step farther, suing GM for $26 million but settling out of court for $425,000. He invested the money in his research and advocacy efforts while continuing to follow an unassailably austere lifestyle.

By taking on corporate America, Nader opened vigorous debates over the government's role in protecting consumers' interests. Should it compel businesses and industries to balance their commitments to profit-seeking shareholders with responsibilities to protect the safety of consumers? What could be done to convince consumers to pay $700 more per car for safety features? Although Nader's efforts led to the passage of laws designed to protect consumers against product hazards, his actions met corporate resistance—and even consumer resistance—at every step.

Consumers' well-being had been a concern even before Nader gained prominence. Both President Kennedy's Consumer Advisory Council and President Johnson's Committee on Consumer Interests gave consumers a voice in the White House. The Consumer Federation of America became the umbrella group for coordinating the efforts of consumer, rural cooperative, labor, and other groups wishing to promote a consumer program.

NOTES

1. *Newsweek*, May 24, 1965, 28.
2. *Life*, December 22, 1961, 135.
3. Rachel Carson, *Silent Spring* (Boston: Houghton Mifflin, 1962), 1–3.
4. Ibid., 12–13.
5. Ralph Nader, *Unsafe at Any Speed: The Designed-In Dangers of the American Automobile* (New York: Grossman, 1965), vii.

4

Consumers in the Material World

Consumers attending to their material needs went shopping, and by the 1960s that meant going to shopping centers. Such centers traced their origins to the increased use of automobiles and the growth of suburbs. The first—including such well-known and distinctive ones as the Country Club Plaza in Kansas City, Missouri—were built in the 1920s and 1930s. Construction accelerated rapidly following World War II, and by the end of the 1960s there were more than 10,000 shopping centers of all sizes and descriptions. Most notable were the new creations of the 1960s, the enclosed shopping malls. Only homes, schools, and jobs claimed more of the American people's time than shopping malls.

Shopping Centers and Malls

The malls developed in the 1960s had features that have since been refined. By today's standards the early malls seem unsophisticated. Although each had distinctive architectural features and each sought to set itself apart from others, a monotonous predictability prevailed. In mall after mall, the climate-controlled interiors with replanted landscapes blurred indoor and outdoor sensations. No sounds of nature were to be heard—only Muzak, music intended to remove silence without requiring listening.

In Disneyesque fashion, malls reproduced images of the small town. Missing, however, as one scholar has noted, were pool halls, bars, second-hand stores, and the kind of people who patronize them.[1] From one mall to the next, even the shoppers seemed to look the same: white, middle-class, suburban. So did those who were there just to hang out, or to meet over a cup of coffee and a doughnut, or to walk routes where rain and snow, cold and heat, never interfered.

A main purpose of malls was to create a community of shoppers. Walk in, they seemed to say, and feel at home. Listen to the folksingers. Visit Santa Claus. See the temporary art gallery in the center court. Give blood. Gather around the automobile on display. Spend a few minutes at the antique fair, the science fair, or the history fair. Forget about the elements. Slip into a store and buy something. Feel safe. Malls have never been free of crime, of course, but they are intended to make shoppers feel that they are.

Fashion   Being unfashionable is at times itself fashionable; in the early 1960s, as ever since, the fashionable and unfashionable complemented each other. High fashions and low came increasingly to stand side-by-side, leading to the eventual lowering of boundaries between them. Boundaries between styles of the generations fell, too, as parents and even grandparents became comfortable in attire like that of their offspring. However, the most extreme versions of clothing worn by youth did not find favor with their elders. In fact, clashes over proper dress were common.

The refined taste of Jacqueline Kennedy—her pillbox hats, conservative two-piece suits or dresses, solid colors, low-heeled shoes—set the tone for a short while, but imitators were found mainly among the wealthy. When tackiness in fashions among all social classes seemed inevitable, many tried to give tackiness a sleek look. Loose-fitting bell bottoms worn by both women and men followed this route for respectability. In 1963, the casual look featured shifts—simple waistless dresses. Around the same time sneakers, variations on running shoes, replaced the saddle shoes of the 1950s as the modish footwear.

Then came the miniskirt. So sexy were they, says Ellen Melinkoff, "that we could never have worn them in public without thinking, 'I can handle it.' Psychological armor was a fashion accessory. . . . To wear a mini was to work from a position of strength. It still made us sex objects, but we were sex objects with a sense of our own power." Accordingly, although the mini appeared to be a step backward for women's liberation, says Melinkoff, "it was a breakthrough." Remnants of modesty, though, and the danger of excessive exposure while climbing steps or bending over, prompted the wearers of the mid-thigh skirts to wear tights under them, and that inspired a 1966 innovation regarded as the longest-lasting legacy of the mini—that is, pantyhose.[2]

New fabrics played a big part in fashion trends. By 1966 double knits of acrylic, dacron, orlon, and other synthetics made possible the pantsuits that became popular with women and the leisure suits worn by men.

Before long, synthetic fabrics were used widely in clothes of traditional styles.

If some fashions came and went, one in particular came and stayed. Blue jeans, which had evolved from shapeless work clothes, had been around for decades, but they were sometimes a point of contention between elders and the youthful. Could they be worn to school? That was a question raised around 1950. The answer: by boys, but only if they wore belts. But the casual look of the 1960s gave jeans a new status. Jeans were a political statement. Moreover, they concealed the wearers' sex, especially when both men and women sported long hair. Designers and the fashion industry, however, saw profits in such attire; so if the political statements and the unisex appearance intended by such attire faded, the industry found ways to make them as conventional as the stuffier garments they replaced.

Since World War II, eating and drinking has amounted to more than meeting bodily needs. In *Eating in America*, published in 1976, Waverly Root and Richard de Roche-mont, summarized their observations on practices that were well under way by the early 1960s: **Eating and Drinking**

> Americans are consuming, along with unheard-of amounts of valuable proteins in their meats and cereals, and along with vast quantities of fruits and vegetables full of good nutrients and vitamins, tens of billions of dollars worth of packaging, additives, and advertising, as part of their total estimated two hundred and fifty billion dollar contribution to the food industry, agribusiness, and the conglomerate corporations that decide what we will be allowed to eat.[3]

What was new in this "great glob," as the writers called it, that made up the American diet? By the early 1960s, what nutritionists called junk food had claimed a big place in the fare American people consumed. This included sugared breakfast foods and synthetic "fruit" drinks containing little fruit juice promoted by Saturday-morning cartoons, along with much of the fatty, salty, and sugary goods passed over the counter at fast-food restaurants. If Americans were improperly nourished, they were at least not underfed.

Just as important as the quantity and quality of what the young and old in America ate is when and where they ate it. In 1965 one meal in four was eaten outside the home, with the number on the rise. When meals *were* eaten at home, they were less likely to be occasions for families to come together. This is not surprising, given the many commitments to jobs, school, and leisure and cultural activities of all generations in the typical family.

Dieting   Fashion consciousness, particularly that inspired by the "Twiggy" look that came into vogue in the 1960s, and health concerns made many Americans sensitive to being overweight, so it is not surprising that dieting became something of a national pastime. The most prominent organization in the weight-loss industry was Weight Watchers, begun in 1961 and incorporated for granting franchises in 1963. It gained adherents by using a combination of "group therapy" in weekly meetings and menus that prescribed foods low in fat and high in protein; the diet prohibited foods not fitting this description. Although Weight Watchers changed its prescriptions and prohibitions through the years, and the character of its approach evolved with the times, Weight Watchers continued to attract followers. Other diet formulas and plans have enjoyed bursts of popularity and then faded away as new ones took their place.

Dieters had more than mere weight loss as their concern. Reports on relationships between nutrition and health appeared regularly. For example, the Food and Nutrition Board of the National Academy of Sciences published a calorie table showing dietary allowances based on one's age and desired weight. The American Heart Association recommended that people reduce the amount of fat they eat and begin "reasonable substitution" of vegetable oils and polyunsaturated fats for animal fats. Previously the Association had suggested dietary changes for persons judged to be vulnerable to heart attacks. Now, for the first time, it called for changes in the eating habits of the general public. Sharp controversy followed, with representatives of the dairy industry leading the attacks on the recommendations.

Fitness and Sports   In keeping with his image as a young and vigorous president, John F. Kennedy urged the American people to get out of their armchairs and do something to get in shape. In fact, he charged the President's Council on Youth Fitness with developing a program to improve the physical condition of the nation's schoolchildren. The Council proposed standards for measuring fitness and urged schools to provide children with at least fifteen minutes of vigorous activity daily. Running became a popular activity for many people, even an obsession, and the commercial world encouraged a running craze. German shoes imported to meet new demands included Adidas, designed by Adi Dassler, and Puma, the product of his brother Rudi. From Japan came Tiger Marathons. New Balance, a Boston manufacturer of orthopedic footwear, designed a new type of shoe for runners. Before long other companies produced their own versions. Reports on testing and rating of shoes appeared as regular features in magazines on running, and shoes became status symbols.

Other sports such as tennis and golf also flourished, as did spectator sports. Major league baseball gained fans in cities through the expansion or relocation of franchises. In the process, other fans were left behind or left out. The process began in 1953 when the Boston Braves moved to Milwaukee; the St. Louis Browns to Baltimore in 1954, becoming the Orioles; and the Philadelphia Athletics to Kansas City in 1955. The bigger news came in 1958 when the Brooklyn Dodgers moved to Los Angeles and the New York Giants to San Francisco, reflecting the westward shift of the population in general. Over the next dozen years, a fan-boggling shuffling of franchises occurred. Three more existing franchises moved: the Kansas City A's to Oakland, the Milwaukee Braves to Atlanta, and the Washington Senators to Minneapolis–St. Paul, becoming the Minnesota Twins. Eight new ones were created: the Los Angeles/Anaheim Angels; the Washington Senators, becoming the Rangers when the team moved to Dallas–Fort Worth; the Houston Astros; the New York Mets; the Montreal Expos; the San Diego Padres; the Kansas City Royals; and the Seattle Pilots, which became the Milwaukee Brewers. The expansion prompted the American and National Leagues to form two divisions in 1969, with league playoffs determining competitors in the World Series.

Baseball fans had new records to talk about during these years: Roger Maris hit 61 home runs in 1961, breaking Babe Ruth's 34–year record. The fact that his teammate, Mickey Mantle, was close on his heels made the race for the record all the more exciting. The next year Maury Wills stole 104 bases for the Los Angeles Dodgers, breaking Ty Cobb's previous record of 96. His teammate, Sandy Koufax, struck out 18 batters in a nine-inning game. In 1965 Koufax struck out a record 382 in the season and pitched a perfect game, his third no-hitter. Television's coverage of such feats made them nationally celebrated events.

Developments in football made it possible for that sport to challenge baseball's dominance as the national pastime. The National Football League (NFL) and the American Football League (AFL) merged in 1966 and agreed to a playoff game between the leagues. Thus was born in 1967 the Super Bowl. At first the NFL dominated, but in 1969 Joe Namath, the charismatic quarterback of the New York Jets, led his AFL team to victory over the Baltimore Colts.

These were interesting years in boxing, too, as much outside the ring as inside it. A young athlete from Louisville gained fame by his actions in the ring and infamy by his words outside of it. Cassius Marcellus Clay, the 1960 light-heavyweight gold-medal winner in the Olympics, came into his heavyweight title match with Sonny Liston four years later as an 8:1 underdog, but he won. Then he announced that he had joined the Nation of Islam, renounced his "slave name," and, following the lead of another black Muslim, assumed the name of Cassius X. A few weeks later he said that henceforth he would be known as Muhammed Ali, adding another dimension to controversies about him. More than any other heavyweight champion, except possibly Joe Louis in the 1940s, Ali became the subject of conversations across the land, and controversies involving him would become more intense later in the decade.

Medicine and Health   Consumer interests played a part in advancements in medicine. The development of an improved form of polio vaccine in 1961, for example, met the public's desire for better ways to battle dreaded diseases. As penicillin and antibiotics came into more common usage, doctors frequently found themselves under pressure from their patients, or their patients' parents, to prescribe them even when they had doubts about the medications' effectiveness. Doctors' fears that overuse of such medications might pose problems were realized when the bacteria at which they were aimed developed resistance to them.

Other medical matters had significant, continuing social and economic implications for American consumers. Based on persuasive evidence produced through years of research, the Surgeon General's Advisory Council reported in 1964 that it had found a statistical relationship between smoking (particularly cigarette smoking) and a number of respiratory diseases, including lung cancer. This report and the stream of subsequent studies linking smoking with cancer, emphysema, and cardiovascular illnesses led the tobacco industry to market adaptations of cigarettes—longer ones, or ones with filters, for example—purported to reduce the health risks of smoking. At the same time, the industry continued to challenge the scientific accuracy of the studies to which it was responding.

The 1965 Cigarette Labeling Act required that beginning on January 1, 1966, packages had to carry this warning: "Caution: Smoking May Be Hazardous to Your Health." Whether warnings, even after they were made more forceful and applied more broadly, had the effect of discouraging smokers to kick the habit is not known, but they did seem to protect cigarette manufacturers against liability suits brought by survivors of persons who had died from illnesses caused by smoking. After all, the manufacturers could say, the victims had been warned.

The public's response to the reports, studies, and warnings was not immediately encouraging. In 1966 the tobacco industry produced 570 billion cigarettes. That was 30 billion more than in 1964, the year of the surgeon general's report, and it represented a 1 percent increase in per capita consumption over the previous year.

The American Cancer Society distributed this poster in January 1966 to call attention to the link between cigarette smoking and lung cancer confirmed by the Surgeon General's Report on Smoking and Health in 1964. *American Cancer Society.*

NOTES

1. Richard Francaviglia, "Main Street USA," quoted in William Severini Kowinski, "The Malling of America," *New Times*, May 1, 1978, 35. See also Neil Harris, "American Space: Spaced-Out at the Shopping Center, *The New Republic*, December 13, 1975, 23–25.

2. Ellen Melinkoff, *What We Wore: An Offbeat Social History of Women's Clothing, 1950–1980* (New York: Morrow, 1984), 119–20.

3. Waverly Lewis Root and Richard de Rochemont, *Eating in America: A History* (New York: Morrow, 1976), 443.

5

The Other America

The preceding chapters might create the impression
that the general prosperity enjoyed throughout   *The Other America*
America reached into all homes and families. But if
migration to suburbs was a sign of affluence, the city neighborhoods and
the people left behind soon showed the many faces of poverty. Poverty
was abundantly evident in rural America as well, particularly in Appa-
lachian regions of West Virginia, Kentucky, Tennessee, and North Carolina. Although industries had moved from the North to the South,
particularly in textile and furniture manufacturing, it was the prospect
of paying lower wages that lured them, so increases in living standards
were slow in coming. Most African Americans who earlier had migrated
from the South to what they saw as the promised land in northern cities
found poverty rather than promise there. Slums and derelict housing
projects populated almost exclusively by blacks became common in major cities, and racial discrimination posed barriers as formidable as those
existing in the South.

Some economists and social activists who had kept an eye on the conditions faced daily by America's poor proposed strategies for economic
development to ameliorate them, but action did not come quickly. President Kennedy's slight margin of victory in 1960 would have hobbled
any major reform efforts he might have proposed, and his conservative
instincts probably discouraged him from recommending ambitious plans
anyway. His measures to stimulate the economy had some positive effects, as the gross national product (GNP) grew at an average annual
rate of 5.3 percent between 1961 and 1964, compared to the 3.2 annual

average of the 1950s. But problems of unequal distribution of wealth—
indeed, of outright poverty—persisted.

Just as *Silent Spring* and *Unsafe at Any Speed* had stimulated interest in
environmental and product safety concerns, Michael Harrington's passionate book *The Other America* (1962), changed what many people
thought about problems of poverty. Although Harrington sprinkled statistics throughout the book, it was his description of the "invisible poor,"
particularly the elderly, the young, and minorities, that gave the book
its power. "In a sense," he wrote, "one might define the contemporary
poor in the United States as those who, for reasons beyond their control,
cannot help themselves. All the most decisive factors making for opportunity and advance are against them. They are born going downward,
and most of them stay down. They are victims whose lives are endlessly
blown round and round the other America." Forty to 50 million of them,
he estimated. Harrington asked his readers "to respond critically to
every assertion, but not to allow statistical quibbling to obscure the huge,
enormous, and intolerable fact of poverty in America. For, when all is
said and done, that fact is unmistakable, whatever its exact dimensions,
and the truly human reaction can only be outrage."[1]

Although Harrington chose not to use statistics to dramatize the condition of the "other Americans," one can see in the numbers of the early
1960s that daily life differed dramatically according to where one stood
on the nation's economic ladder. The 20 percent of Americans on the top
rungs of the ladder owned more than 75 percent of the nation's wealth;
the 20 percent on the bottom rungs owned only 0.05 percent. Those on
the bottom rungs received 23 percent of the total money income; those
on the top, 77 percent.

**Making War on
Poverty**

The Other America captured President Kennedy's attention and stirred him and other national leaders to face
the issues it raised. His administration was developing
proposals for action when he was assassinated. Taking
up more aggressively where Kennedy left off came naturally to Lyndon
Johnson. His origins in rural Texas had included few of the material
advantages that had been Kennedy's from childhood. On his first full
day as president, Johnson asked his advisors to come forward with specific proposals, which reached him in time to permit him to declare "un-
conditional war on poverty in America" in his 1964 State of the Union
address. "The richest Nation on earth," he said, "can win it. We cannot
afford to lose it."

Circumstances were right in the mid-1960s for the nation to attack
poverty through legislation and executive and other actions. The assassination of John F. Kennedy seems to have inspired national leaders to
believe that if they could not undo that wrong, they could at least right
other ones. In President Lyndon Johnson, who had been majority leader

in the Senate until he became vice president in 1961, they had someone who knew how to pull legislative strings and mobilize public sentiment more effectively than most presidents before him. Unrest stirred by the civil rights and student movements promoted the kind of introspection that leads nations as well as individuals to change what they can while they can do so on their own terms. The space race with the Soviet Union led schools across the country to insist that teachers teach better and students learn more and learn it faster. More extensive homework assignments and more demanding instruction, particularly in the sciences, were widespread, demonstrating a national mood to not let the Soviets win. This mood made it natural for education to be a weapon in the War on Poverty as well.

Besides, these were times of economic expansion, and with no military war being waged, a War on Poverty could be a war of choice. In August 1964, responding to Johnson's War on Poverty proposals, Congress enacted the comprehensive Equal Opportunity Act. Although conservatives in both parties opposed it (185 in the House and 34 in the Senate), the opponents were largely soft-spoken, fearful that opposition might be taken as indifference to poverty. The act was a noble effort, almost a heroic one, to solve the problems Harrington and others had identified. Each of its major parts held potential for changing the daily lives of countless Americans: It provided job training for the poor, programs to teach marketable skills to unemployed youths in inner cities, arrangements for recruiting middle-class volunteers to work in programs in poverty-stricken areas, funding for public-works projects in poor areas, and structures for making loans to indigent farmers and small businesses. The Head Start program gave disadvantaged preschool children training in basic skills—more than 500,000 youngsters in 2,400 communities participated in 1965, the first year of operation. The 1965 Elementary and Secondary Education Act was designed to stimulate innovation in schools and make educating America's poor children a priority. Upward Bound helped youth from poor families attend college. The Office of Economic Opportunity served as the operational center in the War on Poverty, and the Community Action program encouraged grassroots involvement in program development. Its goal was to empower the poor to better look after their own interests.

Although this would seem to be a boon to cities, big-city politicians and state governors did not like the Community Action program at all. They resented what they took to be loss of control to tenant unions in public housing. They opposed organized voter registration drives and resisted other efforts by activists to give poor people the power to deal effectively with their own problems. The Community Action program therefore became the target of hostility and attacks. This in turn created fear that the War on Poverty would lead to class warfare, and it neutralized the effectiveness of other programs.

But troubles in the War on Poverty did not dampen President Johnson's enthusiasm for shaping what he called the Great Society. Proposals poured forth from the White House in 1965 and 1966, and Congress enacted laws on Capitol Hill at a pace not seen since the famous Hundred Days at the beginning of Franklin Roosevelt's first term in 1933 when Congress enacted fifteen major laws between March 9 and June 16. Although the effectiveness of the legislation was mixed, partly because Johnson and his aides were more interested in enacting it than in implementing it, the impact on daily lives of the intended beneficiaries and those who implemented the programs was considerable.

Urban Programs The Housing and Urban Development Act of 1965, for example, offered reduced interest rates to builders of housing for the poor and elderly, thus benefiting builders and construction workers as well as those who were to live in the units they built. It also provided funds for health programs, beautification of cities, recreation centers, and rent supplements for the poor. The new cabinet-level Department of Housing and Urban Development assumed responsibility for coordinating the creation of urban and regional planning agencies. The Urban Mass Transportation Act of 1966, establishing the cabinet-level Department of Transportation, provided funds and structures for development of mass transit systems in urban areas. The Model Cities Act of 1966 provided over $1 billion for slum clearance and urban renewal.

Education and Immigration The Elementary and Secondary Education Act, passed in 1965, designated more than $1 billion for educationally deprived children. However, because the funds were ultimately under the control of local school districts they were frequently diverted to other purposes. The Higher Education Act of 1965 established a scholarship and low-interest loan program for financially needy college students and library grants to colleges and universities. The Immigration Act of 1965 eliminated the discriminatory quotas designed to exclude certain national groups, or to admit them on a restricted basis, that had been in effect for forty years and reaffirmed just thirteen years earlier.

Health-Care Insurance As life expectancy increased, resulting in growth of the elderly population that continues to the present day, provisions for caring for the elderly became more critical. Elderly persons worried about this, as did their children whose houses and urban apartments did not have space for additional dwellers and whose incomes were typically not sufficient to provide for institutional care. After the Democratic landslide in the 1964 election, sentiment for new laws providing for medical care for the elderly enabled those who backed them to surmount the opposition, including that of the American Medical Association.

The Medicare program enacted by Congress in 1965 provided insurance to cover most hospital charges, diagnostic tests, home visits, and in some instances nursing home costs for the elderly. Participants in Medicare could volunteer to purchase supplementary coverage, subsidized by the government, to take care of other medical expenses, including visits to doctors' offices. Prescription drugs, eye glasses, and hearing aids were not covered. At the end of Medicare's first year of operation, approximately 17.7 million elderly persons (93% of those eligible) enrolled in the voluntary medical insurance program. Also included in the Medicare bill were funds for nursing schools, medical schools, and medical student scholarships, all intended to train personnel to provide health-care services.

The Social Security Act of 1935 was the first step toward providing the elderly with means to be cared for by others if they were unable to care for themselves. Sometimes the care was given in not-for-profit nursing homes. The more **Care for the Elderly** extensive benefits provided through Medicaid—a companion program to Medicare that provided funding to states to pay for medical care of the poor of all ages—quickly spawned a lucrative for-profit industry. Nursing homes, one observer noted, "changed from a family enterprise to big business. Major corporations, including several hotel/motel chains, purchased large numbers of facilities and nursing home issues became the hottest item on the stock exchange." Between 1960 and 1976, nursing homes increased in number from under 10,000 to 23,000; the number of residents more than tripled, to 1 million. The number of employees increased during this period from 100,000 to 650,000. Impressive though these numbers are, they do not compare in magnitude with the 2,000 percent increase in revenues received by the industry. Almost 60 percent of the more than $10 billion in revenues was paid by taxpayers through Medicare and Medicaid. While these numbers were all skyrocketing, the population of senior citizens increased by only 23 percent.[2]

Who were the grandpas and grandmas in nursing homes? In the mid-1960s they were moving toward the profile that existed a decade later: More than 70 percent were over 70 years of age; women outnumbered men by 3 to 1; 63 percent were widowed, 22 percent had never married, 5 percent were divorced; only one in ten had a living spouse. In fact, many residents were *not* grandpas and grandmas; more than 50 percent had no close relatives. More than 60 percent had no visitors at all. Fewer than 50 percent were able to walk. The average stay in nursing homes was 2.4 years, and only 20 percent of the residents ever returned to their homes. The vast majority died in the nursing homes, with a small number succumbing in hospitals.

President Lyndon Johnson honors former President Harry Truman by signing Medicare into law at the Truman Library in Independence, Missouri, on July 30, 1965. Also present were Mrs. Johnson, Vice President Humphrey, and Mrs. Truman. *LBJ Library Collection.*

Such a profile means that in addition to worries over health and finances and fear of being a burden to others, many elderly people lived in dread of having to move to a place other than their own home. "It is a time of no tomorrows," wrote former senator Frank Moss in 1977, "a time of no hope. Death lurks like a mugger in a dark alley. The elderly await the inevitable, when they are reduced to the simple act of breathing and eating—and less."[3]

An initial appropriation of $6.5 billion got Medicare started, and increased Social Security payroll deductions were to provide for its long-term funding. However, Medicare and Medicaid planners underestimated the rate at which increases in doctors' fees and hospital charges, as well as the longer lives of the elderly, would create spiraling costs.

To celebrate the enactment of Medicare, President Johnson traveled to Independence, Missouri, where he signed the new bill into law in former president Truman's presence. Truman then became the first person to hold a Medicare card. What the two presidents celebrated, however, was a limited victory, for the American Medical Association had succeeded in restricting Medicare to bill-paying functions. The government had virtually no role in redesigning health-care systems or controlling costs. By the 1990s, with expenditures for both Medicare and Medicaid having multiplied more than tenfold, problems continued that might have been dealt with better when the programs were first created.

Programs in the War on Poverty had significant effects on the daily lives of millions of beneficiaries and benefit providers, even though they received only modest funding. The proportion of Americans recorded as being below the federal poverty line dropped from 20 to 13 percent between 1963 and 1968, and the ratio of African Americans living in poverty declined from 40 percent in 1960 to half that figure in 1968; but the problems of poverty remained daunting.

Looking Back on the War on Poverty

In attempting to account for the bursts of optimism that inspired the War on Poverty and public confidence in it, it is useful to reflect on the words of Lyndon Johnson, the War's mastermind. Speaking to Howard University students on June 4, 1965, Johnson laid out his vision for America, and particularly for the black students he was addressing. Members of their race were disproportionately represented among the poor, and he was sensitive to their circumstances. The breakdown of the family, President Johnson said, flowing from "the long years of degradation and discrimination, which have attacked [the Negro man's] dignity and assaulted his ability to produce for his family," was the main cause. So strengthening families was essential. To accomplish this and to solve all the other problems society faced, Johnson said, there was no single easy answer. Jobs were part of it, as were decent homes, welfare and social programs, and care for the sick. But another part of the answer is what moved President Johnson: "An understanding heart by all Americans."

NOTES

1. Michael Harrington, *The Other America: Poverty in the United States* (New York: Penguin, [1962] 1981 reprint), 15.

2. Frank E. Moss and Val J. Halamandaris, *Too Old, Too Sick, Too Bad: Nursing Homes in America* (Germantown, Md.: Aspen Systems Corp, 1977), 6–7.

3. Ibid., 8–9.

6

Mind and Spirit

The most striking changes in education in the early 1960s
affected adults, who enjoyed new opportunities in higher   **Education**
and continuing education. A burst of enrollment in higher
education had followed the GI Bill in the years after World War II. Of
14 million persons eligible, 2.2 million veterans jumped at the chance to
have their college tuition paid as partial compensation for their military
service. Eventually, nearly 8 million took advantage of the Bill's educational benefits. This set the stage for continued growth of colleges and
universities in the 1960s. In states with rapid population growth the expansion was breathtaking. In Florida, for example, where in the early
1940s there had been one university for men, one for women, and one
for blacks, along with one public junior college, by 1972 there were nine
public coeducational universities and twenty-eight community colleges.

The demand for such institutions increased in part because of the enrollment of women. The proportion of women in college populations
grew from around 33 percent in 1960 to more than 40 percent a decade
later. The increased enrollment of both women and men was served
mainly by the establishment and enlargement of public institutions. In
1940 about 47 percent of the 1,494,000 students enrolled in colleges and
universities were in private, denominational, or sectarian institutions. By
1970 the enrollment reached 7,136,000, with nonpublic institutions serving only 28 percent of the total.

The establishment of community colleges—160 between 1960 and
1966—opened doors for many young people and brought back to school
adults seeking to acquire new knowledge and skills. In the five years

preceding 1968, enrollment of full-time students in community colleges increased from 914,000 to 1,909,000, and part-time enrollment rose from 489,000 to 888,000. Priding themselves on the comprehensiveness of their offerings, community colleges enabled students to lay the groundwork for transferring to four-year institutions or to equip themselves for better jobs by enrolling in two-year vocational programs. Community colleges also provided credit and noncredit continuing education courses of almost limitless variety, some of them designed to improve job opportunities, some for intellectual and artistic growth.

Arts and Humanities
Visits at established museums rose in the decade before 1962 from 83,189,000 to 184,767,000, indicating that times were right for opening new museums—as happened in cities, counties, and towns across the nation. Similarly, although the number of major metropolitan symphony orchestras remained constant at around 25, the number of community orchestras rose from under 600 to more than 1,000 in the fifteen years preceding 1965. In the early 1960s, with community interest in the arts and humanities demonstrating that these were fields of interest not only to elites, efforts were undertaken to develop mechanisms for providing federal support to supplement and encourage local fund raising. The result was the creation in 1965 of the National Endowment for the Arts and the National Endowment for the Humanities. Through its programs, the Arts Endowment made grants to provide partial support for activities in the visual and performing arts in communities across the country, and the Humanities Endowment did the same for studies and activities in such fields as literature, foreign languages, history, and philosophy. Some of the federal funding from both Endowments was channeled through agencies created in each state; these agencies, like their federal counterparts, used public monies to generate additional support from private sources.

Religion
A revival of interest in religion as the 1960s approached was another sign that religion had come to be regarded by many as a commodity to be chosen or disregarded according to the needs of their daily lives. Church membership and participation were less likely than in the past to be traditions continued from generation to generation. In the later 1950s, church membership increased at a rate slightly higher than the growth of the population, reaching an all-time high in 1960. Nearly two-thirds of the population claimed to be church members.

Did increases in membership mean that church-related activities were a part of the daily life of large numbers of Americans? Polls taken in the 1960s revealed a relatively high measure of participation, but the picture was mixed. A Louis Harris poll in 1965, for example, showed that roughly half the U.S. population claimed to attend church weekly. The numbers for Protestants were substantially lower than for Catholics. Another poll reported that regular weekly church attendance declined from 49 percent in 1958 to 45 percent in 1965. A third poll indicated that in 1957, 69 percent of those polled believed the influence of religion was growing, but that figure dropped to 33 percent in 1965. In fact, 45 percent thought religion's influence was declining.

Numbers aside, religious ferment in these years was noteworthy. A spirit of "ecumenism," that is, of promoting unity among religions, became evident. At the very least, interdenominational rivalries cooled. The editor of a Lutheran periodical probably spoke for many when he wrote near the end of 1963 that "some of the expressions Protestants have long been using about Roman Catholics will necessarily and in all fairness have to be drastically qualified. Wince though we might at first, we won't be able to escape thinking and speaking of Romans in much more deliberate and 'defrosted' tones."[1]

Nonetheless, although desires for unity led to discussion of mergers and collaborative efforts, church denominations maintained their identities and distinctive practices. Individual members did not witness sweeping changes in their own places of worship. To a greater extent than their churches' leaders, they had probably always been more open to acceptance of religious pluralism—that is, to the sense that rivalries between denominations were self-defeating. Supporters of pluralism believed that allowing the free practice of religion and avoiding the concentration of power and authority in one church was in accord with American ideals and preserved the freedom of all.

Sometimes powerful forces caused church members to ignore denominational lines. Protestants, no matter what their formal affiliations were or their views on evangelist Billy Graham's methods or message, could not ignore him or the movement he represented. In the years following his huge rally in Madison Square Garden in New York in 1957, Graham intertwined his message of the Christian Gospel with expressions of faith in American progress. The fact that he became a favorite of presidents and the news media helped to establish him as an important public figure. At the same time, his rallies broadcast over television brought him into the private lives of millions of Americans. Other evangelists built followings by emulating Graham. Going further, adapting their preaching styles to the settings of show business, these "televangelists" carried on lucrative ministries.

The work of Father John Courtney Murray, the principal figure in leading American Catholics to understand the meaning of religious freedom, prepared them **Vatican Council** for the changes in Church practices that were to come from the Second Vatican Council. The Council, held in Rome in four sessions between 1962 and 1965, was convened by Pope John XXIII to reassess the role of the Church in the modern world. Continued by his successor, Pope Paul VI, the Council issued a number of documents, the most important for American Catholics being the Declaration of Religious Liberty. This document asserted one's right not to be coerced by individuals or society into acting contrary to one's conscience or into not following one's conscience in religious matters. By this time, the election of a Roman Catholic to the presidency of the United States and the conduct in office by John F. Kennedy had persuaded many Americans that Catholicism was no threat to American democracy.

As Pope John XXIII intended, the Council "threw open the windows" of the Church. Changes in practices among American Catholics resulting from the Council have been striking. Regular attendance at mass remained an integral part of life for many Catholics, but after November 29, 1964, priests offered the liturgy in English rather than Latin. Removal of restrictions in everyday life, such as one prohibiting the eating of meat on Fridays, gave Catholics a greater sense of being in mainstream America. So did the Church's softened opposition to easing civil divorce laws. At the same time, the Church's official opposition to the use of contraceptives of any kind—affirmed formally by Pope Paul VI in 1968 in the encyclical *Humanae Vitae*—kept it at odds with Catholics and non-Catholics who accepted birth control as morally right. Also at odds with the Church were those who advocated birth control because of fears that a "population bomb" would explode if growth was not kept under control.

Judaism   The Vatican Council's Declaration on the Church's Relations with Non-Christian Religions had considerable significance for Jews as well as Catholics. It condemned displays of anti-Semitism and denounced all prejudice and discrimination on the basis of race, religion, nationality, or tribe. Will Herberg, author of *Protestant-Catholic-Jew*, helped Jews come to understand and strengthen their place in the religious scene in America. At the same time, their assimilation into the cultural mainstream posed a threat to their distinctive identity, as wartime and postwar Jewish immigrants established themselves in America and joined migrations to suburbs, leaving behind their enclaves in the city. So too did the growing frequency of interfaith marriages. Jewish leaders recognized that even though the practice of religion among Jews as measured by synagogue attendance and religious observances in their homes was minimal, their identity was inherently associated with religion. Consequently they encouraged establishment of Hebrew day schools and after-school religious studies programs. Nearly two-thirds of the nation's 1 million Jewish children engaged in formal study of religion. Jewish leaders also supported efforts to increase the number of programs in Jewish studies in American colleges and universities. The number of such programs increased from 10 to 70 in the 20 years preceding 1965.

Jewish leaders also participated in interfaith confer- **Further Changes**
ences aimed at combating prejudice and implementing
the Vatican Council's Declaration on the Church's Relations with Non-Christian Religions. These conferences affirmed the acceptance of Jews in the trio of faiths Herberg had described in
Protestant-Catholic-Jew. Mainstream Protestants began to purge their Sunday School materials of portions that seemed to justify anti-Semitism. As
Protestants, Catholics, and Jews gradually felt more secure in the plu-
ralistic religious scene, they were more ready to accept into it believers
in Islam, Buddhism, and other religions.

Perhaps religious denominations lowered their voices in speaking of
one another because they recognized the need to work together against
forces in American life that ran contrary to beliefs they shared. The leadership that black churches in the South provided in civil rights struggles
compelled their white counterparts to examine their own teachings and
practices. Such self-examination almost always led to formal and informal support of those seeking an end to racial segregation.

Some church members believed that decisions of the U.S.
Supreme Court in 1962 (*Engel v. Vitale*) and 1963 (*School*   **Religion in**
District of Abington Township v. Schemp) finding school-   **Schools**
sponsored prayer and devotional Bible reading in public
schools to be unconstitutional were signs of the power of anti-religious
forces. In the first case (involving the recitation of a prayer composed by
the New York Board of Regents) Justice Hugo Black, writing the opinion
for the majority, observed that the daily classroom invocation of God's
blessings as prescribed in the prayer was a religious activity. The opinion
stated:

> [W]e think that the Constitutional prohibition against laws respect-
> ing an establishment of religion must at least mean that in this
> country it is no part of the business of the government to compose
> official prayers for any group of the American people to recite as
> a part of a religious program carried on by government. . . . When
> the power, prestige and financial support of government is placed
> behind a particular religious belief, the indirect coercive pressure
> upon religious minorities to conform to the prevailing officially ap-
> proved religion is plain.[2]

So intense in some quarters was the reaction that U.S. Congress held
hearings on a proposed amendment to the Constitution that would permit such religious activities. In these hearings and in additional statements by church leaders, it became clear that there were good reasons

for drawing a line between private and public devotional practices. Mainly, it protected children from having imposed on them teachings that were at odds with their own beliefs. Besides, the greater forces in the secularization of America were found in the commercial and entertainment worlds, and they were not likely to be turned back by reinstatement of school-sponsored prayers and devotional Bible readings in the schools.

NOTES

1. Quoted in Myron A. Marty, *Lutherans and Roman Catholicism: The Changing Conflict, 1917–1963* (Notre Dame, Ind.: University of Notre Dame Press, 1968), 53.
2. *Engel v. Vitale*, 370 U.S. 421 (1962).

7

Technology in Daily Life

Technology plays an important part in almost every
aspect of American life: business and industry, farm-   **Benefits and Costs**
ing, urban development, health care, law, politics,
banking, courtship, marital relationships, childrearing, schooling, religion, housekeeping and home maintenance, cooking and dietetics, shopping, social interactions, the spending of leisure time, and more. But the
benefits of technology often have a price. For example, its relentless quest
for "the new" necessarily makes our present possessions obsolete. Determination to keep up with "the better" or "the different" imposes challenges on both bank balances and human emotions. Technology
encourages uniformity and predictability, thereby erasing the distinctiveness of communities and cultures.

Technology's solutions to one generation's problems often create new
ones for the next. Disposable diapers, for instance: Widespread usage
did not begin until around 1970, when increasing numbers of mothers
of infants and small children found employment outside the home. But,
since their introduction, there have been concerns about their effects on
the environment. By the early 1990s, soiled diapers amounted to 1.4 percent of the bulk in landfills, according to a study conducted in Arizona.
Was that too much? And whatever the quantity, should disposable diapers be banned for other environmental reasons—for seepage of waste
into groundwater, for example? Not necessarily. Debates over compar-
ative environmental costs and benefits of using disposable as opposed
to laundered diapers typically end in a draw. Washing diapers consumes
energy and puts both human waste and detergents—another technolog-

ical advance with harmful environmental consequences—into sewer systems and larger bodies of water where the wastewater flows.

                I'll Buy That!, published in 1986 by *Consumer Reports* mag-
Automobiles   azine, identified and described "50 Small Wonders and
                Big Deals that Revolutionized the Lives of Consumers"
during the magazine's fifty-year history. The attention that the book's pictures and essays give to the automobile reveal the important role this technological wonder has played in American life. Through the years American-made cars grew bigger and more technologically complex. In the 1960s, automatic transmissions became standard on cars of all sizes. Power brakes, power steering, and air conditioning came first in larger cars, then in cars of all sizes. In 1966, Oldsmobile introduced the Toronado, the first domestic car with front-wheel drive. Before long, this innovation, too, became a standard feature as well.

    I'll Buy That! pointed to the 1965 Mustang as a symptom of change in Americans' buying habits. The editors describe the Mustang as neither a sports car nor a family car, but a "personal car." A 1962 version was a two-seater, but then, say the book's editors, there was a further corporate vision. "Put a young couple in something as romantic as a Mustang and they might just be fruitful and multiply and three into two doesn't go."[1] So the design was scrapped in favor of "two-plus-two"— that is, two seats in front, plus a small rear seat for two children. Of course, not by chance did the Mustang gain popularity. The Ford Motor Company launched it with a $10 million publicity campaign, calling it a "school bus," a "shopping cart," and a "dream boat." "Join the tide of history," one advertisement said, "with a car that scoots through traffic . . . hoards gas . . . and sports a low price tag." Creating the sense of need for the Mustang was just as important as creating the car itself.

    The Volkswagen "Beetle," a tiny car with its engine in the rear, established its own popularity through unconventional advertising: "Think small" and "Ugly is only skin deep," for example. Despite the car's many inconveniences and crudities, VW owners drove their Beetles with immeasurable pride. Still, the Beetle was not a family car. The Toyota Corona, introduced in 1965, was. Its acceptance as an economical but comfortable car encouraged other Japanese manufacturers, particularly Honda and Nissan (known then as Datsun), to enter the American market; within a decade the three Japanese companies claimed about 20 percent of the U.S. market. This jeopardized the very existence of Chrysler Corporation and dented the prosperity of General Motors and Ford, the other two manufacturers in the Big Three. The popularity of smaller cars had implications for automobile safety, as tests showed that their drivers were more vulnerable to accidental injury or death than drivers of larger vehicles. Also affected by the increasing popularity of imported cars were the thousands of families whose breadwinners worked in manufacturing plants that now faced cutbacks caused by declining sales of American-made automobiles.

Ever since its invention, the automobile had played an important role in the development of America. By 1960, wrote historian Kenneth Jackson, "the best symbol of individual success and identity was a sleek, air-conditioned, high-powered personal statement on wheels." The presence of plain, low-powered, low-prestige foreign vehicles did not threaten that symbol. The imported vehicle often served as a family's second car, providing transportation rather than luxury. Nonetheless, it contributed to a phenomenon noted by Jackson: between 1950 and 1980 the American population increased by 50 percent, but the number of automobiles increased by 200 percent.[2]

Americans' reliance on the automobile led President Eisenhower to propose and Congress to approve the Interstate Highway Act in 1956, providing for a 41,000-mile system of limited-access highways. Construction proceeded rapidly, with little regard for the farmland and urban neighborhoods that lay in the highways' paths or for the consequences of highway-spawned "sprawl." Connecting urban highways to the Interstate system meant the construction of spaghettilike interchanges and resulted in the loss of more neighborhoods and the migration of more residents to suburbia. In the 1960s, factories, offices, and shopping centers also migrated to the suburbs, so that by 1970, according to Jackson, in nine of the fifteen largest metropolitan areas the suburbs were the principal sources of employment. In some cities, such as San Francisco, almost three-fourths of all trips to and from work were by people who did not live or work in the core city. Similar patterns in other cities explain why extensive public transportation systems were usually hopeless dreams.

Romance with the automobile helped create a "drive-through" culture. The "drive-in" culture restaurants, where car-hops served patrons who ate in their cars, disappeared rather quickly as new technologies had customers shouting their orders into a loudspeaker and passing a window to pick up their orders. Drive-through banking was its counterpart, along with drive-through cleaners and drive-through pharmacies. Eventually there were even some drive-through funeral homes, where friends could pay their respects to the deceased without getting out of their cars. A drive-through bridal chapel was yet to come.

The automobile's place in American life and the improvements in vehicles and roads were continuations of processes set in motion early in the twentieth century. Other technological developments of the 1960s had more recent origins. Among these, computers stand out in importance. The first electronic digital computers, built in the 1940s, were huge machines that were usually dedicated to a single purpose. The development of the transistor in the early 1950s

Computers

made possible integrated circuits, and old vacuum tubes swiftly became obsolete. The patenting by Texas Instruments in 1961 of a silicon wafer, known as a chip, opened the way for further changes in computer technology. No bigger than a postage stamp, the silicon chip eliminated the miles of wires required in earlier machines.

Although personal computers did not become common in American households until several decades later, IBM's production of a primitive word processor in 1964 was a first step in that direction. However, IBM failed to anticipate what was to come as far as personal computers were concerned. Not until 1981 did it market its first one.

As computer technology came to play a larger role in American life, it was not limited to such obvious processes as financial record management, credit card accounting, airline reservation systems, and word processing. In 1966 it took a small first step into the daily lives of users who were unaware of how it worked and even of its existence, as British technologists developed the first computer-controlled, fuel-injection automobile engine. Such advances, while making life easier in some respects, also made it more confusing—as backyard mechanics would soon discover.

Space Ventures   Computer technology played an essential role in America's first flights into space. In 1961, Navy commander Alan Shepard and Air Force captain Virgil Grissom each piloted space capsules in suborbital flights of just over 300 miles, preparing the nation for the big moment to come the following winter. At 9:47 A.M. on February 20, 1962, with schoolchildren bunched around television sets in their classrooms and their parents interrupting tasks at work and at home, an Atlas missile at Cape Canaveral, Florida, launched the space capsule *Friendship 7* into orbit around the earth, with Colonel John Glenn aboard. Minutes short of four hours later, CBS newsman Walter Cronkite narrated Glenn's reentry into the atmosphere and his splashdown in the Caribbean Sea. In orbit, the capsule had reached a velocity of 17,500 miles per hour, and in the four hours between launch and recovery from the water Glenn had seen three sunrises. Viewers cheered what they saw and buzzed with excitement as they talked about it. Still, the way it was carried out was so precise that it looked routine, matter-of-fact, predictable. It had all the marks of a choreographed theatrical production. Surely this was American progress, the success of modern times.

There was more to come: Three months later, astronaut Scott Carpenter repeated John Glenn's feat, this time taking control of functions done by computerized instrumentation in the first flight. The following October, Navy commander Walter Schirra completed a nearly perfect flight of more than nine hours, circling the earth six times and making a pinpoint landing in the Pacific Ocean. Television viewers began to take success for granted, but even bigger things were yet to come.

Based on the counsel of the National Aeronautics and Space Administration (NASA) and his advisors, and at the urging of Vice President Lyndon Johnson, President Kennedy declared in a speech before Congress on May 25, 1961: "This nation should commit itself to achieving the goal, before this decade is out, of landing a man on the moon and returning him safely to earth. No single project . . . will be more exciting, or more impressive to mankind, or more important for the long-range exploration of space; and none will be so expensive to accomplish." The cost? Likely to be $30 to $40 billion, with those dollars contributing little to economic growth. The cold war explains why American taxpayers were willing to pick up the tab. Johnson was correct in saying he did not believe "that this generation of Americans is willing to resign itself to going to bed each night by the light of a Communist moon." Anyone doubting that the Soviet Union saw the contest in the same terms should remember that every day thousands of Russians pass a statue of Yuri Gagarin mounted on a pedestal 40 meters tall on a main thoroughfare in Moscow. Gagarin was the Russian hero whose single-orbit flight on April 12, 1961, three weeks before Alan Shepard's suborbital flight, showed America that the Soviet Union could beat the United States in launching a man into spatial orbit.

The only immediate benefit of the space flights for the American people seemed to be bolstered pride in the nation's technology. The flights had been accomplished in full view of the American people, via television. So what if comparable feats had occurred earlier in the Soviet Union. They had been done in secret. How could we know, Americans asked, how many failures had preceded the Russians' successes?

More tangible benefits were to come, space scientists claimed, as by-products of space exploration would reach into many quarters of daily life. One such benefit became apparent by mid-1962, with the placement in orbit of AT&T's Telstar communications satellite. The satellite permitted transmission of the straight-line waves of television, unhampered by mountains or oceans. When more orbiting stations were launched later, continuous transmission via satellites became possible. Television networks and weather forecasters soon came to rely on satellite transmissions, and eventually homeowners willing and able to mount a "dish" in their yards or on their roofs enjoyed the benefits too. Meanwhile, the American people maintained their interest in space flights, particularly those with two men tucked tightly into the Gemini capsules. In a period of twenty months, twenty astronauts in Project Gemini conducted a variety of experiments in space. Despite scary moments, NASA called each one of them an unqualified success.

Medicine Technology has always been the essential link between science and the practice of medicine, and between 1960 and 1966 technological innovations were many. A list of these innovations is truly impressive, but the items in it take on particular meaning for the countless individuals and families who benefited from them at the time and the many more who have since been affected by the further medical progress those innovations made possible. In these years, among many other things,

- lasers were used for the first time in eye surgery,
- the first liver and lung transplants occurred, made possible in large part as a result of improvements in anesthesia,
- a prominent cardiac surgeon used an artificial heart to sustain his patient during surgery,
- pacemakers allowed persons with heart conditions to live normal lives,
- home kidney dialysis became possible,
- vaccines proved to be effective against German measles and rubella (which, if contracted during pregnancy, could injure the fetus),
- methods were perfected for dealing with the Rh factor, a blood condition that threatened the survival of babies at birth,
- an improved polio vaccine led to virtual eradication of the disease,
- the key antigen for development of a hepatitis B vaccine was discovered,
- development of antibiotics continued,
- radioactive isotopes were used widely in diagnosis and treatment of diseases, and
- more sophisticated forms of chemotherapy for cancer treatment showed improved effectiveness.

Meanwhile, scientists engaged in basic research were laying the groundwork for technological innovations that would arrive in later years.

The Autonomy of Science and Technology Immersion in technology, for all its benefits, has complicated life in America. As it gained dominance, writes historian Daniel Boorstin, American civilization lay increasingly at the mercy of the internal logic of advancing knowledge. Science and technology had a momentum of their own: each next step was commanded by its predecessor. To fail to take that next step was to waste all the earlier efforts.

Once the nation had embarked on the brightly illuminated path of science, it had somehow ventured into a world of mystery where the direction and the speed would be dictated by the instruments that cut the path and by the vehicles that carried man ahead. The autonomy of science, the freedom of the scientist to go where knowledge and discovery led him, spelled the unfreedom of the society to choose its way for other reasons. People felt they might conceivably slow the pace of change . . . but they wondered whether they were in a position to stop it.[3]

NOTES

1. Editors of Consumer Reports, *I'll Buy That! 50 Small Wonders and Big Deals That Revolutionized the Lives of Consumers* (Mount Vernon, N.Y.: Consumers Union, 1986), 64.

2. Kenneth Jackson, *Crabgrass Frontier: The Suburbanization of the United States* (New York: Oxford University Press, 1985), 246.

3. Daniel J. Boorstin, *The Americans: The Democratic Experience* (New York: Random House, 1973), 597.

8

Cultural
Transformations

As the Great Society changed the political and economic face of America through legislative and presidential actions, and as the civil rights movement and technology brought other changes in American life, still other forces transformed American culture. With college youth drawing the most attention for their challenges to established practices in American life and rejection of conventional sexual mores and practices, they were joined in quieter ways by men and women of all ages.

In the 1960s the traditional practices of courtship rather suddenly disappeared. New patterns of interaction between **Courtship** the sexes began to take their place. As Beth Bailey explains in *From Front Porch to Back Seat*, the differences between what had been and the new "lay not only on the surface, in the changing acts of courtship, but in underlying understandings of value and values, in presumptions about how the world works, and in ideas about the proper relations between men and women."[1] It would have been surprising, of course, if old ways of dating had survived in a culture where sexual mores and social conventions were changing rapidly.

Dating had implied certain conventions: Calling in advance to arrange for the boy to pick up the girl, and appearing in appropriate attire for "going out." If it worked, "going out" led to "going steady"; if not, back to "playing the field." In the former there was security; in the latter, competition. There were rules, determined by age, for holding hands, kissing, necking, and petting, with warnings against "going too far." Parents set hours to be home. Colleges made rules *in loco parentis* (in the place of parents). Boys played masculine roles—providing transportation, determining where to go, and paying the bills. To be feminine, girls were expected to be coy and deferential.

In the 1960s, Bailey says, a new context emerged. In this one, "Sex appears to be the normal, if not unproblematic, medium of contemporary courtship."[2] Freedom to express love, or hints of love, or simply masculinity and femininity through sexual relationships, replaced the conventions of earlier times. Dispensing with rituals, men and women (in earlier times they would have been called boys and girls) began to move informally, in crowds, with uncertain destinations, pairing off as opportunities and hormones prompted. Coed dorms in colleges and universities did not cause the changes in relationships between the sexes, as critics contended, so much as they reflected them.

As the youth of the 1960s sought "freedom, honesty, love, and equality," Bailey acknowledges, many of their elders saw them as having found only "meaningless sex, loneliness, and lack of commitment," resulting in "epidemics of teen pregnancy and sexually transmitted diseases" as young people were left without rules essential for both stability and romance.[3]

Even as courtship changed in character and practice, many men and women never courted or were courted. By chance or by choice, opportunities never came their way. For some, even if they gave courtship a try, it did not lead to marriage. On the other hand, many men and women, rebounding from failed marriages, found themselves courting again. Experiences on the road to marriage influenced their conduct in later courtships. Children and alimony were both likely to be complicating elements in post-divorce relationships.

Sexual Mores   If old conventions disappeared quickly, new ones were somewhat slower in taking shape. Consequently, uncertainties over what was right and wrong, proper and improper, created anxieties for the transition generation. Nonetheless, forces at work clearly put established conventions on the run. The launching by Hugh Hefner of *Playboy* magazine, filled with photos of nude "playmates" and philosophizing about sexual standards, had that effect. Hefner and his writers judged existing standards to be hypocritical and repressive; what they had to say foreshadowed and fostered changes to come. Between 1953 and 1960, *Playboy's* circulation grew from 70,000 to more than a million. By 1967 it had reached 4 million, and it peaked at 7 million in 1972.

Before the end of the decade, Helen Gurley Brown made *Cosmopolitan* magazine *Playboy's* counterpart, without the nude photos. David Farber calls readers of *Playboy* and *Cosmopolitan* "the original yuppies." They asserted, he says, "that hardworking young urban professionals (well-paid men) and young, independent pink-collar workers (poorly paid 'girls') deserved all the pleasure they could get. In their vision, good sex and material comfort added up to the good life." This was not the model the counterculture cared to embrace, Farber continues, but "it was an important part of the sexual revolution, and central to the sexually charged national conversation young people joined."[4]

Increasing openness on sexual matters had other sources. Beginning in 1946 and several times thereafter, the Supreme Court struck down as unconstitutional laws restricting publication and distribution of sexually explicit materials. When the Food and Drug Administration approved the marketing and use of oral contraceptives—that is, "the pill"—restraints on sexual promiscuity caused by fear of pregnancies were lessened. By 1963 more than 1 million women were taking the pill; by 1970 the number had grown to 12 million, despite controversies concerning possible side-effects and the Catholic Church's continued condemnation of its use. Interestingly, research through the years showed that the pill's effects on sexual practices were greater within marriages than within premarital relations, allowing married couples sexual freedom that fear of pregnancy had not previously allowed.

Advocates of birth control also succeeded in challenging restrictions on its use. For example, the Supreme Court's decision in *Griswold v. Connecticut* (1965) established rights of privacy, implicitly erecting barriers against intrusions by persons who would impose what they regarded as publicly endorsed standards of conduct. Accounts of sexual matters became more and more explicit in books and movies, including those shown on television. In 1966 William Masters and Virginia Johnson, sex therapists in St. Louis, attracted considerable attention by documenting the greater openness about sex in their book *Human Sexual Response*. They provided physiological evidence of women's sexual responsiveness, altering both male and female assumptions about satisfying sexual relationships.

Changes in sexual mores and practices were just one part of the interwoven forces that created an American culture **Rock Music** quite different from that of a generation earlier. Rock music, with its increasingly explicit sexual themes, was another. Herbert London contends that "like the inscriptions on the Rosetta stone that solved the mystery of hieroglyphics, rock music provides a key record of the Second American Revolution that may unlock its inner logic." Not wishing to overstate the case, he adds that "rock is a spectator at the cultural storm, not its ruler. It may rekindle the ashes with a spark, but it cannot make the original fire."[5]

Historians trace the origins of rock music to several sources. One was the rock 'n' roll craze of the 1950s, featuring black musicians like Chuck Berry and Little Richard, as well as white ones, including Elvis Presley, Jerry Lee Lewis, and Buddy Holly. The new phenomenon, writes historian Edward P. Morgan, "represented a merging of such traditional strains as black blues, jazz, gospel, and white country music." A second source, Morgan says, lay in "traditional folk music—protest songs from the labor movement, antiwar tradition, ballads, and folk-blues." By the mid-1960s, a gentler phase of folk music, with Bob Dylan, Joan Baez, and Peter, Paul, and Mary as leading artists, yielded to more critical variations. These variations reflected the alienated perspectives of the Beat movement characterized by the poetry of Allen Ginsberg and Jack Kerouac and the countercultural lifestyle of the 1950s that was called Beatnik.[6]

As rock music evolved with its merged traditions, much of it expressed the political sensitivities of the civil rights movement and antipathy to the arms race with the Soviet Union. Performers also attacked what they regarded as repressive social mores. In other words, like music of earlier eras, it reflected the times. While the majority of the population regarded the lifestyles of the rock musicians and their most devoted followers as countercultural, the ingredients of rock music gradually infiltrated the larger culture. That may explain why it became the subject of so much scholarly analysis such as that provided by James Haskins and Kathleen Benson, who, in *The 60s Reader*, outline three distinctive characteristics of rock music.

First, rock's sexually explicit lyrics revealed society's new sexual permissiveness. Those who found it offensive contended that its sexual themes also fed this permissiveness, something those who "dug it" could hardly deny. Second, rock music not only belonged to the youth culture, but the youth's elders could scarcely tolerate it. To them it seemed raucous and incoherent, its lyrics unintelligible. Television shows like *Hit Parade*, starring Rosemary Clooney and appealing to audiences across generation lines, disappeared. Third, rock broke down the barriers between white musicians and their black counterparts. By the 1960s, the new music, aimed at both blacks and whites, was well established, and a distinctive, affluent teenage market wanted more.

A "generation gap," encouraged if not created by the sound, lyrics, and staging of rock music, soon became a matter of concern to older generations. Indeed, Haskins and Benson say that "nowhere did that gap present itself more clearly than in the controversy over rock 'n' roll and over its most popular purveyor at the turn of the decade, Elvis Presley. He rode in a gold Cadillac, he dressed in gold lamé suits, he gyrated his hips so sensuously that when he appeared on television the cameras never showed him below the waist. Parents were enraged; young people were delighted. A generational tug-of-war resulted." Attempts at censoring rock music on the radio and banning rock stage shows failed to reduce its seemingly inevitable appeal to the younger generation.[7]

Three developments of the 1960s proved wrong any thoughts that

American performers would be unable to sustain enthusiasm for rock 'n' roll or that the appeal of its performers might wear thin. One was the enduring strength and adaptability of folk music. Continuing the tradition of Woody Guthrie and Pete Seeger (whose music had been inspired by social conditions of the 1930s and 1940s), Joan Baez, Bob Dylan, Judy Collins, and others, as well as groups like The Kingston Trio and Peter, Paul, and Mary, now appealed to millions with their songs of alienation and protest.

The second was the arrival of groups from England, particularly the Beatles in 1964 and the Rolling Stones a year later, to be followed by others such as The Who. These performers, Morgan says, bypassed "the more tepid rock and roll imitations" and "reached back to the blues roots of rock and roll and figures like Chuck Berry. Together with a kind of working-class stance and each group's distinctive signature—the Beatles' path-breaking chord combinations and harmonies, the Rolling Stones' swaggering alienation—resulted in a burst of new energy in popular music."[8] David Chalmers describes the appearance of the Beatles on *The Ed Sullivan Show* in 1964 as "electrifying." "Their well-scrubbed look, their Teddy Boy dress and the hair down over their ears, their wit, their ensemble performance that did not submerge the individual personalities, their compelling but not overwhelming acoustical beat, and their lyrics of love and holding hands created a powerful personal chemistry. They came across as real."[9] The very power of the Beatles, Jeff Greenfield observed later, "guarantees that an excursion into analysis cannot fully succeed." Even so, he writes, "they helped make rock music a battering ram for the youth culture's assault on the mainstream, and that assault in turn changed our culture permanently."[10]

The third was the success of Motown Productions, a Detroit-based music empire closely tied to the civil rights movement of the mid-1960s. Its success lay in grooming, packaging, marketing, and selling the music of black performers, such as The Supremes, to masses of white Americans. Using methods practiced by the Detroit automobile factories in which he had worked, its founder, Berry Gordy, according to David P. Szatmary, "ensured the success of the Supremes by assembling the parts of a hit-making machine that included standardized songwriting, an in-house rhythm section, a quality-control process, selective promotion, and a family atmosphere reminiscent of the camaraderie fostered by Henry Ford in his auto plant during the early twentieth century." The Temptations and other groups assembled later were all part of the Motown machine. The machine itself enjoyed success from 1964 until things came apart in 1967, but the sounds and the stars it got started continued.[11]

The sudden burst in popularity of rock music should not obscure the

The Supremes, the popular Motown trio, performing in 1965.
UPI/CORBIS-BETTMANN.

fact that other forms of popular music—jazz, country, and traditional
folk music, for example—also thrived.

Counterculture   The emergence of rock music and its claims on a prominent and lasting place in American society did not oc-
cur by chance. Rather, it fit with the times: As the United
States became more deeply involved in Vietnam, racial clashes at home
grew sharper. Themes of protest and dissent made rock music central to
the 1960s. Alongside rock music, the movement known as the counterculture emerged. Even though this counterculture built on the mood and
style of the 1950s' Beatniks, it was different. An observer of the Haight-
Ashbury scene in San Francisco, the capital of the counterculture, described the difference this way: "Beat was dark, silent, moody, lonely,
sad—and its music was jazz. Hippie is bright, vivacious, ecstatic,
crowd-loving, joyful—and its music is rock. Beat was the *Lonely Crowd*
[the title of a popular book published by sociologist David Riesman in
1950]; hippie, the crowd that tired of being lonely."[12] If the hippie crowd
was joyful, it was also alienated from the society surrounding it, partic-

ularly from technology and the controlling "establishment." If it was bright and adventurous, it was so in part because it attracted idealistic rebels and rebellious idealists.

Not all these rebels and idealists were in distant places. Many lived in the homes and neighborhoods of mainstream America and attended schools populated by teenagers who did not share their alienation. Self-conscious youth, uncertain of their abilities to express themselves, were vulnerable to fads that attracted crowds. In this fad, America's youth proved vulnerable to the massages of rock music's sounds, ready to be aroused by new group experiences. Blending sounds from the blues and country music into choruses of protest, rock music's appeal broadened and deepened. Soon those absorbed in it, older persons as well as youth, were puzzled by the opposition it inspired.

The counterculture reflected by rock music and other forces of protest revealed a paradoxical desire to change society while also escaping from it. If rock music offered one means of escape, more powerful ones seemed to go with it: sexual experimentation, communal living, distinctive dress and hair styles, and the use of drugs. And if the counterculture and its communes and enclaves seemed insidious to the surrounding society, it had a profound influence nonetheless. Sexual experimentation spread throughout the dominant culture, resulting in changed attitudes toward marriage and a weakening of its place in society. This also meant a substantial increase in of out-of-wedlock childbirths despite the availability of birth control pills and contraceptive devices. While the percentage of births to unmarried women increased from 4 percent in 1950 to 5.3 percent in 1960, by 1975 fully 14.2 percent of all births were to unmarried women, with larger increases to come later. The fact that these numbers increased at the very time that methods of preventing conception or terminating pregnancies following conception were becoming available is a further indication of changes in attitudes toward marriage. The openness on sexual matters affected not only male-female relationships. It also encouraged homosexuals to emerge from the closet and openly establish relationships that flouted moral codes of the past.

As for the attire of the counterculture, the fashion industry soon discovered that it could produce clothing that appeared washed-out and worn; such clothing became a staple in families where adherents to countercultural ideals would have been unwelcome. Long hair and beards were typically taken as expressions of sympathy for the counterculture and accordingly were detested by the many who considered themselves traditional Americans. Yet, long hair and beards soon became commonplace, even among men whose reaction to other changes in society placed them in the midst of the forces of backlash.

Communes

Because communal groups, in the 1960s as well as earlier in American history, were often formed by men and women who wanted to get away from the society they saw as corrupt, most such groups sought and cherished obscurity. Reports on how many communes existed, where they were located, and what went on in them were few and unreliable. That left much to the imagination of both critics and sympathizers.

Looking back, we know that some were "retreat" communes. These tended to be small, anarchistic, loosely organized, predominantly rural, and youth-oriented. Based on protest, they were largely negative in character. Drugs played an important part in their routines. Others were communes with a mission. Their members sought to interact with society, hoping to change it without compromising their own beliefs and ideals. Such communes had at their core political or scientific ideologies, or social commitments, or artistic interests, or religious beliefs. Each commune had its own rules, routines for daily life, and practices concerning such things as ownership of property. No two were alike.

Sociologist John Hostetler has identified discernible ideals among the communal groups he studied, each one of which challenged mainstream Americans who encountered them to rethink the nature of the society in which they lived or wished to live. Communes, he suggests, attracted those who believed that real needs must be distinguished from material needs; that alienated men and women must return to a natural, human habitat; that human relationships must be restructured in such a way as to allow for sharing of the whole person—not only intelligence, but also body and spirit; that living in communities provides means for self-discovery and exposure to a broader range of human potential; and that longevity is not the criterion by which to measure the success of a commune.[13] Those who studied new communes estimate that more than 2,000 were established by 1970. Membership ranged from just a handful to perhaps several hundred, but because the population was so fluid it was difficult to determine the size of most of them. At their peak, membership in communes represented no more than 0.03 percent of the population of the United States.

Advocates of communal living, acknowledging that many communes were short-lived, insisted that individual fulfillment was the appropriate measure of success. After all, they noted, many so-called "successful" communes "repressed creativity, individuality, intellectual activity, and even sexuality," noting sardonically that among the most successful institutions for maintaining continuity are prisons.[14]

There was more to the counterculture than rock music, communes, clothes, and beards. As David Farber points out in *The* **Drugs**
Age of Great Dreams, "the consumption and distribution of illegal
and experimental drugs, more than any other single factor, was responsible for the creation and development of America's many countercultural enclaves." They were indispensable to these enclaves' economic well-being, social order, and cultural outlook. Moreover, Farber says, "the dissemination of drugs outside of these enclaves was also the single most important factor linking the small counterculture with the vast majority of going-to-school, living-at-home young people. The spread, lure, promotion, and open use of illegal and experimental drugs was also the main reason a majority of adult Americans feared and even hated the counterculture."[15]

Those wary of drug use were concerned that the gentler drugs like marijuana, known for giving a mild high—giddiness, goofiness, and rapture—would lead to the use of more dangerous ones. In the 1960s and thereafter, the sequel to marijuana for many has been LSD, known as "acid." Although the effects of LSD vary with each person, the desired one is hallucination—that is, the "unblocking or unlocking of the conscious mind." According to the more spiritually inclined, says Farber, "acid put a person on another plane of reality in which the here-and-now physical world was given new meanings by a 'higher' realm of consciousness. In places as public as the Haight-Ashbury and as private as farms in the Kansas countryside, young people dropped acid, imagined the impossible, and then tried to bring it to life. Along the way, a few people died and others lost their minds."[16]

If older generations despised the counterculture, it was not because they had nothing in common with it in their daily lives. Through what Farber calls "a legal pharmaceutical revolution," these generations had become dependent on drugs "far more powerful and dangerous than marijuana, in mind-numbing quantities." In 1965, he says, doctors wrote 123 million prescriptions for tranquilizers and sedatives and 24 million for various amphetamines, helping their patients to relax or speed up, depending on the situation. In the mid-1960s, about 3,000 Americans died annually of overdoses of legal drugs. Parents and elders in vast numbers were also hooked on alcohol and tobacco, and their unwillingness or inability to break their dependency on these drugs made them less credible when they admonished their younger counterparts to stay away from drugs.[17]

For the nation's youth, marijuana held appeal despite the fact that it was illegal—or maybe because it was. More significant in encouraging drug use in the youth culture was its prevalence in the lives of its cultural heroes, that is, rock musicians. Not only were popular performers users themselves, but they romanticized drug use in their lyrics. Not that the messages in the lyrics caused the drug use or that the drug use made the messages appealing; rather, it happened simultaneously, merging into a way of life.

Even though the sale and distribution of drugs was illegal, it became a big business carried on surreptitiously through small deals on street corners and in school corridors. Figures on sales, revenue, and profit are therefore impossible to determine. The other part of the equation—that is, rock music—quickly became a big business; the youth culture, particularly white youth, was ready to spend enormous sums buying the labels of its idols. Tour promoters had no trouble filling halls and stadiums for the star performers, and special productions also became big business. It all became very profitable, even for segments of society that had little use for the sound and lyrics of rock music and the culture that loved it.

Conclusion   The products and byproducts of the counterculture of the 1960s gradually became part of the daily lives of many Americans, contributing to cultural changes that seemed unstoppable and, in subsequent decades, irreversible. But there were other contributing forces. Technology was a powerful one, with television being a prime example of its power. Commercial interests played a large but often overlooked part in the cultural transitions. Advertising, for example, transformed consumers' wants into needs, seducing them with promises of lifestyles they otherwise could scarcely have imagined. In less affluent days, practicing self-restraint—duty, loyalty, hard work, and good citizenship—was perhaps made easier by shortages of money and material goods. There were limits on what people could own, where they could go, what they could do, and how they could live. The arrival of post-Depression, postwar prosperity enabled people to own more freely what their hearts desired, go where they wished, do what they wanted, and live as they pleased.

The Vietnam War rattled the social order in countless ways, turning people against one another and testing American claims never to have been involved in an unjust war. The Great Society's War on Poverty played a part in changing American culture by enlarging the role of the federal government in areas previously considered off-limits. Lowered racial and gender barriers allowed people to move out of their traditionally fixed places in society. As they did so, the old order was forced to change. Schools played a part in the cultural changes by experimenting with new ways to meet new obligations. Churches had helped sustain established beliefs and behaviors, but in the new times some of their old teachings lost influence. When churches softened their teachings on matters affecting daily lives, or when they tried to make ecumenism or pluralism work, their grip on their members weakened.

Although ideals described as modern flourished in the early 1960s, they faded with each passing year. New times, not yet named, were at the doorstep; sharper discord was just around the corner.

NOTES

1. Beth Bailey, *From Front Porch to Back Seat: Courtship in Twentieth-Century America* (Baltimore, Md.: Johns Hopkins University Press, 1988), 2.

2. Ibid., 112.

3. Ibid., 2.

4. David Farber, *The Age of Great Dreams: America in the 1960s* (New York: Hill and Wang, 1994), 184.

5. Herbert I. London, *Closing the Circle: A Cultural History of the Rock Revolution* (Chicago: Nelson-Hall), 11.

6. Edward P. Morgan, *The 60s Experience: Hard Lessons about Modern America* (Philadelphia: Temple University Press, 1981), 188.

7. James Haskins and Kathleen Benson, *The 60s Reader* (New York: Viking Kestrel, 1988), 82–83.

8. Morgan, *The 60s Experience*, 189.

9. David Chalmers, *And the Crooked Places Made Straight: The Struggle for Social Change in the 1960s* (Baltimore, Md.: Johns Hopkins University Press, 1991), 90.

10. Jeff Greenfield, "They Changed Rock, Which Changed the Culture, Which Changed Us," *New York Times Magazine*, February 16, 1975, 12; reprinted in Janet Podell, *Rock Music in America* (New York: H. W. Wilson, 1987), 43.

11. David P. Szatmary, *Rockin' in Time: A Social History of Rock and Roll*, 2d ed. (Englewood Cliffs, N.J.: Prentice-Hall, 1991), 134–44.

12. Leonard Wolf, *Voices from the Love Generation* (Boston: Little, Brown, 1968), xxi; quoted in Morgan, *The 60s Experience*, 172.

13. John A. Hostetler, *Communitarian Societies* (New York: Holt, Rinehart and Winston, 1974), 57.

14. Ibid.

15. Farber, *Age of Great Dreams*, 173.

16. Ibid., 178.

17. Ibid., 173–74.

Part II

Troubled Times: 1967–1974

The concluding paragraphs of Part I set the stage for our look at the continuing cultural changes in America in the later 1960s and early 1970s, as well as at new forces in technology and the increasing influence of consumerism. The War on Poverty and the Vietnam War greatly enlarged the role of government in the lives of the American people, and controversies surrounding them produced social turmoil. The civil rights revolution made it clear that domestic tranquility could not be restored apart from equal treatment of all citizens. Demands for change constantly tested the traditions and practices of families, schools, churches and organizations of all kinds. By the middle of the 1970s, the nation the United States had been in the 1950s had been permanently transformed.

9

Changing Families

By 1967, many parents who had begun raising families in the 1950s could say that their hopes and expectations were being realized. Not that they had struck it rich, but they **Family Life** had managed to buy larger homes in suburban neighborhoods. The future looked promising, perhaps because of pay increases and promotions for the fathers. The mothers' willingness to find part-time jobs made a difference, too.

As families' prosperity inched upward, they enjoyed such things as genuine summer vacations. In earlier times vacation travels may have taken them to visit grandparents, aunts, uncles, cousins, and friends. Now, perhaps with borrowed camping gear loaded into low-powered, unairconditioned sedans, they traveled to such events as Expo '67 in Montreal. The innumerable technological wonders displayed at this world's fair dazzled even the most sophisticated visitors.

For the children, each year in school meant a new grade, a new teacher, and, in larger schools, new friends. Studies, music lessons, sports, church activities, friendships, playtime, visits to doctors and dentists, camping trips, other family outings—all these claimed a place in their crowded lives. With the children all in school, mothers had greater freedom to take occasional jobs, such as substitute teaching or trying their hand in retail sales. Some found full-time jobs, although they preferred seasonal ones that allowed them to be at home in the summer with the kids.

Such families no doubt regarded their way of life as normal, although they did not think too much about what *normal* meant. They did not strive to live up to some fantasy of an ideal family. Yet their composition—mother, father, and three or four children—represented a large portion of the American population. So did their everyday activities. Children and parents, occasionally joined by grandparents, worked together around the house. Mowing the lawn, raking leaves, and in other ways maintaining their homes as do-it-yourself suburbanites provided all family members with creative diversions from workday and school-day worlds.

Countless families of the late 1960s, however, would have considered this depiction as atypical. Single-parent families facing lives of hardship and discrimination in urban ghettos, for example, would surely have thought so. Rural families in the South and Jewish families in New York would have had little in common with the social circumstances of these suburban families. Asian immigrants in California, and Hispanic families in the Southwest or Harlem, would have seen their own lives as much different. Indeed, all generalizations about families have exceptions. Yet despite differences in their daily lives, it is possible to consider matters that touched most of them.

Family Tensions   Tensions existed in all families, even in ones regarded as rock solid. Placing sunrise-to-sunset child-rearing responsibilities on mothers caused some tensions. So did missed career and personal opportunities resulting from demands at home. Issues faced by families show more possibilities for tension: If both mothers and fathers pursued careers outside the home, how were they and their children affected by placing the children in the care of others during the workday? How did the division of labor in child rearing and home management affect relations between husbands and wives? In single-parent homes, what did placing all the responsibilities of child rearing and home management on one person do to that person's relationship with her or his child? What kind of social lives were possible outside the home?

In most two-parent families, the commitments of husbands and wives to stability for their children and to faithful, life-long marriages made the division of domestic and wage-earning responsibilities acceptable, at least temporarily. Their family relationships seemed part of the natural order of things. Not that these relationships would necessarily continue in future generations, but for them they worked.

Changes in Families   The natural order soon changed, resulting in different patterns of family life. As increasing numbers of women found employment outside the home, time for tasks inside the home diminished sharply. In some families the husbands and children pitched in, but a survey in the late 1980s showed that housework was still almost exclusively women's work. One observer wrote that "men recognize the essential fact of housework right from the beginning. Which is that it stinks."[1]

Two trends established during the 1960s, rising divorce rates and declining birthrates, continued throughout the next three decades. Between 1960 and 1967 the divorce rate increased from 2.2 per 1,000 population to 2.7, but this gradual increase began to accelerate rapidly, so that by 1974 it stood at 4.6 per 1,000. The birthrate per 1,000 population declined annually: from 23.7 in 1960, to 17.8 in 1967, to 14.9 in 1974.

Another trend that accelerated in later years was the increase in single-parent families. In 1970, 87.1 percent of households with children included both a father and a mother; by 1980, the number had dropped to 78.5 percent, and by 1990, to 71.9 percent. The numbers for white households in each year were slightly higher, but for black households dramatically lower: 64.3 percent of households with children had two parents in 1970, 48.1 percent in 1980, and 39.4 percent in 1990. In the earlier years, men in white families were the single parent in about one in seven instances, although the number gradually increased. In black families, women were the single parent more than thirteen times as often as were men.

Changes in family patterns and activities reflected a gradual shift in cultural values. Reverence for marriage **Families and** and parenting diminished as desires for other forms of per- **Cultural** sonal happiness and fulfillment gained prominence. Well- **Standards** publicized emphasis on healthy marriages led husbands and wives to place greater importance on finding sexual fulfillment and intimacy with each other, in addition to providing economic security and parental guidance for their children.

The gradual coming of age of the 75 million Americans born between 1946 and 1964, known later as baby **Baby Boomers** boomers, also contributed to changes in family life. Simply by growing up and leaving home, the baby boomers caused changes in the households left behind. So did the way baby boomers made their presence felt elsewhere. Some older ones went to war in Vietnam, some went to college to avoid the military draft and join campus protests against the war, some went to college to earn degrees and prepare for careers, and some drifted into the counterculture. Many simply got jobs, married, and established families of their own, expecting their lives to be much like those of their parents. They had not known either war or depression, however, and they were influenced by cultural forces unlike anything their parents had experienced, so their expectations were naive.

The baby boomers were big players in the emergence of a "singles culture" that gave rise to bars, clubs, and apartment houses catering to unmarried persons. Women who wanted their own careers outside the home—not only for economic reasons, but for a sense of fulfillment and independence—found pleasure and satisfaction in the singles culture. For them, motherhood and homemaking could wait, at least for a while.

Men, too, found enjoyment in the singles culture. It offered both men and women companionship free of obligations.

Courtship   In an earlier chapter we noted changes in courtship, showing that male-female relations began to exist on different terms.

The changes occurred not merely in conventions (that is, in standard, by-the-rulebook way of doing things), but also in conduct. Women felt increasingly free to accept roles that previously had belonged exclusively to men. Accordingly, they occasionally initiated an evening out, provided transportation, and paid part or all of dinner or admission costs. As conventional rituals were discarded, sexual relationships developed at younger ages and earlier in acquaintanceships. Relations between men and women not involving sex became easier and more relaxed. Coed residence halls at colleges were common by the late 1960s, and many institutions that had previously enrolled only men or only women became coeducational. Yale, for example, began to admit women in 1968, and Vassar admitted men in 1970.

Among teenagers, interactions at school led to the loose formation of groups for "hanging out" at shopping centers or in the family rooms of understanding parents. Armed with audiocassettes, a crowd of youth might make half a dozen stops in an evening. Sometimes they dropped in on a football or basketball game at school. Sometimes they took in a movie. Sometimes they gathered at a park. Dating and going steady were less formal than in the past, although pairing off was still common.

Older persons who did not find the "bar scene" satisfying as a way to meet persons of the opposite sex sometimes turned to match-making services. Operation Match, a corporation founded in 1965, reported two years later that it had 5 million clients seeking mates and 130,000 who had married. It is hard to say whether these figures mean that many who hoped for courtship and marriage were disappointed or simply concluded that marriage was not for them. Perhaps they satisfied their sexual desires outside of marriage, since they no longer faced the sanctions imposed in earlier times. In any case, as marriage rates declined the numbers of permanent singles increased, giving rise to a subculture within the singles culture.

The new relationships among unmarried persons did not always deliver the freedom, honesty, love, and equality that the participants claimed to be seeking. Nor did they win the approval of most parents, who saw no need to change the terms of courtship by which they had found each other or the practices that had governed their own relationships. The new terms also brought pregnancies outside of marriage in record numbers, particularly among teenagers, along with sharp increases in sexually transmitted diseases. Confusion and loneliness are not new emotions in the young, but the youth of the 1960s seemed to experience them more deeply, in part because they were unable or un-willing to make and keep commitments of honor and trust.

Some of these problems beset older men and women, too. If the price of freedom was partnerships without romance, sex without love, cohab-itation without marriage, some found the price too high. But as the cul-ture changed and as sexual mores continued on the course set in the early 1960s, it was difficult for individuals to go against the grain. Some did so, finding support in their families, churches, and schools, but the odds were increasingly against them. Pollster Daniel Yankelovich re-ported in 1974 that 32 percent of the general population believed mar-riage to be obsolete, compared with 24 percent expressing that sentiment six years earlier. In the same six-year period, the percentage of young people who said they were looking forward to marriage themselves de-clined from 66 to 61 percent.[2] Often overlooked in reports like these is the fact that majorities on all these matters remained, so to speak, on the traditional side of the fence.

The easing of sanctions against sexual activity outside of mar-riage and the lowering of expectations of virginity before marriage **Sex** occurred rather suddenly. This should not be taken, however, as brand-new interest in sex. The baby boom itself is good evidence that sex had played an important part in the lives of the boomers' parents, presumably with pleasure and satisfaction. Furthermore, the substantial number of baby-boomers born before their parents had been married for nine months indicates that rules on premarital sex had not always been honored. Now, though, any remnants of the belief that the exclusive purpose of sexual intercourse was to produce babies were regarded as quaint. Freer relations between the sexes outside of marriage and within it was part of what is called the sexual revolution.

Controversial reports by Alfred Kinsey in 1948 on *The Sexual Behavior in the Human Male* and in 1953 on *The Sexual Behavior in the Human Female* became bestsellers, despite their statistical content and clinical tone. They opened the way for more sensational books on sex in the following de-cade. Titles appearing between 1969 and 1971 reveal the new character of books on sex and reflect at least the interests, if not the fantasies, of their readers: *The Joy of Sex; Everything You Always Wanted to Know about Sex but Were Afraid to Ask; The Pleasure Bond; "J," the Sensuous Woman;* and *"M," the Sensuous Man*. These and similar books sought to show that sexual relations existed for pleasure and fulfillment rather than simply as a passage into "normal" society through marriage, giving birth to children, and parenting.

Critics worried that these books had stripped sex of its mysteries, re-placed love and romance with eroticism, and pushed aside ethical ques-tions pertaining to sexual relationships. The pictures of nude women and the articles on the "philosophy of sex" in the increasingly popular men's magazines raised further concerns. Not surprisingly, with the greater openness came more explicit uses of sex appeal in advertising.

Marriage and Divorce Neither the sexual revolution nor the rising divorce rate meant that the American people had given up on marriage. Between 1961 and 1967, the number of marriage licenses granted increased from 8.5 per 1,000 population to 9.6, and the number of marriages passed the 2 million mark in 1968. This figure was previously exceeded only in 1946 when marriages were deferred while men were away at war. The increases in both rates and numbers resulted from children of the baby-boom generation reaching marriageable age: The number of persons aged 18–24 increased from 16 million in 1960 to 22 million by 1968, an increase of about 37 percent. Furthermore, remarriages were occurring at an increasing rate, more than doubling between 1960 and 1972.

Parenting In the late 1950s American women, on average, had 3.7 children over the course of their lifetime. By 1990 this figure had dropped to 1.9. The explanation was not that fewer women were having children, but that women were having fewer children. One reason was that they were older when their first children were born, a consequence of two trends. First, the age of marriage gradually rose: In 1960 the median age at first marriage was 20.3 for women and 22.5 for men; by 1988 it had risen to 23.7 and 25.5, respectively. Second, women now sought to establish themselves in careers before bearing children. As a result, time for having more children and interest in doing so diminished. Children under age 18 therefore came to constitute an ever-smaller proportion of the population, diminishing from more than one-third in 1960 to just over one-fourth in 1990.

The increasing number of women entering the workforce, particularly middle-class women, contributed to changing attitudes and behavior concerning parenting. In 1967, 26.2 percent of the women in two-parent homes with children 17 years old and younger were employed outside the home. By the end of 1974 that number had grown to 32.9 percent. Consequently, more families had to make arrangements for their children to be cared for by others—whether by persons who came to their homes or in child-care centers or preschools. The number of children placed in "preprimary programs" (such as Head Start, day care, and arrangements administered by public schools) indicates the trend. In 1967 there were 3,868,000 such children; by 1974 the number stood at 4,698,000, a 21 percent increase.

Homosexuality Sex, intimacy, love, pleasure, and adventure had long been ingredients in homosexual relationships. Now the homosexual culture began to define itself more clearly by drawing distinctions between homosexuality and being gay. Charles Thorp, a gay activist, put it this way in 1970: "Homosexual is a straight concept of us as sexual. . . . But the word gay has come to mean . . . a life style in which we are not just [a] sex machine. . . . We are whole entities. . . . Gay is a life style. It is how we live."[3] Although lesbians did not consider themselves exact counterparts to gay men, their lifestyles were just as distinctive.

As homosexuals defined themselves by their orientation toward distinctive lifestyles, rather than simply by their sexual desires and practices, homosexuality gained more prominence and gay men and lesbians became more open in their relationships. Medical judgments concerning the nature of homosexuality also began to change. In 1973 the American Psychiatric Association removed its categorization of homosexuality as a mental disorder. Proponents of the action said that diagnostic categories should describe conditions succinctly and accurately, and that was not the case with homosexuality. The public's perception of homosexuality also changed. Although antipathy toward homosexuals in some segments of the population remained strong, attitudes toward individual homosexuals became more tolerant.

With matters involving sex becoming more open for discussion, abortion was discussed more freely. Opponents of **Abortion** restrictive laws challenged them in the courts. The seeds for intense, bitter, and long-lasting controversies were sown in 1973 when the Supreme Court ruled in *Roe v. Wade* that laws prohibiting abortions violated rights of privacy. Battles between persons taking what were called pro-life and pro-choice positions continued throughout subsequent decades.

NOTES

1. Pat Minardi, "The Politics of Housework," quoted in Judith Babbits, "Household Labor," *Encyclopedia of American Social History*, Vol. 2 (New York: Charles Scribner's Sons, 1993), 1430.

2. Daniel Yankelovich, *New Morality: A Profile of American Youth in the 70's* (New York: McGraw-Hill, 1974), 59.

3. Charles Thorp, "Leadership and Violence," in *Out of the Closets*, eds. Karla Jay and Allen Young (New York: Doublas/Links, 1972), 353; quoted in Steven Seidman, *Romantic Longings: Love in America, 1830–1980* (New York: Routledge, 1993), 164.

10

Civil Rights and Group Identities

By the late 1960s it was obvious that if enacting civil rights laws was difficult, changing practices was going to be even harder. Still harder was changing attitudes. Growing impatience by blacks was understandable. A year after his **African Americans** speech at the Lincoln Memorial in 1963, when he spoke hopefully of his dream that "someday" freedom would ring in America, Martin Luther King, Jr. published a book entitled *Why We Can't Wait*. Challenges to his leadership by more radical figures—Malcolm X, Stokely Carmichael, and the Black Panthers, among others—and changing circumstances in 1967 compelled him to become more radical too.

Television networks that year brought the nation live coverage of riots in Detroit. Scenes of looting, fires, injuries, and deaths reminded viewers of the riots in Watts two years earlier. The next year a commission appointed by President Johnson to investigate the causes of civil disorders formally reported that the United States was moving toward two societies, "one black, one white—separate and unequal."

Did it have to be that way? In the year that Martin Luther King, Jr. spoke passionately of his dream for **The Fire Next** America, novelist James Baldwin acknowledged that cre- **Time** ating one nation had proved to be "a hideously difficult task." The past that blacks had endured, a past "of rope, fire, torture, castration, infanticide, rape; death and humiliation; fear by day and night, fear as deep as the marrow of the bone," had forced them each day to "snatch their manhood, their identity, out of the fire of human cruelty that rages to destroy it." In so doing, Baldwin wrote in *The Fire*

Next Time, they achieved their own unshakable authority. Blacks had the advantage, he claimed, of never having believed the myths to which white Americans cling about the heroism of freedom-loving ancestors, about American invincibility, about the virility of white men and purity of white women. They were free to take on the problems they faced. But they could not do it alone:

> If we—and now I mean the relatively conscious whites and the relatively conscious blacks, who must, like lovers, insist on, or create, the consciousness of the others—do not falter in our duty now, we may be able, handful that we are, to end the racial nightmare, and achieve our country, and change the history of the world. If we do not now dare everything, the fulfillment of that prophecy, re-created from the Bible in song by a slave, is upon us: *God gave Noah the rainbow sign, No more water, the fire next time!"*[1]

By 1968 it looked as though the fire was coming. The assassination of Martin Luther King, Jr., on April 4 led to more urban riots. Before the decade was over, riots occurred in more than 100 cities and resulted in at least 77 deaths. Thousands suffered injuries, and property destruction was incalculable. The well-publicized purpose of a civil rights law passed one week after King's death was to prohibit racial discrimination in housing policies and practices. However, a provision insisted on by Senator Strom Thurmond of South Carolina showed the ambivalence of white politicians toward militant blacks. This provision made it a crime to use the facilities of interstate commerce "to organize, promote, encourage, participate in, or carry on a riot; or to commit any act of violence in furtherance of a riot." Robert Weisbrot, a historian of the civil rights movement, has observed that the bill's priorities were clear: "modest federal involvement in black efforts to flee the ghetto, but overwhelming force to curb all restiveness within it."[2]

Before his death, Martin Luther King, Jr., had planned a "Poor People's March on Washington" to shift the focus of the civil rights movement from racial to economic issues, believing that this might attract broader support. Leadership of the Campaign fell to his successor in the Southern Christian Leadership Conference, Ralph David Abernathy. Even under ideal conditions, the prospects of success were limited, but the weather in Washington at the time of the march was miserable. The political climate the campaigners faced was even worse, and their well-intentioned efforts seemed only to call attention to the powerlessness of poor blacks and their isolation from poor whites.

Nixon's Southern Strategy
The death of King, the riots, and exhaustion took much of the impetus out of the civil rights movement. The election of Richard Nixon in November 1968 dealt it an additional blow. His "southern strategy" played on the resentments of whites. At the same time, supporters

of civil rights turned to Congress for laws calling for affirmative action policies in hiring and protective measures of other kinds. The notion of establishing race-conscious policies and preferential treatment for blacks to remedy past injustices caused strains among supporters, both black and white. Some contended that the struggle should be for a "color-blind" society, with neither advantages nor disadvantages resulting from the color of one's skin. Race-conscious policies also intensified the back-lash by those who thought the movement had already gone too far too fast. Pursuit of civil rights goals in the courts also encouraged the back-lash, particularly on the matter of busing to achieve school desegregation. A period that had begun on a note of gloom ended on an even gloomier one.

Hoping to serve the interests of African Americans more effectively, black leaders sought to increase their representation in executive positions at the local level and in state legislatures and the Congress of the United States. By 1971 twelve African Americans held seats in **National Black Political Assembly** the House of Representatives, and a number of cities had African American mayors, but this did not have much effect on the daily lives of African Americans. Policy changes to achieve success would require that they hold more political power.

With that in mind, the Congressional Black Caucus, formed in 1971, cooperated tactically with the more militant blacks in planning a National Black Political Assembly in Gary, Indiana, in March 1972. The Assembly was the largest black political convention in U.S. history; about 3,000 official delegates attended, representing almost every faction and viewpoint. An additional 9,000 persons attended as observers. Historian Manning Marable refers to the Assembly as a marriage of convenience between the aspiring and somewhat radicalized black petty bourgeoisie and the black nationalist movement. The collective vision of the convention, he says, "represented a desire to seize electoral control of America's major cities, to move the black masses from the politics of desegregation to the politics of real empowerment, ultimately to create their own independent black political party."[3]

The fiscal, social, and demographic problems faced by urban blacks were awesome, for as the affluent populations of cities had fled to the suburbs, the tax base **A Grim Picture** declined sharply. Racial conflicts over dwindling job opportunities were common. Civil service laws protected the jobs of insensitive or racist city bureaucrats. States and the federal government were losing interest in coming to the cities' rescue. At the national level, President Nixon made no moves to increase the voting power of African Americans. He supported only voluntary efforts to integrate schools, did little to push integration of federal housing programs, and failed to provide adequate funding for black entrepreneurs seeking to start businesses.

The laws passed in the 1960s with the intention of making things better, or at least of offering hope that things would change, instead magnified African Americans' sense of hopelessness. If by working together they could not overcome their disadvantages, how could they hope to do so as individuals? If the government could or would not help them, who could?

Hispanics Except in southwestern regions of the United States, Miami, and New York City, it was easy for Americans to ignore the presence of persons of Hispanic descent. The diversity of this population complicates generalizations about them. Even finding suitable terminology is difficult. Today's officially adopted and most commonly used term, *Hispanic*, cannot adequately encompass the Chicano farm workers in California, Latinos from Central America living in Los Angeles, Mexican Americans in Phoenix or Albuquerque, Cuban Americans in Miami, Puerto Ricans in Harlem, and others with a Spanish surname.

Although shaping a movement with political clout has always been difficult for Hispanics, they learned lessons of strategy from the movement for civil rights for African Americans. Chiefly, they learned the importance of solidarity and group pride, and they became more confrontational and increasingly active in politics. Those living in the southwestern and western states began to create a new identity by adopting, for a time, the term *Chicano* as a rejection of the cultural assimilation suggested in *Mexican American* or *Latin American*.

Given their diverse interests, it made sense for all who are today identified as Hispanics to concentrate their efforts on gaining political power and influence at the local level. The League of United Latin American Citizens (LULAC), formed in 1929 and revitalized in the 1960s, sought to force desegregation of some public facilities and schools. It worked in particular against discrimination in housing and employment. To achieve its goals, it helped elect the first Mexican American officeholders in the Southwest. By the end of the 1960s, under the leadership of Jose Angel Gutierrez more Mexican Americans were winning local elections in Texas, inspiring them to form the La Raza Unida party.

Wherever similar but less well-known groups took shape, their leaders and followers were moved by common concerns, mainly inequities in the schooling, language barriers, and poverty. Of the many efforts by Hispanics to improve their lot, only one gained regular coverage in the national news media. The United Farm Workers, led by Cesar Chavez, achieved prominence by striking against grape and lettuce growers in California in 1965. Walter Reuther, head of the United Auto Workers, and Senator Robert Kennedy offered well-publicized support, as did various church groups helping to persuade sympathizers to join boycotts of growers of grapes and lettuce in California. Although the strike and the boycotts achieved modest success, at best the American people came to realize through the work of Chavez that the lives of the migrant workers who picked the grapes and cut the lettuce served on their tables were unenviable.

Native Americans, or American Indians (here, too, the preferred term is elusive), faced conditions that were in many respects more distressing than those of African Americans and Hispanics. In 1973 the Census Bureau reported an Indian population of nearly 800,000, an increase of more than 50 percent since 1960. Nearly half of them lived in urban areas, about 29 percent on 115 major reservations and the rest on smaller reservations and in rural areas. Most who lived on reservations suffered from abject poverty. Those in cities fared somewhat better, but their tribal identity was lost or weakened. **Native Americans**

Wherever they lived, American Indians could learn from the movements of other minorities, but their circumstances made forming an effective one of their own extraordinarily difficult. Even as they became more confrontational in the latter part of the 1960s, marches and rallies did not make sense. They were most concerned with protecting their land rights against encroachments by states and the federal government. Consequently, they did not hesitate to file lawsuits charging violations of treaty rights. In the first of a number of decisions favoring the Indian position, the Supreme Court in 1967 upheld a judgment by the Indian Claims Commission that the government had forced the Seminole tribe to cede their land in Florida in 1823 for an unjustifiably low price. The Court required that additional funds be paid. When New York State wanted to build a superhighway through a portion of the Allegany reservation, it tried to gain the land through condemnation proceedings. The Seneca tribe resisted, forcing the government to exchange other land and pay cash for an easement through the reservation.

The National Congress of American Indians, established in the 1940s, worked as a lobbying group and undertook litigation on behalf of American Indians. In 1972, about 500 Indians organized by the American Indian Movement (AIM) seized control of the Bureau of Indian Affairs (BIA) building in Washington and demanded changes in the agency. They agreed to leave about a week later, but they took with them artifacts, paintings, and thousands of government documents. A shake-up in the BIA followed, and policy changes and other actions seemed to commit the government to responding to AIM's grievances. **Indian Organizations**

In 1973 the American Indian Movement, led by Russell Means and Dennis Banks, protested against unfair treatment of Indians by officers of the law. The protests resulted in well-publicized confrontations and eventually led to the seizing of a trading post at Wounded Knee, South

Dakota. Staged in a perfect setting for a media event, the seizure revived memories of the Seventh Cavalry's brutal crushing of an Indian protest there in 1890. Again the focus of the Indians' grievance was on what they regarded as a trail of broken treaties. In staging the seizure, AIM challenged tribal authorities as well and thereby created divisions in the leadership among Indians.

Serving to remind American Indians of their goals—and whites of their obligations—were two moving books. N. Scott Momaday's 1968 Pulitzer Prize–winning novel *House Made of Dawn* gave both Indians and whites a better understanding of the Indians' plight. Vine Deloria's *Custer Died for Your Sins*, published in 1969, stated the case for Indian rights in terms that boosted Indian hopes and that many whites found persuasive. Even as they sought support from whites, Indians realized that improving their condition depended to a great extent on their own initiative. With that in mind, Indian tribes began to establish colleges, such as the Oglala Lakota College in the Badlands of South Dakota.

Asian Americans   The term *Asian American* came into use in the late 1960s, as immigration from Asia was increasing rapidly. In the 1970s, Asians accounted for 34 percent of all legal immigration, compared with only 5 percent in the period 1931–1960. As with Hispanics, except perhaps more so, the number of distinctive groups lumped together under this term makes it a misleading one. The 1980 census recorded the presence in the United States of sixteen specific groups with Asian roots. It identified another group as "Asians not specified," and it placed eleven more groups in the "all other Asian" category. In addition, it noted about twenty Polynesian, Micronesian, and Melanesian groups under the broader heading "Pacific Islander." Perhaps because they are so diverse, no demonstrations or other activities on behalf of Asian Americans gained national attention during the turbulent 1960s and early 1970s.

White Ethnics   Racial minorities were not the only groups who were moved to protest their condition. Michael Novak's passionate *The Rise of the Unmeltable Ethnics*, published in 1972, made the case that virtues in the earthy eastern European past contrasted favorably with the powerlessness of white American masses. His book reflected the mood felt in ethnic enclaves across the nation. Czechs, Slovaks, Poles, Italians—any ethnic group that regarded itself as having been in some way placed at a disadvantage in America—sought to cultivate group pride and protect its interests. Second-generation Americans had in many instances been embarrassed by the languages, manners, and fashions of their immigrant parents, and the third generation's identity with the nationality of their immigrant grandparents had diminished considerably.

Around 1970 an ethnic revival occurred. The Ethnic Heritage Studies

Center bill of 1972 authorized grants to school systems to develop curricula that would teach children from various ethnic groups about their heritage. The bill provided only enough money for pilot programs, but in so doing it established a sentiment for studying ethnicity. Grants from other sources also contributed to the scholarly study of ethnic groups. Although these were intellectual rather than political manifestations of ethnicity, they helped turn the anger of white ethnics from protest politics toward cultural concerns. The impact on the everyday lives of members of the ethnic groups was slight and indirect, but the whole movement made ethnic identity respectable.

In 1965 Congress revised the immigration laws that had **Immigration** established national origins quotas favoring immigration from western and northern Europe. The revision placed all countries of the world on an equal footing. By 1970 it was apparent that large numbers of immigrants would be arriving from China, Japan, the Philippines, and elsewhere in Asia, as well as from Mexico, Central America, and South America. The influx from Puerto Rico and Cuba under other laws continued. By their arrival, the immigrant groups of the late 1960s and early 1970s changed America's racial and ethnic patterns. As they were assimilated into American life, they often encountered difficulties similar to those faced by earlier immigrant groups— learning a new language and adapting to new customs and different values, for example. Along with the protesting minorities already in the United States, they tested the nation's commitment to cultural diversity. More testing was to come later in the 1970s, when the influx of immigrants increased again.

Growing numbers of middle-class women took fulltime jobs outside the home, not to show a commitment to **Women's** women's rights but because their families needed the ad- **Movement** ditional income. For a while, these women and their employers simply accepted the fact that the jobs they filled were "women's work," characterized by low pay and few opportunities for advancement. The women's movement, however, struggled to improve their employment opportunities and working conditions and to help women better understand themselves and the surrounding society.

Publications played an important role in accomplishing these purposes. For example, in 1973 a women's health collective—a discussion group of eleven women, itself a sign of the times—published *Our Bodies, Ourselves,* encouraging women to understand and control their own bodies. By 1976 it had sold 850,000 copies. *Ms.* magazine, founded in 1972 by Gloria Steinem, sold 300,000 copies of its preview issue in eight days and had 250,000 subscribers by the end of its first year of publication. *Ms.* dealt with issues of sexuality, employment, discrimination, and other feminist issues, whereas the traditional women's magazines such as *La-*

dies Home Journal and *Good Housekeeping* continued to focus on domestic interests, celebrities, and romantic fantasies. Use of the term *Ms.* in place of *Miss* and *Mrs.* was controversial for a number of years, and only gradually did it gain acceptance. The *New York Times* began to use it in 1986.

Not all American women supported or even sympathized with the women's movement. Some saw no need to change the way things were. Some saw the movement as contemptuous of women who stayed at home to do traditional tasks. Many women of color, while sympathetic to the goals of the movement, found themselves in situations quite different from their white sisters. For them, problems of race were more critical than problems of gender. For all races, the different life situations of men and women, particularly in childbearing and childrearing, complicated efforts to achieve complete equality between the sexes.

NOW and the ERA
In addition to encouraging women to assume new roles, the National Organization for Women pressed for such things as equal employment opportunities, child care centers, and reform of abortion laws. The "for" in the organization's name showed that it was these causes that mattered and that men were welcome to help pursue them. NOW also led the quest for congressional passage and ratification of the Equal Rights Amendment (ERA), which stated: "Equality of rights under the law shall not be denied or abridged by the United States or by any state on account of sex."

Some in the women's rights movement wanted more radical changes in understandings of women's sexual identity and a swift end to male domination and social exploitation. Even though the pursuit of radical goals failed to win widespread support, and even though the Equal Rights Amendment eventually failed to be ratified (despite approval in thirty-five states and polls showing support by 60% of both men and women), changes in both attitudes and practice revealed by several surveys in the early 1970s are worth noting. One showed that in a two-year period the number of college students who believed that women were oppressed doubled. Others showed that women interested in entering such fields as business, medicine, engineering, and law were outnumbered by men in 1970 by a ratio of 8 to 1; by 1975 the ratio stood at 3 to 1. The number of women entering law schools between 1969 and 1973 increased fourfold.

Senior Power
As minority groups and women worked to improve their status, others followed their lead. Growing numbers of elderly men and women of all races and classes exerted influence on legislation concerning such matters as Social Security, medical insurance and care, and mandatory retirement. Many belonged to the increasingly powerful American Association of Retired Persons, founded in 1958, and some joined the Gray Panthers, organized in 1970. Writing letters and making phone calls got legislators' attention. So did

showing up by the busload in Washington, D.C., and waving "Senior Power" placards, as they did in 1973. Surrounding the offices of the Department of Health, Education, and Welfare, they made sure the federal government knew that they would not be ignored.

A series of riots in late June and early July 1969, sparked by a police raid on the Stonewall Inn, a gay bar and dance club in Greenwich Village, has come to be **Gay Liberation** recognized as the birth of the modern gay and lesbian movement. Bars had served as important meeting places for gay men and lesbians since the 1940s. Sexual identities revealed more openly during World War II, when men and women found themselves in single-sex environments that allowed discovery of mutual homoerotic desires, led to the formation of associations of homosexual men and women. These were little known to the general public. Now, though, gay men and lesbians began to abandon their silence and fight openly for an end to discriminatory practices in their jobs and elsewhere. Their increased visibility as advocates for lifestyles that made some Americans uneasy and enraged others did not deter them from using tactics similar to those employed by racial minorities and women. The issues raised by the Gay Liberation Front, formed after the Stonewall riot, and its allies could not be wished away by those who were reluctant to deal with them.

Although the most visible campus struggles were directed against racial discrimination and the U.S. role in the war in **Students** Vietnam, the noise students made and the force they exerted compelled college and university administrators to be more mindful of student concerns, whatever their origins. Students were invited to serve on advisory committees, contribute to reshaping curricula, and help institutions become less bureaucratic. Programs in gender and ethnic studies appeared in many places. The activism on campuses did not last long, but many of the changes wrought during the turbulent decade of activism continued.

It is misleading to say that until the 1960s white men enjoyed unquestioned dominance in American life. The vast ma- **Backlash** jority could truthfully say that if they enjoyed dominance anywhere, it was only in their own homes. Even there most men practiced the art of accommodation. In their jobs, most of them did the bidding of others. Still, until the 1960s one might have concluded that domestic tranquillity, such as it was, depended on the willingness of all groups to stay in their place. The natural order of things in American life gave the biggest place to white men.

Activists for change increased in number in the latter part of the 1960s, but they still represented only a tiny minority of the population. Although many in the majority supported their goals, their methods met with opposition. Those known as white ethnics gained the first attention for expressing resentment toward actions and groups they regarded as extreme, but by 1969 opposition to the protesters became more wide-spread and noisier—even though President Nixon called them the "silent majority." Seeing flags burned and policemen called pigs was bad enough. Seeing men referred to as male chauvinist pigs was worse. So was listening to the demands of the poor and witnessing the deterioration of housing projects well-intentioned taxpayers had built for them. Hearing strident demands for Black Power and watching urban riots on television was intolerable.

Middle-class Americans saw themselves as having worked for what they got, as having played by the rules. They were loyal, trustworthy, taxpaying citizens. What did they have to show for their patriotism, hard work, monogamous lifestyle, and religious commitments? What were the payoffs in the status quo they preferred? Perhaps a small house with a large mortgage. A low-paying job with unrewarding duties and little job security. Plenty of worries about the future. Their own place in society was in jeopardy, however, not because they were economically vulnerable but because their values were being threatened by those who would upset the social order. Everything seemed to be coming apart, collapsing, disintegrating, right before their eyes. If the violence they witnessed on television was far away, the way of life they cherished every day, right at home, was nonetheless under assault. So they protested, too, against the protesters.

Polarization   Circumstances were right for someone to play the politics of polarization. Richard Nixon, despite his campaign slogan "Bring us together," was skilled at playing it. With George Wallace, governor of Alabama and the American Independent party's candidate for president in 1968 being even more skillful and aggressive in dividing the American people, Nixon was able to avoid being labeled an extremist. Appealing to what he called the "silent majority," he pulled to his side many, such as blue-collar workers, whose economic interests would have made them more at home in the Democratic party. When New York's mayor John Lindsey attacked Nixon and his policies, Nixon encouraged construction workers to demonstrate against Lindsey and the antiwar protesters. On May 8, 1970, they responded by assaulting the protesters near New York's City Hall, beating them with their own placards. They forced City Hall officials to raise to full-staff the flag that had been lowered to half-staff in memory of the shooting victims at Kent State University several days earlier. New York police officers appeared to watch in amusement. Later, a leader of the construction workers traveled to the White House to present President Nixon with a hard hat of his own, celebrating the events in New York. In 1970 Nixon encouraged Vice President Spiro Agnew to attack the protesters in his speeches, as he himself did from time to time.

Neither side in the confrontations was blameless. Both paid a price.

New York construction workers wave flags as they disrupt an antiwar rally on Wall Street, May 8, 1970, several days after the shootings on the Kent State University campus. *UPI/CORBIS-BETTMANN.*

Before long the protests lost their steam, but resentments lingered. In the long run, Nixon and his heirs benefited from the backlash. Yet in the 1990s, critics of the protests and protesters blame the 1960s for problems that evolved in the intervening decades. The cultural standoffs of the succeeding decades have their origins in the confrontation of the 1960s. So, too, does the inclination of disadvantaged groups to practice "identity politics," in which their sense of being victims is a powerful motivational force.

NOTES

1. James Baldwin, *The Fire Next Time* (New York: Dial Press, 1963), 111–20.

2. Robert Weisbrot, *A History of America's Civil Rights Movement* (New York: Norton, 1969), 272.

3. Manning Marable, *Race, Reform and Rebellion: The Second Reconstruction in Black America, 1945–1982* (Jackson: University Press of Mississippi, 1984), 136–37.

11

Securities Shaken

Changes in the economy occurring around 1970 were
worrisome. Not that everything had gone wrong. Good   **The Economic**
things had happened and continued to happen. But even   **Picture**
those who held no corporate stocks or bonds and cared
nothing about Wall Street sensed uncertainties.

In the 1960s the gross national product had increased at an average
rate exceeding 4 percent. By the end of the 1970s the increases had declined to 2.9 percent per year. Between 1970 and 1973 purchasing power,
adjusted for inflation, grew by 7 percent. In the remainder of the 1970s
there was no growth at all. The inflation rate by the end of the 1970s
had risen to 12.5 percent. Americans had always prided themselves on
having the highest standard of living in the industrialized world, but in
the 1970s it dropped all the way from first to tenth. There were reasons
to believe that in fighting the war in Vietnam, continuing the cold war,
and waging war on poverty the United States had taken on too much.

The personal security of families and individuals depended mostly on
good jobs with good wages. The unemployment rate in the civilian labor
force in 1967 was 3.8 percent. After slight annual fluctuations it rose to
5.9 percent in 1971, declined slightly over the next two years, and shot
up to 8.6 percent in 1975. The median family income in 1974 was $12,836,
In constant dollars, that was below the level of the two previous years
and barely above the level of 1970. In contrast, the median family income
had increased by more than 15 percent between 1965 and 1970.

A mild recession in 1969 and 1970 did not hurt the majority of wage
earners, but it deepened their worries. A variety of economic concerns,

many of them related to international trade, caused President Nixon to worry too, and he ordered several economic policy changes. The most startling was his imposition of a wage-price freeze for ninety days, ordered without warning on August 15, 1971. Except among labor leaders, the freeze was well received and produced generally good results. Even so, anxieties over what would happen when the freeze was lifted created new uncertainties. Economists believed that if the wage-price freeze did not boost the economy as much as initially claimed, neither did it do short-term or long-term damage. Ordinary Americans seemed to take both the freeze and the surrounding controversy in stride—a sign that they were in a "try *something*" mood. Nonetheless the national economy remained weak, and by 1974 the effects of a deep, broad, and prolonged slump affected many families.

Labor Unions　　From the mid-1930s until the 1960s labor unions had played an important part in improving the economic security of many working-class Americans. By 1970, however, the unions' influence had begun to erode, not only in the workplace but in politics too. They had built their strength in earlier years by taking an aggressive approach to organizing and bargaining, but now their implicit partnership with the Democratic party tempered their actions.

In only two respects did unions maintain or increase the strength they had enjoyed in the 1950s and early 1960s. First, as women entered the workplace they formed two organizations—the National Association of Working Women (known as Nine to Five) and the Coalition of Labor Union Women. Recognizing the potential power of women in the labor movement, the AFL-CIO, labor's largest organization, endorsed the Equal Rights Amendment in 1973. In subsequent years unions provided support on what came to be called women's issues, such as affirmative action, child care, and pay equity.

Second, unions representing government workers at all levels gained power and influence. By 1970 membership in public employees' unions exceeded 4 million, making it ten times larger than it had been fifteen years earlier. Particularly powerful were the American Federation of State, County, and Municipal Employees, the American Federation of Teachers, and the National Education Association, along with unions of police officers, fire fighters, nurses, and postal workers. Yet their power was limited by the fact that work stoppages—some legal, some illegal— by public servants directly affected the lives of those whom they served, thereby arousing resentment.

Unions' Problems　　The recruitment of women and the growth of government workers' unions were insufficient to offset the decline of industrial unions. That decline reflected many changes in economic processes that attracted little attention until their consequences were widely felt. One was the increased automation of manufacturing processes, making assembly line workers dispensable. Another involved the rising aspirations of families that had moved to the suburbs and worked their way into white-collar jobs. They sent their children to college with expectations that the children could reach even higher rungs on the employment ladder through individual rather than collective effort.

More significant was the process known as deindustrialization. In the 1970s the United States became an exporter of raw materials and an importer of more cars and steel, as well as electrical, electronic, and other manufactured goods. The U.S. share of global manufactured exports declined significantly and trade deficits ballooned. Large corporations invested their money in mergers, so much so that in 1968 the Federal Trade Commission launched a sweeping investigation of the causes and consequences of runaway conglomerate mergers. The chairman of the Commission referred to these conglomerates—the joining of companies engaged in unrelated or remotely related businesses—as a "virus" threatening the health of the American economy. Corporations also acquired related business enterprises and invested in overseas operations. Consequently, workers found themselves competing more strenuously against one another for jobs in the United States and against poorly paid workers in other countries. This allowed businesses to call for concessions, or "givebacks," as they were known. These included reductions in pay, elimination of formerly protected jobs, and the scaling back of such fringe benefits as medical insurance.

Also affecting unions' effectiveness was something unseen by most Americans, that is, the development of more than a thousand consulting firms that specialized in advising corporations on how to keep union organizers and sympathizers out of the workplace. These firms also showed how to defeat a union when elections could not be avoided and helped employers find ways to "decertify" unions that had won elections.

In 1965 President Johnson, applying the principles of the 1964 Civil Rights Act, issued an executive order requiring federal contractors "to take affirmative action to ensure that applicants are employed . . . without regard to their race, creed, color, or national origin." A series of court cases followed that dealt with the barriers to affirmative action principles. In a 1971 decision involving a standard written examination for employment, *Griggs v. Duke Power Co.*, the Supreme Court ruled that so-called objective criteria for hiring employees could in fact be discriminatory. Specifically, the Court said that the aptitude tests being challenged were illegal because they resulted in a relative disadvantage to minorities without at the same time having a "compelling business interest." To be permissible, the knowledge and

Discrimination in the Employment Market

skills they evaluated had to be directly applicable to the jobs for which the employers used them. The Court later extended the principles of this ruling to recruitment practices, job placement, transfers, and promotions. The Court rulings made it possible for women and minorities to get jobs from which they had previously been excluded, but unequal pay remained a problem.

Crime

Reports of violent crimes, often sensationalized, filled the airwaves and newspapers, probably giving an exaggerated sense of the perils people face in their daily routines. Increases in crime were nonetheless a legitimate concern. Between 1967 and 1974 crime grew rapidly, partly because of the bulge in the population profile of young men between the ages of 17 and 24, the years when some youths are most susceptible to committing crimes of violence and property. Among new reminders of the threat of crime was the increasingly common installation of burglar alarms. The routine screening of airline passengers to prevent hijacking, begun in 1973, was a reminder of a relatively new kind of crime.

Crime and Politics

As a candidate for president in 1968, Richard Nixon capitalized on people's fears by making "crime in the streets" an issue. His campaign theme of "law and order" seemed to be a transparent effort to take advantage of concerns generated by riots in African American areas of Los Angeles, Detroit, and other cities, but it worked. It fit well with his party's "southern strategy," aimed at wooing whites who disapproved of the policies on race pursued by the party to which they and their forebears had belonged for a century (the Democratic party).

The killing of African Americans by others of the same race accounted almost completely for the dramatic rise in urban homicide rates. The prevalence of such homicides puzzled scholars. Among their explanations, the most plausible is that African American populations in northern cities grew just as the industrial opportunities that had induced them to migrate there from the South all but disappeared. Consequently, they did not develop the customs and responsibilities shaped by regular employment that reduce inclinations to commit crimes. Poor schools and broken families contributed to a climate in which the commission of crimes lost much of its stigma.

Insecurities of the Poor

In 1968, 13 percent of the American population still lived below the poverty line as defined by the federal government. This compared with 20 percent at the beginning of the decade. Twenty percent of African Americans remained below the poverty line, down from 40 percent eight years earlier. These improvements meant that the Great Society's War on Poverty could claim only a partial victory.

When Richard Nixon became president in 1969, he supported modest growth in the size and cost of a few Great Society programs, went along with legislation that increased Social Security benefits, and approved construction of subsidized housing and expansion of the Job Corps. More significant, he offered a bold and ambitious plan for welfare reform. The Family Assistance Plan (FAP), would have ended piecemeal allowances and guaranteed every family of four an annual income of $2,400, with a maximum of $3,600 for a family of eight or more. The FAP passed the House of Representatives but died in the Senate, caught between liberals who thought it too conservative and conservatives who thought it too liberal.

Before long, changes in economic conditions, partly due to the drain caused by the war in Vietnam, meant **Public Housing** the end of concerted efforts to eliminate poverty. But poverty persisted. A good way to comprehend the dilemmas involved in dealing with poverty is to consider a specific project that represented the hopes, failings, and ultimate destruction of a major effort supported by both parties to improve conditions for the poor. In St. Louis in 1958 the federal government constructed housing that, upon first impression, would seem to have answered the needs of families looking for a good place to live. Known as Pruitt-Igoe, this housing project consisted of 33 towers, each 11 stories high.

Pruitt-Igoe, and other projects like it, concentrated a large number of poor people in a small geographic area. That would have been bad enough, but design flaws made matters worse. Inadequate wiring made installation of window fans or window air conditioners impossible, causing the apartments to be miserably hot in the sweltering summers of St. Louis. Elevators stopped only on the fourth, seventh, and tenth floors. Residents on other floors had to walk up or down a level from the one on which the elevator stopped. Children were not always able to judge the time it would take to make a bathroom run from the playground to their apartments, and before long the elevators were filled with wretched odors and filth.

Perspectives of those who lived in Pruitt-Igoe differed from those who did not. To a resident, "a project ain't nothing but a slum with the kitchen furnished and an absentee landlord; except we know who the landlord is—it's the city and government." To an outsider, "whether it is a pig pen or not isn't important. When people have done nothing to contribute to the society but make an application for welfare, a housing project is more than they deserve."[1] Either way, Pruitt-Igoe had no future. Poor management, poor maintenance, too heavily concentrated living arrangements, and crime made the apartments uninhabitable within

Eleven-story buildings in the Pruitt-Igoe public housing complex in St. Louis are demolished by dynamite on April 21, 1972. *UPI/CORBIS-BETTMANN.*

a decade. Judged to be beyond repair and too poorly conceived to justify salvage efforts, the buildings were imploded with dynamite in 1972.

After the midterm elections in 1970, President Nixon tried a different approach to problems of poverty. First, he refused to spend poverty program funds Congress had authorized. Then he announced a program of "revenue sharing" that called for allocation of federal funds **New Economic Policies and Problems** to state and local governments to be used for social services. Although Nixon was enthusiastic about the new law, which was passed in October 1972, downturns in the economy resulted in deep cuts in spending, and poverty programs in some cities got worse rather than better. Various measures—including a ninety day freeze on wages, prices, and rents, followed by federal controls on the size of later increases—helped the economy improve, but uncertainty remained throughout 1974 and worsened in 1975.

Part of the uncertainty stemmed from the crisis over oil. Prices had shot up in 1973 as a result of an embargo on exports by Arab producers. This hit the United States particularly hard, since one-third of the petroleum used domestically was imported. The crisis drove up consumer prices for all petroleum-based products by 12 percent in 1974 and 11 percent the next year, causing panic by threatening the critical role of automobiles in the American way of life. Consequently, the American auto industry suffered severe blows. The big "gas guzzlers" that had been the industry's mainstay soon became too expensive to operate; and smaller, more fuel-efficient models failed to prevent imports from increasing their share of the market. The oil crisis also increased dramatically the costs of keeping homes warm in the winter and cool in the summer. On top of all this, the power demonstrated by the Organization of Petroleum Exporting Countries (OPEC) represented a shift that angered and frustrated Americans already disturbed by the war in Vietnam.

Economic worries at home had their political counterparts in international affairs. With both the Soviet Union **International** and China supporting the foes of America's allies in Viet- **Concerns** nam, escalation in the war there meant heightened possibilities of danger elsewhere. But even as the escalations occurred, a vague sense persisted that the nation was on the brink of nuclear war and non-nuclear confrontations with our longtime foes. Occasional reminders that our missiles were pointed at theirs, and theirs at ours, made Americans uneasy; but the uneasiness passed quickly, even after a showdown over Soviet missiles based in Cuba in 1962.

The numbers of persons directly involved in the war in Vietnam provide a sense of the war's broad and **War in Vietnam** powerful impact in America. Of the almost 27 million men of draft age during the war, 11 million were drafted or enlisted. The remaining 16 million who never served included some who enlisted in the National Guard or were granted conscientious objector status. Some were exempted for physical reasons. Others had educational, vocational, marital, or family hardship, or other reasons for exemption. An estimated 250,000 men, many from urban ghettos, did not register at all. Fifty thousand evaded the draft or deserted the military by exiling themselves to Canada and other places.

Of the 2.7 million persons who served in Vietnam, 300,000 were wounded and 58,000 died. For their parents, spouses, siblings, and friends, the pain caused by the loss of loved ones was indescribable. Even though the flow of daily life in the United States seemed in some respects to be undisturbed, the loved ones of those who served and returned, those who evaded service, and even those who were exempted from it endured anxiety and heartache. For the rest, the daily reports on casualties, the commentaries on the war, and the protests the war inspired meant that happenings far away were affecting the lives of everyone.

U.S. Marines use a tank to recover their comrades killed on the battlefield near Con Thien in Vietnam, July 2, 1967. *UPI/CORBIS-BETTMANN. Photo by Dana Stone.*

Antiwar Protests
Protests against U.S. involvement in the war between North and South Vietnam began in the early 1960s. As troop levels went up, so did the numbers and vehemence of the protesters. On April 15, 1967, 125,000 Americans gathered in New York to rally against the war. More than 55,000 joined in a comparable event in San Francisco. Organized by a coalition known as the Spring Mobilization to End the War in Vietnam, the demonstrations had the support of a broad range of groups and such prominent individuals as Martin Luther King, Jr. and Dr. Benjamin Spock, whose book on baby and child care had been relied on by the parents of many of the protesters.

The efforts of antiwar protesters, most of them college-educated and middle-class, initially met with indifference. As the protesters became more insistent and more vocal, however, they increasingly alienated working-class people who knew that those fighting the war came primarily from their ranks. In December 1967 a Louis Harris poll reported that more than three-fourths of the population believed the protests encouraged the enemy to fight harder. Seventy percent of the respondents expressed the belief that antiwar demonstrations were "acts of disloyalty" to the soldiers fighting the war. A poll several weeks later showed

Antiwar protesters, including Dr. Benjamin Spock and Coretta Scott King (wife of Martin Luther King, Jr.), gather outside the White House gates on May 17, 1967. *Robert Knudsen, LBJ Library Collection.*

that 58 percent favored continuing the war and stepping up military pressure on the Communists. Sixty-three percent opposed halting the bombing of North Vietnam as a tactic to see if the Communists would be willing to negotiate a peace settlement.

Yet the demonstrations showed that opposition to the war could not be taken lightly. The antiwar sentiment of some demonstrators sprang from moral outrage over the loss of American lives in what seemed to be a lost cause, of others from long-standing pacifist commitments. Still other demonstrators believed it made sense to cut losses in a war that was simply an imprudent endeavor.

Even though the antiwar movement failed to attract multitudes of followers, televised reports on marches and acts of civil disobedience created widespread uneasiness about the war. Critics of the news media, particularly Presidents Johnson and Nixon, were outraged by what they considered to be antiwar bias. Since then other critics have claimed (contrary

Reactions to Protests

Gaylord Chris, age 14, carries a peace symbol in a crowd of some 100,000 antiwar protesters gathered in New York, April 15, 1967. *UPI/CORBIS-BETTMANN.*

to persuasive evidence) that the United States could have won the war if the media had reported more fully and accurately the U.S. military successes in Vietnam, rather than embracing the antiwar arguments.

Careful analyses show that most of the media, at least until 1968, held positions sympathetic to President Johnson's policies. Most continued to support the government's actions well into the Nixon presidency. On the other hand, the media's reports on antiwar activities tended to focus on violent or bizarre behavior by the protesters. *Time* magazine, for example, dismissed the April 1967 protests as a "gargantuan 'demo'" that was "as peaceful as its pacifist philosophy, as colorful as the kooky costumes and painted faces of its psychedelic 'pot left' participants, and about as damaging to the U.S. image throughout the world as a blow from the daffodils and roses that the marchers carried in gaudy abundance."[2] By failing to give serious attention to the arguments advanced by the protesters—admittedly difficult to do in collages of short clips and sound bites—the media failed to give viewers and readers insights into the ideas and ideals of those who genuinely thought the war wrong.

The agony caused by an offensive launched by the North Vietnamese in January 1968 did more to turn **The Tet Offensive** sentiment against continuing U.S. involvement in Vietnam than anything the antiwar movement might have done. The media provided uncensored coverage of that offensive, named for Tet, the Vietnamese New Year. The North Vietnamese attacked at many points, but the focus of news coverage was on a siege at the combat base known as Khe Sanh. The siege lasted from January 21 until April 14 and included fierce battles, reported daily. At one extreme, television viewers saw hand-to-hand combat with knives, rifles, and grenades. At the other, they saw the dropping of 220 million tons of bombs by American planes in the area. By the time the siege ended, about 300 U.S. soldiers had been killed and 2,200 wounded, but estimates of enemy casualties ranged from 2,500 to 15,000.

Military and political leaders in the United States claimed that the Tet Offensive had failed. Nonetheless, as Nancy Zaroulis and Gerald Sullivan explain vividly in *Who Spoke Up?*, Tet was a turning point in the minds of many Americans who had previously supported the war effort or were neutral about it. Savagely fought contests struck raw nerves. Perhaps even more so did a photograph showing South Vietnam's police chief shooting a Viet Cong suspect in the head on a Saigon sidewalk. Or hearing a U.S. major say about the fighting at Ben Tre, a city of 35,000, "It became necessary to destroy the town to save it." When CBS anchorman Walter Cronkite, in his "Report from Vietnam" on February 27, 1968, expressed doubts about prospects for U.S. success, those doubts spread. They spread further when the Business Executives Move for Vietnam Peace, which claimed 1,600 members, said that "as businessmen we feel that when a policy hasn't proved productive after a reasonable trial it's sheer nonsense not to change it." Even the *Wall Street Journal*, always a spirited antagonist of the antiwar movement, published an editorial on February 23, 1968, stating that "everyone had better be prepared for the bitter taste of a defeat beyond America's power to prevent."[3]

In subsequent months, more and more people expressed opposition to the war. They wrote letters to members of Congress and the president, placed advertisements in newspapers, signed petitions, and joined in vigils in public places, including military installations. They supported candidates who took antiwar positions, most notably presidential candidates Eugene McCarthy and Robert Kennedy in 1968 and George McGovern in 1972. A few refused to pay taxes, or to register for the draft, or to be inducted. A few burned draft cards and participated in strikes on campus and occasionally in workplaces. By engaging in nonviolent civil disobedience, they became subject to arrest, jailing, and court trials. More extreme actions included raids on offices of draft boards to destroy records by burning or pouring blood on them, as well as trashing, burning, or setting off bombs in buildings and, in several instances, committing suicide.

In the aftermath of the Tet Offensive and two weeks after a weak showing in the New Hampshire primary, President Lyndon Johnson announced on March 31 that he would not seek reelection. Vice President Hubert Humphrey, who hoped to be Johnson's successor, had been reluctant to question Johnson's policies, thus making himself the object of bitter and ferocious criticism by the war's opponents. The assassination of Robert F. Kennedy, Humphrey's leading rival for the nomination, added to the Democratic Party's turmoil. The Democratic National Convention in Chicago was a nasty affair. Protesters made the conventioneers angry, and Chicago police officers attacked the protesters, resulting in what came to be called a police riot.

As opposition to the U.S. role in Vietnam increased, Republican presidential candidate Richard Nixon claimed that he had a secret plan for ending the war. Humphrey gradually let his opposition to the war be known, and his strong campaign finish made the results of the election surprisingly close: Nixon received 43.4 percent of the popular vote, Humphrey 42.7 percent, and George Wallace 13.5 percent.

President Nixon and the War
After the election, the antiwar movement lost whatever coherence it ever had and fell into general public disfavor. The Nixon administration's misleading statements of its intentions and its denunciations of the movement's leaders, along with divisions within the movement, were partly responsible. Probably more important were the excesses displayed by radical campus groups, such as the Weathermen, and the news media's willingness to be wooed by Nixon's foreign policy advisor, Henry Kissinger. Still, opponents of the war were able to mobilize for a Vietnam Moratorium Day on October 15, 1969. An organization of Republicans known as the Ripon Society, the liberal Americans for a Democratic Society, the United Auto Workers, and the Teamsters union, along with many political and religious leaders, endorsed the moratorium. A number of Vietnam War veterans were among the millions of participants in local protests across the nation.

Growing Conflict
Conflicts between supporters and opponents of the war continued into 1970, most notably on university campuses. During the academic year ending in the spring of 1970, there were nearly 250 bombings and about the same number of cases of arson, resulting in at least six deaths. The event that brought into sharp focus the conflict between those who opposed the war and those who defended U.S. policies and actions occurred on May 4, 1970. Five days earlier Nixon had shocked the nation by announcing

that U.S. troops had invaded neutral Cambodia to wipe out enemy strongholds there. Ohio National Guardsmen, apparently in panic as they faced protesters of this action at Kent State University, fired sixty-one shots into a crowd of students, killing four and wounding nine. Students around the nation, reacting to what they had seen on television, threw their own campuses into turmoil, forcing some 400 colleges and universities to end the semester prematurely.

By mid-1970 the lines between opposing sides in the conflict over the war in Vietnam seemed fixed. While casualties mounted, protests continued. In April 1971, Vietnam War veterans marched in Washington, D.C., some on crutches. Others rode in wheelchairs. Thousands of veterans gathered at the U.S. Capitol, removed medals awarded them for bravery, and threw them away. But the demonstrations changed few minds. Nixon's policy of "Vietnamization"—that is, of turning the fighting of the war over to the Army of the Republic of Vietnam—meant that more U.S. troops returned home. The number of U.S. troops in Vietnam dropped from 536,000 in 1968 to 156,800 by the end of 1971. By March 1972 troop strength was down to 95,000, including only 6,000 combat troops. Those coming home made difficult reentries into the routines of everyday life, and the lives of those who remained in Vietnam changed: Estimates on drug use by troops in 1970 stood at about 50 percent. By March 1972 nearly 250 underground antiwar papers were circulating among U.S. troops. Reenlistment rates dropped sharply, and desertions spiraled upward, as did "combat refusal" incidents. Officers feared rebellion in their ranks, and some found their very lives in jeopardy.

Many Americans greeted with skepticism Secretary of State Henry Kissinger's announcement on October 26, 1972, that "peace is at hand." Even so, the nation was not ready to oust Richard Nixon from the presidency, and he easily defeated George McGovern in the **Ending the War and Continued Protest** presidential election the following week. The next month, peace talks made no progress, and again Nixon ordered bombing of North Vietnam. This prompted some who had not previously joined in protests to attend services of prayer and repentance, believing that as citizens they were party to morally indefensible actions. One such service, attended by persons of all ages, was led by Francis B. Sayre, Jr., who had been dean of the Washington National Cathedral for twenty-one years. He was the son of a diplomat, the grandson of Woodrow Wilson, and the last person to have been born in the White House. After the service, most in attendance marched silently with Dean Sayre to the White House, where they were ignored.

Despite the strength of their feelings, protesters found it hard to sustain the momentum of protests against the war. When Richard Nixon was inaugurated for a second term on January 20, 1973, a counter-inaugural demonstration drew a crowd of more than 60,000 persons at the Washington monument. The mood there, write Nancy Zaroulis and Gerald Sullivan, was "one of witness. Most were there because they were unable not to be. They had come to manifest silent concern for a war in which, as Lincoln's [Second Inaugural Address] had put it, 'Neither party expected . . . the magnitude or the duration which it had already attained'." But "the stale rhetoric from the monument platform on a day when little remained to be spoken that had not already been said many times before could not hold the audience. Most wandered off in the direction of Pennsylvania Avenue to watch, unbelieving, the inaugural parade and its anticipatory bicentennial theme of 1776."⁴ (No one knew then, of course, that by 1976 both President Nixon and Vice President Spiro Agnew would have resigned in disgrace.)

Two days later Nixon announced in a televised statement that representatives of the United States and North Vietnam had initialed the Agreement on Ending the War and Restoring Peace in Vietnam. "Peace with honor," he declared, had at last been achieved. A cease-fire began several days later. Withdrawal of the remaining 23,700 troops was to be accomplished in sixty days, and all American prisoners of war were to be released. The agreement left South Vietnam, known as the Republic of Vietnam, at the mercy of North Vietnam. The South Vietnamese managed to continue their struggle for two more years, but as American aid dwindled, they saw their capital, Saigon, fall on April 30, 1975. It was left to President Gerald Ford to issue a proclamation stating that May 7, 1975, was the last day of the "Vietnam era."

Whether any actions on the part of war protesters through the years accomplished the results they sought was debatable then and remains so. Attempts then, as well as more recently, to portray those opposed to the war as irresponsible "anti-Americans" who committed treasonous acts under orders from communist leaders run contrary to facts. Like every mass movement, the one opposing the war in Vietnam included some radicals, and the radicals in this one engaged in bizarre, violent, destructive acts. But the movement was homegrown and eventually included persons of all ages from across the political spectrum. Leaders and followers in the movement, with rare exceptions, believed deeply in their American heritage as defined in the Constitution and built into their political traditions.

NOTES

1. William Moore, Jr., *The Vertical Ghetto: Everyday Life in an Urban Project* (New York: Random House, 1969), 3–4. The author does not identify the project of which he writes as Pruitt-Igoe.

2. *Time*, April 21, 1967, 20.

3. Nancy Zaroulis and Gerald Sullivan, *Who Spoke Up? American Protest against the War in Vietnam, 1963–1975* (Garden City, N.Y.: Doubleday, 1984), 152–53; this note includes all quotations in this paragraph.

4. Ibid., 402.

12

Cultural Reflections/ Cultural Influences

The 1960s was the second decade of television's dominance of home life. The average number of hours of viewing per home per day increased from just over five hours in 1960 to almost six hours in 1970, nearly 18 **Home Life and Television** percent. With more channels, there were more programs to watch. Although virtually no homes were hooked to a cable television system in 1960, the increase to 8 percent in 1970 was the beginning of an accelerating trend. The 2,350 cable systems, up from 640 a decade earlier, principally served isolated areas; but when the Federal Communications Commission allowed cable channels to enter major markets, they began to increase program options for viewers in urban areas, too.

Television did not become, as some had expected, a theater in the home with featured attractions being the center of attention. Although a set might be on most of the time, it did not interfere with the activities of people in the room. One study showed that about one-fifth of the time it played to an empty room. For another fifth, those in the room did not look at it at all. This study reported that children "eat, drink, dress and undress, play [and] fight . . . in front of the set," and that is where adults "eat, drink, sleep, play, argue, fight, and occasionally make love." Almost always the viewing was discontinuous. Hours spent in front of television sets were greater among persons of lower income and lesser education than among the wealthier and better educated, for whom other activities were within reach and within budgets.[1]

The age of television. © *Stan Hunt.*
The New Yorker. Used by permission.

Television
        Popular programs from a decade earlier—*Andy Griffith, Red Skelton, Gunsmoke, Bonanza,* and others—maintained their appeal. Joining them as favorites were *Gomer Pyle* and *Rowan and Martin's Laugh-In,* neither of them particularly edifying shows. What mattered to program sponsors was not edification but whether they attracted audiences. Sponsors, networks, and local stations, showing sensitivity to the diverse composition of their audiences, increased the numbers of blacks, Hispanics, and Asian Americans appearing as performers and newscasters. In 1971, producer Norman Lear introduced a show intended to deal with questions of racial tensions in an unconventional, controversial, but appealing way. The star of *All in the Family,* a lovable bigot named Archie Bunker, became the mirror against which many Americans examined their own vocabularies and conduct on racial matters.

Three changes in television programming had significant effects for viewers. First, the creation by the federal government of the Corporation for Public Broadcasting (CPB) in 1967 made possible high-quality, commercial-free programs. The Public Broadcasting Service (PBS), supported by the CPB, initially had difficulty attracting audiences for its programs for adults, rarely gaining as much as 5 percent of the viewing audience.

Sesame Street, a popular program for children introduced in 1969, fared better. Big Bird, Oscar the Grouch, and Cookie Monster created their own set of fans. The Children's Television Workshop sought to use *Sesame Street* to change children's attitudes toward learning and adults' under-standings of children's capabilities. Network programs like *Captain Kangaroo,* a friend of children since 1955, survived the new competition, but many local programs for children lacked the sophistication of *Sesame Street* and soon disappeared.

Second, events in this period allowed television to become a dominant journalistic force in America. Coverage of the civil rights movement demonstrated television's power to instantly transmit newsworthy images, and reports on the war in Vietnam prompted networks to increase time given to news programs. NBC led the way in 1965 by extending its evening newscasts from 15 minutes to 30 minutes. Four years later, CBS's *Morning News* became the first hour-long news show. When the Watergate scandal began in 1972, all the networks gave it intensive coverage. The debut of *60 Minutes* on CBS-TV in September 1968, the first of the "news magazine" programs, gave television news an entertainment quality that increased in later years. Production costs for such news programs were substantially lower than for other entertainment, so other networks created variations of *60 Minutes.*

Third, the creative work of ABC's Roone Arledge changed the character and content of sports programming. Arledge made his first mark in 1960 as a producer of telecasts of college football games who gave casual viewers a sense of being there. His innovations included cameras mounted on cranes and in blimps, field-level cameras, shots of players and coaches on the sidelines, close-ups of beautiful women, shotgun-mikes to capture sounds, and instant replays. From college football, Arledge moved quickly to make all sports a commercial entertainment business by creating *Wide World of Sports.* His decision in 1970 to broadcast National Football League games on Monday nights was the next big move. His team of announcers included Howard Cosell, a tough-talking New York lawyer who had gained fame principally through his interviews with Muhammed Ali. Cosell's role on Monday nights was to be the man Americans loved to hate, the irritant charged with arousing controversy. He succeeded, and the viewership increased dramatically.

As other networks imitated Arledge's innovations, sports programs claimed increasing shares of television time. Gone as main features were the largely humdrum boxing and wrestling matches. Worries about television hurting gate receipts of professional football and baseball generally disappeared. By the mid-1970s television and sports were so thoroughly intertwined that television held a firm grip on the scheduling of sporting events. Athletes, coaches, team owners, and team sponsors saw it as the medium that could propel them to fame and fortune.

Radio   Advertising revenues were the mainstay of both television and radio. By 1968 television's revenues had reached about $2 billion, roughly twice what radio advertising yielded to stations and producers. By other measures, however, radio continued to play a big part in the lives of Americans, as it found ways to maintain and enlarge audiences. One way was through the growth of FM stations. Because they could broadcast in stereophonic sound, manufacturers began to produce sets capable of receiving both AM and FM bands. By the end of the 1960s, in contrast to the beginning of the decade, few homes were without FM receivers.

Specialized programming enabled both AM and FM stations to attract audiences. They increasingly concentrated on such styles as rock 'n' roll, country and western, contemporary hits, adult contemporary, big band, gospel, easy listening, or classical music. Each station's choice of styles reflected the advertisers' belief, based on market research and demographic data, that listeners' preferences were shaped by their responses to what they had heard previously. Country music, for example, seemed to reach listeners who not only had on their minds the travails and triumphs of the vocalists they wanted to hear but who had lived through the kinds of things the songs dealt with. The gospel songs of Aretha Franklin touched the hearts of those whose beliefs the songs echoed. To keep listeners listening, experts said, stick with the standbys. Specialized programming also resulted in expansion of "talk radio," that is, call-in programs. In its early days, talk radio sought mainly to be informative rather than controversial and sensational.

Just as the creation of the Public Broadcasting Service allowed for high-quality, noncommercial programming on television, it also brought something new to radio through programs of National Public Radio (NPR). *All Things Considered,* an NPR program of detailed news and feature stories, began broadcasting in 1971. In 1979 NPR added a counterpart, *Morning Edition.* Public radio stations also served the interests of listeners who appreciated classical music in stereophonic sound delivered to their homes. These noncommercial stations relied in part on the financial contributions of their listeners, and they geared their programming to satisfy contributors' preferences.

Movies   Although critics and the public might debate each movie's artistic merit and dramatic achievements, movie producers were in the business to make money. Thus they produced movies intended to satisfy viewers' tastes and provide diversions from daily concerns. Some films succeeded with humorous or dramatic qualities or provocative messages. Others served tastes best described as juvenile or crude, or both. Film producers learned how to push depiction of sex and violence to the limit. The stars around whom the movie industry built its productions and on whose success its profits rested made real the fantasies of those who watched them. Movie magazines enabled fans to follow the stars in their private lives, too, thereby extending the fantasies.

Three themes evident in the most significant movies of this period mirrored the condition of the society that found them attractive. All three were variations on alienation and loneliness. *M*A*S*H* (1971), by mocking the standard war pictures, revealed American disillusionment with the war in Vietnam. *A Clockwork Orange* (1971) portrayed violence and extreme versions of the practice of behavior modification advocated by some psychologists. *The Godfather* (1972) and *The Godfather II* (1974) showed a deeply pessimistic side of American life, portraying a patriarchal, closely knit family dominated by a tough, protective godfather as a refuge from society's pervasive ills.

At the beginning of the 1960s, the Motion Picture Association's (MPA) decades-old censorship code still enjoyed token observance. The MPA continued to allow the Catholic Church's Legion of Decency to screen movies and pass judgment on their content. Before long, however, the censorship code did not work anymore. Primarily as a public relations move, the MPA in 1968 adopted a rating system—G (general audiences), PG (parental guidance), R (under age 17 not admitted without an adult) and X (persons under age 17 not admitted). The MPA expected the rating system to work against the films rated the most wholesome and in favor of those that tested the limits of acceptability, as indeed it has. (PG-13 was added in 1984 and NC-17 in 1990.) The popularity of three films confirmed this expectation: *Blow-Up* depicted frontal nudity in dramatic situations, and *Bonnie and Clyde* and *The Dirty Dozen* represented choreographed violence.

Relaxation of standards regarding what could be shown on movie and television screens seemed to give sexual activities depicted there a stamp of approval. The mixture of frankness and voyeurism in **Magazines and Cultural Mores** Hugh Hefner's *Playboy* magazine did the same. *Playboy's* success at gaining readers—or at least viewers of photographs of nudes that filled its pages—invited competitors. As more sexually explicit material published in Robert Guccione's *Penthouse* magazine attracted growing numbers, the contents of *Playboy* became more sexually explicit too. Nevertheless, *Penthouse*, founded in 1969, overtook *Playboy* in newsstand sales in just six years.

Rock Music
As rock and roll evolved in the later 1960s, many groups of performers sprang up, some of them attracting huge followings. Listing and describing these groups in any detail is unnecessary, but several happenings in the world of rock music demonstrate what an important part the performers played in the cultural transitions of the late 1960s and early 1970s.

Among the most striking was that a number of rock and roll superstars—leaders of protests against "the establishment"—became big moneymakers. According to *Forbes* magazine, in 1973 at least fifty superstars earned an estimated $2 to $6 million annually. Overlooked in this report, of course, are the sums earned by mainstream American businesses through production and sale of the superstars' records and promotion of their concerts. By the early 1970s seven corporations accounted for 80 percent of all sales, and those sales were enormous. In 1950, record companies' sales totaled $189 million. Five years later they reached $277 million. By 1971, sales of records and tapes amounted to $1.7 billion in the United States alone. In two more years sales stood at $2 billion (compared with $1 billion in network television and $1.3 billion in the film industry). That was only part of the story: In 1973 sales of records and tapes reached $555 million in Japan, $454 million in West Germany, $441 million in the Soviet Union, and $384 million in the United Kingdom.

The stars and superstars paid a high price for the money and adulation they enjoyed. Heavy performance and recording schedules and frenetic lifestyles, saturated with drugs and alcohol, sometimes ruined them. Janis Joplin, whose intense performances were laced with obscenities, died of an overdose of heroin in 1970. Jimi Hendrix, known as the most extreme acid-rock guitarist, was the victim of an overdose of sleeping pills in the same year. And Jim Morrison, whose dialogues with the audience were filled with raw sexuality, died of a heart attack in 1971, his body ravaged by the excesses of his lifestyle. Joplin, Hendrix, and Morrison were all 27 years old when they died. Elvis Presley died at age 42 in 1977, the victim of a dissipated life.

As rock music gained wider acceptance, not by moving closer to mainstream America but by drawing mainstream America closer to it, some performers gained critical acceptance with their distinctive styles and sounds. The lyrics of Bob Dylan, set to folk melodies, were ambiguous enough to express the protests of almost anyone. Mostly, though, the performances of his touring group, The Band, reflected the outlook of his own baby-boom generation. Some consider Dylan's style as marking the beginning of the use of the term *rock* instead of *rock and roll*.

Other performers helped extend the influence of rock music. As young people played the record albums of Simon and Garfunkel, for example, their parents picked up both the lyrics and the tunes. Perhaps they shared the performers' concern over the "sounds of silence," of "people talking without listening"; or perhaps they too hoped to find a "bridge over troubled waters." The Beatles had caught on quickly with youth in the United States, and they attracted older listeners by experimenting with exotic instruments, melodies from classical music, and sophisticated recording techniques, creating something called studio rock. Although the Beatles disbanded in 1970, their records continued to gain in popularity. Until the death of John Lennon in 1980, and even thereafter, rumors of a comeback persisted.

The wider acceptance gained by Bob Dylan, Simon and Garfunkel, and the Beatles, among others, displayed the adaptability of rock music and the swiftness with which it changed. The folk-based performers' style came to be known as soft rock. Some groups, such as the Rolling Stones, drew fans with a blues-based, hard rock style. In the late 1960s, as experimentation with drugs moved through the counterculture and permeated the youth culture, acid rock gained popularity with its dissonant, glass-shattering sounds. Jefferson Airplane and The Grateful Dead were the two best-known acid-rock groups. Also gaining fans in these years were groups modeled on Led Zeppelin, whose loud, blues-based music combined with a macho stage show was called heavy metal.

Consciousness-raising, a popular term in the late 1960s, was applied to almost anything that enabled people to **Rock Festivals** see things in different ways. Rock music's main consciousness-raising events were the festivals staged by promoters in various parts of the country. While those who attended—perhaps as many as 2.5 million fans between 1967 and 1969—often displayed boundless enthusiasm, media coverage of the biggest festivals attracted much unfavorable attention to the music, the performers, and the fans.

The Monterey International Pop Festival in 1967 was the first large gathering of rock bands and superstars. The event that let the whole nation know that a new phenomenon had arrived, however, was the Woodstock Music and Art Fair. Held in a large pasture in the Catskill Mountains at Bethel, New York, for four days in August 1969, it appeared to be an event of young people simply coming together for a good time. But it was not a spontaneous happening. Rather, like other rock festivals, it was a well-calculated business venture. It was planned by John Roberts, a young millionaire who had graduated from the University of Pennsylvania, and his partner, Joel Rosenman, a Yale Law School graduate. Working with Michael Lang and others who gave the event stronger connections with the counterculture, they intended to make money from the performances by rock stars but also from the sale of food and souvenirs (such as posters of the late Che Guevera, the rev-

Some 300,000 to 400,000 participants head home from the Woodstock Music and Art Fair at Bethel, N.Y., in mid-August, 1969. *UPI/CORBIS-BETTMANN.*

olutionary ally of Cuba's Fidel Castro who had been killed in 1967). They also sold movie and recording rights to the festival. One of the promoters observed that although those who came "fancied themselves as street people and flower children," he and his partners were in fact "a New York corporation capitalized at $500,000 and accounted for by Brout Issacs and Company, tenth largest body of CPAs in New York City."[2]

Despite careful planning, events at Woodstock were so chaotic that no one was certain how many were there. Estimates ranged between 300,000 and 460,000. They came from all over America to hear acid-guitarist Jimi Hendrix, folksinger Joan Baez, Jefferson Airplane, The Who, The Grateful Dead, and other rock stars and groups. Traffic jams were horrendous. Torrential rains accompanied by intense heat made mud bathing and nude parading a natural pastime. Shortages of food, water, and medical facilities contributed further to making Woodstock a mess. In the midst of the mess, loving and sharing went on everywhere, and everywhere folks were using marijuana, LSD, barbiturates, and amphetamines. Yet round-the-clock entertainment helped maintain a measure of orderliness—and even peacefulness. Supporters of Woodstock hailed it as an example of the better world to come. There were no signs of violence. Looking at it from a distance, mainstream America could not imagine a place for such things in their everyday lives. The generation of youth that thrived on such events wore the term *Woodstock* proudly. Others regarded it with contempt.

Four months after Woodstock, a rock festival at a stock-car racetrack near Altamont, California, was the climax to an American tour by the Rolling Stones. With about 300,000 in attendance, promoters hired members of a motorcycle gang known as Hell's Angels to keep order. From the outset the crowd was rough and rude. When a naked, obese man climbed on the stage and began to dance, the cyclists triggered a melee by beating him to the ground. By the end of the festival an 18-year-old black youth had been stabbed to death, and three others died from accidents, drug overdoses, and beatings. If this, too, was the wave of the future, a sign of cultural transitions in the making, it was an unsettling one.

Nonetheless, the back-to-nature notions of rock music conveyed by the festivals continued to strike a responsive chord in urban youth. At the same time, a brief turn to a gentler, more reflective style enabled rock music to continue its progress across generational lines and into the American mainstream. The evolution of rock was not over, however, as blendings with folk, blues, and country music continued.

Amateur theatrical productions in community playhouses, as well as those staged by schools and colleges, have long at-   **Theater** tracted substantial audiences, but their productions are not theater in the eyes of those who know and love theater. To them, to know theater means to know Broadway—the playwrights, the actors, the box-office hits, the artistic successes and failures, the financial bonanzas and busts.

The 1960s were not good times on Broadway. Except for *Fiddler on the Roof* and *Hello Dolly* in 1964 and *Cabaret* two years later, high-priced musicals and plays failed to attract large audiences. The action for serious theatergoers took place "off-Broadway," or even "off-off-Broadway." There imaginative writers and producers gambled with more imaginative and less expensive productions. One off-Broadway production made it big, and its impact reached much farther. The musical *Hair* blended elements of the hippie culture into a "tribal love-rock musical." Protesting against commercialism, it became a commercial success when it opened in April 1968. Word of brief moments of nudity (on a darkened stage) created a controversy in New York. When it moved to Broadway and later toured the country, the controversy went with it. Nonetheless, it started a fad of plotless rock-music productions with sensational scenes. The most notable successor was *Oh! Calcutta*, a 1969 musical that treated nudity as a stage costume and confirmed changing attitudes toward sex.

It is hardly accurate to say that a fitness craze swept America in the 1960s, for many Americans   **Fitness and Sports** continued to lead sedentary lives. Still, running claimed the interest and time of millions of Americans. Many runners became insatiable consumers of running gear, causing rapid growth of new companies. Nike, a company founded in 1972, soon gained a dominant role in many sports.

Bicycling reached new levels of popularity in the early 1970s, when for the first time since 1897 Americans purchased more bicycles annually than automobiles; 60 percent of the bicycles were purchased by adults. Other nonteam sports such as golf and tennis held their appeal, and multitudes were hooked on team sports made for the occasional athlete, such as slow-pitch softball.

Spectator sports, however, particularly as they were carried into homes on television, consumed far more of the ordinary American's time. Regular season games drew substantial audiences, but playoff games hooked viewers to a much greater extent. The playoffs that gained enormous popularity in the 1960s and 1970s were the NCAA basketball tournaments played each March and April. The astonishing success of the UCLA teams, coached by John Wooden, was particularly intriguing. After winning the championships in 1964 and 1965, they missed the next year; but then, for seven consecutive years, 1967 to 1974, they were the big winners.

Other records, especially those established over long periods, gripped sports fans—especially if they contained an element of controversy. When Hank Aaron broke Babe Ruth's career home run record by hitting his 715th on April 8, 1974, some wondered if he could have done it if he had not played about 25 additional games as a result of the lengthening of the major league baseball season from 154 games to 162 in 1962. Denny McLain's 31-victory season for the Detroit Tigers in 1968 was made more interesting by McLain's reckless lifestyle, which ultimately cut short his career and landed him in jail. Other events in sports proved controversial, such as the decision of the American League to install a gimmick advocated by the unconventional owner of the Oakland Athletics, Charles Finley: the designated hitter, known as the DH, became the regular pinch-hitter for pitchers in 1973. The National League refused to use the DH, creating odd situations when teams from the two leagues met annually in the World Series and All-Star games.

Most controversial among sports fans was heavyweight champion Muhammed Ali, whose request for conscientious objector status on the basis of his adherence to Muslim teachings was denied. For refusing to be inducted into the military, Ali was arrested on April 28, 1967, given a five-year prison sentence, and fined $10,000. Boxing authorities had earlier stripped him of his title. An outrage, said some. Just what he deserved, said others.

Ali, always a fountain of words on any subject, had his own say: "The power structure seems to want to starve me out. I mean, the punishment, five years in jail, ten-thousand-dollar fine, ain't enough. They want to stop me from working. Not only in this country but out of it. Not even a license to fight for charity. And that's in this twentieth century. You read about these things in dictatorship countries where a man don't go along with this or that and he is completely not allowed to work or to earn a decent living."[3]

Hippies—the "now generation," the "love genera-
tion"—were completely alien to the daily lives of most **Counterculture**
Americans. Many never even heard the term used to
describe them: *counterculture*. Nor did they know fellow Americans who lived in "the underground" or followed an "alternative lifestyle." The movement identified as the counterculture did not have a widely accepted name until Theodore Roszak published *The Making of a Counter Culture* in 1969. Not until later were the words combined into one. Yet those who knew nothing about the counterculture, as well as those who empathized with it and those who loathed it, were unquestionably affected by it. We have already noted the counterculture's influence on the wardrobes and hair styles of young and old, as well as on music and entertainment. These were superficial influences, even though they proved to be widespread and durable. The counterculture had deeper and more profound effects in its encouragement of the use of drugs. In the early 1970s, polls showed that as many as 60 percent of college students had used marijuana.

The most significant influences came from the counterculturalists' questioning of things long accepted as given: Was truth attainable? Was reason overvalued? Who needed progress? What made traditional ways the right ways? If the social order worked to the disadvantage of so many, was it not time for a new order? The counterculture's emphasis on intuition and experience as guides for action helped push modern times into the past and lay the groundwork for many things postmodern.

A 1967 *Time* magazine cover story captured the significance of what was happening in a story on hippies during the "Summer of Love." If there were a hippie code, the story said, it would include these flexible guidelines: "Do your own thing, wherever you have to do it and whenever you want. Drop out. Leave society as you have known it. Leave it utterly. Blow the mind of every straight person you can reach. Turn them on, if not to drugs, then to beauty, love, honesty, fun."[4]

Contrary to later judgments, the 1960s counterculture was not concocted by conspirators or crackpots. For the most part it attracted intelligent, caring people who saw things they thought were wrong with society and created new communities as a way to change them. This raises interesting questions: What conditions in America made a counterculture appealing to those who attached themselves to it? Was the emergence of a counterculture in the 1960s inevitable? Might a continuing backlash against the counterculture, apparent yet in the 1990s, lead to the creation of a new counterculture, maybe even a similar one, in the future?

As drug use spread in the counterculture and its communes, it
Drugs   also made its way through the larger society, reaching into colleges and high schools, even in rural areas. No one knew for
sure how far it reached, but estimates of the numbers of drug users
during these years offer clues. The numbers shot upward rapidly, as
figures reported by the National Institute of Mental Health (NIMH) reveal. The NIMH estimated in October 1969 that 5 million Americans had
used or experimented with marijuana, generally considered the point-of-
entry drug, in part because of its easy accessibility. Just five months later
the estimate was raised to 8 million. By June 1970 the figure stood at 20
million.

Despite efforts to curb drug use in the military, it rose there too. In
June 1970 the Army reported that in the previous year drug use by
troops had doubled—from 1.2 percent to 2.4 percent. Nobody believed
these figures, so new research was necessary. By August 1970 new estimates were that three out of ten soldiers had at least sampled marijuana
and hard drugs such as heroin. Another survey indicated it might be as
high as six in ten, at least at one military base in North Carolina. The
increases outside the military may not have been as steep everywhere,
but in some places they apparently were. In New York City, where statistics were probably the most accurate in the country, deaths from heroin rose more than fivefold in the 1960s, and the increase of deaths
among teenagers was at least tenfold.

NOTES

1. George S. Comstock, *Television in America* (Beverly Hills, Calif.: Sage
Publications, 1980), 29–30.

2. David A. Szatmary, *Rockin' in Time: A Social History of Rock-and-Roll* (Englewood Cliffs, N.J.: Prentice-Hall, 1991), 195

3. Leonard Shecter, "The Passion of Muhammed Ali," *Esquire*, April 1968, 130.
See also Thomas Hauser, *Muhammed Ali: His Life and Times* (New York: Simon
& Schuster, 1991).

4. *Time*, July 7, 1967, 20.

13

Material Aspects of Life

In this chapter we sample some of the most interesting changes in four material aspects of life around 1970—food and drink, fashion, shopping, and health care.

The American people were, in the words of historian David Potter, "people of plenty." Even so, **Grocery Shopping** many were distressed by the high prices of foods— so much so that in 1966 and again in 1970 and 1973 consumers in various parts of the nation organized boycotts of supermarkets. A Gallup poll showed that the 1973 boycott involved 50 million people, or 25 percent of all consumers. Boycott participants acknowledged that the increases in per capita spending on food resulted in part from their demand for more meat, bakery products, delicacies, and easy-to-prepare foods, but these were matters within their control. Beyond their control were such things as the amount of money producers and retailers spent on advertising, promotions, and trading stamps. Buyers "earned" trading stamps with their purchases, placed them in savings books, and exchanged them for such premiums as toasters, can openers, and electric blankets. Enthusiasm for stamps peaked in the early 1960s, and by the end of the decade most consumers regarded them as a nuisance. Some consumers, however, remained passionate stamp collectors who would shop anywhere to get them.

In the midst of plenty, *well fed* does not always mean *well nourished*. In recent decades consumers have **Food Packaging** gained more knowledge about nutrition than in earlier times, but increased knowledge has not always led them to better eating habits. Appealing advertisements aimed especially at children, catchy promotional jingles, and attractive packaging have often had more to do with choice of food than has its nutritional content.

The Fair Packaging and Labeling Act passed in 1966 was intended to assure consumers that packages and labels told the truth. So powerful was the lobby opposed to this act, however, that it required only that manufacturers print their name and address on the label, display the net weight prominently, state the size of servings, and stop using terms like *giant* and *jumbo*. Several packaging mandates came later, one requiring that a label list all the ingredients in a packaged product and another that package sizes be standardized. These requirements were poorly enforced, however, and by the end of 1969 the commissioner of the Food and Drug Administration could only guess that 70 percent of the packages were in line with the law.

Had the labels been required to list all of a package's ingredients, what might have caught the consumer's eye? Artificial flavoring and sweeteners and such natural flavorings as salt and sugar to change food's taste. Food colorings to change its appearance; chemical preservatives to lengthen its shelf- or refrigerator-life; thickeners and thinners to change its texture; such ingredients as caffeine to change its effects. Revelations about the effects of some 3,000 food additives, many of them poorly tested, gradually led to new labeling requirements. In 1973 the Food and Drug Administration required standardized nutrition information on food labels and began to require the listing of such things as calories and grams of protein, fat, and carbohydrates per serving. As the printing of this information on labels became more widespread, competition induced some marketers to include information that the regulations may not have explicitly required.

Just as important in changing the nutritional qualities of foods with additives were practices that removed important ingredients. Refining processes often removed fiber, now known to be important in preventing certain diseases. Canning, freezing, heating, and dehydrating destroyed at least part of such water-soluble nutrients as thiamin and various vitamins, enzymes, and proteins. Here, too, consumers heard wake-up calls and began to change their eating habits. Perhaps these changes reflected a change in the character of the American people, for, as anthropologists contend, to know what, where, how, when, and with whom people eat is to know the character of that society.

Natural Foods   Advertising for foods thrived on ambiguities. Foods were called "natural" without particular attention given to what that meant. Restaurants served "shakes" containing no dairy products. Producers of imitation "chocolate" bars synthesized frcm various agricultural products, made tasty with an artificial flavor, mixed with bulking agents, and given the appearance of chocolate, could describe them as "all natural." Such developments, along with the profusion of foods to which chemical fertilization and pesticides had given a misleading appearance of wholesomeness, encouraged interest in "organically grown" foods. In their growth and processing, these foods were not touched by chemical fertilizers or pesticides or additives.

Despite quickened lifestyles and changes in family structures, much good cooking continued to be done at home. **Cooking** Would-be gourmet cooks used high-tech food processors and cookbooks filled with nutritious and tasty recipes. Newspapers and women's magazines had long contained recipes, but now, as more and more men helped out with home cooking, sometimes taking over completely, food sections in newspapers moved from women's sections to lifestyles pages, and special magazines devoted to cooking began to appear. Television programs also featured cooking ideas, examples, and recipes.

According to estimates in 1973, one meal in three was eaten outside the home—many of them hastily at fast-food **Eating Out** restaurants, the number of which doubled between 1967 and 1974. McDonald's, described by *Time* magazine as "the burger that conquered the country," had fewer than 1,000 restaurants in 1967 and more than 3,000 in 1974. New ones opened at the rate of one every day. In 1972 McDonald's passed the U.S. Army as the biggest dispenser of meals; by then it had served more than 12 billion burgers. Numbers like this are only part of the story. McDonald's managers' greatest achievement, according to *Time*, was "taking a familiar American institution, the greasy-spoon hamburger joint, and transforming it into a totally different though no less quintessential American operation: a computerized, standardized, premeasured, superclean production machine."[1] The fact that its menu items were loaded with fats and calories—almost 1,100 in a meal consisting of a Big Mac, a chocolate shake, and a small order of fries—did not keep customers away.

It was difficult in 1969 to avoid news reports of possible hazards in food, even in the milk of breast- **Hazards in Foods** fed children. The Sierra Club reported that mothers' milk contained four times the amount of the pesticide DDT than was permitted in cows' milk sold in stores. High concentrations of DDT in coho salmon in Michigan lakes and streams led the state to restrict the spraying of crops with DDT. Baby-food producers discontinued use of monosodium glutamate (MSG), a flavor enhancer, when tests showed that mice fed large amounts suffered brain damage. Test rats given excessive amounts of artificial sweeteners known as cyclamates developed cancer in their bladders. The Food and Drug Administration (FDA) then removed cyclamates from its "generally recognized as safe" list and revealed plans to remove products sweetened with it from stores. Later, however, serious doubts were raised about the validity of the tests. The

Sample food stamps. *Courtesy of the U.S. Department of Agriculture.*

next year the FDA ordered the recall of large quantities of canned tuna because the mercury levels were thought to be too high. Despite the scare, it turned out that only 3 percent of canned tuna exceeded the FDA-prescribed limit.

Hunger in America   Throughout the nation's history there have been people who have gone hungry, particularly in times of depression. A 1968 CBS documentary, *Hunger in America*, revealed how serious the problems of hunger could be, even in relatively prosperous times. In the same year, a nutrition investigator claimed that malnutrition in some parts of the United States was as grim as any he had seen in India or any other country. At one school, he reported, children had vitamin A deficiencies worse than those who have gone blind as a result of this deficiency.

Buying food stretched the budgets of many beyond their limits. To help such persons, the government established a program to provide "food stamps" to purchase certain items in grocery stores. By Thanksgiving 1967, three years after this Great Society program was launched, 2.7 million Americans received food stamp assistance. That was just the beginning. By 1969 the number of participants climbed to 7 million, on the way to 19.6 million in mid-1975. Between 1969 and 1974, funding for the program increased from $4 million to $3 billion. Urban food-stamp recipients typically had to pay more for food than more affluent suburbanites, since their parts of town had no supermarkets and prices in the small stores located there were higher. When government programs provided free or reduced-cost meals for schoolchildren in areas where feeding a family was difficult, these meals were often the best, if not the only, meals some children ate. The programs also benefited farmers and helped reduce government-financed food surpluses.

Champagne to toast newlyweds, a martini at a cocktail party, wine with dinner, a bottle of beer at a picnic, a gin and **Drinking** tonic at a bar—such customs came to America with immigrants from early times and have never disappeared. Drinking establishments, from the corner tavern to the bar in exclusive clubs, have long been fixtures in the American social landscape. With the drinking go friendly conversations, political arguments, television watching, and hanging out.

The other side of the story is also part of daily lives: poor schoolwork done during repeated hangovers, tragedies caused by drunken drivers, families ruined by alcohol-related conflicts, jobs lost because of excessive absences caused by drinking binges, homeless men and women clutching bottles barely concealed in giveaway brown bags, and illness and death caused by excessive drinking.

Although the effects of excessive drinking are well known, knowledge alone does not restrain those who are tempted to drink too much. By the mid-1960s the National Institute of Mental Health began to encourage research into causes and consequences of alcoholism, and in 1966 two federal appeals court decisions supported contentions that alcoholism was a disease. Two years later the Supreme Court took note of these decisions, observing that experts were divided on the matter; the Court then ruled that arrests for public intoxication were permissible. The next logical step was for Congress to establish an agency to direct federal efforts to deal with alcohol-related problems. The National Institute on Alcohol Abuse and Alcoholism made it possible for treatment, research, and educational activities to be conducted at new levels. One result was a recommendation that states remove many alcohol-related legal infractions from the criminal justice system, substituting medical treatment for punishment.

In the early 1970s, a way to be fashionable was to show more of the body. So there were short skirts, sleeveless and **Fashions** backless dresses, hot pants (preferably worn with boots), skin-tight T-shirts, see-through dresses, and increasingly brief swimming suits. These were years, however, of no predominant look. Ellen Melinkoff, whose offbeat social history of women's clothing avoids all the usual stuff about what was in and what was out, says of 1970, "Walk a block or so on any big city street, you'd see women wearing Indian block-print bedspread dresses, tight tie-dye T-shirts and hip-hugger jeans, afros, boots that hooked up the front, long calico dresses, rose-printed black-challis dirndl skirts, maxicoats, and microminis (slips that year came in twelve-inch lengths!)."[2]

But that was neither the beginning nor the end of fashion. With some, the sloppy, studied, uniform, somewhat weird, casual hippie look remained in style for a while. With others, conservative attire—full blouses, longer skirts—was the choice. Those in the dress-for-success school wore tailored shirts and suits and conservative dresses, recognizing that if clothes made the man, they also made the woman. Synthetic fabrics continued to grow in importance despite environmental concerns, and cotton fabrics became less common.

Among men, trends were toward looser fitting, more colorful shirts and slacks. As the width of ties and the boldness of their colors changed, going tieless became more common. Long hair, too, became popular. The hippie look called for it to be scruffy, but professional men began to patronize beauty salons to have their hair styled with conditioners and sprays, and the blow-dried look became common.

Given the variety of attire in vogue in the 1960s and into the 1970s, it seemed unlikely that waves of fashion changes would ever again sweep across the nation in controlling ways. Freedom in fashion seemed securely established, whether the purposes were utilitarian, status-seeking, or seductive.

Discount Stores The shopping malls that developed in the 1950s and 1960s found counterparts in another addition to the commercial landscape in the 1960s—vast, low-overhead, self-service operations called discount stores. Signs hanging from the ceilings in warehouse-like buildings identified the departments. In 1962, Kmart, Target, and Wal-Mart stores all entered the world of discounting as updated versions of the bargain basements found in conventional department stores. Kmart was founded by the corporate owner of the S.S. Kresge dime-store chain. Target was begun by Dayton-Hudson, a large Minneapolis-based chain of department stores. Sam Walton, an entrepreneur from Arkansas who owned a Ben Franklin store, launched Wal-Mart with a strategy of using small-town locations. By 1965 these and other discount stores surpassed in sales volume all the traditional department stores combined. Target had eight stores in 1967 and Wal-Mart had 19. Kmart, with 250 stores, had challenged the leading discounter, E.J. Korvette, in total sales, and it had six times as many stores. Before long, discount department stores were joined by

Fashions know no boundaries in the Western world. Mini- and maxi-skirts worn by these women on a street in London in 1967 were becoming common in the United States, too. *UPI/CORBIS-BETTMANN.*

discount specialty stores, like Toys "R" Us, Circuit City, T.J. Maxx, Office Max, Office Depot, and Best Buy.

Catalog Shopping   As malls increased in number and size and discount stores sprang up in large cities and small towns, another sector of retail marketing expanded and diversified. Mail-order houses ("at-home malls, " one might call them) had been around for decades. Montgomery Ward began filling orders through the mail in 1872, and Richard Sears in 1886. Sears, Roebuck, and Company published its first general catalog in 1896 and four years later surpassed Montgomery Ward in sales. A few specialty companies, like L.L. Bean, founded in 1912, were well established. Its net sales increased from around $2 million in 1960 to $4.75 million by 1967. It was then that Leon Leonwood Bean died at age 94 and his grandson became president of the company. Sales have increased annually since then, reaching more than $1.078 billion in 1995. At the same time, new competitors appeared. Land's End, for example, specializing in "cut and sewn" products, was established in 1963. Its product lines were limited and it grew relatively slowly in the early years, but by 1995 its net sales totaled nearly $1.03 billion.

As these and other companies prospered, their colorful catalogs became more appealing, keeping step with tastes and trends of the times. Later, some mail-order enterprises established stores in shopping malls, but they conducted their big business through the mail. Rather, they distributed their catalogs through the mail—a practice that increased so that by 1987, according to one estimate, the average household received 116 catalogs each year—more than one every third day. Most buyers of catalog merchandise placed their orders by phone, using toll-free numbers, and much of the merchandise was delivered by private carriers such as United Parcel Service, rather than the U.S. Postal Service.

Effects on Cities and Towns   Before shopping centers, discount stores, and specialty mail-order houses became plentiful, most consumers shopped in locally owned stores. Even big department stores were owned by hometowners, or at least by local businesspeople from nearby towns. One study reported that in each decade after 1950, more than three-fourths of the towns with populations under 2,500 suffered net losses of such retail and service businesses as gas stations, farm implement dealers, and lumberyards, as well as grocery, hardware, and furniture stores.[3] Population decline accounted for some of the losses, but the readiness of small-town residents to drive fifty miles or more for the variety and savings offered in shopping malls and discount stores made a bigger difference.

In cities, stores on main thoroughfares served people in their neighborhoods, while big department stores lured them downtown. Competition from malls and grocery supermarkets put many neighborhood stores out of business and emptied the downtowns. Ironically, mall de-velopers eventually discovered that the vacant spaces they had helped create in America's downtowns might be ideal for malls, so that is where, in the 1970s and 1980s, they began to build them.

Millions of Americans took advantage of credit cards issued by banks to pay for goods and services. Holders of **Credit Cards** BankAmericards (changed to VISA in 1975) increased from 2 million in 1966, to 14 million in 1968, to 26 million in 1974. For Master Charge (later Mastercard), the number of cardholders climbed from under 5 million in 1966 to 33 million in 1974. Loans out-standing on credit cards increased, too, many of them at interest rates around 18 percent per year.

BankAmericard and Master Charge were not the first credit cards. Din-ers Club and American Express had served travel and entertainment needs, and Montgomery Ward, Sears, J.C. Penney, and many local and regional department stores had their own cards, as did oil companies. BankAmericard and Master Charge, however, were the first ones known as "universals" or "third-party" cards, that is, cards that could be used in a wide variety of establishments. Initially, restaurants and hotels stuck with Diners Club and American Express, and stores and stations resisted accepting the universal cards, but eventually they made breakthroughs that opened up the entire credit card industry.

The increased use of credit cards had several long-term effects. It made shopping more convenient, particularly catalog shopping. It made it eas-ier for ordinary Americans to go into debt, month-by-month, sometimes with little appreciation of its consequences. It laid the groundwork for the development of a largely "cashless" and increasingly "checkless" society.

Many changes in health care that made headlines during these years resulted from technological advances that will **Health-Care** be treated in Chapter 15 on technology. Less newsworthy **Changes** than changes in technology, but undoubtedly more signif-icant in the daily lives of the American people, were the dramatic re-ductions in infectious diseases occurring between 1960 and 1970, continuing a trend that had begun in the postwar years. Reported cases of measles, for example, which had increased from 319,124 in 1950 to more than 440,000 in 1960, dropped to 47,351 in 1970. Between 1960 and 1990, cases of diphtheria declined from 918 to 4, and poliomyelitis from 3,190 to 7. On the other hand, while deaths per 100,000 population from infectious diseases continued to decline, the decade-to decade increases in deaths caused by cancer also continued to rise, as they would further in subsequent decades. Deaths from cardiovascular and kidney-related causes began to decline for the first time in the 1960s, although they remained ten times as high as deaths caused by infectious diseases and three times as high as those caused by cancer.

                    The federal government took steps to deal with shortages of
Physicians   physicians caused partly by the broadened availability of
                    health care resulting from the instant popularity of Medicare
and Medicaid. In 1971, Congress enacted legislation offering government funding for medical schools that increased their enrollments. Two years later it passed a law encouraging the development of health maintenance organizations (HMOs). These HMOs, consisting of groups of physicians and other medical providers, offered comprehensive health care to members of groups who paid fixed monthly premiums.

Decades earlier, physicians had stopped making house calls. Now the medical profession made other changes affecting doctor-patient relationships. Patients with acute illnesses and serious injuries were more likely to be referred by their primary doctors—family practitioners, pediatricians, obstetricians/gynecologists, and internists—to persons in specialized fields. Hospitals preferred having only "board-certified" physicians on their staffs, and health insurers paid higher fees to board-certified specialists, so the American Medical Association and other medical societies began to insist that every physician be certified in a specialty. Family practitioners, the primary care physicians who gradually replaced those known as general practitioners, also required certification. After 1970, therefore, almost all physicians-in-training served multiple-year residencies to be certified.

As medical specialization increased, physicians were more inclined to form group practices. Some groups included physicians with the same specialty, such as orthopedics or obstetrics/gynecology. Some included individuals or groups from a broad range of specialties, making it possible for them to provide comprehensive medical care through in-group referrals.

In 1970 more than 93 percent of the nation's physicians were men. By 1990 women physicians were beginning to claim a larger place in the profession, as the percentage of male physicians declined to below 83 percent.

                    Most aspects of health care depend on the willingness of
Smoking and individual Americans to exercise responsibility for their
Health   own health. The most persistent preventable health problems were caused by smoking. By 1967 the surgeon general's warning on the hazards of smoking had induced many smokers to tackle the difficult challenge of quitting, and smoking-withdrawal clinics appeared across America.

It is difficult to estimate the numbers of persons whose attempts to quit smoking succeeded. Many quit for short periods, but their addiction to nicotine was so powerful that they ultimately returned to their old habits. Nevertheless it appears that between 1966 and 1970, 13 million Americans gave up smoking. The percentage of adult men who smoked dropped from 52 to 42, and of women from 34 to 31, although smoking among teenagers increased. The decreases and increases seem to have evened out the per capita consumption of cigarettes, for the figures for 1960 and 1970 were almost identical. By 1980, however, there had again been a slight increase in total consumption. The National Association of Broadcasters announced a plan in 1969 to phase out cigarette advertising on radio and television over a three-year period beginning on January 1, 1970. Publicity accompanying this announcement may have influenced some smokers to quit.

Smoking came to be regarded as a more serious threat to health and a greater social stigma after the surgeon general issued a warning in 1972 that second-hand smoke may pose health hazards for nonsmokers. Gradually thereafter restaurants began to provide nonsmoking areas, and hotels sometimes honored requests by hotel guests for rooms in which smoking was not permitted. Meetings and social gatherings that would once have been held in smoke-filled rooms began to be free of smoke. Laws calling for smoke-free workplaces and lawsuits demanding them carried restrictions against smoking even farther. Tobacco companies fought the laws and challenged the evidence on the damaging effects of smoking, but they could only slow the imposition of restrictions.

Dieting and Diet-Related Illnesses

Whether from eating too much, or eating the wrong foods, or failing to adequately exercise, many American men and women jeopardized their health and appearance by being overweight. Diet plans promoted on television, in books, and through programs like Weight Watchers all attracted believers and followers. Some nutritionists placed the emphasis on healthful, balanced diets. Others called for drinking nutritious concoctions in place of solid foods. The range of gimmicks for losing weight was impressive; but then as later, most who managed to lose weight by following one plan or another quickly regained it when they returned to their pre-dieting habits.

During these years a number of psychophysiological eating disorders began to receive greater attention. The most common were anorexia nervosa and bulimarexia, or simply bulimia, whose victims were typically women. The symptoms of anorexia include an abnormal fear of being fat, a distorted image of one's appearance, aversion to food, and, consequently, extreme loss of weight. Victims of bulimia go on eating binges followed by periods of depression and guilt. To deal with their insatiable appetites, they try extreme diets, fasting, and self-induced vomiting and diarrhea. For persons suffering from these disorders, the problem is not unavailability of food but inability to cope with its presence.

More and more people, faced with increasing complexity
Mental Health   in their lives, sought counseling from psychologists and
psychiatrists. Many received effective treatment through counseling and medication. At the same time, there was an increase in so-called pop psychology, that is, do-it-yourself approaches to coping with stress, depression, and other troubling conditions. Doctors and counselors on radio programs provided ready-made answers for questioners seeking help, but probably more significant were books promoting self-help. The first bestseller in what was to become a self-help industry was *I'm OK, You're OK* (1969), a popular rendition of the principles of a field of treatment known as transactional analysis, by Thomas Harris, M.D. Transactional analysis was used widely by psychiatrists, though not without controversy, and it became something of a game, a means for people to discover much about themselves and others. One practitioner remarked, "Tom Harris has done for psychotherapy the same thing Henry Ford did for the automobile: made it available to the average person."[4]

Patients, doctors, hospitals, pharmaceutical compa-
Health-Care Costs   nies, and providers of health insurance were all re-
sponsible in some way for steep increases in health-care costs. As patients learned more about medications and medical procedures, they began to insist on treatments their physicians might not otherwise have administered. In some cases patients could receive insurance benefits only if they were hospitalized, and that drove costs upward. In others, sympathetic or ill-informed physicians, operating largely without guidelines or restraints, kept patients in hospitals longer than necessary. To protect themselves against malpractice charges, doctors prescribed medical tests that may have been unnecessary. Hospitals installed costly equipment and facilities, some of which were underutilized, possibly because they duplicated equipment and facilities located nearby. The high cost of drugs paid for with federal funds got the attention of President Johnson, when he learned the varying costs of twelve prescriptions of thirty tablets of prednisone. "The taxpayer should not be forced to pay $11 if the $1.25 drug is equally effective," he said. "To do this would permit robbery of private citizens with public approval."[5] Insurers typically paid hospital benefits on a cost-plus basis without scrutinizing the charges as carefully as they would do later. In other words, they reimbursed hospital charges without reference to uniform standards. During these years the seeds were planted for the crisis in health care that descended on the nation two decades later. It was not a crisis of quality of care, but of the costs of paying for it.

NOTES

1. *Time*, 17 September 1973, 84. Growth figures cited in this paragraph were provided to the author in an information packet from McDonald's, July 1995. McDonald's home office is in Oakbrook, Illinois.

2. Ellen Melinkoff, *What We Wore: An Offbeat Social History of Women's Clothing, 1950–1980* (New York: Morrow, 1984), 119–20, 165.

3. Richard Lingeman, "Village and Town," *Encyclopedia of American Social History*, Vol. 2 (New York: Charles Scribner's Sons, 1993), 1256.

4. Quoted in *Time*, August 20, 1973, 45.

5. Quoted in *Time*, March 15, 1968, 71.

14

Environmental and Consumer Protection

The American people in the 1960s had reasons to worry about the air they breathed, the water they drank, the food they ate, and the hazardous wastes found in their communities or transported through them. Industrial processes that produced much-desired consumer goods also produced waste that was dumped into streams or blown into the atmosphere. Automobiles consumed huge quantities of natural resources and pumped substantial quantities of pollutants into the air. The streets and roads on which automobiles traveled and the space required for parking took up large parts of the landscape. Tankers that brought petroleum to the United States burst open when they ran aground, and off-shore oil wells were susceptible to leaking, as happened in the Santa Barbara channel in 1969.

Environmental Worries

A spokesman for the Public Health Service (PHS) reported that annual household, commercial, municipal, and industrial wastes totaled 360 million tons. Only 6 percent of the nation's 12,000 landfill disposal sites, according to the PHS, met even less-than-minimum standards for sanitary landfills. Of the 300 incinerators used for disposal of waste, 70 percent were without adequate air pollution control systems. Consumers' preference for disposable cans, bottles, and other packaging, as well as their general resistance to recycling, caused the bulk in landfills to multiply. Consequently, before pointing fingers at others, consumers had first to look in mirrors to see the source of many environmental problems.

Survival may not have been an immediate concern, but the welfare of generations to come caused worries. When the sources of worry were specific and close to home, men and women who had never before plunged into political action organized and took steps to protect themselves. Even when immediate concerns were absent, Americans faced the hard question of how to preserve and improve the natural environment at the same time that their rising standard of living posed serious threats to it.

Environmentalism and Conservation   To understand the nature of the grassroots environmental organizations that sprang up in the 1960s and those that followed in the next several decades requires drawing a distinction between *environmentalism* and *conservation*. The conservation movement since the latter part of the nineteenth century had sought to achieve more efficient, less wasteful use of America's physical resources. As historian Samuel Hays points out, however, conservation is an aspect of the history of *production*, inspired by technical and political leaders, whereas environmentalism is a part of the history of *consumption*. Environmentalism stresses new aspects of the American standard of living—specifically, something we call quality of life.[1] Inspired by concerns like those described by Rachel Carson in *Silent Spring*, environmentalism developed from a broad base, always pressing its case against reluctant leaders and opposing forces.

Even though environmentalism has consistently had ties to conservation and has benefited from the financial support of conservationists, the values of the two movements, Hays adds, have continually been at loggerheads. Conservationists are moved by concerns for continuing industrial and agricultural development; they want more and more production. Environmentalists take a more cautious approach to development, wanting to know what its impact will be on health, beauty, safety, and the preservation of natural resources.

Education and Action   The culmination of what might be called the first phase of environmentalism came on Earth Day, April 22, 1970, when ordinary Americans, displaying grassroots power, participated in street demonstrations, parades, and rallies in leading cities. Comparable activities occurred on as many as 1,500 college campuses and in 10,000 schools. An estimated 20 million people joined in what Wisconsin senator Gaylord Nelson, who had proposed the observance of Earth Day, called "nothing short of incredible."

Paul Ehrlich, author of *The Population Bomb* (1968), had helped stir many of the environmentalists to action. The several million persons who purchased his book and many more who heard him interviewed were sensitive to potential dangers of overpopulation. Although Ehrlich insisted he was not making predictions, his descriptions of prospects confronting the world if population controls were not put in place inspired concern, if not fear. The fact that population growth in the United States was within the people's control may explain the popularity of Ehrlich's views.

The offbeat *Whole Earth Catalog*, also published in 1968 (and annually to 1971 and again in 1994), spread environmental ideas of the counterculture and marketed gadgets popularizing the cause. The founding in 1969 of Friends of the Earth, an aggressive offshoot of the Sierra Club, gave environmentalism further impetus. Educational efforts by environmentalists included publications and reports in news media, conferences, and teach-ins on university campuses. Leading environmental organizations in the 1970s doubled the size of their membership in just a few years. The Sierra Club increased fivefold in a decade.

To translate their ideals into action, the environmentalists pushed for new laws to protect the natural environment, hoping to complement the material aspects of their rising standard of living. They covered a remarkable array of concerns: assurance of clean water and fresh air; protection of oceans, forests, croplands, and rangelands; wise use of minerals, energy, and nuclear power; safe disposal of industrial and agricultural waste; protection of endangered species (a new term in the vocabulary of many Americans); and, not least, control of the burgeoning human population worldwide. A Sierra Club handbook described environmentalists' methods as "ecotactics . . . the science of arranging and maneuvering all available forces in action against the enemies of earth."[2] The main ecotactics included education, litigation, and political action.

The best way to gain a sense of the environmentalists' impact is to identify the most important laws enacted in response to their efforts. Congress had dealt with environmental issues early in the 1960s, but because powerful economic interests would be affected by legislative action—in other words, their operating and production costs would go up—initial steps were hard to take. Accordingly, such legislation as the 1960 Clean Water Act and its amended version three years later were cautious and limited. In 1965, the Water Quality Act went farther than the law that preceded it, and the Solid Waste Disposal Act broadened that arena of legislative action.

Environmental Laws

An earlier, rather weak Clean Air Act was strengthened in 1967, with indications of more to come. Between mid-1969 and mid-1970 members of Congress introduced more than 140 bills concerning the environment. Most failed to become law, but they helped environmentalists sharpen their sense of how to accomplish their goals. Of the laws enacted, the most important in showing the influence of the environmental movement was the National Environmental Policy Act in 1969, which led to the establishment of the Environmental Protection Agency (EPA) and the Council on Environmental Quality (CEQ) the following year. This put the federal government in the environmental management business, not because it wanted to be but because the movement put it there. The act also instituted the practice of requiring environmental impact statements for all major federal actions that had the potential to significantly affect the environment.

Also important in addressing matters of environmental security were the Occupational Safety and Health Act and the National Industrial Pollution Control Council, both established in 1970. The Water Quality Act was strengthened in 1970 and again in 1972. Known simply as the Clean Water Act, it sought not only to ensure citizens pure water, but to preserve ecological integrity by protecting wetlands against development. The Natural Resources Defense Council called it "one of the strongest environmental laws ever written."

Additional legislation included the Water Pollution Control Act Amendments, passed over President Nixon's veto; the Noise Control Act, which empowered the Environmental Protection Agency to set limits on noise from trucks, buses, and railroad trains and to set noise standards for newly manufactured products; and the Pesticide Control Act, which required registration of all pesticides on the basis of safety data and prohibited the sale of pesticides not bearing registered labels. In June 1972 the EPA announced a ban on the use of the pesticide DDT on crops, effective at the end of the year. The Endangered Species Act, passed the following year, reaffirmed the nation's commitment to preserving wildlife habitats. The Safe Drinking Water Act, passed in 1974, set standards to guard against toxic contaminants.

Consequences of the Laws

At first glance it seems particularly impressive that much of this legislation was enacted during the administration of President Richard Nixon. Although his heart was on the side of business and industry leaders who complained about the cost of implementing it, he went along with most of it. He and members of Congress were also no doubt mindful of the threat and the reality of lawsuits by persons facing environmental crises. New laws would help define the limits of such suits. In fact, the laws enacted were neither as sweeping nor as vigorous as they might have been. As Kirkpatrick Sale points out, "In all of this . . . the clear purpose was to respond to the public without jeopardizing the status quo so revered by federal legislators—without, for example, forcing automobile manufacturers to adopt stringent emission-control standards, or banning heavy metals from sewage-treatment streams, or restraining the output of untested chemicals—but it was unquestionably a beginning, a camel's nose under the tent."[3]

What could be done to guarantee that electricity, the lifeblood of America, would continue to flow without interruption? Government experts and utilities execu- **Nuclear Power** tives knew that demands for electrical power would increase dramati- cally in coming years. The threat of blackouts and "brownouts," which occurred when power had to be cut back because reserves had fallen too low, demanded answers. Electricity generated by nuclear power plants seemed to provide them. The Atomic Energy Commission estimated that by the year 2000 half the electrical power consumed in the United States would be generated by nuclear fuel. Building more nuclear-powered plants made sense.

Consequently, by 1966 half the new generators planned or being built were nuclear-powered, even though serious but unpublicized accidents in nuclear reactors had occurred since testing first began on nuclear gen- erators in 1949. In January 1966 the first nuclear-powered plant, the En- rico Fermi, located on Lake Erie between Detroit and Toledo, went into operation. The following October a malfunction caused the reactor to overheat. Safety devices and extraordinary efforts by plant workers averted a potentially enormous disaster. The Detroit police were able to call off their plans to evacuate the city, thus sparing something that would have been much more than a mere interruption in daily life. After being out of commission for several years, the Enrico Fermi reactor was eventually dismantled.

Thus nuclear power brought the American people a new environmen- tal worry. Problems with other nuclear reactors—mainly accidents and difficulties in finding ways to store wastes that would remain radioactive for thousands of years—dashed hopes that nuclear power would be safe and relatively inexpensive. Nuclear power was not going to be the ul- timate technological fix, the cure-all for energy shortages.

By the mid-1960s, environmentalists had counterparts in another movement committed to enhancing the quality of **Consumer** American life—that is, the consumer protection movement. **Protection** Like environmentalists, consumer advocates sought to edu- cate consumers about abuses in the marketplace, called for laws to pro- tect consumers against those abuses, and filed lawsuits when necessary. Education of consumers had of course been going on for a long time. Since 1936, for example, the Consumers Union had published *Consumer Reports*. Regulation of matters affecting consumers had for years been the responsibility of such agencies as the Federal Communications Com- mission, the Food and Drug Administration, and the Federal Trade Com- mission.

Consumerism took on a new character with the work of Ralph Nader, whose book *Unsafe at Any Speed* (1965) had prompted enactment of the

National Traffic and Motor Vehicle Safety Act. Within a year or two a consumerism bandwagon was rolling, perhaps driven in part by the belief that American society had solved its "level of production" problem. In other words, with fear of economic depression gone and unemployment no longer a dominant problem, political leaders concluded that they could protect consumers even if it meant adversely affecting the growth of business. Consumer groups had a broad range of objectives, including:

- assurance of accuracy in weights and measures and the prominent display of such on packages,
- elimination of dangerous additives to food products,
- elimination of unsafe products from the market,
- protection against fraudulent and misleading advertising,
- establishment of procedures for dealing with consumer complaints,
- creation of product standards and grade labels showing performance characteristics and safety,
- evaluation of the performance of goods and services by impartial experts and publication of the results, using brand names,
- development of programs for the education of consumers,
- effective representation of consumers before commissions making decisions affecting them, and
- assurance that the market would remain competitive, preventing domination by business interests to the disadvantage of consumers.

The passage of a number of consumer protection laws demonstrated the effectiveness of consumer advocates in legislative arenas. The most important laws were the Wholesome Meat Act in 1967, the Consumer Credit Protection ("Truth in Lending") Act in 1968, the Wholesome Poultry Products Act in 1968, the Child and Toy Protection Act in 1969, and the Consumer Product Safety Act in 1972. The last of these sought to bring virtually all consumer products under federal control. It also empowered the government to ban the sale of products judged to be unsafe. Federal laws had counterparts at the state level, as a growing number of states pursued consumer protection interests.

Responses from Business
Consumerism prompted responses from businesses, of course, and these responses also affected the lives of Americans. The responses included denying complaints, blaming abuses on irresponsible firms, embarking on public relations campaigns to neutralize negative public im-

pressions, and seeking to weaken proposed legislation. Sometimes manufacturers continued to sell products they knew to be hazardous, as Ford did with its Pinto, a vehicle with a gas tank and bumper configuration that invited explosions if it was struck from the rear. Foes of consumerism also attacked the truthfulness and character of critics, as General Motors had done with Ralph Nader. If these efforts failed, they engaged in studies to determine the validity of the complaints and decide what, if anything, needed to be done. Of course, if changes sought by consumer advocates actually materialized and increased production or distribution costs, those costs would in turn be passed along to consumers. Accordingly, not all consumers were enthusiastic about consumerism.

NOTES

1. Samuel P. Hays, *Beauty, Health, and Permanence: Environmental Politics in the United States, 1865–1985* (New York: Cambridge University Press, 1987), 1–30.

2. Quoted in Victor B. Scheffer, *The Shaping of Environmentalism in America* (Seattle: University of Washington Press, 1991), 115–17.

3. Kirkpatrick Sale, *The Green Revolution: The American Environmental Movement, 1962–1992* (New York: Hill and Wang, 1993), 26.

15

Technology's Small Steps and Giant Leaps

In 1974 the Amana Refrigeration Company began to market small microwave ovens for home use. However, probably because meals cooked in them seemed less attractive and less tasty than those prepared in regular ovens, microwaves did not catch on for general use. Rather, they became "heat-things-up" devices, increasingly useful for families that found it impossible to gather around the dinner table at the same time. Also, as baby boomers headed off to their own apartments and as childless families became more numerous, microwaves proved useful for heating prepackaged dinners and leftovers. Another small but important technological device that was installed unobtrusively in many homes deserves mention: smoke detectors became household necessities after their introduction in 1970.

Technology in Homes

In 1970, although one family in five had no automobile, Americans' reliance on automobiles showed no signs of diminishing. Nor did the automobile industry escape numerous technological problems. One had to do with air pollution caused by automobile emissions. The California legislature, responding to complaints about the smog that was suffocating cities, became the pacesetter in setting emission control standards. It imposed limits on the amount of carbon monoxide and hydrocarbons permitted from automobile exhausts. The federal laws that followed permitted California to enforce stricter ones, as atmospheric conditions there differed from other parts of the country. Had mass transit—buses, subways, streetcars, and trains—held greater appeal, pollution problems might have been less

Automobiles

severe, but mass transit could not compete with the convenience, power, and pride derived from automobiles. Nationwide between 1945 and 1967, mass transit rides fell from 23 billion to 8 billion.

More vexing for the American makers of big cars was consumers' growing preference for small ones, caused mainly by rising fuel costs resulting from the oil crisis. Japan's Datsun (known later as Nissan) and Toyota were serious about doing business when they entered the U.S. market. By 1968 they had been joined in the American market by other Japanese manufacturers (principally Honda, Mitsubishi, and Mazda), and Japan had passed Germany as the world's second-largest producer of motor vehicles.

In response, American makers marketed what were called captive imports. Mitsubishi made the Dodge Colt and Mazda made the Ford Courier pickup. General Motors owned 35 percent of Isuzu, maker of the LUV, marketed by GM. When imports reached 10 percent of all sales of passenger cars, the American automakers began producing their own subcompacts. The Ford Maverick and American Motors Hornet, introduced in 1969, and the Chevrolet Vega, Ford Pinto, and American Motors Gremlin in 1970 did not distinguish themselves as high-quality vehicles, but they positioned the American automobile industry to take on the greater challenges to come.

Petroleum Dependence
Those challenges arrived with the petroleum crisis that began in 1973, a crisis resulting from a situation President Nixon described in an address to Congress on June 29: "While we have 6 percent of the world's population, we consume one-third of the world's energy output. The supply of domestic energy resources available to us is not keeping pace with our ever growing demand." The demand for petroleum in the United States was 17 million barrels per day, but domestic output was little more than 11 million barrels per day.

The situation worsened in October 1973. The Yom Kippur War between Israel and its Arab neighbors prompted Middle Eastern oil-producing countries to impose an embargo on exports to countries regarded as sympathetic to Israel. Included were the United States, Canada, all of western Europe, and Japan. While the embargo was in effect, until the spring of 1974, panic buying caused long lines at gas stations. To keep their tanks full, drivers would fill up when they needed as little as three gallons. In January 1974, President Nixon signed into law a 55-mile-per-hour speed limit act, after having asked Congress to set the limit at 50 miles per hour. The reduced speed limit conserved an estimated 3.4 billion gallons per year, and highway fatalities in 1974 fell to 45,196 from 54,052 in the previous year. They soon climbed again as motorists flouted the unpopular law. Some states imposed limits on quantities of gas that could be purchased, causing drivers to go from station to station.

"The Summer of 73," by Paul Szep. *Reprinted courtesy of The Boston Globe.*

Others restricted days on which cars with even- or odd-numbered license plates could fill up. Many communities organized carpools, and state highway departments provided lots to enable drivers to park their cars and share rides with others.

Anger over the problems the oil shortage caused was plentiful. After all, a way of life seemed in jeopardy. Those who suspected conspiracies believed that oil companies seeking to raise prices were responsible for the shortages. They claimed there were loaded tankers waiting offshore and supplies of gas hidden in the tanks of abandoned stations, all ready to be released when the price was right.

The computerization of America accelerated rapidly in the late 1960s and early 1970s, with each step affecting more **Computers** directly the lives of Americans. Until the mid-1960s, most computer applications were found in large businesses and the military, but they spread quickly to smaller settings. Office secretaries who had learned to use the IBM Selectric typewriter when it was introduced in 1961 were struggling with electronic typewriters by the end of the decade. Soon they faced the intricacies of primitive word processors.

In 1971, when Intel of California introduced the microprocessor—essentially a computer on a silicon chip—a whole new industry opened up. That meant new jobs in the production of both hardware and software. Boom times came to places like Silicon Valley, the 25-mile strip in California between Palo Alto and San Jose.

As computers entered the workplace, those who used them did not need to understand how they worked. Previously, processors of data worried about stacking and storing the punch cards or magnetic tapes carrying the data they worked with. Now they simply used hard drives and floppy disks to enter, manipulate, store, and retrieve data, all in unprecedented amounts and with impressive speed. But the picture was not all rosy for computer users. The repetitive nature of their work, as they sat in the same position hour after hour with their eyes focused on a screen with moving images, made them vulnerable to new physical maladies, particularly something called repetitive strain injury or cumulative trauma disorder.

As computer users became more adept and productive, they unwittingly caused the underemployment and unemployment of other employees who were displaced. Their work also unwittingly increased the prospects that confidential financial, legal, medical, military, and other records would be vulnerable to invasion by persons who had no right or reason to see them. Another worry was that records would be improperly transferred, scrambled, destroyed, or simply lost in the system. A problem that has persisted results from the perpetual introduction of new generations of hardware and software. Data generated and stored in obsolete generations cannot be retrieved in the next and are forever lost. This might not affect the immediate operations of an organization, but it is a concern to those who attempt years later to come back to original records.

High-Tech Agriculture Mechanization of agriculture had been occurring for centuries, but going high-tech was another matter. It affected the nature and quality of the food Americans found on their dinner tables. A publication of the U.S. Department of Agriculture in 1968 explains how. It observed that "machines are not made to harvest crops; in reality, crops must be designed to be harvested by machines," as in fact happened.[1] The tomato is but one of a number of examples. In 1961, two University of California researchers marketed a mechanical tomato harvester and a strain of tomato plant to go with it. The tomato would ripen on schedule, remain on the vine for thirty days without deteriorating, survive mechanical harvesting, and withstand shipment. A miracle—except for one thing: The tomato turned out to be hard and tasteless. Nevertheless, by 1967 this tomato and the harvester were used in combination on 90 percent of California's tomato acreage, representing a majority of the nation's crop. Consumers presumably got cheaper tomatoes, though less tasty ones, and an estimated 32,000 migrant tomato pickers lost their jobs. Even as California's tomato acreage increased, about three-fourths of the state's farmers sold their land to larger growers. Comparable harvester-producer combinations were used in lettuce, grape, and other crop production, with similar effects.

Sometimes consumer preferences, rather than the technology of harvesting, caused agricultural products to change. In consumers' eyes, what is more beautiful than a bright red, shiny, flawless apple—one that keeps its alluring look despite having been picked weeks earlier and having traveled long distances? On its way from blossom to the store, such an apple has been sprayed with insecticide, fungicide, and maybe a coat of wax. It is, says Thomas Hine, "a largely successful attempt to outwit time, place, mortality. You can always have the same apple anyplace, anytime."[2] Does tastelessness or dry, coarse texture matter in this state-of-the-art apple, this apple for the eye?

A committee formed by grocers and manufacturers of food products, wishing to improve the productivity of their workers, issued a recommendation in 1973 calling **Shopping and Computers** for a Universal Product Code (UPC) for all supermarket items. The code on each item would permit electronic scanners at checkout counters to read and record the price automatically, thereby eliminating checker errors and streamlining inventory control. For a time, retailers balked at installing the costly equipment this would require, and consumers protested that individually marked prices would be eliminated. When it became clear that the benefits to the retailers would offset the costs, the UPC went into use. More than one-fourth of the nation's supermarkets used electronic scanners by the end of 1975, and their use increased rapidly thereafter. The use of scanners and the UPC eventually spread to all kinds of merchandise and a variety of operations requiring packaging and sorting. Besides improving the speed and accuracy of checkout procedures, the system made inventory control much easier. This, in turn, made it possible for stores to predict demand and thus keep inventories smaller.

As the Gemini space capsules scored successes in the mid-1960s it became only a matter of time before a **Space Ventures** moon landing would be attempted. In May 1969, *Apollo 10* astronauts took their lunar module into orbit within nine miles of the moon before reconnecting with the command module. On July 20, hundreds of millions of Americans listened to communications preceding the landing on the moon of "the Eagle," *Apollo 11*'s lunar module, by astronauts Neil Armstrong and Edwin Aldrin. When it touched down, their television sets enabled them to watch events as they occurred. Speaking the first words on lunar soil, Armstrong called the venture "one small step for a man, one giant leap for mankind." The astronauts conducted experiments on the lunar surface, collected about 45 pounds of rock and soil samples, and returned safely to the command module for the journey back to earth.

"After centuries of dreams and prophecies," wrote *Time* magazine, "the moment had come. Man had broken his terrestrial shackles and set foot on another world. Standing on the lifeless, rock-studded surface he could see the earth, a lovely blue and white hemisphere suspended in the velvety black sky."[3] One of the six remaining missions, *Apollo 13*, survived a near-disaster without a moon landing, but the other five were successful, the last one in December 1972. In that year the National Aeronautics and Space Administration (NASA) began a space shuttle program to provide means for further scientific exploration, and possibly future colonization and commercial activities. In the meantime, though, NASA faced deep budget cuts. Some were caused by the costs of waging war in Vietnam, others apparently by the belief that the big goal, reaching the moon, had been accomplished. By 1970, NASA's employment force of about 136,000 was roughly half of what it had been five years earlier.

What were the dividends of the space program for the American people, the payoff on the $25 billion it cost them? Photographs of the lunar surface. Rock samples of great geological interest but no known practical significance. Considerable knowledge concerning how to maneuver vehicles in space. Improved technological bases for telecommunication via satellites and weather surveillance worldwide. Information that would prove useful in advances in medicine. Most important, perhaps, was the restoration of American morale that had been damaged when the Russians sent *Sputnik* into orbit twelve years before the moon landing. Never mind that the Soviet Union used unmanned moon landings to accomplish many of the same results as the manned landings of NASA. Of the tangible benefits of space technology, one cited frequently, sometimes sarcastically, is Velcro. This had been designed to help space travelers keep track of pencils and other hand-held objects in the zero gravity of space. The prototype of video cameras that later came into common usage was developed for space missions, as were electronic stethoscopes, fire-resistant fabrics, lightweight insulation materials, dehydrated foods, computer technology for automated control of highly sophisticated equipment, and many other things.

Technological advancements in medicine and sci-
ence ranged from those that seemed distant and exotic   **Medical Miracles**
to those that affected the daily lives of millions of peo-
ple. Sometimes the speed with which a rarity became commonplace was
stunning. Within a decade of the first implantation of pacemakers to
control irregular heartbeats, these devices enabled thousands of men and
women to enjoy longer and happier lives. The same was true of coronary
bypass surgery. Sometimes medical miracles captured worldwide attention, as when Christiaan Barnard, a South African surgeon, transplanted
the first human heart on December 3, 1967. That it could be done was
amazing; whether it was worth the time and expense required to extend
one life for eighteen days, as happened in this instance, was debatable.
Four days later, the first transplant patient in the United States lived
only a few hours.

While there was no shortage of patients waiting to receive transplanted
hearts, the number of hearts available for transplant was always very
low. However, the shortage of organs available for transplants—of
hearts, livers, lungs, kidneys, and corneas—was not the main obstacle to
making transplants routine. Nor was it a lack of surgeons with technical
skills for performing transplants. Rather, it was the limitations of drugs
to prevent rejection of the implanted organs. In the seven years after Dr.
Barnard's feat, more than 250 patients received transplanted hearts, but
only about 20 percent lived more than a year after the surgery. For them,
life each day was a reminder that the medical miracle performed by their
surgeon was worth it, but general questions about transplant surgeries
continued to raise ethical, medical, and financial questions.

Mental health remained a concern for millions of
Americans. Such illnesses as schizophrenia were the sub-   **Mental Health**
ject of ongoing research, as were depressive illnesses that   **and Medicine**
prevented their victims from functioning well in daily
life. Antidepressant medications, along with electro-convulsive therapy,
had been used for a number of years to bring about recovery from bouts
of manic depression, but the quest continued to find something that
would prevent recurrences. In 1970 lithium carbonate was made available by prescription for treatment of acute depression and maintenance
of relatively normal lives by manic-depressive patients. This required
close monitoring of side-effects. Lithium is regarded as the first successful preventative medication in the treatment of psychiatric patients.

Not all medical breakthroughs were exotic and con-
troversial. An example of a simpler, more widely used   **Contact Lenses**
technological development was the soft contact lens,
which received approval by the Food and Drug Administration in 1971.
Soft lenses were more comfortable than the hard lenses that had been

introduced in 1939, but they were intended to last only a year. At an initial cost of $300 (more than $950 in 1990 dollars), they were unavailable to many wishing to use them; but before long their price dropped considerably.

Diagnostic Tools   Some technological developments during these years vastly improved physicians' ability to diagnose diseases and injuries. Three diagnostic tools were developed almost simultaneously during the early 1970s. Computerized axial tomography (CAT) which provided cross-sectional views of internal body structures, was introduced in England in 1972 and marketed in the United States a year later. Initially, CAT scans required patients to be perfectly still for the views to be read. They were therefore used primarily to diagnose head injuries and diseases, since the head can be held in a fixed position longer than other parts of the body. As the instruments improved, wider usage became possible. Nuclear magnetic resonance (NMR), used to measure the absorption of radio waves in a magnetic field, enabled physicians to distinguish healthy tissue from diseased tissue. Ultrasound, marketed in 1974, made use of ultrasonic waves to visualize such things as the development of a fetus. It could also be used to apply deep heat in the treatment of body tissues. Each year increasing numbers of persons benefited from CAT scans, NMR's, and ultrasound. As they did, their medical bills went up. So did frustration for doctors and patients, as diagnostic breakthroughs continued to run far in advance of treatments and cures.

Side-Effects   As technological advancements in medicine occurred, people found it necessary to be on the alert for reports of side-effects. For example, in the decade following the introduction of the birth control pill as a presumably safe method of contraception, there were recurring concerns over its safety. In 1968, research sponsored by the National Institutes of Health reported that the pill could cause blood clots and might pose other health hazards. The Food and Drug Administration, in turn, ordered packages to carry warnings of these potential effects. One critic complained that the Food and Drug Administration had initially ruled the pill to be safe on the basis of tests involving 132 women in Puerto Rico. These women had stayed on the pill for a year or more, but only sixty-six of them had taken it for more than two years. The critic claimed that researchers had not investigated the deaths of three subjects from blood clots. Writing in 1970, she claimed that in the previous eight years "the FDA has fathered a steady stream of government reports and 'Dear Doctor' letters, each certifying the Pill as safe, but each crawling closer to an admission of serious side-effects."[4]

A medication that had been used since the 1930s to prevent miscarriages (diethylstilbesterol, known as DES) was found to cause cancer in some of the children born of those pregnancies. Hexachlorophene, which had been widely used as a disinfectant and as an antibacterial agent in soaps, was ordered off the market by the FDA when it was discovered to cause brain lesions in monkeys and suspected as a possible cause of death in several newborn infants. Even such an ordinary household item as aspirin made the news when it was reported to be a possible cause of ulcers.

Sometimes technological solutions to medical prob- lems brought problems of a different kind. Deaths and **New Problems** illnesses of children who had been poisoned by drugs they had taken from easily opened containers left within their reach prompted the Food and Drug Administration to require that packages containing certain drugs be made "childproof." Once this process was set in motion, pharmacies, perhaps recognizing legal liabilities in any incident involving medication, began to use childproof containers for all prescriptions. The result was a backlog that forced the FDA in 1972 to postpone the deadline for compliance several times. The requirement posed a longer-term problem for elderly persons who found the new packages difficult, if not impossible, to open.

NOTES

1. R. E. Webb and W. M. Bruce, "Redesigning the Tomato for Mechanized Production," *U.S. Departments of Agriculture Yearbook [1968]*, 104, cited in Howard P. Segal, "Technology and Social Change," *Encyclopedia of American Social History*, Vol. 3 (New York: Charles Scribner's Sons, 1993), 2318.

2. Thomas Hine, *Facing Tomorrow: What the Future Has Been, What the Future Can Be* (New York: Alfred A. Knopf, 1991), 207–8.

3. *Time*, Special Sixtieth Anniversary Issue, October 5, 1983, 142.

4. Judith Coburn, "Off the Pill?" in *In the Marketplace: Consumerism in America*, eds. Frank Browning and the editors of *Ramparts* (San Francisco: Canfield Press, 1972), 52–53.

16

Hard Knocks
for Schools

School administrators, board members, and teachers in those years wrestled with such issues as minimum competency testing, community advisory councils, programs in "values clarification," bilingual educa- **Challenges Facing Schools** tion, and questions about textbooks. In their student populations were some judged to be at-risk, others gifted and talented, and still others learning disabled (a term used initially in 1963). For the latter, that most likely meant separate classrooms, since mainstreaming was not yet a part of schools' responses or vocabularies.

Moreover, until the twenty years of enrollment growth ended in 1970, school administrators faced overcrowded schools and classrooms. Predictably, but with seeming suddenness, enrollment problems shifted into reverse in 1971, as a long downward spiral began. Soon decisions over which schools to close became battles between neighborhoods within school districts. Convenience of location was one issue. The perception that an empty school building signaled neighborhood decline was another.

As school systems grew larger and more bureaucratized, teachers felt increasingly alienated from school administrators. Rather quickly, they stood on **Teacher Militancy** opposite sides of a number of issues. Almost overnight the National Education Association (NEA), once the symbol of a united profession, became chiefly a collective bargaining agent. Whether teachers chose to affiliate with it or its rival, the American Federation of Teachers (AFT), or simply to maintain unaffiliated local organizations, they became more militant.

They demanded better wages and benefits; improved teaching conditions, including smaller classes; and a greater voice in school affairs. Membership in the NEA grew from 700,000 in 1960 (including many administrators and college professors) to 1,700,000 in 1978. In the same period, the AFT increased its membership from 50,000 to 500,000.

Teacher militancy affected schoolchildren and their families when it produced improved conditions for learning, but when it led to strikes its effects were more obvious and immediate. A strike by the American Federation of Teachers in New York in 1967 disrupted the normal routines of 1,100,000 children and their families for fourteen days. A thirteen-day strike did the same for 300,000 children in Detroit. Similar occurrences of varying length marked the opening of the school year in cities large and small for the remainder of the 1960s and throughout the 1970s.

Funding Problems The teachers' militancy reflected the schools' perennial scarcity of funds. A snapshot of the budget picture of schools in 1970–1971 reveals their plight. In that year, about 52 percent of the $39.5 billion spent to operate public elementary and secondary schools was raised by local taxes, typically on property; 41 percent came from state taxes on sales, income, and property; and 7 percent came from the federal government under a variety of programs. A report on school finance showed that in 1970 voters approved only 48 percent of school bond issues, compared with 81 percent a decade earlier. In other words, as the public increased its demands on schools it also became more reluctant to foot the bill. Unequal distribution of dollars among schools and school districts caused another budgetary problem: Where the tax base was low, so was tax revenue, and the schools suffered. Poor children attended inferior schools. Court decisions over the next several years achieved only limited success in equalizing the resources of school districts.

School Desegregation Schools continued to deal with three matters they had faced since the 1950s. The first was desegregation. In some parts of the country, school districts with racially segregated schools had for more than a decade defied the Supreme Court's 1954 ruling in *Brown v. Board of Education* that such schools had to be eliminated. They changed school boundaries, redrew bus routes, and offered "voluntary choice" programs to perpetuate segregation. A series of Supreme Court rulings, however, particularly one in 1968, declared that the federal courts would insist on proof of racial integration in areas that formerly had segregated their schools by law. In 1971 the Court upheld busing of schoolchildren as a means to achieve racial balance where segregation still had official local sanction and where school authorities had not offered acceptable alternatives to busing. By 1976, as a result of court orders, 77 percent of black schoolchildren in the South attended schools that had at least 10 percent white students.

In 1972 the Court ruled that segregated schools resulting from residential segregation must be treated as the result of deliberate public policies, just as if they had been segregated by law. Such schools were judged to be in violation of the Constitution, and remedies to eliminate segregation were required. Busing and the creation of magnet schools— schools offering special programs in the arts or the sciences, for example—were the most common remedies. "Pairing" schools was another remedy, with a portion of black students bused to a predominantly white school and vice versa. School desegregation proceeded slowly, partly because many families moved to avoid sending their children to newly desegregated schools. So-called white flight meant that neighborhood populations changed swiftly and dramatically, and desegregation plans had to be updated almost yearly. Thoughtful persons wondered aloud why the task of desegregating society was being given mainly to children, but where they were given a chance, the children showed they were capable of making desegregation work.

Desegregation posed many challenges. Children of both races found themselves in classrooms with other children from whom they had been taught, or even required, to keep their distance. Teachers encountered children who had been denied solid educational opportunities and who therefore had difficulty meeting their expectations. Administrators were compelled, often against their personal wishes, to design desegregation plans and make them work. Parents worried about the effects of desegregation on their children and often resisted it passionately. In Charlotte, North Carolina, for example, the Parents Concerned Association vowed to boycott schools if busing plans were implemented. "I'm willing to go to jail if I have to," one parent said.[1] Even if Board members and community leaders supported school desegregation, they had to cope with the resistance of citizens who did not.

But the simple and obvious truth was that the only way to eliminate schools attended solely by black children was to enroll those children in schools with whites. Controversies over school policies, court decisions, and legislative and executive actions at both state and federal levels aimed at desegregation continued throughout the 1970s. Some of them became violent. A much larger effect of the Supreme Court's decisions, as well as of decisions by lower courts, was that color-consciousness and sensitivity to group identities came to permeate virtually all decisions in schools, particularly in urban districts.

Members of an anti-busing group in Memphis bury an ancient school bus in a symbolic protest against court ordered busing, February 22, 1972. *UPI/CORBIS-BETTMANN.*

School District Reorganization The second matter affected many more schools and communities but fewer students and teachers. It, too, required elaborate busing plans. Communities across the nation, mostly in rural areas, reorganized and consolidated their school districts, for they recognized that small school districts no longer had the resources—the diverse curricula, teachers in specialized fields, science laboratories, and instructional technology, for example—to prepare children for life in an increasingly complex world. Between 1953 and 1963 the number of school districts declined from more than 67,000 to around 31,000. In 1932 there had been almost 128,000. By 1980 the number would drop to under 16,000. In some states, the shrinkage in numbers of districts was stunning. In Colorado, between 1953 and 1963, the number of school districts declined from 1,147 to 222; in Iowa, from 4,558 to 1,164; in Mississippi, from 1,417 to 150; in Nevada, from 185 to 17; and in Wisconsin, from 5,463 to 741.

School district reorganization inspired fears and resistance. Some fears echoed those expressed in school districts facing orders to desegregate: Local control of the schools would be lost. The school plant would be located elsewhere and children would be transported far from home (by "forced busing"). Personal and financial interests in the school would end. Parental influence would weaken. Taxes would increase while the level of service decreased. Close relationships between home and school would be destroyed. The community itself might disappear. Sometimes reorganization occurred with financial incentives provided by the states, or under state mandates, but this kind of governmental intervention sometimes heightened rather than lessened local fears.

The primary mission of schools might have been to pursue high standards through rigorous curricula, but many other obligations made such pursuit difficult. Improving the per- **Changing Missions** formance of educationally disadvantaged children, a third challenge, was one such obligation. The influx of poorly educated children to urban schools from rural areas, particularly in the South, imposed heavy obligations on schools undergoing desegregation. Recognizing that as society became more complex and technologically sophisticated, the plight of the unskilled and minimally educated would only worsen, the schools sought to bring everyone's skills and knowledge above minimal levels. The obligation to give special attention to children with learning or behavioral disabilities consumed substantial resources. As the quality of home life declined, schools were called on to provide what formerly had been offered by families, such as hot meals and after-school care programs. Schools also faced the challenge of conservative forces objecting to the content of textbooks they regarded as unfit for use in schools. The books, they said, included filthy language and unsavory themes, subverted traditional values, and were unpatriotic.

Other criticisms of schools during these years were also severe, but for different reasons. One widely read **Criticisms and** author charged schools with being intellectually and so- **Reforms** cially cruel to children, with racism playing a part. Another attacked insensitive school bureaucracies. A third showed how schools stifled the excitement of learning. In sum, critics maintained, schools destroyed children's souls, regardless of race or class. As Diane Ravitch contends in *The Troubled Crusade*:

> The underlying assumptions in the various approaches [of the critics] were, first, that there was little in the schools worth preserving; second, that anything innovative was bound to be better than whatever it replaced; third, that the pathology of the schools was so grave that the only change worth attempting must be a fundamental, institutional, systemic kind; and fourth, that the way to change society and to turn it against war and racism was to change (or abandon) the schools.[2]

Calls for such things as "deschooling," "alternative schools," and "open education" poured forth, gaining popularity here and there and tried where disciples generated support and allies. Open education caught on rather widely, thanks largely to the efforts of Charles Silberman, author of the bestselling *Crisis in the Classroom*. Even though his ideas were seldom adopted in their entirety, they brought innovations that changed the daily experiences of schoolchildren in modest ways. Students played a larger role in selecting their own activities, for example, and students' initiative in determining course content was given freer play. Traditional courses were replaced by those seeming to have greater "relevance"—a key word in school reforms of the 1960s and early 1970s. Other changes included less rigid scheduling of school time, less emphasis on letter grades, and less grouping for instruction according to levels of ability. The public perceived discipline in the schools to be a serious problem, according to a 1969 Gallup poll, and the loosening of teachers' authority did nothing to improve it. Many parents found changes in school routines to be unsettling, in part because the changes made the children's experiences different from their own.

Politicization of Schools
One thing everyone could agree on is that public schools had become the subject of political discord. Why? Lawrence Cremin, a distinguished historian of education and president of Columbia University's Teachers College, said that the answer lay in the "longstanding American tendency to try to solve social, political, and economic problems through educational means, and in so doing to invest education with all kinds of millennial hopes and expectations." Educational institutions, he said, sought to be more relevant to the daily concerns of ordinary men and women and to nurture social, civic, and economic competencies in their students. Education became "a leading weapon in everything from the fight against race discrimination to the war on poverty to the drive for political and economic competitiveness."[3]

Federal Involvement in the Schools
The 1965 Elementary and Secondary Education Act (ESEA) provided federal funds for remedial training in basic skills for children in schools with a high percentage of low-income families and for programs for learning disabled children from families of all income levels. However, local school districts sometimes used federal support to replace local dollars for such programs, so the funding increases for these purposes were not as significant as had been intended. In 1967 the renewed ESEA provided funds for bilingual education, and seven years later the Supreme Court ruled that schools were obliged to meet the educational needs of children who were not proficient in English.

Women's rights advocates urged schools to give girls the same opportunities in such fields as mathematics and the sciences as were open to boys, to prepare for careers formerly closed to them. An eventual result of these efforts was Title IX of the Educational Amendments of 1972, which also led to greater equality in support for participation by girls in athletics and other school activities. While this was going on, textbook publishers began to provide a better balance in portraying the roles of men and women in all aspects of American life.

The turmoil that rocked college and university campuses in the mid-1960s continued for the rest of the decade and **Turmoil in** into the next. Academic year 1969–1970 was particularly tu- **Colleges and** multuous. Weapons were brandished at Cornell University, **Universities** and students took over administrative offices in all kinds of colleges and universities. A riot at San Francisco State University caused its closing for several months, and disturbances at Brooklyn College, Duke University, and the University of Wisconsin brought intervention by state troopers or the National Guard. The bloodiest confrontation, described earlier, occurred at Kent State University in May 1970. Student uprisings protested such things as the presence of ROTC units and military recruiters on campus, government contracts for military research, restrictive campus rules, and the absence of black studies or Hispanic studies programs.

Although fewer than 2 percent of college students were thought to be intent on committing destructive acts, that was small consolation to those who saw what they regarded as the collapse of civility in the very settings where it ought to be sturdiest. Furthermore, the 2 percent figure meant that there were some 100,000 radical protesters—enough to persuade observers that they constituted a serious threat to society. A Harris poll found most Americans to be shocked and dismayed by the disorder and unable to comprehend black demands for separatism, one of the causes of disorder. The poll revealed that 68 percent of the public regarded the campus demonstrations as unjustified and 89 percent supported calling in police or the National Guard to restore order.

In academic year 1971–1972 campuses remained relatively quiet, with disillusionment a prevailing mood. **Quiet, Unsettled** In April 1972 a study entitled *The Changing Values on* **Campuses** *Campus* showed that seven in ten students counted themselves as "mainstream," two in ten called themselves "conservative," and one in ten "left radical." More striking, as many as 30 percent of the college students surveyed said that they would prefer to live in another country.[4] The apparent calm suggested by the numbers was misleading, for when President Nixon ordered heavy bombing of Hanoi-Haiphong in December 1972, protests again erupted on many campuses.

The unsettled character of college campuses can best be understood in the larger context of higher education between 1967 and 1974. These were times of opportunity for many young and not-so-young people who were the first in their families to attend college. Until the 1960s a person with a high school education could, by hard work and a little luck, still get comfortably into the middle class, with a reasonable chance for secure, long-term, fringe-benefit employment with a single company. Times were changing, though, and colleges and universities faced the challenge of serving a new clientele while also coping with disorder prompted by circumstances in the larger society.

Community Colleges   Rapidly growing community colleges played an important role in serving the new clientele. They provided many opportunities for persons wishing to acquire knowledge and skills that would enable them to launch or change careers. Some who enrolled already held college degrees. Others were so ill prepared for college-level work that remedial programs, sometimes called compensatory, were essential. This was true not only in community colleges; four-year colleges and universities, too, had to find ways of dealing with the circumstances reflected in the decline of SAT scores over the course of the decade.

Expansion and Change   In 1967, enrollments in all colleges and universities increased to 6,911,000—almost a million more than just two years earlier. Part of the increase reflected the fact that more women were attending; the proportion of women in college enrollments grew from around 33 percent in 1960 to more than 40 percent a decade later. The U.S. Office of Education predicted that the college population would increase four times as fast as the national population over the next decade. This meant that enrollments would grow by nearly 50 percent.

Construction, too, was booming. In academic year 1966–1967, more than one-third of all U.S. institutions of higher education received federal aid to build or remodel classrooms, laboratories, and libraries. Grants and loans to 877 institutions under the Higher Education Facilities Act of 1963 helped generate almost $2 billion in construction. Between 1963 and 1969, the professional staff of colleges and universities became 50 percent larger. Doomsayers had a hard time finding an audience that year.

By 1973–1974 the picture was less promising. Failure to realize excessively optimistic projections left colleges and universities with an estimated 600,000 vacant spaces. Responding to the need to compete for students as never before in order to balance budgets, admissions offices began aggressive recruitment campaigns using increasingly sophisticated materials and techniques. Nonetheless, the total enrollment in 1973–1974 exceeded 10 million. Tuition increases driven by general inflationary pressures put private institutions out of the financial reach of many students, who enrolled instead in public ones. In 1960, more than 40 percent of college and university students were enrolled in private institutions. In the next thirteen years, the percentage declined to just under 25. By 1990, fewer than 22 percent attended private institutions. Not that private colleges and universities failed to grow, but rather that public institutions grew much more.

The appetite of the American people for learning showed itself also in ways that did not require atten-   **Informal Learning** dance in school. Television and radio were constant sources of informal learning, and some programs on the Public Broadcasting Service and local stations offered the possibility of earning college credits. During these years bookstores began to pop up in shopping malls, laying the groundwork for the chains of larger stores that came a decade later. An unfortunate side-effect of the use of technology in shopping-mall bookstores was that sophisticated sales records enabled them to anticipate the likely continuing demand for books they carried, and those with forecasts of low sales had a short life on the shelf. That, in turn, meant that the time between publication and consignment to the "remaindered" tables became shorter and shorter.

Learning continued through magazines and newspapers, although changes here were striking. The weekly *Saturday*   **Magazines** *Evening Post*, a general-interest staple in many American homes for 148 years, went out of business in 1969. Even though it had 3.5 million subscribers, its advertising revenues were insufficient to make it a profitable enterprise. *Look* magazine folded in 1971 and *Life* magazine ceased publication in 1972. Both publications had been known for illustrating their news and feature stories with photographs. In 1974 Time, Inc., launched *People*, a breezy magazine focused on the personalities and lives of celebrities. Its photographs and short features were intended to appeal to readers conditioned by television to accept superficiality and ephemera as the daily fare of "celebrity journalism." By this time the circulation of the weekly *National Enquirer*—for half a century the source of stories on crime, gore, miraculous and bizarre occurrences, gossip, and sex—reached 4 million.

NOTES

1. *U.S. News and World Report*, March 16, 1970, 30.

2. Diane Ravitch, *The Troubled Crusade: American Education 1945–1980* (New York: Basic Books), 237–38.

3. Lawrence A. Cremin, *Popular Education and Its Discontents* (New York: Harper & Row, 1990), 92–93.

4. Nancy Zaroulis and Gerald Sullivan, *Who Spoke Up? American Protest against the War in Vietnam, 1963–1975* (Garden City, N.Y.: Doubleday, 1984), 380–81.

17

Spiritual Matters

Matters of faith and practice cannot be ignored if we wish to understand everyday life in the late 1960s and early 1970s. Jewish children had bar mitzvahs and bas mitzvahs, Christian children celebrated first communion **Religion in Everyday Life** and confirmation, and Muslims learned early in life the place of prayer in their daily routines. Hundreds of religious bodies flourished. Leaders continued to strive for church unity, even though their efforts had few discernible effects on individual lives. Similarly, they advocated positions on social issues of war and peace, racial and civil strife, economic justice, and world hunger; but except for activists in their midst, church members often failed to support or even accept those positions.

Many Americans found inspiration, guidance, and fellowship in their churches, synagogues, mosques, and meetinghouses; but because these were human institutions, they were also places for contests over doctrine and practice and disputes over budgets, programs, personnel, and facilities. Many long-time church members could recount strife with fellow members in their congregations, and official and unofficial schisms within denominations were common. That may explain why many who claimed to have religious convictions had no formal religious affiliations and why polling data on church membership and attendance fluctuated.

In 1967, Gallup polls showed that 98 out of every 100
Preferences,   Americans had a preference for some church. About two-
Practices, and   thirds called themselves Protestants and one-fourth said
Perceptions   they were Catholics. Jews accounted for 3 percent, and
                         "all others" the same. The slight changes in the next eight
years might lead one to believe that not much changed in the world of
religion, as the total expressing some preference dropped by only four
percentage points. The numbers claiming to be Protestant or Jewish declined slightly, and Catholic and "all other" preferences showed slight
increases.

But as early as 1968, evidence was beginning to grow that the American people were pessimistic about the state of religion and morality. A
Gallup poll that year showed that 50 percent of those polled believed
life was "worse" as far as religion was concerned, and 78 percent said
morals were declining. A series of five polls conducted over a period of
eleven years showed a decided increase in the number of persons who
saw religion's influence as waning. The 67 percent in the polling sample
who believed religious influence was diminishing matches almost exactly
the 69 percent in 1957 who saw it as increasing. Between 1968 and 1970
the respondents believing religious influence was being lost increased
from 67 to 75 percent. However, by 1974 that figure had dropped all the
way down to 56 percent, confirming notions that these were years of real
uncertainty about the status of religion.

There were other signs of an uncertain future for religion. Total attendance in churches and synagogues declined, reaching the point where
only four in ten claimed to be regular churchgoers. While regular church
attendance reported by Protestants declined from 39 to 37 percent during
these years, among Catholics the decline was from 66 to 55 percent. Financial contributions also declined, and, measured in constant dollars,
money spent on church construction decreased in five years by more
than one-third from the $1 billion spent on it in 1970. Yet another wor-
risome matter was a sharp decline in the numbers of persons studying
in seminaries to be pastors and priests.

One explanation for the uncertain state of church mem-
Changing   bership lies in changes in the age distribution within the
Circumstances   population. The disproportionately youthful population
                        apparently felt less need for religious affiliations, or per-
haps they believed churches failed to serve their needs. Changes in family structures and commitments and increased demands on family time
also had affected involvement in religious activities. Some individuals
probably became dropouts to protest against their churches and denominations for positions taken on social issues, whether too liberal or too
conservative.

Perceptions of decline must also take into account the search by many

Jesus People of the House of Shiloh, a community of political radicals and fundamentalist Christians, gather by the Naches River northeast of Yakima, Washington, for a baptism in April 1973. *Photo by Mike Frazee. Reprinted with permission from Joe Peterson* and *Communities magazine, 138 Twin Oaks Rd., Louisa, VA 23093.*

for alternatives to the religions they had come to question. In almost all denominations there were "underground" movements of individuals who believed that traditional places of worship had become stagnant and unresponsive. They sought to create a different kind of worshipping community, simpler in structure and free of trappings and traditions. Often these communities were simply groups of men and women who gathered in the homes of their members. Few lasted more than a year or two.

Some who sought alternatives to traditional forms of religious practice found it in the Jesus movement that sprang up in California in the late 1960s. The first ones in the movement were known to the bemused public as "Jesus freaks," young persons claiming to be "born again." Their lives had lost meaning and purpose, they said, and finding it neither in drugs nor in the counterculture, they responded emotionally to calls to focus everything on Jesus. Their ecstatic version of faith resembled that displayed in earlier Christian revivals. For many, it was the "ultimate trip." The apparent innocence, simplicity, and spirit of community displayed by the Jesus

The Jesus Movement

people helped the movement to spread rapidly, often through campus networks. In 1971 the Religious News Writers Association called the Jesus movement the news event of the year in religion.

The most radical members in the Jesus movement formed highly disciplined "families" and repudiated everything they regarded as "establishment." Typically living communally, sharing everything, they required their members to renounce their biological families and the churches in which they had been raised. Distraught parents, believing their offspring to be the victims of mind control, sometimes tried to retrieve them with the aid of "deprogrammers." In less radical ways, the Jesus movement broadened its boundaries. The emotions of the movement drew favorable responses from persons in established Christian churches who would not have considered joining it in its informal communal or coffeehouse days. Just as effects of the counterculture had seeped into the lives of people in mainstream America at the very time when it was itself vanishing from the scene, so it happened with the Jesus movement. Its effects, particularly its "born again" themes, continued after the movement itself was gone.

Beginning of "Christian Rock" The continuation resulted in part from the work of musicians like Pat Boone and Johnny Cash, who fused Christian lyrics with rock music to reach vast numbers with the Jesus movement's message of sin and salvation. Families playing the musicians' tapes learned the words and tunes without connecting them to their origins. Church youth groups that went to see *Godspell*, which opened a long run on May 17, 1971, had by then no reason to connect the lyrics to the movement that inspired it. Nor, as moms and dads sang along with their records of Andrew Lloyd Webber's popular musical *Jesus Christ Superstar*, which opened on October 10 of the same year, did they think about the emotion-filled movement that had popularized the message it carried.

Movement Counterparts The spirit and practice of the Jesus movement had counterparts among Pentecostalists, who believed they were restoring and maintaining practices neglected since Christianity's early days. Prophesying, interpreting prophecy, speaking in tongues, and performing miraculous acts of healing played an important part in Pentecostal ministries. Their distinctiveness did not prevent Pentecostalists from finding a place in the American religious scene, alongside the growing evangelical and fundamentalist churches. Regarded as either evangelical or fundamentalist or both were Baptists, Assemblies of God, Seventh-Day Adventists, Nazarenes, and various churches known simply as "Christian." At the same time, mainline Protestant churches suffered declining membership, among them the Methodist, Lutheran, Presbyterian, and Episcopalian churches, the Disciples of Christ, and the United Church of Christ.

Although people identifying themselves as fundamentalists and evangelicals have much in common (indeed, many claim to be both), it is useful to draw distinctions. Fundamentalists stress a belief in the "inerrancy" of the Bible, meaning that the Bible is free of error. They regard the Bible as the absolute authority on religious matters. Many fundamentalists apply biblical authority to secular matters as well. Evangelicals stress their "born again" conversions, their acceptance of Jesus as their personal Savior and the Bible as the authority for all doctrine, and their obligation to spread the faith through personal witness and by supporting missionaries. Billy Graham, the best known of the evangelicals, embodied these convictions. Graham's eloquence as an evangelist and the efficiency of his organization enabled him to maintain national prominence and respect throughout the 1960s and 1970s and into the 1980s and 1990s.

During these years, the Roman Catholic Church maintained its vitality as its members adapted to changes initiated by the Second Vatican Council. The aggressive mission practices of the Church of Jesus Christ of Latter-day Saints (Mormons) resulted in its **Other Religious Bodies and Groups** rapid growth. The astonishingly swift triumph of Israel in the Six-Day War with Arab States in 1967 revitalized Jewish communities in the United States, but problems resulting from assimilation and dispersal of Jewish people in America continued to threaten Jewish identities.

Also during these years, groups sometimes described as cults claimed a share of public attention. Hare Krishna followers, for example, handed out literature, tried to sell books, and begged for contributions in major airports. The Unification Church of the Reverend Sun Myung Moon was an aggressive recruiter of new members (known as "Moonies" for their absolute subservience to the leader). Various Eastern religions, transcendental meditation, and quasi-religious "technologies of the spirit" also attracted followers, but they represented such minute slivers of the population that their impact was negligible in mainstream America.

18

Not Ready for New Times

Changes in the everyday life of ordinary Americans occur so gradually that often they are discovered only after they have gained momentum and resulted in new structures and patterns of living. Looking back on the years 1967–1974, we see continuities in everyday life being broken. Lines between private and public lives became so blurred that it became virtually impossible to draw distinctions between them. The descriptive term *modern* fit less well than before, although *postmodern* did not fit well either. Thoughtful men and women of all ages had reason to ponder the meaning of what they saw around them.

They could ask, for example, where idealism had got them: personal insecurity still existed. Some continued to suffer from hunger or lack of decent clothing or shelter. Some were unemployed or lacked the skills for economic advancement. Distribution of wealth was grossly unequal. Some Americans remained victims of discrimination in their quest for housing, jobs, and education and as producers and consumers in the marketplace. Some were politically powerless; some who had power abused it. They could wonder whether the Voting Rights Act of 1965 did much to change the circumstances of the African Americans who were previously denied the right to vote, or whether lowering the voting age from 21 to 18, (achieved through ratification of the Twenty-Sixth Amendment in 1971) conferred significant power on America's youth.

How long did the forces driving the cultural changes of the 1960s last? Did the counterculture leave a permanent mark on America? Many of the changes of these years were most visible among youth on college campuses, so one way to answer those questions is to compare life and ideals there in the early 1970s with what they had been in the late 1960s. Polling studies done by Daniel Yankelovich between 1967 and 1974 and reported in *The New Morality* showed, among other things, that by the early 1970s what might be called the everyday life on campuses was different in these ways:

- the campus rebellion was moribund;
- new lifestyles were scarcely connected to radical politics;
- students sought self-fulfillment within conventional careers;
- criticism of America as a "sick society" had lessened;
- campuses were free of violence;
- gaps between generations in mainstream America had narrowed on values, morals, and outlook;
- the new sexual morality prevailed in both mainstream college youth and mainstream working-class youth not enrolled in college;
- the work ethic seemed stronger on campuses but was growing weaker among noncollege youth;
- criticisms of major institutions were tempered on campus but taken up by noncollege youth;
- criticism of universities and the military had subsided;
- although campuses were quiet, signs of latent discontent and dissatisfaction appeared among working-class youth;
- concerns for minorities had lessened;
- the number of radical students was significantly smaller and there was greater acceptance of requirements for law and order;
- public attitudes toward students showed few signs of anger and little overt concern about them.[1]

Obviously, the revolt of the 1960s had ended. "Youth no longer appeared as a major force on the national political scene, in search of new institutional patterns and interpersonal relationships," writes David Chalmers in *And the Crooked Places Made Straight: The Struggle for Social Change in the 1960s*. Even though the war in Vietnam was over, "military budgets escalated. No organization spoke for black America. Preachments about radically changing America were more likely to be heard from the Right than the Left. The poor were still poor, particularly the children." Although it may not be proper to blame the 1960s and the consumer culture, he adds that "three of the saddest developments in the following decades derived from both too little and too much affluence and freedom. By the eighties, teen-age pregnancy among the poor, and drugs among the young, had become national epidemics, while the dark shadow of AIDS hovered over sexual liberation."[2]

By 1974, the times of one kind of troubles were over. Other troubles remained, however, as America entered a period of readjustment. The cultural transitions we have considered became cultural standoffs that intensified throughout the years. Given their multiple causes and terrains, the term *standoffs* is intentionally used here in the plural. If the opposing sides in the standoffs wish to find common ground, it will be necessary to learn that fixing blame for what went wrong and claiming credit for what went right will not accomplish that.

NOTES

1. Daniel Yankelovich, *The New Morality: A Profile of American Youth in the 70's* (New York: McGraw-Hill, 1974), 3–5.

2. David Chalmers, *And the Crooked Places Made Straight: The Struggle for Social Change in the 1960s* (Baltimore, Md.: Johns Hopkins University Press, 1991), 144–45.

Part III

Times of Adjustment, 1975–1980

By the mid-1970s, the war in Vietnam had ended. Embittered war veterans and disillusioned antiwar protesters kept their distance from each other. The War on Poverty had faded away with neither a victory nor a truce. The Nixon presidency had collapsed in the shame of Watergate. The civil rights revolution had lost its steam. The backlash of reaction against the forces of the 1960s had become more subdued, or at least more subtle.

The 1960s may have been over, but many who abhorred the legacies of that decade clung to the modern ideals that had lost dominance in its early years. Accordingly, coming to terms with the cultural changes wrought by the 1960s required a period of adjustment. So did organizing resistance against these changes. The mid-1970s to the early 1980s proved to be such a period.

Not that domestic tranquillity prevailed as adjustments occurred. Rather, continuities with the recent past included simmering and polarizing controversies. Opposing ideologies led to conflict that laid the groundwork for the cultural standoffs to be considered in Part IV of this book. Happily, amidst the controversies and conflict there was also a special celebration that reminded the American people of their common—and uncommon—heritage and the promise it held. Celebration of the Bicentennial of the Declaration of Independence in 1976 brought moments of accord in a decade of discord.

19

Family Changes Continue

Trends begun in the early 1960s continued:

- The median age at the time of marriage rose for both men and women, and the number of men and women in all age groups who never married increased.
- Families had fewer children, and more couples were childless.
- By 1975 the "typical nuclear family," consisting of a working father, a homemaker-mother, and two children, represented only 7 percent of the population.
- The size of the average family was 3.43 persons, down from 3.58 in 1970 (and from 4.3 in 1920). The average household declined in size from 3.1 to 2.8 persons during the decade.
- More unmarried women gave birth to babies.
- The number of single women heading families increased by 50 percent in the 1970s, to 8 million.
- More children lived in single-parent homes.
- Children in greater numbers spent time in the care of persons outside their immediate family, usually with a relative or a sitter coming to their home.
- Divorce rates doubled between 1965 and 1975, and continued to increase until the mid-1980s.
- The number of persons living alone increased by 60 percent in

the 1970s; by the end of the decade nearly one-fourth of American households consisted of one person.

- The number of unmarried men and women living together increased by 50 percent between 1970 and 1980.

Concern for the Family
The apparently unstable family structures and the changing nature of family relationships were cause for concern: (1) that the gradual movement toward sexual equality threatened the well-being of families, (2) that improved employment opportunities for women would lessen interest in marriage and child-bearing, (3) that women's new opportunities would erode men's desire to live in families, particularly men who prided themselves on being the breadwinner; (4) that sharing roles within the family by husbands and wives would weaken the emotional aspects of their relationship—in other words, that genuine love and regard for one another might not survive; (5) that cohabitation outside of marriage would harm the individuals involved and society in general.

Of particular concern was the fate of children in families. As the pace of life quickened, would there still be a place for them? Would the increasing number of mothers spending more time and energy at full-time jobs outside the home have resources left for parenting? Would fathers take up the inevitable slack in caring for the children? How would wives, husbands, and children be affected by reduced family size and the increasing frequency of divorce? What would be the effects on the growing number of children placed for longer hours in the care of others outside the home? What hazards did "latch-key children" face as they were left unattended by parents or other adults for hours at home before and after school? How would the increased mobility of families, which placed children at great distances from grandparents, aunts, and uncles, affect the stability of family relationships?

Research on Families
Such questions were on many minds, but scholars drew largely inconclusive answers. Marriage, they reported, was not about to wither away, even though declining birthrates and increasing numbers of wives employed full time outside the home were changing its character. The rising divorce rate meant not that more marriages were troubled, but that husbands and wives sought alternatives to troubled unions. Moreover, the fact that remarriage rates kept pace with divorce rates indicated that it was a specific partner, rather than the institution of marriage, that was being rejected. The decline of the family's role in caring for children, researchers concluded, was more myth than reality. As for the children themselves, the most significant was the fact that there were fewer of them and that those

Preschools like this one became more affordable for parents in the smaller families of the 1970s, and children lacking siblings at home found playmates there. © *Myron Marty.*

who lived with a single parent were almost invariably less well off economically. The rapid increases in cohabitation outside of marriage, out-of-wedlock childbirths, and single-parent homes were too recent in 1980 for their long-term effects to be measurable.

More significant than the scholars' findings are the changes in popular attitudes. Cultural biases against divorce, working mothers, premarital sex, and out-of-wedlock births did not disappear, but they carried much less force. "Guilty" persons **Changing Attitudes** were treated with more understanding than would have been imaginable two decades earlier. Although parents of young unmarried couples living together might withhold approval, the trend this growing practice represented did not cause much of a stir. Self-realization and fulfillment came to be seen as more important and more acceptable than compliance with standards of conduct the sexual revolution had challenged.

In the 1970s, new laws concerning divorce reflected changing attitudes, but they also presented new problems. California **Divorce** implemented "no-fault" divorce in 1970, but by the end of 1977 all but three other states had taken similar action. In nearly one-third of the states, irretrievable breakdown of a marriage or irreconcilable differ-

Although family life changed in many ways, home
maintenance was still done by family members, as
in this father-and-sons scraping and painting project.
© *Myron Marty* .

ences were established as the only grounds for divorce, and roughly the
same number of states added it to existing grounds. In no-fault divorces,
offending spouses—adulterers or deserters, for example—were not pe-
nalized and intolerable relationships were simply dissolved. Before long
women discovered that no-fault provisions often had harmful effects for
them and their children. Court-mandated settlements typically failed to
offset their low earnings with sufficient alimony and property awards,
resulting in increased poverty for women and children in their custody.
Presumptions that they had been full economic partners in a marriage,
perhaps encouraged by feminist rhetoric in the 1960s, were almost always shown to be false.

Baby Boomers and American Culture

Changes in family life established themselves quickly even though older persons held to old beliefs and old ways. A new generation brought new beliefs and new ways, and its impact in the mid-1970s was so notable because that new generation was so large. By the mid-1970s, nearly two-thirds of the 75 million Americans born between 1946 and 1964 were making their presence felt as adults. In 1980 more than 64 million of them were 18 years old and older, and baby boomers represented more than 28 percent of the total American population. Never before had a new generation represented such awesome numbers.

It would be a mistake to think that all baby boomers were of one mind on anything. The early baby boomers witnessed the arrival of television as a common fixture in almost every home. They experienced television's pervasive and often corrosive influences, but not when they were youngsters, not during the years when their outlook on life was being shaped. Younger baby boomers grew up in the constant presence of television, and the more frequent and more explicit depictions of sex and violence held little shock value for them.

Baby boomers stood on opposing sides of almost every issue of the 1960s. The war in Vietnam provides an example: some fought in it, and others protested against the war. Perceptions of racial tensions, gender relations, economic issues, and political corruption differed, sometimes reflecting the ages of the boomers when critical events occurred. More often their race, gender, social class, and economic circumstances accounted for differences among them.

The baby boom generation nonetheless made distinctive contributions to American culture. It made acceptable what previous generations had rejected. Their attitudes toward sex, marriage, parenting, and divorce generally differed from that of their parents. Many of them viewed the use of drugs less harshly. Although many women regarded it desirable to find a husband or live-in partner in college, unlike most of their mothers they also had careers in mind. The careers might be interrupted by childbearing, but not too soon and not too often.

Just as the parents of baby boomers had fared better economically than their grandparents, the boomers expected to surpass their parents. The economic slowdown of the mid-1970s that continued into the 1980s, however, dampened their hopes and helped shape their social and political outlook.

20

The Peoples of America

The initial successes of the civil rights movement persuaded many Americans that working together with others in their racial or ethnic group held promise of improving their lot. Further, if all racial and ethnic minorities, women, and others in groups sometimes referred to as "marginal" could achieve a sense of common purpose, sweeping changes in America's social structure might be possible. Legislation and court decisions over several decades had worked in their favor, but the potential of a backlash remained considerable.

The civil rights movement on behalf of African Americans in the mid to late 1970s contrasted sharply with what it had **African** been a decade earlier. During the latter period, there were **Americans** few organized protests, as civil rights leaders reexamined their strategies in the face of strengthened opposition. An extension of the Voting Rights Act that abolished literacy requirements was the only civil rights law enacted during these years. In 1977 the Supreme Court upheld the use of racial quotas in reapportioning legislative districts, but by then there were signs that court actions favoring the cause of African Americans were less promising.

In a case that attracted national attention, the Supreme Court heard arguments in a lawsuit brought by Allan Bakke, a white man who contended that his denial of admission to the medical school at the University of California at Davis was unconstitutional. A quota plan, he claimed, allowed the admission of less-qualified blacks and Hispanics, resulting in his exclusion. Many observers believed this to be the Court's most important civil rights case since its unanimous ruling in *Brown v.*

Board of Education (1954) that segregated schools were unconstitutional. In a 5-to-4 decision the Court ruled in 1978 that the admissions program at the California medical school had indeed violated Bakke's constitutional rights and that he should be admitted. Even though the Court concluded that the particular plan Bakke challenged was invalid, five justices held that race and ethnicity *could* be taken into account in making admission decisions as long as strict quotas were not imposed. In effect, then, both sides won.

In another closely watched case, *United Steelworkers v. Weber*, the Supreme Court ruled in 1979 that it was legal for private employers to give special preference to black workers to achieve "manifest racial balance" in jobs that were traditionally limited to whites. This gave blacks a measure of assurance, whereas whites who opposed it charged that they were the victims of "reverse discrimination" and were being made to pay for century-old offenses in which they had played no part.

Although many court decisions dealt with schools, they broke little new ground. In some cities, though, most notably in Boston, racial conflicts were severe and neighborhoods were torn apart. The stabbing of a black student closed South Boston High School for four weeks. When it reopened in January 1975, almost 500 policemen and state troopers were present to control a crowd of 300 whites who were determined to disrupt the arrival of 31 black students. Months of negotiations between school officials, citizens groups, the mayor, and U.S. District Judge W. Arthur Garrity resulted in agreements that led to a hostile calm. Generally, however, these were years of neither progress nor regress in the civil rights of blacks. The backlash against blacks became more visible, however, and no one was quite sure how to deal with it.

Hispanics   Mexican Americans, the largest subgroup of persons classified as Hispanic, were concentrated in five southwestern states, from Texas to California. In 1980, fully 83 percent of the Mexican American population lived in these states, nearly three-fourths in California and Texas. Between 1970 and 1980 this population group nearly doubled in size—from 4.5 to 8.7 million. The relative youthfulness of the Mexican-American population helps to account for its rapid growth. However, about one-third of the increase resulted from legal and illegal immigration, with illegal immigrants outnumbering the legal ones by about 2 to 1.

There was also a considerable influx of Central Americans, as economic and political instability in their nations prompted them to look for new opportunities in the United States. Of the more than 330,000 persons residing in the United States in 1980 who had been born in a Central American nation, more than one-third had arrived in the previous five years and another one-fourth between 1970 and 1974. Whatever the country of their origin, Hispanics were also affected by the backlash that slowed the progress of blacks. Although the 1965 Voting Rights Act was extended in 1975 to include Spanish-speaking Americans and other "language minorities," the revised law had little effect on the daily lives of Hispanics. Their wages were nearly one-third below the average of white males' earnings, and jobless rates were well above the national average. The perception shared by many whites that Hispanics were unwelcome competitors in a tight labor market complicated efforts to improve their status. César Chavez remained the most prominent leader in Hispanics' struggles for improvement. In 1979 he led the United Farm Workers through a bitterly contested eight-month strike against California lettuce growers, but his successes were less impressive than they had been a decade earlier. The strike was marred by violent clashes between strikers and nonunion harvest crews, and lettuce growers found ways of working around the nationwide boycott of lettuce grown by producers struck by his union.

Although the American Indian Movement (AIM) continued its militant activities, such as seizing an **Native Americans** unused Roman Catholic seminary in Wisconsin in 1975 and demanding that it be turned over to the Menominee tribe, other groups, such as the Navajo Tribal Council resisted such aggressive tactics. Yet, there remained room for organized action by Indians. In July 1980, 7,000–10,000 people from twenty-three Indian nations and thirty-five nations around the world assembled for ten days on the prairies of South Dakota in an International Survival Gathering. There they contemplated the destruction, devastation, and demoralization they faced, much of it resulting from exploitation of the natural resources of their lands and the indifference of outsiders to their health and welfare. Their purpose was to work toward the common goal of survival in dealing with forces beyond their control.[1]

At the same time, many Indian leaders advocated abandoning protest and violence and seeking redress of grievances through Congress, the Bureau of Indian Affairs, and the courts. Issues had to do mainly with control of natural resources on or affecting Indian reservations, such as mining, water supplies, and fishing rights. In 1975 the Indian Self-Determination and Education Assistance Act gave Indian tribes greater control over their own affairs and provided grants for strengthening tribal governments. The act also gave Indians a more significant role in deciding how funds allocated for the education of Indian children would be used in public schools.

Between 1931 and 1960, persons arriving in the United States from Asia represented only 5 percent of **Asian Americans** all legal immigrants. Changes in immigration laws in the 1960s, however, opened the door to more Asians (commonly referred to at the time as Orientals). In the 1970s the percentage of immigrants

César Chavez and his United Farm Workers enjoyed the support of church groups during an 8-month boycott of California-grown iceberg lettuce in 1979. Chiquita bananas, the money-making brand of the parent company of the largest lettuce producer, was also a target. © *Ellen Shub. Used by permission.*

from Asia increased to 34 percent, and in the early 1980s to nearly 50 percent. Until 1980 the Census Bureau recorded separately only a few groups of Asian origin. That year's census, however, recognized that Asians came to the United States from many countries, so the Bureau created the new category of "Asian and Pacific Islander." Although only five Asian groups were listed separately on the census questionnaire, it might have added another twenty. Pacific Islanders included Polynesians, Micronesians, and Melanesians in more than twenty-five subgroups. The diversity of languages and cultures represented in the general category was considerable. Given this diversity, it is difficult to identify efforts intended to improve the status or secure the rights of Asian Americans.

Immigrants from Southern Europe As immigration from Asia increased, the number of persons coming to America from southern Europe declined sharply. In 1977, immigrants from the homelands of those who had claimed attention as white ethnics a decade earlier stood at one-third to one-half the peak years of 1969 and 1970.

Kathryn Smith, a Navajo elder, displays sacred bundles as she participates in the International Survival Gathering in the Black Hills of South Dakota, July 1980. © *Ellen Shub. Used by permission.*

A number of state legislatures placed before voters amendments designed to assure equal rights for women, **Women's** and an Equal Rights Amendment (ERA) to the Constitution **Movement** of the United States had been overwhelmingly approved by the Congress in 1972 and quickly ratified thereafter in many states. But it became apparent in 1975 that hopes of advocates for the amendments would not be realized when organized efforts, led by conservative women, persuaded voters to turn down amendments to state constitutions in New York and New Jersey. By then, North Dakota had become the 34th state to ratify the ERA, bringing the total within 4 of the required 38. However, approval of the amendment had been denied in 13 of the remaining 16 states, making ratification highly unlikely. To revive its chances, the U.S. Senate, following actions taken earlier in the House of Representatives, extended the deadline for ratification of the ERA from March 1979 to June 1982, but prospects for ratification remained dim.

Initial gains in women's quest for equal treatment seemed impressive, as Congress enacted legal guarantees **Women and** of equal pay for equal work, equal access to education, **Equality** equal employment opportunities, and equal access to **Questions** credit. However, delivering on the guarantees proved to be a tricky matter, for reconciling equality between the sexes with the reality of sexual differences is a complex task. As far as career advancement is concerned, for example, what a person accomplishes in the early years is critically important. For women, taking time out for childbearing and child rearing slows and sometimes stalls their career progress.

The difficulty of dealing with issues of childbearing and child rearing became evident in the 1970s. When the Supreme Court ruled that pregnancy was a "voluntary physical condition" rather than a temporary disability, employers were able to exclude pregnant women from disability options provided in their benefits plans. The Pregnancy Discrimination Act of 1978 attempted to offset the effects of court decisions by requiring employers to give women who were temporarily "disabled" by pregnancy the same benefits given to other disabled workers. Employers, claiming disability leaves were too costly, then began to deny such leaves to all workers, with women being most frequently and adversely affected. Whether women should seek special legislation related to pregnancies then became an issue in Congress and among women activists, and it was not resolved until more than a decade later.

Comparable Worth
One problem facing women in the world of employment was the gap between their wages and those paid to men. Where men and women did the same work, with the same expectations in performance, gaps in pay could be easily corrected. However, "occupational segregation" meant that men and women typically did different sorts of work. In order to address the roughly 33 percent gap between income levels of men and women who were employed full-time year-round, advocates for women advanced the principle of comparable worth. They contended that the knowledge, skill, and effort required to perform various responsibilities could be compared, even though jobs are dissimilar in nature. So could working conditions. When the comparisons are complete, they argued, women should be paid equally for jobs of comparable worth. Not until the 1980s, however, were efforts made to resolve issues of comparable worth, and those efforts produced few results.

Military Academies
In highly publicized actions with immediate and direct effects on only a few women but symbolic effects for many, the military academies at West Point, Annapolis, and Colorado Springs began to admit women to their programs in 1975. In the same year, Harvard University changed its practice of admitting men and women in a 5-to-2 ratio and instituted equal admissions instead.

Senior Citizens
By the late 1970s the American Association of Retired Persons (AARP), founded in 1958, had become a powerful lobbying group as well as a provider of insurance, discounts, and other services to persons in their 50s and older. As their numbers increased, AARP members became a political force no politician could ignore. On the one hand, lobbying on behalf of the many who wanted to continue in their jobs led to enactment of the Age Discrimination in Employment Act in 1975, which strengthened earlier laws with

An Elderhostel participant is pleased with his accomplishments in a computer class at Western New England College. © *Jim Harrison*.

the same general purpose. In 1978, Congress raised from 65 to 70 the age at which retirement could be required. On the other hand, the fact remained that many seniors lived at or near the poverty level, although in declining numbers; their desire to continue working was frequently dictated by necessity. Seniors' health problems were grievous and abundant, nursing home scandals made headlines, and worries about the Social Security system persisted.

There was more to life for senior citizens than looking after their economic and physical well-being. Senior citizens **Elderhostel** clubs in churches and communities sprang up, attending to many of their social needs. In 1975, with support from the University of New Hampshire, Martin Knowlton and David Bianco created an organization that would serve the lively interests of seniors with educational and social activities. Known simply as Elderhostel, its purpose was "to continue to expand [senior citizens'] horizons and to develop new interests and enthusiasms." Retirement, Elderhostel's founders believed, "does not represent an end to significant activity for older adults but a new beginning filled with opportunities and challenges." Elderhostel's one-, two-, and three-week programs bringing together groups of fourteen to forty interested persons caught on quickly. By the early 1990s, Elderhostel had more than 300,000 alumni.[2]

**Disabled
Persons**
By 1975, advocates for the rights of physically and mentally disabled persons had joined the civil rights movement and begun to achieve success in having their
concerns addressed. In education, for example, they demanded not simply *education* for children with disabilities but *equal education*. Where possible, they contended, it should be offered side-by-side
with nondisabled children. "Mainstreaming" disabled children, they
claimed, would benefit all children; all would discover that those with
disabilities, just as those without them, were real people.

An estimated 20 to 35 million physically disabled persons in the
United States faced challenges in the routines of daily living: crossing
streets safely, finding convenient parking spaces, entering buildings
through a front door, gaining access to upper levels in buildings, using
restrooms and drinking fountains, and finding and keeping jobs. Persons
with mental disabilities faced comparable problems. Sensitivity to these
unique challenges gradually resulted in positive actions and legislation.
For example, in 1977 the Department of Health, Education, and Welfare
issued orders prohibiting discrimination against people with disabilities.
The movement on behalf of persons with disabilities soon went much
farther, leading to enactment of the Americans with Disabilities Act in
1990.

NOTES

1. Boston Editorial Committee, "People Unite for Survival" (photographs by
Ellen Shub), *Science for the People*, November/December 1980, 17–26; Ellen Shub,
"Saving Ourselves; The Work Goes On," *Sojourner*, October 1980, 10, 29.

2. Eugene S. Mills, *The Story of Elderhostel* (Hanover, N.H.: University Press of
New England, 1993), 5.

21

Security Concerns

By 1975 the economic slump that had begun in 1973, described by some economists as the most severe busi- **The Economic** ness decline since the 1930s, gave signs of coming to an **Picture** end. The economy remained "soft," however, and serious problems continued. Inflation decreased consumers' purchasing power. In response, policymakers raised interest rates so high that by the end of the decade the Federal Reserve Bank's prime rate—the rate banks charge their most creditworthy borrowers—rose to 21.5 percent. High interest rates, in turn, made it difficult or impossible for consumers to borrow money to purchase two essential parts of the American dream: houses and cars.

Federal budget deficits hampered the government's ability to develop creative and effective policies for dealing with inflation. In the first quarter of 1980, inflation reached the incredible rate of 18 percent. Making matters worse, prices for food, housing, energy, and medical care rose appreciably faster than for other items. These necessities accounted for about two-thirds of the spending in four of five American families.

Just as troubling were the persistently high levels of unemployment. In 1975 nearly 8 million men and women—8.3 percent of the labor force—were unemployed. About one-third of the unemployed were out of work for fifteen weeks or longer, indicating the need for retraining to equip them to move into new lines of work. The unemployment figures do not reflect the hundreds of thousands who were unemployed for so long that they gave up looking for jobs and were classified as "discouraged workers." Contracts with leading labor unions awaited negotiation, and the unions' weakened bargaining position increased employment uncertainties. Moreover, unemployment among African Americans was more than double that of whites. Among all teenagers the unemployment rate in 1980 stood at nearly 19 percent, and for African American teenagers it exceeded 40 percent. This figure helps explain the unrest in cities.

Internationalization of Business

American businesses, as well as ordinary Americans, had other reasons for being concerned about the future. The weakened U.S. dollar in European countries and Japan (U.S. dollars were worth less when exchanged for foreign currencies) increased the cost of imported goods and undermined confidence in U.S. economic policies. The search by businesses for cheaper labor led them to expand manufacturing operations abroad, thereby stimulating the global economy and effectively exporting jobs.

Even when jobs were not exported, industrial production in some segments of the economy suffered. The automobile industry, for example, manufactured 20 percent fewer cars in 1980 than in 1979, and the earlier year had not been a good one either. In fact, automobile production by U.S. companies in 1980 was the lowest since 1961. At the end of 1980, more than 200,000 autoworkers were in an indefinite layoff. Part of the problem was that as gas prices spiraled upward, fewer consumers were willing to buy the big gas-guzzling cars produced by American automakers. Autoworkers found that increased automation on the assembly line reduced the need for human workers. Computer-controlled robots could spot-weld, paint, move things on and off conveyor belts, and run quality control tests at high speeds and low cost.

Changes in the Labor Force

As production of manufactured goods provided fewer opportunities for employment in the United States, people sought jobs in the service sector. Such jobs—delivering pizzas, serving as security guards, and working in fast-food restaurants, for example—typically paid less than production jobs, and more of them were offered on a part-time basis and carried few or no fringe benefits. The bargaining power of American workers was obviously weakening.

During these years, changes in the composition of the labor force that had been developing in previous decades became more striking. In the three decades preceding 1976 the number of women in the labor force increased at a rate more than double the rise in female population. Early retirement, sometimes by choice, sometimes resulting from age discrimination, reduced the number of males in the employment market. In 1976 the percentage of men between the ages of 55 and 64 holding or seeking jobs stood at 77 percent, compared with 89 percent in 1947.

The general economic circumstances affected individuals and families in more ways than can be **Effects of** measured by rates of inflation, interest, employ- **Economic Problems** ment, and the value of the dollar. The cost of health care is an example. During these years, with costs rising, there was a need to develop systems of health insurance to cover millions of ordinary people who began to find their lives endangered by lack of adequate care.

The deterioration of what came to be called the infrastructure is another example. Roads, bridges, sewers, water and lighting systems, and other essential systems for contemporary life fell into disrepair, particularly in cities. As suburban areas expanded, flourished, and gained political influence, neglect of the infrastructure made things worse for city dwellers.

Statistics concerning beneficiaries of welfare programs begun in New Deal days and enlarged by the Great Society's War on **Welfare** Poverty show that daily life for many Americans was difficult. Among the 32 million who received Social Security payments in 1975, some had additional benefits from pension programs; depending on the amount of these benefits, they may have lived well. Others had a marginal existence. Also in 1975 almost 25 million persons benefited from Medicare and more than 9 million from Medicaid, 19.2 million received food stamps, almost 5 million drew veterans' benefits, 11 million were covered by Aid to Families with Dependent Children (AFDC), and 25.3 million children took part in school lunch programs. Of course, there was considerable overlap among beneficiaries. For example, a person on Social Security might also be covered by Medicare and Medicaid. Families drawing AFDC funds might also be using food stamps, and their children might be eating free lunches at school.

The appearance of a new class of people lumped together under the label "homeless" brought back memo- **Homelessness** ries of the 1930s. In the years since the Great Depression there had been skid row "bums"—typically single, white, middle-aged or elderly males. More or less confined to dilapidated dwellings in urban slums and cut off from their families, inhabitants of skid row were often afflicted by personal problems, primarily alcoholism. Largely out of sight, they were easy to isolate and control.

But urban renewal projects in the 1960s and 1970s resulted in the removal or renovation of dilapidated buildings and the construction of new ones. This, along with construction of highways through the centers of urban areas, sent inhabitants of skid rows scrambling to neighborhoods throughout the cities. Urban renewal also meant the elimination of small businesses that had formerly offered indigent and unskilled men occasional odd jobs. Many of the homeless suffered from mental illnesses. Dressed shabbily, they carried their possessions in shopping bags and grocery carts and slept in parks and on steaming grates of downtown buildings. One could not walk in cities or drive through downtown areas without seeing the homeless. In the 1980s, when this group included younger men, families, and more racial minorities, as well as increasing numbers of persons with mental and physical disorders, dealing with the homeless became a critical problem in most cities.

Violent Crime   As had been the case in almost every year since 1960, crime continued to rise or remained steady in most categories, with only occasional slight declines. Even though local reports of violent crimes alone were enough to make ordinary Americans worry about their security, high-visibility crimes made them aware that even the rich and famous were vulnerable.

White-Collar Crime   Bribery, tax evasion, fraud, and other so-called white-collar crimes were probably more pervasive in American life than crimes against persons and property, and they affected the lives of others more widely. Higher prices, higher taxes, and insecure investments were among the harmful effects of white-collar crime. Perhaps more serious was the loss of confidence in government when federal, state, and local officials were involved—for example, in 1978, the former acting director of the Federal Bureau of Investigation was indicted for having approved illegal break-ins and searches of the properties of a radical antiwar group. In the same year four U.S. congressmen were indicted on various charges; three of the four were subsequently reelected in their districts. Critics of the Federal Bureau of Investigation wondered how many convictions of white-collar criminals there would have been if FBI agents devoted as much time and energy to making cases against them as they did to other crimes.

Energy Crisis   The establishment of the Department of Energy in 1977 was evidence that awareness of the use of the nation's energy resources had reached a new high. Nonetheless, President Carter's energy plan, designed to promote conservation by imposing tax penalties on gas-guzzling cars and raising other taxes to encourage more conscientious use of energy, drew strong criticisms from business interests. Carter's appearance on television to call for support for the plan was ineffective, and foes poked fun of him for wearing a sweater to show that there was an alternative to turning up the thermostat in a chilly room. The Carter plan did not make it through Congress. The next year Congress passed a measure that put less emphasis on conservation and more on offering incentives to expand fuel supplies. Consequently, a chance to engage the American people in solving energy problems was lost.

In early 1979, disruptions in the flow of oil to the United States again drove up prices and caused shortages and panic buying. Long lines appeared at stations as drivers tried to keep their cars' tanks full.

In the mid-1970s enthusiasm for laws and regulations to protect consumers against fraudulent and dangerous goods **Consumer** and practices began to cool. Accordingly, when the Federal **Protection** Trade Commission in 1975 announced complaints about such things as diet pills, mail-order firms, and tax-preparation services and proposed guidelines to curb deceptive advertising, some citizens were riled even though others were pleased. Business opposition to proposals by President Carter to establish an agency to monitor the performance of all regulatory agencies led to the proposals' defeat in 1977 and 1978. Consumer advocates had apparently achieved about as much success as was within their reach. By the late 1970s, rather than seeking to have new laws enacted, they had to fight to preserve their earlier accomplishments.

Pressure for deregulation from airline, rail, trucking, communications, banking, and other industries led to re- **Opposition to** laxation of a variety of laws and regulations. Complaints **Regulations** from business interests impelled Congress to slash the powers of the Federal Trade Commission (FTC), forcing it twice to shut down briefly by denying it operating funds. Among other things, Congress placed restrictions on the FTC's authority to investigate the insurance industry, halted probes of pricing practices of agricultural cooperatives, prohibited requiring used car dealers to give buyers warranties, insisted on relaxation of regulations proposed to govern funeral-home practices, and forbade actions on advertising on the grounds that advertisements' content was unfair. Perhaps more significant, Congress established a "legislative veto" that permitted both the House and the Senate to reject any FTC rule within ninety days of its proposal. The consumer-protection pendulum was obviously swinging the other way. The swing occurred even though polls of consumers showed strong public support for more, not less, regulation over product hazards and unfair practices in the marketplace. Consumers simply lacked the political clout to translate their desires into law.

Nonetheless, protection of consumers remained possible under existing laws, as the Firestone Tire & Rubber Company **Recalls** learned when it was forced in 1978 to recall about 13 million unsafe Firestone "500" steel-belted radial tires. The after-tax cost of the recall was estimated at $400 million, a sum that would have been much higher had Firestone not been served by well-connected Washington lawyers. Tires, of course, were not the only safety problem with automobiles. In 1977 there were more than 12 million automobile recalls to correct safety defects, with high numbers also preceding and following that peak year.

The Environment
In 1977, President Carter launched a study that resulted in *The Global 2000 Report to the President*. The report identified environmental, resource, and population stresses that were intensifying and would increasingly determine the quality of human life on planet earth. It projected deterioration and loss of resources essential for agriculture at an accelerating rate, and it forecast the extinction of 500,000 plant and animal species over the next twenty years and deforestation leading to the loss of almost all accessible forests in less developed countries.[1] Despite the thorough documentation of the report's concerns, it attracted little attention. Perhaps the problems it cited seemed too far from home, too unlikely to affect ordinary persons in the United States.

Endangered Species
One of the species threatened with extinction was the three-inch-long snail darter, a fish whose only known habitat was the Little Tennessee River. Under provisions of the 1973 Endangered Species Act, a federal court of appeals in 1977 ordered the Tennessee Valley Authority to stop construction of a dam as it neared completion on this river to preserve the snail darter's habitat. Although $116 million had already been spent on constructing the dam, the Supreme Court affirmed the decision in the following year. In his decision, Chief Justice Warren E. Burger asserted that Congress in enacting the Endangered Species Act clearly regarded the value of endangered species as incalculable. Scientists gave various reasons for defending endangered species. Some contended that observing these species might add to humankind's biological knowledge or provide substances for the development of drugs. Others simply said that destroying the life of any plant or animal diminishes the lives of humans, too. The victory for the snail darter and environmentalists was short-lived. In 1979, over angry objections, President Carter "with regret" signed legislation that exempted the dam from any laws that might prevent its completion.

Fluorocarbons
Events in the 1970s provided dramatic evidence of the environment's fragility. Sometimes the evidence was subtle or unseen. For example, it hardly occurred to users of aerosol cans, as they sprayed vaporized deodorants and insect repellents, that the propellant in the spray contained ingredients considered harmful to the environment. In the mid-1970s, however, scientists fixed part of the blame for the gradual destruction of the ozone shield on the molecules of fluorocarbons in aerosol propellants. The ozone shield prevents the most harmful ultraviolet radiation from reaching the earth's surface. Its destruction, experts said, would cause increases in

skin cancer and cataracts, and possibly genetic damage to plant and animal life.

Environmentalists called for a ban on fluorocarbon gases, but producers opposed a ban, claiming that producing, packaging, and marketing them amounted to an $8 billion industry with nearly 1 million workers. Nonetheless, manufacturers gradually switched to another propellant, partly because consumers who were sensitive to environmental concerns had begun to turn away from chemicals they regarded as dangerous. By 1979, when the Food and Drug Administration began to prohibit shipment of hair sprays, deodorants, and other products with propellants using fluorocarbons, most manufacturers had already replaced them with other substances.

Workers in all kinds of trades touched and breathed potentially toxic chemicals every day, often without adequate protection. Sometimes, as in the **Chemical Hazards** case of lead and benzene, restrictions imposed by the Occupational Safety and Health Administration (OSHA) resulted in lengthy court battles. Nonetheless, recognizing the danger that many chemicals posed, OSHA in 1980 produced a list of 107 substances used in industrial operations suspected of causing cancer. The purpose was to generate data and discussions regarding these substances. In response, companies and labor unions provided OSHA with much toxicological and epidemiological data to be used in determining which ones should be put on a list of suspected substances to be issued in early 1981. When OSHA issued regulations in 1980 that gave employees and their representatives, along with OSHA itself, access to a company's medical and exposure records, the move was not welcome. Companies protested that such orders represented invasion of their privacy and threatened trade secrets.

Some regarded OSHA's activities as excessive governmental intrusion into business and industrial practices. Yet the requirements OSHA sought to enforce were drawn initially from voluntary standards developed through the years by private safety groups and industry associations. Each OSHA requirement therefore had advocates, which explains why any effort to repeal them involved a lengthy process.

A dramatic example of the environment's fragility attracted national attention in 1978. In a residential neigh- **Love Canal** borhood known as Love Canal in Niagara Falls, New York, a chemical dump that had been buried there more than twenty years earlier began to bubble up in lawns and basements. Given the toxic nature of the bubbling chemicals, the state of New York bought the property bordering the Love Canal and moved 239 families to new homes. However, not only did the toxic chemicals migrate beyond the evacuation line, but nearby residents reported diseases believed to have been

Supporters of the Coalition for a Non-Nuclear World include other causes in their demonstration at the Pentagon in 1980. © *Ellen Shub. Used by permission.*

caused by the chemicals. By 1980, studies seemed to show that the chemicals were indeed responsible for the diseases, but the studies' adequacy and accuracy were disputed. The federal government offered funds to residents who wanted to move, but the distraught residents could not do so until they sold their homes, for which there was no demand. In 1980 a new federal law, passed four years earlier, went into effect, providing for strict controls on toxic waste disposal. That was small comfort, however, to families across the country who lived near one of the 50,000 toxic waste disposal sites that in one way or another resembled Love Canal.

Three Mile Island Wastes created in generating nuclear power were another concern, tempering hopes that nuclear energy might be the answer to dependence on oil for producing electric power. On March 28, 1979, an accident at the nuclear power plant at Three Mile Island near Harrisburg, Pennsylvania, heightened fears that such plants posed too dangerous an environmental hazard to be trustworthy. Assurances by the Nuclear Regulatory Commission that this plant did not have to be permanently closed failed to convince many environmentalists that nuclear power would ever be safe. For years thereafter, the term *Three Mile Island* was sufficient to arouse fears of nuclear disaster.

Events such as this made the concerns reported in the *Global 2000* report less than startling. Even so, those opposed to strict environmental regulations continued their efforts to reverse what had been accomplished, and legislators seemed unwilling to believe the report's conclusions. Environmentalists feared the election of Ronald Reagan in 1980 would lead to a reversal of the gains they had made in enactment and enforcement of environmental protection laws. Reagan was critical of the movement and its leaders and stated that he would do such things as invite coal and steel industries to propose revisions in clean-air laws.

NOTE

1. Council on Environmental Quality, *The Global 2000 Report to the President of the U.S., Entering the 21st Century: A Report* (New York: Pergamon Press, 1980).

22

Television, Movies, and More

By the mid-1970s about half of the American households had two or more television sets. The sets had become, in **Television** historian Cecelia Tichi's words, the home's "electronic hearth," the focal point in a room. Viewers absorbed their radiating warmth and flickering images. They were also a home's window to the world, as the programs and commercials shaped viewers' needs, interests, habits, and values. Television's manipulated portrayals of reality became indistinguishable from reality itself.[1] "As seen on TV . . ." validated claims and opinions.

Given television's dominant role in American life, it is not surprising that its images altered viewers' ways of apprehending the world. In contrast to the way one reads—from left to right across a line, top of the page to the bottom, page after page—television follows no predictable or essential lines. Viewers move quickly, not necessarily randomly but seemingly so, from one scene to another with subtle transitions or no transitions at all. Reading is another matter: One *learns* to read books, magazines, and newspapers, typically going through "reading-readiness" exercises and then moving from elementary to more complex material.

No one *learns* to watch television. Many programs, and particularly commercials, are designed to simultaneously hold the attention of 6-year-olds, 16-year-olds, and 60-year-olds. As television holds viewers' attention hour after hour it becomes what Marie Winn has labeled "the plug-in drug." Viewers may not be in a perpetual state of stupor—perhaps they cheer about what they see or talk back to those they hear—

but they are addicted to viewing nonetheless. In her book *The Plug-In Drug* (1977) Winn described how the addiction changes viewers' ways of learning, thinking, and being, as well as their relationships with others and their environment. She focused particularly on television's narcotic effects on children, but adults suffered from them as well. These effects were by now widespread.[2]

Teleconsciousness

The popularization of remote control units encouraged channel hopping, allowing viewers to multiply the seeming randomness of television's offerings and serving well those with short attention spans. At the same time, it probably enabled viewers to cultivate abilities to shift attention quickly from one thing to another—from the screen to a book or a game or a conversation, and back again to one or the other. Tichi calls this multicentered consciousness, characterized by intermittent viewing, "teleconsciousness."[3] Widespread beliefs among viewers that program choices were getting worse, or at least not getting any better, no doubt encouraged channel hopping and teleconsciousness.

Cable Television

Cable channels grew in number and reach during these years. By May 1978, subscribers were seeing cable broadcasts in an estimated 12 million homes. Two years later, 4,200 cable systems had about 17 million subscribers. In 1980, Cable News Network (CNN) began its 24–hour news service and quickly attracted substantial numbers of viewers.

TV Guide

Watching television did not mean the end of reading. Sometimes television programs might even encourage it, as viewers sought more information on topics treated in the programs. Popular specials sometimes caused a run on books in libraries and bookstores. In one respect, at least, television encouraged reading. When *TV Guide* celebrated its twenty-fifth anniversary in 1978, it had long had a larger circulation than any other weekly magazine. Two years earlier, *Business Week* reported that approximately 24 million women and 20 million men followed *TV Guide* in choosing the programs they watched. As a money-making venture it was also out in front, well ahead of *Time* and *Newsweek* and earning nearly twice as much as *Sports Illustrated* and *Reader's Digest*.

Television Programming

As urban markets grew, television aimed its programming at younger, more commercially lucrative markets. Not one of the top ten programs in the Nielsen ratings of 1968–1969 remained there five years later. *Gunsmoke* went off the air in 1975 after a twenty-year run (but reruns would continue). By then, television programs had acquired an ethnic mix more representative of the American population. Norman Lear's *All in the Family*, which broke taboos by poking fun at bigotry in terms previously forbidden on television, remained popular, perhaps because of its blue-collar appeal. Ranked third in the Nielsen ratings was *Sanford and Son*, featuring scenes from rough-and-tumble aspects of African-American life, with African-American actors as junkyard dealers. These programs and others in the top ten reflected greater permissiveness in language, plot, and depictions of sex, as well as the importance of being relevant to American life. Other new programs, such as *Saturday Night Live*, a mix of slapstick and satire, showed the same characteristics. NBC aimed this program, introduced in 1975, specifically at baby-boomers.

Soap operas attracted 20 million viewers daily, and not just bored housewives and shut-ins. College students were **Soap Operas** among those hooked on the daily dramas featuring troubled characters in life's continuing crises. As in their earlier days on radio, soaps were typically sponsored by manufacturers of household products. In 1976, television networks carried fourteen daytime soap operas, totaling forty-five hours each week. Those who missed episodes could learn what happened by reading plot summaries in the *Daytime Serials Newsletter*. The shooting of J.R. Ewing in the 1979–1980 season's final episode of a prime-time soap opera, *Dallas*, prompted summer-long speculation on "Who shot J.R.?" An audience of about 83 million tuned in to the show in November 1980, when the culprit was revealed.

To poke fun at soap operas, Norman Lear produced *Mary Hartman, Mary Hartman*, a program that drew large audiences in both daytime and late-evening slots. Although soap operas were regarded as insipid by many, some psychiatrists saw in them therapeutic value for patients able to relate to characters with similar problems. Mary Hartman provided the model: As she recovered from a nervous breakdown, she was encouraged to watch soap operas. Perhaps such programs, with their exaggerated portrayal of aspects of American life, proved to be cathartic even for healthy viewers.

In 1977 a serial of a different nature attracted the largest audience in the history of television. Running on consecutive **Television** evenings for a total of twelve hours, Alex Haley's *Roots*, a **Specials** dramatic and melodramatic depiction of the harsh life experienced by his slave ancestors, gripped the emotions of as many as 130 million viewers. Among black Americans it inspired a new sense of pride, and whites were compelled to confront a legacy of guilt for the cruelty and exploitation inflicted on slaves by their forebears. Vernon Jordan, executive director of the Urban League, called *Roots* the "single most spectacular experience in race relations in America." That aside, it also stirred viewers to explore their own families' roots. In the months following *Roots*, the National Archives in Washington, D.C., showed a 40 percent increase in visitors, and the number of black genealogists using the Archives' resources tripled. Two years later, *Roots: The Next*

Generation, a fourteen-hour series in a seven-night run, drew an estimated 110 million viewers.

Sex and Violence on Television   By the mid-1970s, criticism of depictions of sex and violence began to grow. Broadcasters wanted to satisfy the tastes of viewers who enjoyed programs with sexual themes and episodes of violence, but they faced criticism by those who were offended. In response, the National Association of Broadcasters (NAB) agreed to something called Family Time. The NAB's code policy stated that "entertainment programming inappropriate for viewing by a general family audience should not be broadcast between 7 and 9 P.M. Eastern time." This gave the impression of promoting two hours of "cleanliness and virtue," even as the later evening hours were being filled with more explicit sex and violence.

The Writers Guild of America challenged the NAB policy in court, claiming that it violated the First Amendment. The Guild's lawsuit charged that even though the policy seemed to have been adopted voluntarily, the threat of government action had in fact made the adoption less than voluntary. Ruling in favor of the plaintiffs, the court said that networks could adopt a Family Hour on their own, but not through the NAB or under pressure from the Federal Communications Commission. None of the networks was ready to act alone, and Family Time was gone.

Television and the Olympic Games   Through the years the Olympic Games have attracted large television audiences, and in 1976 many fans of the Olympics traveled from the United States to Montreal, Canada, to see the Summer Games in person. The 1976 Winter Games held at Innsbruck, Austria, also offered television viewers considerable pleasure and excitement.

The Summer Games in 1980 were another matter. To protest the invasion of Afghanistan by troops from the Soviet Union, the U.S. Olympic Committee, under intense pressure and threats from President Carter, voted to boycott the Games. In the United States, instead of having more than 150 hours of Olympic television to enjoy in their family rooms, viewers settled for brief daily reports. The success of the Winter Games at Lake Placid, New York, later that year offset some of the summer disappointment, particularly when viewers saw the U.S. hockey team upset Russia in the semifinals and defeat Finland in the finals to win the gold medal.

VCRs   In 1975, Sony's video-recording system known as Betamax arrived in the United States, but it could only be purchased in a console package containing a videocassette recorder (VCR) and color TV that cost as much as $2,295. Even though the price soon dropped almost by half, JVC's Video Home System (VHS) soon displaced Betamax. The systems were incompatible, and VHS eventually won out (partly because of its longer recording time and lower cost) leaving Betamax owners with technology that was almost instantly obsolete.

But VCRs quickly overcame consumers' misgivings, and by the end of the 1980s about two-thirds of American households with television sets owned at least one unit. With a VCR connected to their set, viewers could for the first time arrange to watch whatever they chose, whenever they chose. Television schedules no longer controlled meal times and evening activities. Appreciated just as much was the ability to fast-forward through commercials as viewers watched programs they had recorded, although knowing how to program VCR's for recording was always a challenge. VCRs were used most frequently for watching rented VHS videocassettes. Within a decade, consumers were spending almost $2 billion on rentals and purchasing about 50 million videocassettes.

Television found yet another way to claim time in the daily lives of Americans. Video games, introduced by **Video Games** Atari in 1975, were soon on their way to becoming a national craze. Initially they were played through computerized control boxes that converted television screens into fields for simulating games of hockey and tennis. Such things as math quizzes and games of war and adventure were also popular. The imagination of the games' designers matched the enthusiasm of their buyers, and by 1976 video-game sales reached $250 million. Video-game arcades became popular in shopping centers, restaurants, airports, and other public places.

Television did not bring about the demise of the motion picture industry, as some had predicted years earlier. The industry **Movies** held its own partly by producing made-for-television films and selling broadcast and videotaping rights of movies after they had run in theaters. Sales in foreign countries also helped. Most of the industry's revenue, however, poured in through box offices, as going to movies remained a popular social activity. People were still willing to pay more to see the film on a big screen. In 1975, box-office revenue broke the record set the previous year. Higher admission prices accounted for part of the increase, but the average weekly attendance of 21 million, up 10 percent from the previous year, was the main reason. These figures are notable mainly because they represent a reversal of the 25–year downward spiral from the average attendance of 80 million in pre-television days.

Blockbuster films brought in much of the industry's revenue. In 1975, Steven Spielberg's spine-tingling *Jaws* was the big moneymaker. The violence and terror wrought by a huge man-eating white shark in a resort community evidently appealed to the tastes of vast numbers of the reading and movie-going public. Like other popular films, it was based on a novel; when the film was released, there were 5.5 million copies of Peter Benchley's novel in print. Another film based on a novel, *One Flew over the Cuckoo's Nest*, did very well at the box office and achieved critical acclaim with its portrayal of life and medical treatment in mental institutions. In 1977 came another blockbuster: *Star Wars*, a movie saturated with special visual and sound effects. Some of this film's appeal lay in its depiction of the romance of fighting a "just" war; some lay in the drama of science fiction.

Newspapers   Even though public opinion surveys in the late 1970s indicated that television had lost some of its luster as a fixture in American life, its dominance continued. That dominance affected newspapers adversely. Across the nation circulation declined to around 60 million in the mid-1970s after having reached a high of 63 million half a dozen years earlier. Increases in subscription prices and second-class postal rates also contributed to the decline. Of the 1,789 daily newspapers operating in 1975, 80 percent were distributed in the late afternoon—a percentage that was to change swiftly in coming years, as these publications found it impossible to compete with the evening news on television. Some independent newspapers that had once enjoyed prosperity and claimed a prominent place in their communities were acquired by larger chains. Sometimes they surrendered their independence for greater profits, often simply to survive. Survival eluded the *New York Tribune* and the *Chicago Daily News* and they shut down in 1978.

Radio   Radio broadcasting held its own during these years, although listening habits continued to change. In 1979 for the first time more people listened to FM stations than to AM. The specialization of radio formats that began a decade earlier continued. One observer counted twenty-four different formats, ranging from adult contemporary to easy listening to big band. Talk radio continued to increase in popularity, with some stations devoting their entire schedules to talk shows.

Rock Music   The big names in rock music in the mid-1970s included Elton John (the first performer to fill Dodger Stadium in Los Angeles since the Beatles had done so in 1966), Billy Joel and Stevie Wonder, to whom Motown Records offered contracts guaranteeing $13 million over seven years. New performers occasionally hit it big. Critics compared one of them, Bruce Springsteen, to Bob Dylan, Elvis Presley, and Buddy Holly, claiming that his style demonstrated the power that had characterized rock music in the 1960s. Springsteen's appearance on the cover of both *Time* and *Newsweek* showed the mainstreaming of rock music. So did the sale of 2 million Elvis Presley records within a day of his death in 1977.

The evolution of rock continued, with blues-based hard rock and heavy metal increasing in popularity. Punk rockers, most notably the Sex Pistols, took things in another direction, emphasizing rebellion and featuring such things as screaming obscenities and hair dyed orange. Pop rock offered a softer sound that was more appealing to middle-of-the-road audiences. Art rock attempted to mix classical sounds with rock and jazz.

Disco was another music phenomenon of these years. Re-**Disco** garded initially as dance music by black singers, it captured at-tention with *Saturday Night Fever*, a 1978 movie starring John Travolta. The Bee Gees' album of its sound track sold 30 million worldwide. Disco blended pop, rock, and black styles, accompanied by repetitive rhythms and dance beats. Discotheques attracted dancing revelers of all ages. Disco garb, including skin-tight Lycra jeans and dresses slit thigh-high, appeared everywhere. The disco beat filled the airwaves. Disco record sales zoomed upward. *Newsweek* described disco as "rhythm without blues; a body trip, not a head trip. It is relentlessly upbeat and unabashedly embraces the consumer society's latest trendy goods."[4] Disco's popularity soon faded, but for a time it was all the rage.

Popular music—rock, jazz, soul, traditional pop, **The Big Business** country, and disco—was big business getting bigger. **of Popular Music** In twenty-three countries, sales of recordings totaled $8.6 billion in 1977; the U.S. share, $3.5 billion, was 28 percent higher than the previous year. Sales increased by 18 percent in the next year. Revenues surpassed the receipts of movies, the theater, and professional sports, sometimes several times over. In 1979, however, sales spiraled downward by as much as 40 percent. One reason, the Recording Industry Association of America complained, was radio's growing practice of playing record albums without commercial breaks; this encouraged listeners to tape-record new releases on their units at home.

Contemporary music accounted for nearly two-thirds of the records sold. Who bought them? Not just teenagers, as some might have thought. Teenagers from earlier times had grown up and kept on buying. Three studies reported that in the late 1970s about 40 percent of the buyers were in their 30s and another 36 percent in their 20s; teenagers accounted for less than 25 percent of sales. Buyers of records spent large sums attending concerts, too, as big-name performers drew large, enthusiastic, and often boisterous crowds. The Rolling Stones, for example, grossed $13 million on their 1975 tour.

Stressing the money-making aspects of popular music obscures the fact that there were bands across the country playing in clubs and bars, and sometimes just for themselves, simply because they liked the music and they liked to play. Their musical energy found a good partner in the energy of the music.

Classical Music

Classical music offered another creative leisure activity, and concert-going was popular, at least among older persons. Most symphony orchestras and opera companies, however, faced annual deficits, caused not by poor attendance but by high labor and production costs. In their 1976–1977 season, the 200 largest performing arts organizations had deficits totaling an estimated $125 million. Some, such as the New York City Opera Association, were threatened with bankruptcy. After failing to reach agreements with its various unions, the Association canceled its 1980–1981 season, but two months of mediation and compromise made it possible to salvage part of the season. Similar problems shortened the seasons for the North Carolina, New Jersey, Denver, and Kansas City symphonies. Because admission receipts covered only a small part of arts organizations' costs, the more performances they gave, the greater their losses. These woes extended to the lives of individual artists, for whom chronically low pay alternated with unemployment. As performers sought to better their individual lots by demanding higher wages, they put in jeopardy the organizations with whom they performed.

Museums

Visits to museums were a popular activity, providing artistic and intellectual stimulation and enriching lives otherwise trapped in routine. Visitors numbered about 300 million annually in the 1970s. A survey conducted in 1980 by the Institute of Museum Services, an agency founded in 1976, revealed that nearly three-fourths of the approximately 5,000 museums in the United States were small, with operating budgets under $100,000. Nearly half were founded after 1960, nearly half were run by private nonprofit organizations, and nearly half were history museums. Unfortunately, as crowds grew and operating expenses increased, budgets tightened. Consequently, museums were compelled to raise the price of admission, shorten the hours they were open, and close completely on some days during the week.

Theme Parks

Amusements parks—such as Coney Island in New York, Forest Park Highlands in St. Louis, and variations in almost every city—had long been popular places for fanciful fun. Offering games, shows, and thrilling rides on roller coasters and Ferris wheels, they seemed to transport visitors into carefree worlds. Carnivals did the same at state and county fairs.

Following the lead of Disneyland in Orange County, California, established in 1955, entertainment villages known as theme parks imitated the most appealing features of amusement parks and carnivals. Theme parks that developed in the 1970s—such as Astroworld in Texas, Cedar Point in Ohio, Knott's Berry Farm in California, Opryland in Tennessee, and

Six Flags over America in five states, set themselves apart from amusement park and carnivals in at least four ways. First, they tried to give coherence to their rides, games, and shows by connecting them with loosely developed themes. Second, their youthful employees were invariably clean-cut in appearance and proper in manner. Third, the settings of theme parks were clean and orderly. Gone were the seediness and tackiness of the older amusement parks. Fourth, unlike amusement parks found near the center of cities, theme parks typically sought isolation in the countryside, although Disneyland was an exception and Disney World in Orlando, Florida, created its own urban area. These aspects help explain why theme parks attracted tourists from around the world.

Running continued to be a popular activity, so much so that Jim Fixx's *The Complete Book of Running*   **Fitness and Sports** found 620,000 buyers in 1978. Health clubs, with their elaborate exercise equipment, prospered by attracting men and women who spent their days behind desks. Stock-car racing, widely regarded as a blue-collar sport, attracted many participants and fans, particularly in the South.

Around home, skateboarding gained popularity, particularly among teenagers. Sometimes skateboards were used for stunts, sometimes simply as a sporting way to get to school. Before long skateboarding became competitive, with cash prizes awarded in regional events. Parents who held their breath or turned away as their offspring performed daring stunts must have been surprised when a study by the Consumer Product Safety Commission in 1975 showed that skateboarding ranked twenty-fifth in danger among activities measured, whereas bicycling was rated the most dangerous. An alternative to skateboards made a quiet arrival in 1980 when Rollerblade, Inc., a Minneapolis firm founded by a 20–year-old Canadian hockey player, perfected the design for in-line roller skates with "blades" of polyurethane wheels and a molded boot like those worn by skiers.

Sporting events, such as Muhammed Ali's regaining the heavyweight title by beating Joe Frazier in 1975 and losing it to Leon Spinks three years later, gave sports fans something to talk about, even if these matches were carried only on closed-circuit television. Other subjects of conversation were the skyrocketing salaries of athletes made possible when they gained free agency rights. Fans began to get a taste of things to come when O.J. Simpson agreed to a three-year, $2.9 million deal to complete his football career with the Buffalo Bills and when baseball player Jim "Catfish" Hunter left the Oakland As to sign a contract with the New York Yankees in 1975 for $2.85 million. Hunter led the Yankees to championships in 1977 and 1978.

A different kind of conversation began at the 1976 Super Bowl, when television cameras panning the sidelines focused on the Dallas Cowboys cheerleaders. Dressed in tight-fitting, low-cut, skimpy outfits, they drew oohs and ahs from male television viewers and complaints from those who considered this another instance of sexual exploitation for commercial purposes. But then, everything done in professional sports—and much of what occurred in college sports, too—was designed to have consumer appeal. Highly paid stars in professional sports played the same role as did the stars in the movie industry: their success at the box office mattered more than their success on the field, although the two were usually inseparable.

NOTES

1. Cecelia Tichi, *Electronic Hearth: Creating an American Television Culture* (New York: Oxford University Press, 1991), 8–9.
2. Marie Winn, *The Plug-In Drug* (New York: Viking Press, 1977).
3. Tichi, *Electronic Hearth*, 117–28.
4. *Newsweek*, April 2, 1979, 56–68.

23

Cares of Daily Life

Food continued to be plentiful for most of the American population, but concerns regarding nutrition were well founded.   **Nutrition**
A report by a Senate committee in 1977 estimated that deaths
in the United States caused by heart disease could be reduced by 25
percent through better diets. In addition, improved nutrition would reduce infant mortality by half and eliminate or minimize the effects of
other diseases. Healthful diets included more fruits, vegetables, whole
grains, poultry, and fish, and smaller quantities of meat and salty, high-
fat, high-sugar foods. It is not surprising that meat, dairy, and egg producers took issue with the report. Word that the American Medical Association questioned the report's scientific justification lessened its
impact, but it nonetheless gave the American people reason to be more
conscious of the nutritional content of foods they consumed. Such consciousness, furthered by heavy advertising campaigns, resulted in modest dietary changes. For example, sales of bran cereals and breads with
higher fiber content increased significantly.

Concern for nutrition received more attention at home
than when eating out. Fast-food restaurants, with satisfy-   **Eating Out**
ing but not notably wholesome or healthful fare, contin-
ued to grow in popularity. Two-income families, with only one or two
children, could afford to eat out more frequently than could larger families a decade or two earlier. McDonald's restaurants doubled in number
between 1974 and 1980 (from 3,000 to 6,000) and other fast-food chains
also expanded.

Concern over food additives continued, with ordinary
Food Additives consumers sometimes finding themselves caught between the conflicting results of scientific studies. The
use of nitrates and nitrites in curing meat is an example. It had been
known since the early 1960s that interactions between nitrites and substances existing naturally in meats resulted in compounds generally
known to cause cancer. That knowledge was confirmed in the late 1970s.
At the same time, a study found that the chemical additives also protect
against the formation of a deadly food poison. So it was a matter of
weighing one health risk against another. In 1980, a thorough review by
the Department of Agriculture and the Food and Drug Administration,
as well as by independent scientists, concluded that there was insufficient evidence to link nitrites with cancer.

Questions concerning food coloring were settled more decisively. In
1977 the Food and Drug Administration banned the use of Red No. 2 as
an additive in foods, drugs, and cosmetics, and Red No. 4 in maraschino
cherries.

Quests for ways to lose weight quickly were understand-
Dieting and able; according to the National Center for Health Statistics,
Diet-Related Americans on average weighed fourteen pounds more in
Illnesses 1978 than fifteen years earlier. Concern for both health and
appearance tempted overweight people to try to shed
pounds too quickly, leading to another kind of health problem. For example, liquid protein diets gained popularity by making weight loss
seem both quick and easy. The Food and Drug Administration, however,
issued warnings in 1978 against consuming liquid-protein concoctions
only, since at least forty deaths had been traced to near-starvation resulting from their use.

Researchers at the University of Iowa confirmed the in-
Drinking and creasingly popular theory that a tendency toward alco-
Drunk Driving holism might be inherited. Children of alcoholics had a
high incidence of alcoholism even when they had been
adopted and raised by nonalcoholics. Theories aside, the reality of the
1960s and 1970s was clear: Between 1960 and 1975, the annual per capita
consumption of alcoholic beverages increased by one-third. Was this a
return to earlier times? Not quite, since the average consumption remained at a level half as high as in 1830. The increase came in part from
the fact that teenagers began drinking at earlier ages and in larger numbers. Further, with liberation of women from old constraints, their drinking levels approached those of men. As far as consumption of hard liquor
("distilled spirits") was concerned, 1978 was the peak year in recent
times. Then came a steady decline, continuing to the mid-1990s.

Excessive drinking harmed the health of the drinkers, of course, but it also did damage to others—particularly when accidents resulted from drunk driving. Drunk drivers were involved in half of the 45,000 fatalities caused annually by automobile accidents between World War II and 1980. Mothers Against Drunk Driving (MADD), founded in 1980, became the most powerful organization striving to reduce drunk driving, particularly among the young.

Surgeon General of the United States Julius B. Richmond continued the efforts of his predecessors to publicize findings about the relationship between smoking and health. In 1979 he called smoking the "most important **Smoking and Health** environmental factor contributing to early death." In 1980 he reported that cases of lung cancer in women were increasing rapidly and that lung cancer soon would lead to more deaths than breast cancer. In March of the same year came reports on research at the University of California at San Diego that produced the first scientific evidence that breathing "second-hand smoke"—that is, other people's cigarette smoke—is harmful for nonsmokers. This report and others boosted efforts to limit smoking in public places.

The surgeon general's reports caused some smokers to fight their addiction and sometimes to win. Between 1970 and 1980 smoking dropped 28 percent among men age 20 and older, 13 percent among adult women, and 20 percent among teenage boys. Among teenage girls, however, it increased 51 percent in the dozen years preceding 1980.

The 1970s, according to observers of the fashion world, amounted to a reversal of the 1960s. Indifference to appearance influenced by hippie lifestyles gave way to concern for **Fashions** self-image. The styles of the 1960s made political statements through nonconformity, although the numbers of persons adopting scruffy appearances meant simply that there was a new kind of conformity. In the 1970s, comfort and neatness mattered, even as fashions changed. The soft look introduced in 1977, for example, with loose-fitting, oversized garments, was intended to be both comfortable and striking in appearance. The next year, with the same intent, came free-flowing silhouettes to give a slimmed-down look. Even the "conscious dishevelment" of the calculated "rumpled, crumpled look" designed to suggest liberation was expected to have an element of neatness.

The new styles were not really new; rather, they were old ones revived and recirculated. What was new were the attempts by designers and manufacturers to popularize the stylish by paying huge sums for commercial endorsements by celebrities from the sports and entertainment worlds. The endorsements created an elite that would become larger and more prominent in the 1980s.

Home Furnishings

Trends in home furnishings resembled those in clothing fashions. Changes were slower in gaining acceptance, however, because furniture, appliances, and other features of home decor cost more than garments and were expected to last longer. Besides, styles regarded as "traditional" always remained popular. Changes occurred, nonetheless, seemingly with increased speed. Paying attention to space limitations imposed by smaller houses and apartments, as well as to energy questions and cost, consumers looked for furniture that was functional and versatile enough to be used for several purposes. The sofa sleeper became increasingly popular, as did pull-down or extendable dining tables and beanbag chairs. So did "knockdown furniture" stocked in large quantities and packed in cartons to be taken home and assembled there by the purchasers themselves.

Medical Miracles

During these years the technological developments in medicine of the preceding decades were refined, but stunning new medical procedures captured the headlines. Although they were initially rare, just as organ transplants had been at first, new procedures offered hope to victims of various conditions. Perhaps the best example is the "test-tube" baby as an answer to problems of infertility. The first test-tube baby was born in London in 1978. She had been conceived when an egg extracted from her mother was fertilized in a laboratory by her father's sperm. The fertilized egg remained in a Petri dish until it had developed into an eight-celled embryo; it was then implanted in the mother's uterus, where it developed as a fetus until delivered as a healthy 5-pound, 12-ounce baby. Other such conceptions and births followed as use of the procedure spread.

Medical Fears

Fears of potential dangers to health sometimes spread rapidly. In 1976, frightened by reports of the probable arrival of a "swine flu" epidemic, 48 million Americans received flu shots. The government spent $135 million in the effort to avert an impending disaster. The alarm proved to be false, as only six cases of swine flu were recorded. At least 535 of those who received the inoculations developed a rare paralytic disorder known as Guillain-Barré Syndrome; hundreds of lawsuits against the government followed. Another medical scare came in the same year, as twenty-nine persons attending an American Legion convention at a hotel in Philadelphia died suddenly. The incident gave the name "Legionnaires' disease" to the rare form of pneumonia that caused the deaths.

Mental Health

Reliance on medication by persons suffering from stress and physical pain had grown rapidly in the 1960s and early 1970s, so much so that drug manufacturers began to worry about dependence on it. They endorsed warnings to physicians by the Food and Drug Administration that tranquilizers not be prescribed for the stress of everyday life. Perhaps in response to such warnings, legally filled prescriptions for tranquilizers (the most widely used of which was Valium) dropped from 88.3 million to 62.3 million between 1975 and 1979.

Treatment of mentally ill persons changed in other ways as well, the most notable being that fewer of them were confined in institutions. In earlier times persons judged to suffer from mental illness could be institutionalized without their consent. To gain their release, they had to prove their sanity and ability to handle freedom. In 1975 the Supreme Court ruled that mental patients could not be confined against their will unless they were a danger to others or could not care for themselves. As a result, and also in reaction to worries inspired by reports of mistreatment in mental institutions (as depicted in Ken Kesey's 1962 novel *One Flew over the Cuckoo's Nest*, made into a film in 1975), mental wards were emptied. Mental patients, in many cases, were simply put out on the streets to become homeless.

Technological advances played a part in pushing health-care costs upward. So did the increased longevity of the population. Another contributor, medical malpractice insurance, had grown in significance for a decade and reached crisis levels in the mid-1970s. Doctors and hospitals purchased malpractice insurance as protection against justified and unjustified claims of mistakes or negligence. Insurance funds were used to investigate the claims, provide legal defenses against them, and pay damages to patient-victims in court judgments or out-of-court settlements. Between 1969 and 1975, according to authoritative estimates, claims had increased by about 180 percent. One doctor in ten, on average, was sued, and the size of awards by juries rose during these years. **Health-Care Costs**

A number of factors played a part in the increase, including: sharply rising doctors' fees, of patients' beliefs that they were not given personal attention, lack of personal relationships between specialists and patients, and, apparently, the belief that greater sophistication in medical techniques should make doctors and hospitals infallible. The popularity of the television program *Marcus Welby, M.D.* seems to have encouraged notions of medical infallibility. The fact that awards in court cases and settlements were reaching into the millions of dollars also encouraged avaricious patients and lawyers to file claims. Even though the plaintiffs lost about 80 percent of the cases that went to trial, the cost of defending them was often so high that insurers frequently agreed to pretrial settlements. In the decade prior to the mid-1970s, insurance premiums for neurosurgeons and orthopedic surgeons increased more than tenfold, and practitioners in less-risky specialties also saw sharp increases. Where state insurance commissions refused to approve rate increases, insurance companies withdrew coverage. In such instances, some doctors declined to perform anything but emergency procedures. Even as solutions to the insurance problems proved elusive, most states tried to find them. Meanwhile, patients covered the cost of increased premiums when they paid the larger fees charged by their doctors.

Automobiles

Despite panic over gasoline shortages and periodic calls for increased use of mass transit or public transportation, dependence on the automobile persisted. So did competition from imported cars. In the late 1970s cars manufactured by Toyota, Nissan, Honda, and others in Japan—along with Volkswagens, Mercedes, BMWs, Audis, Fiats, Citroens, Peugeots, Renaults, Volvos, and others in Europe—claimed about 18 percent of the U.S. market. In part because U.S. success in the competition was limited, even though more than 40 percent of the automakers' production consisted of compact and subcompact cars, the number of autoworkers shrank. This had rippling effects throughout the economy.

Telephone Technology and Service

Until the mid-1970s, the American Telephone and Telegraph Company (AT&T) provided telephone service in almost every home in the United States. AT&T also manufactured, installed, and owned the phones and phone lines. A monthly charge covered a single phone in a home. Second and third phones meant added costs. A long and bitterly contested lawsuit initiated in 1974 by the U.S. Department of Justice, charging AT&T with obstructing competition, resulted in the break-up of the dominant company through an out-of-court settlement in 1982. The dispersal of ownership and the deregulation that occurred with the settlement brought many changes. Most notable, residential telephone users could purchase their own phones and have almost any number of outlets in their homes.

Evolution of telephone technology and applications continued. Beginning in 1951, regions of the country were given three-digit area codes as prefixes to local numbers, and vastly improved technologies made direct dialing of long-distance calls efficient and relatively inexpensive. By 1960 direct dialing had replaced sending calls through an operator in most parts of the country, although in some rural areas that did not happen until 1971. Callers responded in rapidly growing numbers to the invitation to "reach out and touch someone." Touch-tone phones, introduced by AT&T in 1963, gradually replaced the rotary dial models that had been standard for decades, and the entire phone operation was gradually automated. The keypad increased the versatility of the phone, eventually making it possible, for example, for a merchant to check a customer's credit rating or an investor to learn her account balances without speaking with another person.

As reaching for the phone became a habit, the use of toll-free numbers by businesses across the country proliferated. Answering machines gained in popularity, allowing businesses and residences to receive messages from incoming calls when no one was there to respond to the phone's ringing. Such devices had been available since 1950, but their poor quality and high cost had limited their usage until the 1970s. Primitive but expensive fax machines had been in use since the early 1970s, but in 1980 new technology made it possible to convert a printed document to digital signals for faster transmission over phone lines. Throughout the 1980s, the quality of fax printouts improved and prices declined from well over $2,000 per unit to under $400, allowing them to become standard office equipment.

Other technological innovations continued to touch daily lives in ways soon taken for granted. Manufacturers of cameras, for example, introduced something new every year, making them smaller, more automatic, more adaptable, and easier to use. By 1980 most were producing small 35mm cameras that loaded the film, focused, and set the aperture automatically. Another example: The Sony Walkman, introduced in 1979 and soon followed by other manufacturers' models, allowed people to listen to stereo radio or cassette tapes while walking, jogging, biking, riding as passengers in cars, or simply sitting in homes or offices. The convenience of the Walkman also contributed to isolation of individuals, as tuning into the radio/tape player meant tuning out others who were present. Another example: In 1980 the 3M Company introduced an item that sprang suddenly into wide usage and virtual indispensability, that is, the self-stick removable notes known as Post-its.

Technology in Incidentals of Daily Life

A technological device with a large impact had small beginnings in 1976, when Steven Jobs and Stephen Wozniak, college dropouts, founded the Apple computer company. They designed the Apple I, a crude personal computer (PC) most notable for paving the way for Apple II. The Apple II, introduced in 1977, caught on quickly in both homes and schools and set in motion four important processes. The first led to the development of personal computers by IBM, the big company in the computer business. Before long many companies were manufacturing machines more important for the description "IBM-compatible" than for the name of the manufacturer.

Personal Computers

The second came side-by-side with the first: the rapid expansion of Microsoft, founded in 1975 by software-whiz Bill Gates, a 19-year-old Harvard dropout (who had scored a perfect 800 on his math SAT), and his 22-year-old partner, Paul Allen. Before long, Microsoft dominated the software market and Gates was on his way to becoming the richest man in America. Third, costly, complicated mainframe systems gradually came to play a different role in computer operations in businesses, as they accommodated increasingly flexible workstations connected through telephone networks. Fourth, the miniaturization of personal

Television screens provided the monitor for Apple IIe computers like this one. *Courtesy of Apple Computer, Inc.*

computers led to the development in the 1980s of battery-powered laptop models.

In anticipation of the PC's arrival, a scarcely noticed event occurred in 1976 when the German manufacturer of the slide rule presented the last one it produced to the Smithsonian Institution in Washington. For 350 years this venerable device had been the hand-held calculator of mathematicians, scientists, and engineers, and a mystery to the many in the general public who never mastered it.

The development of personal computers and desktop workstations accompanied other trends begun earlier. By 1980 computer technology had established itself in manufacturing and business processes and touched the daily lives of producers and consumers in many ways, from automated assembly lines to banking and credit-card operations, for example, as well as in the operating systems of automobiles and the most intricate surgical devices.

Space Ventures   Early fascination with television spectaculars featuring the accomplishments of the space program had seduced viewers into ignoring its cost. So what, they seemed to say, if with each launching a $200 million Saturn rocket sank into the ocean? As the consecutive launchings and returns blurred together, however, viewers' interest waned. The technical and political milestone represented by the linking of an *Apollo* spacecraft and the Russian *Soyuz* on July 17, 1975, attracted only passing attention. Television showed the exchange of visits by the American astronauts and Russian cosmonauts during the nearly forty-four hours their spacecrafts were linked, but viewers seemed to take this historic occurrence for granted. The same was true when two *Viking* spacecraft landed on the planet Mars in 1976 and sent back spectacular pictures.

24

Arenas of Discord

Pent-up anger among voters over taxation broke loose during the 1970s. At the federal level, Congress enacted a tax reduction bill that President Carter signed reluctantly, disappointed that his more comprehensive tax reform proposal had failed. The bill provided for an increase in "earned-income credits" for the working poor. This gave low-income persons tax exemptions up to a certain percentage of their income and cash refunds to the extent that this exceeded the taxes they owed. It also increased personal exemptions for each taxpayer and each dependent, and made several other adjustments. The most significant breaks largely benefited middle- and upper-income taxpayers and corporations.

The most consequential actions on taxation occurred at state and local levels, where voters insisted that policies change. By mid-1978 legislators in four states had approved measures to limit state and local spending, and similar bills were under consideration in seventeen state legislatures.

In California, voters took things into their own hands. In June 1978 they approved a tax-cutting measure known as Proposition 13, an amendment to the state constitution that had been proposed in petitions signed by 1.3 million Californians. The petition drive and campaign for passage of the proposition by referendum was led by Howard Jarvis, a wealthy industrialist who had long fought for lower taxes and less government, and by Paul Gann, a retired real estate broker. Proposition 13 reduced property taxes to 1 percent of a property's cash value in 1976; this amounted to an overall reduction of 57 percent. Further, it limited increases in the assessed value of any property to 2 percent annually as long as it remained in the hands of the same owner. New state taxes required the support of two-thirds of the members voting in both houses in the state legislature, and new local taxes required the approval of two-thirds of all registered voters. Proposition 13 also boosted the prospects of success for similar efforts in other states.

Few would dispute that taxes had become burdensome to many Californians. Rising property values meant rising property taxes. Rising salaries accompanying inflation lifted many taxpayers into higher brackets. The costs of government, particularly local services, had spiraled upward. The percentage of personal income paid in taxes was more than 40 percent above the national average. Still, the almost instant loss of about $7 billion in tax revenue resulting from Proposition 13 (about 30% of the annual total), offset only by an estimated increase in income tax payments of about $300 million, dealt a serious blow to many California institutions. Loss of matching federal funds for state projects, running into the billions of dollars, made the blow all the worse. Altogether, local governments and schools stood to suffer revenue reductions of about 22 percent. More moderate measures in other states had similar though less crushing effects.

In the competition for tax dollars, local governments were reluctant to cut the budgets for police, fire protection, and sanitation. Cutbacks in school funding were therefore inevitable, and other public services—the kinds of things citizens had come to rely on—were targeted as well. Museums and public libraries, for example, were forced to reduce the hours they were open. Local arts organizations decreased the number of performances they offered. Across the nation, leaders of tax-dependent institutions got ready for the anti-tax wave to reach them, and California-style adjustments occurred in many states.

Politicization of Schools
Schools had long been funded by taxes on real estate and personal property, so how schools were run and what happened in them was a local issue of keen interest. School boards regularly asked voters to approve tax increases and bond issues for school construction. Consequently, public schools could not separate themselves from the political environment surrounding them. In the 1970s a number of developments turned school matters into political issues more intensely than in the past. Local groups, sometimes in coordination with like-minded persons in other localities, challenged the use of certain textbooks and the placement of other books in school libraries. They questioned methods of teaching reading and mathematics and opposed sex education. They criticized schools for being too secular, blaming the 1962 Supreme Court decision that ruled mandated prayers in school to be unconstitutional. They objected to teaching about theories of evolution and supported a

Supporters of Proposition 13 in California celebrate their big victory. *Newsweek* *[James D. Wilson]* © *1978, Newsweek, Inc. All rights reserved. Reprinted by permission.*

movement to include creationism (or "creation science") in school curricula.

Since the mid-1960s the federal government had become increasingly involved in funding schools. With the funding came concerns over loss of local control. The establishment of the Department of Education in 1980 aggravated such concerns. Although the new department provided assistance to schools in a variety of ways, it remained the focal point of criticism by persons who believed that education in America was headed in the wrong direction. With the support of the federal government, schools tried to cope with such things as meeting the needs of children identified as having learning disabilities and those coming from disadvantaged homes, while critics supported a "back to basics" movement emphasizing reading, writing, and arithmetic. Consequently, federal involvement in school funding, even as it did things regarded by many as necessary and desirable, increased the politicization of the schools.

Further Concerns in Schools Public schools, attended by about 88 percent of the nation's children, were larger and had more complex problems than these attacks on them would suggest.

Among the problems: a downward spiral in enrollments; the necessity of closing unneeded neighborhood schools, invariably arousing parental wrath; and resentment by parents who saw no alternative to sending their children to public schools because they could not afford the costs of private or parochial schools.

Schools also faced the challenge of implementing the Education for All Handicapped Children Act (EHA), passed by Congress and signed by President Ford in 1977. Called by its supporters a Bill of Rights for Children, the act required public schools to identify all children with educational, developmental, emotional, or physical disabilities and provide them with special education services. Although the specific regulations for accomplishing the EHA's purposes filled 149 pages, few federal dollars were provided to support the actions local districts were required to take.

Test Scores Reports that the long-term decline of scores on the Scholastic Aptitude Test (SAT) was continuing stirred further concerns about schools. The numbers were indeed discouraging: Between 1962 and 1980, average scores on the mathematics portion of the SAT fell from 502 to 466 and on the verbal skills portion from 478 to 424. Some observers used the lower scores to fault the schools for failing to do their job. Others contended that as a higher percentage of students eligible to take the test did so, the test takers were a less select group than in earlier times. Still others complained that the tests had a built-in bias in favor of white, middle-class students and that the increased numbers of minorities taking them did so at a disadvantage.

Consumer advocate Ralph Nader and his associates issued a detailed report attacking the SAT's sponsor, the Educational Testing Service (ETS). They charged that the tests were not good predictors of college success and that they favored children of affluent parents. Some states passed laws requiring ETS to allow students to see their answer sheets and to publish the test questions. Despite the criticisms, the SAT (along with its somewhat different counterpart, the American College Test or ACT, used primarily in the Midwest) continued to play an important part in college admissions. The news media also used SAT and ACT scores to compare educational attainment in the various states and among selected schools locally.

Given the criticism of schools by various interest groups, the pressing and persistent problems they faced, and the declining test scores, how did schools fare in public opinion? A study done by the Gallup Poll and Kettering Foundation between 1974 and 1979 reported that the percentage of persons sampled who gave schools a grade of "A" dropped steadily from 18 percent to 8 percent, but in 1980 it rose again to 10 percent. In this study, with 28 percent of the respondents expressing a "great deal" of confidence in schools, they ranked second only to churches and ahead of courts and local government (19%), state government (17%), federal government (14%), and big business (13%).[1]

Enrollment in colleges and universities reached a record high in 1980. However, as the Carnegie Coun- **Higher Education** cil on Policy Studies in Higher Education reported, flush times were about to end. Having taken care of the nearly 8 million men and women who attended college under the GI Bill after World War II, and then their baby-boom children, colleges now had to sell themselves to students who knew they were in a buyers' market. So they began intensive recruitment efforts, adopted policies and practices aimed at retaining students, increased offers of financial aid, and showed more concern for high-quality teaching. They also began to cater to students' concerns for convenience by offering classes at off-campus locations and establishing satellite campuses at distant locations. In such arrangements the learning opportunities in courses requiring laboratories and libraries were limited, but students enrolled in low-cost offerings away from the main campuses provided a cash flow that caused many institutions to close their eyes to such concerns.

As enrollment grew in the previous decade, colleges and universities expanded their offerings to satisfy the broad and **Curricular** diverse interests of growing student bodies. Expansion of **Questions** knowledge in academic fields led departments to develop increasingly narrow specializations. In turn, they expected students to narrow the scope of their studies. At the same time, students demanded freedom in their curricular choices to match the freedom they enjoyed in their residential life on campuses, so degree requirements became rather formless. In reaction, many institutions—with Harvard attracting the most attention—began trying to define what an educated person should know and designing programs to make knowing it possible, if not probable. By then, though, curriculum committees faced so many pushes and pulls that the results of their efforts were often notably undramatic and therefore disappointing.

Born-Again Religion   Religious bodies also found themselves in unsettled circumstances. While the Jesus movement described earlier faded away rather quickly, a new one just as quickly succeeded it. Focusing on a new birth through faith in Jesus, those swept up in the born-again movement sought to convert others to beliefs in personal salvation. "I found it!"—a catchy phrase displayed on bumper stickers and billboards—provided a theme for sermons, particularly by televangelists, as well as for pamphlets and person-to-person testimonies. Christians critical of the "I found it!" theme claimed that those using it got it wrong. The message, they said, should be, "He found me"; in other words, it was God who did the finding. Such criticism did not slow the movement. The aggressive bearers of the born-again message, particularly those in the Campus Crusade organization led by evangelist Bill Bright, gained many converts. Complaints that the movement used high-pressure tactics did not faze its followers.

Evangelicalism   The born-again movement represented a part of the upsurge of evangelicalism in the 1970s. Between 1963 and 1978, the percentage of Americans claiming to have been "born again" and having personally experienced salvation rose from 24 to 40. By the end of the 1970s, more than 50 million Americans claimed to be evangelicals. Local congregations played a part in evangelicalism's growing strength, as did church-related colleges, publishing firms, and the denominations sponsoring or supporting them. Evangelicals regarded their Gospel-centered emphasis and clear-cut moral codes, along with their belief in conversion experiences, as standing in sharp contrast to what they perceived to be the consequences of "secular humanism." Evangelicals and fundamentalists, who were more rigid in their Biblical literalism than evangelicals and harsher in their criticisms of societal changes, blamed secular humanism for increases in teenage sexual activity, alcohol and drug abuse, and discipline problems in public schools.

Catholicism   Catholics around the world mourned the death in 1978 of Pope Paul VI, who had had the task of dealing with the changes brought by the Second Vatican Council called by Pope John XXIII. Those changes affected church members in many ways. Liturgical practices continued to evolve, moving farther away from the rituals of the traditional Latin mass. Traditionalists regretted the abandonment of the distinctive black "habits" nuns had worn and objected to seeing priests without clerical collars. More disturbing to Catholic parishioners was the departure in unprecedented numbers of priests, brothers, and sisters who sought dispensation from their sacred vows and left their religious orders or diocesan positions. Men and women entering the orders were far too few in number to replace them. Perhaps more serious for the Church's future, the Catholic parochial schools that had long been an important instrument in carrying out the Church's mission faced cutbacks and closings. For the hierarchy, managing church affairs became more difficult. Although the Pope remained supreme and bishops wielded considerable authority, grassroots assertiveness meant that power was decentralized. In other words, the people in the Church had greater influence in church matters than ever before.

Upon the death of Paul VI, his successor honored the two preceding popes by taking the name of both, becoming Pope John Paul I. However, he died just thirty-four days after his election. His successor, Karol Cardinal Wojtyla from Poland, took the name John Paul II. When the new pope traveled to the United States in October 1979 he was greeted by huge, enthusiastic crowds in New York City, Philadelphia, Des Moines, Chicago, and Washington, D.C. His warm and gentle manner pleased the throngs who came to see and hear him. The pope's pilgrimage had more than creating good will as its purpose, however, for he used the occasion to stress human rights and speak on behalf of the poor. If this meant opposing abortion and criticizing the consumerist culture of the United States, the pope was not reluctant to be candid. One effect of his visit was to give a boost to the claims of religion to a legitimate place in American life.

Certain changes in organized religion begun in the 1960s, such as allowing the ordination of women into the ministry in Protestant churches, proved to be deeply divisive. Although women were ordained with little or no controversy in some denominations, the ordination of 15 women in the Episcopal church created fierce controversy among Episcopalians. Because the church officially opposed ordination of women, those who participated in ordination ceremonies were censured or admonished and sometimes subjected to formal canonical trials. Some Episcopal priests and members of that denomination were so antagonistic to allowing women to be ordained that they led their local parishes into a separate, conservative Episcopal body. Opposition to changes in emphasis and language, along with alternative versions of central rites in the updated version of the *Book of Common Prayer*, added to the resentments of dissenters and gave them another reason for separation.

Ordination of Women

The Roman Catholic Church continued to take strong positions against the ordination of women, with Pope Paul VI and Pope John Paul II speaking forcefully against it. Nonetheless, stirrings for change were evident among lay Catholics and some clergy, who claimed that there were no substantial theological reasons to deny women ordination. The role of women also became a point of controversy in the three strands of Judaism. Several were ordained as rabbis in Reform Judaism, and one became a presiding rabbi in Pennsylvania in 1979. A survey among Conservative rabbis showed that a majority favored ordination of women. Orthodox Jews called for expanded roles for women, but only in keeping with their understandings of religious law.

Churches and Homosexuality   The fact that churches could no longer ignore or evade questions of homosexuality is not surprising, for homosexuals would not allow them to do so. Most of the major denominations experienced turmoil as they grappled with the issue of homosexuals in their churches. Some sought ways to minister to them without condoning homosexuality; but militant conservatives, who regarded them as blatant sinners, opposed openness and efforts to support them. Whether gay men and lesbians could be ordained into the ministry, even in churches less antagonistic toward them, was a particular source of discord. Indeed, homosexuality was potentially the single most divisive issue facing churches since the time of slavery.

Religious Conservatives' Political Action   A decade earlier, religious conservatives had criticized the political actions of mainstream religious leaders on behalf of civil rights or against the Vietnam War. Now, reacting to changes in society that they found objectionable, they became politically active themselves. Besides opposing protection of rights and opportunities for homosexuals, they called for legislation against pornography, worked to defeat the Equal Rights Amendment, and demanded laws to counter the effects of the 1973 Supreme Court decision allowing abortions.

Televangelism   A large part of evangelicals' and fundamentalists' success in political action resulted from their use of television to raise money for promoting their causes. Evangelist Oral Roberts, broadcasting from Tulsa, Oklahoma, showed that it was possible to build an expansive television ministry by combining evangelical preaching with faith healing—healing by placing the healer's hands on the believer and praying fervently. Based in Louisiana, Jimmy Swaggart reached huge audiences, as did Jim and Tammy Bakker's PTL (Praise the Lord; later People That Love) broadcast from South Carolina. Pat Robertson's *700 Club*, featuring interviews with evangelical leaders and carried on the Christian Broadcasting Network (CBN) he founded in 1961, became a powerful force in conservative political causes.

In 1979, televangelist Jerry Falwell used his *Old Time Gos-* **The Moral**
pel Hour, broadcast on more than 300 television stations, to **Majority**
launch an explicit political movement, the Moral Majority.
Falwell, pastor of the Thomas Road Baptist Church in
Lynchburg, Virginia, claimed that the moral ills of society—reflected in
such things as sex education in the schools, the Equal Rights Amendment, and abortion—could be corrected through the political mobilization of moral people. Joining forces with other well-funded conservative
organizations, he aimed to register millions of new conservative voters
for the 1980 election. Success gave him reason to say, "We have enough
votes to run the country. And when the people say, 'We've had enough,'
we are going to take over."[2] In Part IV of this book we shall look more
closely at the role of the Moral Majority and other conservative religious
forces in the cultural conflicts of the 1980s.

Conflict within denominations also affected
church members. The Southern Baptist Conven- **Intradenominational**
tion, the largest Protestant body in the United **Conflict**
States, came under the control of organized conservative forces in 1979. Much the same thing had happened in the 2
million–member Lutheran Church–Missouri Synod a decade earlier,
resulting in strife and schisms. The principal issue dividing Baptists was
"inerrancy," the teaching that the Bible was without error in all respects.
Conservatives claimed that students in Baptist seminaries were taught
that the Bible may not be completely accurate in scientific, historical, and
geographical details. Further, they charged, this doubting of scriptural
inerrancy had made its way into pulpits in Baptist churches and was
threatening the purity of Baptist teachings. Their opponents held diverse
views of biblical authority. Although they also regarded the Bible as the
inspired Word of God, they were willing to apply scholarly interpretive
methods to discover its meaning. The division over this and other issues
continued throughout the 1980s and into the 1990s.

A phenomenon that worried members of all mainline, evangelical, and fundamentalist churches was the appearance of re- **"Cults"**
ligious groups labeled "cults" by their critics and the media.
Typically, these groups sprang up around leaders who based their teachings on claims of revelation beyond traditional religious teachings and
scriptures. They guaranteed salvation and satisfying lives to all who sub-
mitted to their absolute authority and severed all ties with families, jobs,
schools, and friends. While the leaders often lived in royal splendor, they
assigned demeaning tasks to their followers. Indoctrination and repetitive rituals, some of them emotionally and physically dangerous, played
important parts in the leaders' tactics.

Willingness of the groups' followers to surrender unquestioningly to
their leaders was demonstrated most dramatically in November 1978,

when the People's Temple, founded in California by Jim Jones, came to a tragic end. By then Jones had led his followers to Jonestown, Guyana, where they engaged in a mass murder and suicide. The deaths of more than 900 People's Temple members made headline news as television networks carried the story into homes across the nation.

Although members of such groups claimed to belong to them voluntarily, many former members contended that they had been converted by deception and subsequently compelled to endure treatment designed to destroy their egos. In addition to indoctrination, tactics included limiting members' sleep, changing their diet, controlling all conversations, and doing other things to disorient them and make their alienation from society complete. Although the number of people who joined groups with such practices was small, the lives affected by them—the members and the families of members—were affected profoundly. Consequently, discussions were widespread about ways of protecting particularly the young from such groups' advances.

Women's Movement and the ERA

Women styling themselves as traditionalists played a big part in the defeat of the Equal Rights Amendment. Believing that the women's movement had dealt mainly with the concerns of professional women, most of them with college degrees, these traditionalist women found a spokesperson in Marabel Morgan. Her book *The Total Woman*, published in 1975, urged women to scorn the feminists' concerns and "cater to her man's special needs." In other words, traditional roles of men and women should be perfected rather than changed or condemned. Although there were no formal affiliations between those who shared Morgan's views and Falwell's Moral Majority, their general purposes had much in common.

The traditionalists' most outspoken and influential leader was Phyllis Schlafly, an attorney, writer, and political activist who was anything but a stay-at-home mom. She and her followers charged that feminists' criticisms of traditional roles for women were an attack on ways of life that had brought them fulfillment and respect. Schlafly claimed in *The Power of the Positive Woman* (1977) that women who had been good wives and homemakers for decades would be "turned out to pasture with impunity" by what she called "a new, militant breed of women's liberationists." Her foes, she asserted, were willing to sacrifice justice for equality. The next year, when 20,000 women at the National Women's Conference in Houston celebrated the successes of the women's movement, Schlafly rallied a force of about 8,000 antifeminists. She drew cheers by denouncing the ERA, abortion, "lesbian privileges," and child care funded by the government.

Abortions were not illegal in the United States until after
the Civil War, but legislation enacted at that time made those   **Abortion**
performing them and their patients criminally liable. How-
ever, prohibitions against advertising availability of abortions, convictions of persons who performed them, and rising public sentiment stirred
by medical and moral concerns, did not end women's desire to terminate
unwanted pregnancies. According to informed estimates, a million or
more abortions were performed annually in the 1960s, many of them
exposing pregnant woman to physical dangers. The fact that abortions
could be done in ways that reduced the risk, along with fears of overpopulation, sensitivity to economic difficulties faced by large families,
and growing acceptance of abortion as an alternative birth control
method, led legislatures in about one-third of the states to make abortion
laws less restrictive.

On January 22, 1973 the Supreme Court handed down a decision that
would standardize abortion policies across the nation. In *Roe v. Wade*,
the Court ruled by a 7-to-2 vote that all restrictions on a woman's right
to an abortion during the first trimester of pregnancy were unconstitutional. In the second trimester, before a fetus could survive outside the
womb, the Court ruled that a woman's right to privacy required a decision for an abortion to be made only by the woman herself and her
physician. This provision grew out of the Court's determination that persons trained in medicine, philosophy, and theology could not agree on
when a fetus becomes a person. In the third trimester—the last three
months of a pregnancy—abortion was restricted to cases in which it was
necessary to save the life of the mother. Following the Court's decision,
the number of abortions performed increased dramatically. In 1977 doctors performed 1.3 million legal abortions. Every ten live births were
matched by three abortions.

Opponents of abortion rights reacted with horror to
the Supreme Court's decision and its consequences.   **Opposition to**
They began almost instantly to mobilize forces seeking   **Abortion Rights**
its reversal. Annual rallies on January 22, the anniver-
sary of the *Roe v. Wade* decision, were signs of what
was to come in the 1980s, as those opposed to abortions organized a
"pro-life" movement. Before long courts and legislatures were involved.
In a highly publicized 1975 case, Dr. Kenneth C. Edelin, a physician in
Boston, was convicted of manslaughter in the death of a fetus in a therapeutic, second-trimester abortion. The Massachusetts Supreme Court
overturned the verdict in December 1976 on the grounds that there was
insufficient evidence to find him guilty.

The first legislative effort to neutralize the effects of the decision was the Hyde Amendment to the Health, Education, and Welfare appropriations bill in 1976. Named for its sponsor, Representative Henry Hyde of Illinois, the amendment barred the use of federal funds to pay for abortions "except where the life of the mother would be endangered if the fetus were brought to term." In 1980 the Supreme Court upheld the provisions of the Hyde Amendment. By then, Medicaid-funded abortions had declined from nearly 300,000 annually before the Hyde Amendment went into effect to under 4,000.

In response to restrictions imposed by the Hyde Amendment and the attacks on rights legally guaranteed by *Roe v. Wade*, those who believed that abortion decisions should be the prerogative of women in consultation with their physicians organized what came to be called the "pro-choice" movement. As the two sides squared off, middle ground disappeared and abortion became a central issue in the cultural standoffs of the 1980s.

Homosexual Rights

The lines drawn on women's rights and abortion extended rather quickly to another issue, the rights of homosexuals to protection against discrimination. In the mid-1970s, such groups as the Gay and Lesbian Alliance succeeded in persuading states and municipalities to enact gay rights ordinances. These ordinances prohibited discrimination on the basis of sexual orientation. Counterforces acted quickly. They claimed that homosexuality was a sin and that recognizing it simply as an orientation, rather than as a deliberate choice, was further evidence of national degeneracy. To them, guaranteeing rights of homosexuals was simply another part of the corrupt legacy of the 1960s. Battles in Miami were a foretaste of more to come in the cultural conflicts of the 1980s. Miami's 1977 gay rights law claimed national attention when singer Anita Bryant led a crusade against it. If homosexuality were the normal way, she charged, "God would have created Adam and Bruce." By a 2-to-1 margin in a referendum, the law was repealed. Similar referenda soon overturned gay rights laws in other cities.

Discord and Division

The discord apparent in the later 1970s was in many respects nothing new. Since the nation's founding, political differences have been sharply debated. Even so, thoughtful observers worried that things were headed toward the point where pulling together again would be impossible. Many observers got into the blame-fixing game. Perhaps the self-centeredness of what they called the "me generation" of the 1960s was responsible. Members of this generation, however, while pursuing their own interests also worked together to preserve the environment, protect the rights of all citizens, and improve the lot of the poor.

Possibly the economic distress and political turmoil of the 1960s and

Marchers in Boston mark the tenth anniversary of the riots at Stonewall Inn in New York—the birth of the modern lesbian and gay rights movement. © *Ellen Shub. Used by permission.*

the 1970s meant that America had reached a point at which humans could not prosper. Everything was too big and too complex to be manageable: Gasoline shortages, inflation, and declining real wages caused distress, and racial problems defied solution. Changing roles of women upset traditional ways. Environmental problems reminded people that they could not take the future for granted. No wonder the nation was in a bad mood, pulling itself apart.

In 1979 President Carter, searching for a way to pull the nation together and lead it into better times, retreated to Camp David to ponder alternatives. Speaking to the nation on his return to Washington, he described what he perceived to be a moral and spiritual crisis facing the nation. Although he never used the term *national malaise*, reporters, many of whom had difficulty comprehending the style and convictions of a religious, reflective person like Carter, hung the word *malaise* on his speech. His ability to lead thus suffered further blows.

Two decades later, perspectives on the discord of the 1970s remain uncertain. This we know: The backlash against the War on Poverty, the antiwar protesters, and the civil rights movement was already picking up steam in the late 1960s. In 1968 the presidential campaign of Alabama's governor George Wallace against all he thought wrong with the federal government, with the old trump card of anticommunism thrown in, won him followers not only across the South but also in Michigan and Wisconsin. His successes forced Richard Nixon into a more reactionary mode than his previous political record would have suggested, and the forces of backlash gained momentum. Nixon's resignation in disgrace six years later blunted the power of the forces he had drawn together in his presidency. A cautious Democrat—Jimmy Carter—gained the presidency in the 1976 election, but his ineffectiveness meant that the backlash had merely been slowed. The election of Ronald Reagan in 1980 again gave the backlash a platform and set the stage for the dominance of political power by those who styled themselves as conservative.

NOTES

1. Cited in *The 1981 World Year Book* (Chicago: World Book, 1981), 296.
2. Quoted in Paul Boyer, *Promises to Keep: The United States since World War II* (Lexington, Mass.: DC Heath, 1995), 435.

25

Pulling Together

The pulling apart was real enough, but several events between 1975 and 1980 invited Americans to interrupt their everyday lives and rediscover their identity as Americans. We note here three such events, the third of them extending into the 1980s.

The bicentennial of the adoption of the Declaration of Independence in 1776 inspired a wide variety of celebrations. Fireworks filled the skies in communities **The Bicentennial** of all sizes across the nation, and parades, parties, races, games, and historical reenactments occurred in many cities and towns. Some celebrations featured the distinctive styles of ethnic groups, noting the important contribution made by immigrants throughout two centuries. Some celebrated with exhibitions of arts and crafts, often reflecting local or regional distinctiveness. The most American of foods—sweet corn, watermelon, and hot dogs—were on the menu everywhere. Religious congregations assembled to remember with thanks the blessings enjoyed by Americans.

In some cities, spectacular fireworks displays, preceded by concerts and other entertainment, attracted hundreds of thousands of children and adults. Six million persons on the shore of New York Harbor watched an armada of fifty vessels from the U.S. Navy and other countries sail from the Verrazano Narrows Bridge past the Statue of Liberty to the George Washington Bridge. In Philadelphia, where it all began, commemorative activities included striking the Liberty Bell thirteen times, once for each of the original colonies that had united in declaring their independence from the British Crown. Across the nation, bells in

Ships from the U.S. Navy and other countries pass the Statue of Liberty on July 4, 1976. *UPI/CORBIS-BETTMANN.*

churches, schools, and fire departments pealed in response. Television and radio helped to draw everyone into the big party.

In a nation born in protest, some people marked the bicentennial by protesting. In Washington, D.C., for example, the People's Bicentennial called for independence from big business and advocated "democracy for the economy." In Philadelphia, groups of Indians, blacks, and others marched to demonstrate their call for equal rights.

Celebrations on the Fourth of July were only part of the observance of the Bicentennial. The American Revolution Bicentennial Administration (ARBA) distributed the $51 million that Congress had appropriated to finance projects and programs throughout the year. The ARBA's master calendar of observances listed 27,146 active projects and events in 11,639 cities and towns. People from around the world, including Great Britain's Queen Elizabeth II, traveled to America to join in the celebrations, many of them bringing commemorative gifts. Representatives from 36 nations joined others from American communities in the Smithsonian Institution's Festival of American Folklore held on the Mall in Washington, D.C. A 10–car Freedom Train stopped in 140 cities in the 48 contiguous states and attracted an estimated 8 million visitors, who viewed an exhibition of more than 700 objects showing political, technological, and artistic accomplishments of the American people.

As part of the Bicentennial, people joined forces to restore historic buildings and sites, plant trees, build parks, and compile pictorial and oral histories. Citizens in many communities placed memorabilia in sealed capsules to be opened in 2076, letting descendants know how their forebears had marked the special day. On a more personal level, countless families undertook research into their own families' past, and membership in genealogical societies grew markedly.

In about 5,000 town meetings, citizens gathered to identify and analyze the issues facing them and consider possible solutions. Additional discussions of the nation's political, economic, and social concerns occurred as part of the American Issues Forum. Funded by a grant of $7 million from the National Endowment for the Humanities and additional donations, the Forum encouraged exchanges of ideas through newspapers, magazines, radio and television stations, and an array of private agencies and governmental bodies.

Rounding out celebrations of the nation's heritage, museums sponsored exhibitions that celebrated American accomplishments in the arts and sciences. Orchestras performed works of American composers and, with support by the National Endowment for the Arts, commissioned new compositions. Opera companies featured works with American themes or by American composers. Teachers at all levels gave special attention to the meaning of the Bicentennial. Actors and musicians in colleges and schools performed plays and musicals that reflected interest in the legacies of 200 years of history.

Few occasions have drawn ordinary Americans into common celebrations as fully and joyfully as did the marking of the Bicentennial.

An event that occurred thousands of miles away on November 4, 1979, also attracted national attention **Hostages in Iran** and inspired patriotic sentiments, but there were no celebrations until it was over. In Teheran, Iran, militant "students" overran the American embassy and seized more than sixty Americans as hostages. Within several weeks, thirteen lower-level employees—five women and eight blacks—were released, but the others were denied freedom. The pretext for the hostile action of the Iranians was that President Carter had allowed the deposed Shah of Iran to come to the United States for medical treatment. Led by the fanatical revolutionary and spiritual leader in Iran, Ayatollah Khomeini, the Iranians taunted and tortured their hostages for more than a year.

The hostage crisis apparently was made worse by actions that played into the hands of the Iranian extremists. First, President Carter canceled his travel schedule and committed all his time to trying to find a solution to the crisis. The United States broke diplomatic relations with Iran, instituted an economic boycott of Iran, froze Iranian assets in the United States, and cut off various trade and economic aid agreements. The publicity surrounding these actions gave the Iranians the attention they sought. Second, the national media focused relentless attention on the hostages, giving the hostage-taking the kind of publicity that exceeded anything the Iranians' media managers could have desired.

With attention riveted on the hostages and kept there by such things as yellow ribbons tied around trees all across the nation, other things seemed to come to a standstill. An attempt on April 25, 1980, by the U.S. Marines to rescue the hostages, ordered by President Carter, ended in disaster. Dust storms felled three helicopters, forcing those in charge to abort the attempted rescue. A helicopter and transport plane crashed during the evacuation, and eight men were killed. Both the nation and President Carter were humiliated. Showing their contempt for Carter, the Iranians released the fifty-two hostages within minutes of his departure from office on January 20, 1981.

The Vietnam Memorial   Although American participation in the long war in Vietnam had ended earlier, the war itself continued until April 30, 1975. Televised reports of the fall of Hue and Da Nang a month earlier reminded Americans of the price they had paid for their involvement in the war. Footage showing the evacuation of the last 1,373 U.S. troops and 5,695 Vietnamese from Saigon to Navy ships in the South China Sea struck most Americans as humiliating. Refugees numbering more than 140,000 scrambled out of Vietnam on fishing boats, ships, helicopters, and planes. More than 90 percent of them came to settle in the United States.

For decades thereafter, "no more Vietnams" remained a theme in the conduct of U.S. foreign policy. Among those for whom the divisive character of the war exacted a heavy price were the men and women who had served in Vietnam. Whether their tours of duty ended in the mid-1960s or when the war drew to a close a decade later, they returned to civilian life resentful, seeing themselves and their efforts as unappreciated. They had fought the war, and now it seemed they had to sneak back into their own country.

In 1979 Jan Scruggs, a former Air Force officer, decided to do something to recognize the service and sacrifices of the Vietnam veterans. Working with others, he managed to raise initial funds for the eventual building of a memorial tribute to those who had died in the war. Opposition to the memorial by remnants of the antiwar movement did not help, but neither did it hurt Scruggs's cause.

Controversies over approval of the site and design of the memorial continued into the 1980s. So did the seemingly impossible challenge of raising the funds to pay for it and coping with political battles over one thing or another, mainly its design. Eventually, however, the obstacles yielded and the memorial, designed by Yale University student Maya Lin (selected from among more than 1,400 entrants in the design competition), was ready for dedication in November 1982.

Since then, the memorial has seemed to heal some of the war's wounds. Millions of visitors have had reason to share the sentiments expressed by columnist James Jackson Kirkpatrick, who had earlier walked through the mud at the construction site to see what was taking shape. "Nothing I had heard or written," he said, "had prepared me for the moment. I could not speak. I wept. . . . This memorial has a pile driver's impact. No politics. No recriminations. Nothing of vainglory or of glory either. . . . Never mind. The memorial carries a message for all ages: this is what war is all about." Kirkpatrick's conclusion: "On this sunny Friday morning, the black walls mirrored the clouds of a summer's ending and reflected the leaves of an autumn's beginning, and the names—the names!—were etched enduringly in the sky."[1]

The sight of black granite walls bearing the names of 58,000 Americans, listed in the chronological order of their death, unfailingly gives visitors an unforgettable experience. Almost always it is made more so by the presence of families and friends of the war's victims, searching for the names of loved ones and leaving small tributes in their honor.

Discord over the role of the United States in the war in Vietnam lingered, but the memorial remains a place where men and women, no matter their feelings on the war itself, can come together to pay solemn honor to those whose names are inscribed on its black granite walls.

NOTE

1. Quoted in Jan C. Scruggs and Joel L. Swerdlow, *To Heal a Nation: The Vietnam Veterans Memorial* (New York: Harper & Row, 1985), 130.

Part IV

Crossing the Postmodern Divide: 1981–1990

By the 1980s the United States had reached what philosopher Albert Borgman calls a "postmodern divide."[1] Beliefs and behaviors of modern times yielded to new beliefs and behaviors. A framework calling attention to contrasts between modern and postmodern beliefs and behaviors, admittedly stated in extreme terms, helps us understand the changes.

In modern times, progress was an overriding goal. On the postmodern side of the divide, progress is not always seen as attainable or even desirable. Sometimes we pay too high a price for it, as when it destroys the environment. The belief that reason leads to the best solutions to problems has yielded to notions that decisions should be made in one's heart as well as in one's head. Where science was seen as the way to truth, other avenues became plausible. The certainties of modern times have been matched by a tolerance for ambiguities.

In postmodern times, the need for unilateral control by people "in charge" has diminished and relationships have become bilateral and multilateral. We see this in jobs as well as in relations between husbands and wives, parents and children, teachers and students. Appreciation for predictability has been joined by respect for randomness. In modern times, coherence was the ideal. In postmodern times, chaos came to be accepted as normal. Indeed, a book on management by Tom Peters published in 1987 bore the title Thriving on Chaos. In modern times, responsibilities and commitments were meant to be honored. In postmodern times—well, maybe, maybe not; whimsy and indifference have their place.

NOTE

1. Albert Borgman, *Crossing the Postmodern Divide* (Chicago: University of Chicago Press, 1992).

26

Family Variations

The average size of households declined to 2.63 persons in 1990, down from 3.3 in 1960 and the smallest ever. Single-person households increased to one-fourth of the total. Families—that is, households consisting of at least two persons—averaged 3.17 persons, down from 3.67 in 1960. The ratio of households consisting of married couples with children under age 18 declined from 31 percent of the total in 1980 to 26 percent in 1990. Households made up of married couples without children remained constant at around 30 percent, while those with men or women living alone increased to nearly one-fourth of all households.

Households and Families

By the 1980s the strains on families were so great that there were reasons to wonder whether more radical changes in their structures and functions were likely to occur. What did it mean that the percentages of men and women who remained unmarried almost doubled between 1970 and 1990? For men, the increase in "never-marrieds" climbed from under 19 percent in 1970 to almost 26 percent in 1990; for women, from under 14 percent to almost 19 percent. Whether the never-marrieds of both sexes in all age groups remained single by choice or necessity, temporarily or permanently, their presence in the population was notable.

Marriage and Divorce

Divorce rates climbed to much higher levels than they had been in the 1950s. After reaching a peak of 5.3 per 1,000 people in 1981, the rate decreased slightly during the decade, but few expected it to return to the levels of the 1950s. Perhaps trends toward later marriage and cohabitation outside of marriage contributed to declining divorce rates.

The increase of families headed by single parents was one
Single-Parent of the most striking changes in the 1980s. By the end of
Families the decade, 28 percent of the children in the United States
lived with a single parent, a percentage double that of
1970. Almost one-third of these children lived with a parent who had
never married. Many of these parents had given birth as teenagers.
Nearly half of all babies delivered by white teenage mothers in the mid-
1980s were born out of wedlock. For black teenage mothers the figure
was 90 percent. Between 1960 and 1985, the proportion of births to unmarried teenage mothers increased from just over 15 percent to 58 percent. Divorces and separations accounted for the other single-parent
families.

The economic consequences of living in a single-parent household
were stunning. The Census Bureau reported in 1991 that the median
income in two-parent families was more than $40,000; in homes headed
by divorced mothers, around $16,000; and in the homes of never-married
mothers, under $9,000. The never-married mothers were frequently poor
before giving birth to children, and Census Bureau figures for 1985
showed that only one in nine received child support payments from the
father of the children. About 54 percent of fathers who had divorced
their children's mother and not remarried made child-support payments.
For those who had remarried, the figure dropped to 42 percent. When
payments were made, they tended to be meager.

Single-parent homes relied more heavily than others on outside-the-
home childcare arrangements, often of a patchwork nature, with the children placed in the care of family and friends as schedules permitted.
Older children cared for younger ones at earlier ages. More children
spent more time at home alone as "latch-key kids." National surveys
indicated that children growing up in a single-parent family were more
likely than those raised in two-parent homes to drop out of high school,
marry as teenagers, bear children before marrying, and experience un-
satisfying marriages themselves. Even though a majority of children from
single-parent families did not have these experiences, their prospects for
having them were relatively higher.

Paralleling the increase in single-parent families was
Other Variations the growth in the number of families that included
stepchildren, sometimes children from the husband's
previous marriage, the wife's previous marriage, and the new marriage.
Complexity did not end there, as children in these "mixed and matched"
families had links with families of their other remarried parent, and new
sets of grandparents were added to extended families. So common did
step-families become that any sense that they were extraordinary disappeared.

One of the most dramatic increases in the 1980s was in the number of births to unmarried mothers. In the three decades preceding 1990, the percentage of births to unmarried women increased from 5.3 percent of total births to 29.5 percent. In the white population, the 1990 figure of 21 percent was nine times as high as in 1960. Among blacks the percentage nearly tripled, to 65.2. Although the percentage increases reflected in part the fact that married women were having fewer children, statistics presented without percentages also show dramatic increases: In 1960, 15 teenagers per thousand, most of them unmarried, gave birth to babies; by 1990 the number had risen to 44.8.

If bearing children without being married had lost much of its former stigma, so did living together outside **Cohabitation** of marriage. The number of unmarried couples living together increased from around half a million in 1970 (the first year in which the Census Bureau recorded numbers in this category) to almost 2 million in 1985. Among those under 24 years of age, the number increased about eightfold; among those age 25 to 44, nearly twelvefold. About 30 percent of the unmarried couples had children under age 15 living with them.

The sharp increase in numbers of persons living together outside of marriage led observers to believe, for a time, that such relationships would eventually replace the institution of marriage. Looking at cohabitation patterns more closely, however, they concluded that partners in such relationships were not seeking an alternative to marriage. Rather, the arrangement served as a way of finding a compatible partner, a stage of intimacy preceding marriage. One might expect that marriages between persons who "passed the compatibility test" would have lower divorce rates. Studies have shown, however, that such marriages are more likely to break up during the first ten years than marriages in which the partners have not lived together. Observers have surmised that the ethic that allows cohabitational relationships to end when either partner is dissatisfied carries into marriages that result from them.

Because such rapid changes in marriage- and family-related matters as those occurring in the 1970s and 1980s **The Future of** were unprecedented, it is too early to tell whether they **Families** represented irreversible trends or were cyclical. Even if the changes prove to be relatively permanent, it seems likely that families based on marriage will continue to be the prevailing cultural ideal.

A sign of the resiliency of marriage can be found in evidence that relationships between husbands and wives were generally regarded as more rewarding in the 1980s than in the 1950s, which had generally been known as the "golden age" of the family. In the earlier decade, roles of family members were more firmly fixed, if not stereotypical. In the later

Story time at a child-care center in Boston. © *Ellen Shub. Used by permission.*

decade, mutual respect and better understanding of the other's roles in life contributed to healthier relationships.

Household Duties
One thing that changed slowly in families was the role of men in the daily functioning of households.
One survey concluded that even in dual-income families there was not much equality in the sharing of responsibilities for home and family care. Over two decades, the portion of work done by men increased from 20 to 30 percent.

Child Care
Between the early 1970s and the end of the 1980s, the proportion of women with children under the age of 6 who were employed outside the home nearly doubled, reaching almost 60 percent. That meant that more than 10 million children under age 6, about two-thirds of them under age 3, had working mothers. The majority of these mothers came from two-parent families, allowing for sharing of parental duties. In most instances, however, these families also had to find ways to care for their preschool children, as well as for those in school (nearly 20 million of them between the ages of 5 and 14) during nonschool hours. For everyone—regardless of income, marital status, or race—questions of accessibility and affordability of child-care arrange-

ments were ongoing concerns. Reports of sexual abuse in child-care situations made parents particularly attentive to matters of safety, and having to cope with the children's illnesses and emergencies was a constant worry.

Ways of meeting the challenges varied as widely as the circumstances of the families facing them. A 1987 survey showed that about one-fourth of the primary child-care arrangements involved group facilities, typically called day-care centers. In almost as many instances, children were placed in "family day care," usually in the caregivers' own homes. Roughly one child in six was cared for in the home by the father and an almost equal number by a relative or nonrelative; about the same proportion stayed with a relative outside the home. In almost all the remaining instances the mother took the child to work with her. Parents who faced the challenge of finding caregivers for their children during these years knew that although these numbers might represent an accurate picture at a given time, there was considerable movement of the children from one arrangement to another. It was not uncommon for parents to try as many as four or five different arrangements within a single year.

Because employment of women outside the home had become so common, instances of women quitting their jobs to become "stay-at-home moms" were treated as newsworthy. However, stay-at-home moms who found it necessary to return to work were merely statistics, not news.

By the end of the 1980s it seemed certain that the proportion of children cared for by persons other than their parents, and for more hours of the day, would continue to increase, so debates about their care continued. A critical question concerned the short-term and long-term effects on children of being cared for day after day by persons other than their parents. The answers given by scholars who studied the questions were mixed. Other questions usually indicated the need for government involvement: What standards should be required of day-care centers and family-care providers? How much insurance should be required, and how could it be kept at affordable levels? What should be the policies of businesses concerning grants of parental leave to enable mothers and fathers to attend to their newborn or to children who become ill? What should be the government's policies with respect to tax credits for working parents and parental leave?

Addressing the last of these questions, in 1990 Congress passed legislation granting $22 billion in tax credits, mostly for parents in low-income families. It also passed a bill requiring employers to provide up to twelve weeks of unpaid leave to allow employees to care for a newborn or adopted child or for a seriously ill person in their families. President George Bush vetoed the bill, contending that it dealt with matters that should be worked out by employers and employees, not by the government. Attempts to override the veto failed.

Baby Boomers and Senior Citizens   In profiles showing age distributions in the population of the United States, the baby-boomer bulge is always evident. As baby boomers matured, they made their mark in many spheres of society. Some of the young, urban professionals among them were labeled Yuppies. Their ambitious, upwardly mobile, materialistic, and presumably care-free lifestyles contrasted sharply with the hippies of the 1960s, the most radical of whom called themselves Yippies. Admired by some, scorned by many, ignored by most, they probably reflected the values of the culture more than they influenced it. In any case, their impact was sufficient for *Newsweek* magazine to label 1984 the year of the Yuppie.[1]

With the maturing of the baby-boom generation came another demographic phenomenon: The parents of baby boomers were living longer, and the percentage of older people in the population continued to increase. In the ten years preceding 1990, the population over age 65 grew nearly 25 percent, from 16.5 to 20.5 million. This was only the beginning of a long-term trend: The percentage of elderly will continue to increase steadily until about 2030, when their number is likely to be twice as large as in 1990. Probably for the first time in history there will then be more deaths than births in a given year.

Caring for the Elderly   Although many senior citizens remained healthy and vigorous, the lives of some were complicated by infirmities. They required a substantial share of medical services. Although people age 65 and over represented only 13 percent of the population in 1990, they accounted for 44 percent of days spent in hospitals and one-third of the nation's spending for health care. Medicare and Medicaid faced demands that tested their ability to meet them, and the will and ability of the nation to fund these programs became a sensitive political issue.

Much of the hard work of caring for the elderly with infirmities fell on their spouses (usually wives) and children, who were themselves getting up in years. For this and other reasons, many senior citizens had to move to nursing homes; during the 1980s the population of nursing homes increased by 24 percent.

Senior Citizens in American Life   Not everything was gloomy in the lives of the nation's senior citizens. Although most saw their incomes go down, their households were often so well established that they needed to spend little on mortgages or rent, furniture, clothing, and other material goods. Many discovered enjoyment as volunteers in such places as hospitals and museums. Part-time jobs provided more than financial rewards. Sometimes seniors were called back to work by their former employers; sometimes they engaged in work that was entirely new to them. Senior citizens' recreational activities were popular; many traveled widely, sometimes to participate in Elderhostels. Increasing numbers moved to retirement communities in warm climates.

The political power of senior citizens became a force to be reckoned with. Sometimes they exercised their power through the American Association of Retired Persons (AARP), more often simply in voting booths in their own communities. Those between the ages of 65 and 74 could be counted on to vote with greater regularity than persons in any other age group. In some places, senior citizens were major barriers to approval of bond issues or tax increases to support schools: Why, the seniors asked, should they support schools with their limited incomes when they received no direct benefits from them? Rivalries between generations, although not broadly evident, held the potential for discordant consequences. The not-yet-elderly, seeking to prevent the draining of Social Security reserves by wealthier senior citizens, established such organizations as the American Association of Boomers and Americans for Generational Equity (AGE). These organizations, though, were barely visible and could not hope to achieve the power of the AARP, whose magazine *Modern Maturity* had 22.7 million subscribers in 1990, making it the nation's most widely read monthly periodical.

NOTE

1. *Newsweek*, December 31, 1984, cover story.

27

People at the Margins

Efforts to advance the civil rights of racial and ethnic mi-   **Hopes for**
norities and women had lost momentum in the 1970s, but   **Civil Rights**
activists believed that further progress was possible. They
hoped to build on the civil rights laws enacted in the 1960s that protected
voting rights and sought to ensure equal opportunities in employment
and public accommodations. Court decisions, such as the ones that approved busing of children as a constitutional means for achieving school
desegregation, also gave them hope.

The establishment in 1983 of Martin Luther King, Jr.'s January 15 birthday as a national holiday was a sign that there really was an equal place
in American life for persons of African descent. Accomplishments of notable African Americans seemed to be further indications of racial progress. Guion S. Bluford, Jr. was the first black astronaut to travel in space.
Virginia's L. Douglas Wilder was the nation's first African American
governor. Cleveland, Atlanta, Los Angeles, Detroit, and Gary (Indiana)
had elected African American mayors earlier, and now the election of
Harold Washington in Chicago (1983), Wilson Goode in Philadelphia
(1983), and David Dinkins in New York (1990) increased expectations
that the new mayors would better understand the needs of their minority
citizens. So severe, though, were the social and financial problems of the
cities they were elected to serve that success was improbable.

New Times

Even though doors remained open for individual African Americans and other minorities to succeed, commitments cooled for concerted efforts to enhance their prospects for success. Early signs of the new times came with President Ronald Reagan's outspoken opposition to busing to achieve school desegregation. This encouraged the Justice Department and local school districts to withdraw support for busing even where courts permitted or required it. In another move, the Reagan administration announced in August 1981 that it would review rules and guidelines designed to ensure equal employment rights to minorities, no doubt intending to relax them. Several weeks later it proposed easing of antidiscrimination rules for federal contractors.

Despite these shifts into reverse, some forward movement continued. In 1982, for example, Congress enacted and President Reagan signed a twenty-five-year extension of the 1965 Voting Rights Act due to expire that year. It took grassroots lobbying, however, to remove a provision that would have made it harder to prove voter discrimination. Reagan also signed into law the 1988 Fair Housing Amendment Act, thus strengthening laws prohibiting discrimination based on race, color, sex, religion, or national origin in the renting or selling of houses. The act also extended protections against discrimination directed at families with children under age 18, persons with disabilities, and the elderly, and it established a procedure for imposing heavy fines on those found guilty of violating the law.

Actions in Courts

Some actions in the courts looked promising to civil rights advocates. The Supreme Court ruled in two separate 1986 cases that affirmative action programs in the workplace were constitutional when less drastic measures failed to overcome the effects of past discrimination. Furthermore, the Court ruled that hiring goals in affirmative action plans could benefit members of minority groups even though these persons were not themselves the victims of discrimination. The Justice Department had filed lawsuits challenging fifty-one affirmative action plans as violating civil rights laws, but it dropped the suits after the Court's ruling.

Also in 1986 the Court announced that the Voting Rights Act as amended in 1982 allowed blacks and other minority groups to contest redistricting plans that weakened their voting strength. In the following year it approved the use of racial quotas on a temporary basis for both hiring and promotion where there was evidence of severe employment discrimination against African Americans in the past. When the issue reached the Supreme Court again in 1990, it ruled that Congress had the right to enact affirmative action programs to improve employment possibilities for minorities even when they had not personally been subjected to discrimination.

At the same time, there were indications that President
Reagan's conservative appointees to the Supreme Court,   **Reversing**
working with others appointed by Presidents Nixon and   **Directions**
Ford, would bring the Court into line with his beliefs. When
Congress passed the 1988 Civil Rights Restoration Act, which was in-
tended to reverse a 1984 decision that had narrowed the applicability of
federal laws against discrimination, Reagan vetoed it. Both houses of
Congress voted by comfortable margins to override the veto.

In 1989 the Supreme Court limited state and local governments' authority to use affirmative action policies. In the same year, in a series of
five decisions, the Court made it more difficult for minorities and women
to pursue remedies for overcoming the effects of years of discrimination.
Another Supreme Court decision was inconsistent with these five: It
ruled that employers violated antidiscrimination provisions when their
actions were based on sexual stereotypes of their workers—for example,
when they denied promotions because a worker was judged to act in
"unfeminine" ways.

The Civil Rights Act of 1990 passed by Congress was intended to reverse these rulings, but President George Bush   **Actions in**
vetoed it. He believed the act would lead employers to adopt   **Congress**
quotas for hiring and promoting women and minorities in
order to protect themselves against being sued for discrimination. The
dispute over this bill revealed a recurring difference between Democrats
and Republicans: Democrats spoke of establishing "goals" in hiring
plans as a way of requiring employers to make special efforts to recruit
minorities and women; Republicans insisted that the goals would be in-
terpreted by employers and employees as "quotas" that had to be attained. A vote to override Bush's veto failed by one vote in the Senate.

While these presidential, legislative, and judicial actions were occurring, the nation became aware of the   **The Underclass**
existence of a segment of the population known as the
black underclass. *U.S. News & World Report* described it as the "seemingly irreducible core of poor inner-city blacks, those trapped in an
unending cycle of joblessness, broken homes, welfare and, often, drugs
and violence." It estimated that some 2 to 3.5 million persons, about one-
third of the nation's poor blacks, fit the description of underclass. Those
in the underclass were not the only African Americans with dim prospects in America: Half of all black children lived in poverty, half were
growing up without a father. Nearly half of the teenagers were out of
work, one-fourth of the births were to teenagers, and one in every
twenty-one young black men was likely to be murdered.[1]

Even as conditions for blacks had worsened, the national mood shifted
away from providing more assistance programs. Some, including Presi-

dent Reagan, contended that the existing programs had in fact helped create the underclass. Some black leaders agreed with conservative whites in claiming that race was no longer the critical factor in accounting for the plight of the underclass. Declining family values and the ghetto culture, they allowed, were the main problems. These could be dealt with only with a healthy measure of self-help by blacks themselves.

Native Americans   Development of large portions of the West and Southwest depended on access to water and minerals that were technically controlled by Indian tribes. Much of the conflict between Indians and others during these years, usually dealt with in court cases, concerned control of these rights. Another source of conflict concerned Indians' heavy dependence on the federal government, not only for protection of their treaty and civil rights but for economic support as well. The National Congress of American Indians strongly opposed a proposal in 1982 to reduce this dependence through a reorganization of the Bureau of Indian Affairs.

Before long, a more important issue for many tribes concerned their efforts to relieve economic distress by operating bingo games on their lands. Several courts had ruled that state gambling laws limiting bingo jackpots were not applicable to Indian tribes. Thus the tribes were able to offer big prizes to attract large crowds to their games. This was the opening that led to the establishment of full-scale, thriving casinos on many Indian reservations.

Asian Americans   Legislation signed by President Reagan in 1988 was intended to make amends to the 60,000 surviving Japanese Americans who had been held in internment camps during World War II, about half of the total number interned. The internments had occurred because the government, relying on evidence that was highly questionable at best, believed that persons of Japanese descent, both American citizens and legal aliens, posed a threat to U.S. security during the war. The survivors no doubt appreciated the $20,000 awarded to each one, but they probably valued more the government's admission of having treated them wrongly.

Hispanics   Much of the attention focused on Hispanics had to do with the large number who immigrated during the 1980s, many of them illegally. The Hispanic population, which numbered 18.8 million in 1988, was growing at a much faster rate than any other racial or ethnic group. It also was younger, poorer, and less educated. Recognizing the disadvantages at which they found themselves, Hispanics increased their political activity and challenged discriminatory practices in court. During the 1980s the number of Hispanics in Congress increased from six to twelve, and hundreds served in other elective offices. Most prominent were Henry G. Cisneros, Xavier Suarez, and Federico Pena, the mayors (respectively) of San Antonio, Miami, and Denver. Toney Anaya served as governor of New Mexico and Bob Martinez of Florida. The first Hispanic cabinet members were Lauro Cavazos, secretary of education, and Manuel Lujan, secretary of the interior.

As a nation of immigrants, the American people have at times been wary of keeping the doors open for more to **Immigration** enter. Throughout the 1980s there was concern not only over the total number of arrivals but also over what seemed to be a tidal wave of illegal immigrants—persons without proper immigration papers. According to 1981 estimates by the Census Bureau, 3 to 6 million persons living in the United States lacked proper immigration papers. About half of them were Mexicans. The majority lived in California, with a substantial number also in Texas.

Most illegal aliens lived a marginal existence. Schooling for their children and medical care were typically substandard. Their jobs, if they had any, were uncertain and their living conditions poor. Even so, citizens objecting to their presence insisted that the government should do something to, for, or about them. This led President Reagan in 1981 to propose federal restrictions on the hiring of illegal aliens. Employers who failed to observe the restrictions would be subject to fines. He also proposed that illegal aliens be given temporary residency rights but denied welfare and other benefits available to citizens and legal aliens. Congress debated, modified, and sometimes voted on the proposal, but not until the end of 1986 were the two houses able to agree on a law that would allow for fair and orderly treatment of illegal aliens and slow the flow of new arrivals.

A key feature of the law was an amnesty program for illegal aliens who could prove that they had lived in the United States continuously since the beginning of 1982 or earlier. By the midpoint in the program, only about one-fourth of the nearly 4 million considered eligible to apply for amnesty had done so. Extending the deadline allowed a few more to apply, but the total still fell far below the number eligible. The law did not slow the tide of illegal immigrants, nor did it result in massive deportations.

While attention was focused on illegal immigration, many immigrants also arrived legally. A private research group estimated that between 1981 and 1990 the number of legal immigrants, about 8.7 million, would match or surpass the number registered in an earlier period of heavy influx, 1901–1910. The earlier immigrants had come from Europe; now they came primarily from Latin America and Asia. Congress was not yet ready to slow the flow of immigrants. Indeed, the first comprehensive overhaul of immigration laws in twenty-five years, approved in 1990, included provisions to increase the number of legal immigrants. Upon arrival, most of the immigrants established relationships with persons having backgrounds similar to theirs, but soon, even while maintaining those relationships, their jobs and other connections took them into many different avenues of American life. Their capabilities and the initiative they displayed varied so widely that further generalizations about their new lives in America are impossible.

Women's Gains   A number of highly visible events provided evidence of a changing place for women in American life. In 1981, President Reagan appointed Sandra Day O'Connor, a state appellate court judge and former state legislator from Arizona, to the Supreme Court. As the first woman on the Court, she followed in the pathbreaking roles of Justice Louis Brandeis and Thurgood Marshall, respectively the first Jewish and the first African American members of the Court. The following year Congresswoman Geraldine Ferraro was chosen by Democratic presidential candidate Walter Mondale as the first woman to run for vice president. The first woman to travel in space was physicist Sally Ride, and the first to work in space outside a spacecraft was Kathryn Sullivan.

In material terms, women gained from a 1983 ruling by the Supreme Court that differentiating between men and women in determining rates or benefits for group retirement plans was improper. Almost immediately, pension and annuity plans were required to offer equal rates and benefits. Members of Congress then began a move to require a comparable provision in life, health, and automobile insurance policies. Insurance companies, arguing that statistical criteria showing differences in longevity between men and women should be used in determining rates, spent millions of dollars to bring about its defeat.

In 1987 the Supreme Court ruled in a case involving the promotion of a woman by a city transportation system to create a more balanced workforce. Employers were permitted to take gender into account in promotion decisions even if a history of sex discrimination was not proven. Next came a unanimous decision by the Court upholding a New York City law that prohibited private clubs from denying membership to women and minorities. Because many cities had similar ordinances, this decision had a broad impact—although there was no rush by women and minorities to join clubs formerly closed to them, and when they did join there was little disruption.

Less visible but having more effects on the daily lives of ordinary women was their growing importance in the workforce. The numbers of women employed in all kinds of regular, full-time jobs grew steadily, and more women found their way into executive, managerial, and professional positions. They still encountered extraordinary barriers, many

Thanks in part to Title IX, women's basketball gained a more prominent place on university campuses. *Courtesy of Drake University.*

of them rooted in stereotypical notions concerning their capabilities and proper roles, but many women managed to overcome them.

Another sign of changing times for women was their dramatically increased participation in competitive sports, particularly at the intercollegiate level. Although women had proven for many years that they could excel in athletics, their participation was limited by assumptions that athletics did not interest them and by lack of equal funding. The women's movement of the 1960s and 1970s, which had attacked barriers faced in business and politics, helped lower barriers in sports too. By 1985 women outnumbered men as new participants in tennis, bicycling, and softball. The general emphasis on physical fitness contributed further to women's participation in sports.

Women's Athletics

Most important, though, in encouraging women to enter competitive sports was Title IX of the federal Education Amendments of 1972, for which the final regulations for implementation were issued in 1975. Title IX reads: "No person in the United States shall, on the basis of sex, be excluded from participation in, be denied the benefits of, or be subjected to discrimination under any education program or activity receiv

ing federal financial assistance." Because almost all educational
institutions at all levels received some form of federal aid, Title IX regulations became applicable at all levels. Throughout school systems,
sports programs for girls and women had to be made equivalent to
those for boys and men.

Despite opposition before and after the regulations were announced,
schools, colleges, and universities took steps to comply. The results
were dramatic. Between 1972 and 1982, the representation of girls in
high school athletics increased from 5 percent to 33 percent. In the same
period, the proportion of women in college athletics increased from 15
percent to 30 percent. Before Title IX, women's athletics teams received
2 percent of the budgets for competitive sports in colleges and universities. The percentage increased to 16 percent in 1982 and continued upward. Athletics scholarships were virtually nonexistent for women
before Title IX. By 1982 women received more than 20 percent of such
scholarships.

Disappointments To the disappointment of many women, but to the
satisfaction of others, the deadline for ratification of
the Equal Rights Amendment to the U.S. Constitution
passed on June 30, 1982, with only 35 of the necessary 38 state legislatures having ratified it. The National Organization for Women charged
that corporate interests had helped defeat it, since they profited from
paying lower wages to women. There were many other contributing factors, however, including the well-orchestrated campaign against the
amendment led by Phyllis Schlafly. She and her allies played on the fears
of women that the ERA would lead, among other things, to a loss of
special protections women enjoyed in work environments, that women
would be involved in combat roles in the military, and that single-sex
bathrooms in public places would be outlawed. Failure to take into account traditional opposition in southern states to amending the Constitution and other miscalculations caused supporters of the amendment to
assume that ratification was going to be relatively easy. Consequently,
they followed strategies that did not work.

There were other disappointments. Women had been seeking to advance the concept that women and men who hold jobs requiring comparable knowledge, skills, and effort should be paid comparably. The
U.S. Commission on Civil Rights, by 1985 dominated by persons appointed by President Reagan, criticized the concept of comparable worth
as "profoundly flawed." Even though the General Accounting Office asserted that the Commission had defined comparable worth inappropri-
ately, the Equal Employment Opportunity Commission ruled that
unequal pay for comparable jobs did not in itself constitute sex discrimination.

In July 1990 President Bush signed into law the
Civil Rights Laws   Americans with Disabilities Act, a measure that ex-
for Other Groups   tended to an estimated 43 million disabled persons
the same protections against discrimination that the
Civil Rights Act of 1964 provided to racial minorities and women. Later
that year the Older Workers Benefit Protection Act went into effect. It
prohibited denial of benefits to workers on the basis of their age, overturning a Supreme Court ruling of the previous year that such actions
did not violate laws against age discrimination.

NOTE

1. *U.S. News & World Report*, March 17, 1986, 18–21.

28

Security Concerns Continue

In August 1990 the United States began a massive deploy-
ment of troops—230,000 from all branches of the military—   **War Again**
in response to Iraq's invasion of Kuwait. For troops already
on active duty, being sent to a possible combat zone in a desert in the
Middle East was not exactly all in a day's work, but they were expected
to be prepared for such a contingency. For the more than 125,000 reservists and members of the National Guard who were called to active
duty by the Pentagon, readiness for war was another matter. Among
them were men and women from all walks of now-disrupted lives. Not
all were sent overseas, because some were needed to fill positions va-
cated by the full-time troops who had been deployed; but the abrupt
changes in their lives and those they left behind were considerable.

The effects on most Americans of preparation for war had little to do
with strategies or ethics, or even with disruption of their personal lives
by calls to service. Rather, their concerns were with what it cost to fill
the tanks of their cars with gasoline. Before Iraq's invasion of Kuwait on
August 2, the price of gasoline in the United States averaged $1.09 per
gallon. By mid-October it had risen to $1.40, even though only about 9
percent of imported oil had come from Kuwait. Various maneuvers by
the government brought the price down again, but the episode brought
three reminders: First, the reliance of Americans on automobiles was
enormous. Second, the vulnerability of the nation's oil supply was something Americans would rather not think about. Third, oil and automobiles are so central to the American economy that anything threatening

their place shakes the stock market badly. Worries about the war and its implications caused investors to be so jittery that the market lost 20 percent of its value from August to mid-October.

Economic Difficulties   Otherwise, the impending Gulf War did little to distract attention from the cares of daily life. Included among those cares, as always, were those centered on the state of the economy. A survey of the economic landscape in the 1980s reveals disturbing facts in the midst of encouraging ones. Throughout the decade, many workers received minimal wage increases. Sometimes the increases fell below the rate of inflation. Sometimes there were no increases at all.

Furthermore, cutbacks and layoffs heightened employees' sense of insecurity. In 1981, for example, the automobile industry laid off nearly 215,000 workers, about 25 percent of its workforce, and demanded wage and benefit concessions from those who kept their jobs. With auto sales at their lowest point since 1961, dealerships were jammed with unsold cars. This led to the closing of 16 of 220 auto plants and cancellation or postponement of new construction or remodeling of existing plants, and it had ripple effects in the employment market. Things got worse in 1982, with another 50,000 workers laid off indefinitely and more than 20,000 temporarily. In the same year some autoworkers began to find employment as makers of Japanese cars, as Honda opened an assembly plant at Marysville, Ohio. By then, Japanese autos were claiming more than 22 percent of auto sales in the United States, compared with less than 4 percent a dozen years earlier.

Improved auto sales in 1983, resulting in part from Chrysler's introduction of the 1984 minivan (a reinvention of the station wagon), meant that workers could be called back. By the end of the year the number of workers on indefinite layoff was down to 108,000, but 70,000 others had by then been dropped from automakers' employment rolls. At the end of 1984, despite an upturn in the auto industry, employment by the Big Three—General Motors, Ford, and Chrysler—stood at 525,000, compared with 750,000 five years earlier. Sales reached record levels again in 1985, and another recession seemed improbable. But with competition by foreign manufacturers now well established, it seemed likely that the best days for the U.S. automobile industry and its workers were past. Later in the decade, however, sales continued to improve, and automakers were able to call back about 8,600 laid-off workers. As always, there were hopes that the boom-and-bust cycle that had characterized the industry could be replaced by a stability reflecting the commitment of American people to domestically produced automobiles and lessons learned by manufacturers.

There were more symptoms of economic distress as other parts of the economy shared the plight of the auto industry. Unemployment exceeded 8 percent in 1981, on its way to a post–World War II high of 10.8 percent in 1982. Construction companies were particularly hard hit because prevailing high interest rates discouraged prospective builders. Early in the decade, interest rates on home mortgages were very high— between 12 and 13 percent on loans with adjustable rate mortgages— and they remained relatively high for most of the 1980s.

Even though the unemployment rate declined slightly in 1983 and subsequent years (down to 7.2 percent in 1985), economic difficulties continued. Household debt increased dramatically. Credit card delinquencies were frequent. Personal bankruptcies almost doubled between 1984 and 1989, to 642,993. In 1990 they reached 725,484.

Although government policies gradually brought down the high inflation rates, the trade-off was a slowing of economic growth. Increasing numbers of Americans believed that taxes were consuming too large a share of their household budgets, and they responded favorably to the substantial tax cuts enacted early in the decade. Although the tax cuts undoubtedly stimulated the economy, whether they were a major contributor to the ballooning national debt is a disputed matter. In any event, annual budget deficits throughout the 1980s resulted in big increases in the national debt. Between 1981 and 1985 it doubled to almost $2 trillion and rose to $3 trillion in 1989.

Even though the effects of the difficult years lingered, the recovery of the economy in 1983 led to a period of **Better Times?** growth that lasted through 1990, making this the longest stretch of economic expansion during peacetime in the nation's history. The key economic indicators (gross national product, unemployment rate, consumer price index, industrial production, personal income, and corporate profits) were consistently promising throughout this period, although occasionally there were exceptions.

In the midst of prosperity there was always the prospect of an economic slump, and not everything in the picture was rosy. One gray area was inflation, as the consumer price index rose steadily from 1986 to 1990; items that cost $1.00 in 1986 would cost, on average, $1.20 in 1990. The $8 billion trade deficit in 1976, when the United States became a debtor nation for the first time since 1913, was a dark spot. By 1978 the trade deficit had risen to $31 billion before declining slightly again. Big budget deficits, about $200 billion annually, were an even darker spot. Caused in large part by aggressive increases in military spending coupled with substantial tax cuts, the deficits caused the national debt and the interest paid on it to balloon. This did not seem to be of much concern at the time, but it came back to haunt later. Add to this the decay of inner cities, the shambles resulting from conglomerates gobbling up one company after another, along with the continuing effects on workers caused by structural changes in the economy, and it becomes apparent that better times did not make life better for everyone.

The "Working Poor"

Those who benefited least—or perhaps suffered most—from the prosperity of the mid-1980s were those known as the working poor. For them, the recovery from the bad times of the early 1980s meant little. Most working poor lacked the skills to fill the jobs that were available. Because members of minority groups were more plentiful at the lower end of the skills and income scales, they were hit hardest by the downward mobility experienced by lower- and middle-income Americans. In 1987 the unemployment rate among whites was 4.9 percent; among blacks, 28 percent. The median income of blacks was less than 57 percent of the median for whites; the poverty rate was more than triple that of whites. The percentage of black families receiving aid for dependent children was nearly nine times as high as for white families. Of black families headed by women, 52 percent were in poverty—almost double the rate for whites. Even in the years of economic expansion the working poor remained just that, and the poverty of black families remained particularly pervasive.

Poverty and Welfare

Hit especially hard by economic circumstances and policy decisions in the mid-1980s were those Americans affected by the reductions in various welfare programs. President Reagan's inaugural address dramatically revealed his intentions: "Government is not the solution to our problem," he asserted, as he had throughout his campaign; "government *is* the problem." Government generosity and good intentions, he believed, were out of control; he called for "new federalism," a plan to make the down-and-out in society a local and state responsibility. Reductions in federal welfare programs caused worries about whether there would be a "safety net" to catch those losing government assistance.

Statistics on poverty in 1984 reveal the plight of many Americans. More than 33 million, about one-seventh of the nation's population, lived below the poverty level, reversing trends set in motion by the Great Society. The percentage of children living in poverty was higher than that of adults. Among both blacks and persons living in female-headed households, the ratio was one in three. Monthly payments to the 3.7 million families covered by the Aid to Families with Dependent Children (AFDC) program averaged $338. About 21.5 million persons received services funded by Medicaid, with average annual costs of $1,569 per person. Nearly 20 million people were eligible for food stamps, a four-year low resulting from more stringent eligibility requirements.

From time to time Congress attempted to reform the
welfare system, with specific measures aimed at giving   **Welfare Reform**
the poor the job training or education needed to get off
welfare. In 1988 Congress passed a law requiring parents on welfare
whose children were past the age of 3 to enroll in appropriate education,
training, job search, or work programs. The new law, which had an estimated cost of more than $3 billion over five years, allowed for a long
lead-in time, reflecting awareness of the difficulty of moving welfare
recipients into independence: By 1995, 20 percent of those eligible for
welfare would be required to enroll in an appropriate program.

At the very bottom of society were those who lived
with no place called home. Estimates of homeless Amer-   **Homelessness**
icans reached a record high in 1986, but the numbers
were still rising. New York counted 10,000 single people and 5,500 families as homeless. In Chicago the number of homeless was somewhere
between 9,000 and 22,000; in Newark, New Jersey, 4,000–7,000; in Atlanta, 5,000; in Philadelphia, 13,000; and in Los Angeles, 40,000. Included
in the tallies were higher proportions of women, children, and younger
men than in previous decades.

More than a sluggish economy and a tight employment market accounted for the increased numbers of homeless persons. As noted earlier,
in the 1960s and 1970s state and local governments had released mentally
ill people from medical facilities. As a result of "deinstitutionalization"
policies, the population in state mental hospitals dropped from more
than 550,000 in the 1950s to fewer than 150,000 three decades later. Com-
munity-based programs were intended to help them, but these programs
were never sufficiently funded. Those who lacked the mental, physical,
financial, and familial resources to cope with life in the outside world,
and particularly the ability to find and keep jobs, ended up on the streets.
Cities grappled in various ways with the problem of caring for them,
none with notable success.

The economy enjoyed a long period of recovery after a
recession early in the decade, and the stock market   **Stock Market**
surged to highs that few would have imagined. Things
looked promising for investors—promising, that is, until October 19,
1987. Black Monday, as it was called, brought the largest one-day tumble
in the market's history, setting off months-long debates over the sound-
ness of the economy. Some brokers and investment managers referred
to the events of that day and the week that followed as a "market cor-
rection." Some wondered whether structural changes were needed in the
stock market itself. Some worried that investors guided by information
processed by sophisticated computers had so changed things that the

Homeless men find warmth on steam grates near the White House in Washington, D.C. in 1982. *UPI/CORBIS-BETTMANN.*

market might be permanently damaged. Meanwhile, investors gradually regained confidence, and before long the stock market recovered the losses of Black Monday and again climbed upward. The tumble on October 19, however, was a reminder to all investors that they could not count on perpetual prosperity.

Changes in the economy helped to account for the
persistence of unemployment, particularly among   **Structural Changes**
persons with limited education and skills. Auto-   **in the Economy**
mobile manufacturers, steel producers, coal mining
companies, and similar employers in basic industries, once at the heart
of the American economy, required relatively fewer employees each
year. This was due partly to the use of automated processes, sometimes
involving robots, that allowed smaller labor forces to achieve high levels
of productivity. The migration of manufacturing jobs to countries with
lower pay scales was another factor. The effects were impressive: In 1977,
jobs in manufacturing had constituted nearly 24 percent of the nation's
total nonagricultural employment. Six years later they accounted for less
than 21 percent. The actual number of persons employed in manufacturing in the United States was lower in 1983 than in 1977, even though
the nonagricultural labor force had increased by 7 million.

As the numbers of persons employed in manufac-
turing went down, they increased in service indus-   **Service Industries**
tries, most notably in fast-food establishments. Here,
though, most of the jobs were low-paying and part-time, and they offered few fringe benefits and little hope of advancement. Young, ambitious persons used such jobs to earn money for college tuition. They
realized that their dreams of prosperity required more than these jobs
offered, but the jobs were a means to that end. For many, though, low-
paying service jobs were simply a dead-end way to maintain a marginal
existence.

The 1980s got off to a bad start for labor unions when
President Reagan fired 12,000 members of the Profes-   **Labor Unions**
sional Air Traffic Controllers Organization (PATCO) on
August 5, 1981. PATCO had rejected the final bargaining offer made by
the Federal Aviation Authority (FAA), and the traffic controllers went
on strike a week earlier. Because the strike violated federal law, the firings were legal. "Dammit, the law is the law," Reagan said to his aides,
"and the law says they can't strike. By striking they've quit their jobs."[1]
With the firing of the professional controllers, the FAA had to use military controllers, nonstrikers, and supervisors to keep the nation's planes
in the air. The immediate results included a cutback in services, loss of
business from people who were reluctant to fly in uncertain skies, and,
according to the International Air Transport Association, a $200 million
loss by the airlines in the month of August alone.

The symbolic effects of the firings lasted longer. Unions could not expect cordial or deferential treatment from the new administration, particularly the increasingly restive unions of government employees. This,
along with the changing nature of workplaces across the nation, made
it natural for the decline in union membership to continue. Fear of com-

pany shutdowns or permanent layoffs weakened individual union members' readiness to support aggressive tactics by unions in dealing with employers. For ordinary workers, union membership had once symbolized a mutual commitment between themselves and their employers, even in times of difficult negotiations. That sense of commitment gave way to anger and humiliation in the 1980s when unions were compelled to accept distasteful provisions in bargaining agreements. These included such things as lump-sum payments based on company profits rather than permanent wage increases, give-backs of benefits and wage increases bargained for earlier, and systems of pay with two tiers, allowing for lower wages for new employees.

In the early 1980s, organized labor represented about one worker in four; by the end of the decade it represented one in six. With the decline in membership and the disadvantaged positions in which union workers found themselves, the use of work stoppages in disputes with management declined. In 1988, according to the Bureau of Labor Statistics, the forty stoppages involving 1,000 or more workers was the lowest number since it began keeping records forty years earlier.

Agriculture   The nation's farmers, too, faced difficulties in the 1980s. Drought at home hurt production, and a depressed world economy and the worldwide abundance of agricultural reserves damaged the potential for exports. After twelve consecutive years of increases, huge drops in exports in 1982 and 1983 alarmed farmers. Many of them faced cash-flow problems, large debts caused by land purchases, declining land values, and bankruptcies. Government subsidies helped, but farmers were never sure how much they could depend on them, or wanted to. By the end of the decade, though, farm crises experienced in many states had been reversed despite severe droughts in several of the years. In 1989 farm income reached a record high, largely as a result of revived export markets.

Workplace Changes   Another story of the 1980s had both encouraging and discouraging features. By the end of the decade, more than 35 million persons did part-time or full-time income-producing work at home. Increasing most rapidly among them, to a total of more than 5 million, were "telecommuters," that is, employees of companies who did part of their work at home during business hours, most typically involving the use of computers. The trend toward telecommuting was so strong that it seemed likely that it would soon be regarded as unexceptional. Telecommuting served the needs of dual-career families particularly well, as it reduced the need for child care outside the home. Twice as large a number as telecommuters were those who worked at home as freelancers, earning extra income during hours away from their regular jobs—if they had regular jobs.

Yet another change of the 1980s was the growing resistance of employees to management-dictated relocations. Dual-career families found uprootings particularly difficult, even when they involved promotions or pay increases. The costs involved in buying and selling homes also accounted for the reluctance, as did the sense that accepting a move in the new economic times would not necessarily guarantee job security. Employers had increasingly come to regard their employees as a "contingent" workforce, to be retained or dismissed depending on immediate circumstances. Employees responded by regarding themselves as entrepreneurs seeking advancement where it best served their interests.

The consequences of these and other indicators of economic change jeopardized faith in an important **Home Ownership** part of the American dream: Home ownership had become increasingly elusive for many. Young couples in particular found it difficult to scrape together a down payment for a home purchase. Because renting typically costs more than ownership, particularly after tax deductions for interest paid on home mortgages is taken into account, the scraping became harder rather than easier. That may explain why, by the end of the 1980s, only 51.5 percent of households headed by someone under age 35 owned their own homes, down from 61.1 percent a decade earlier. Persons in these households may have been spending their money instead on other things, like cars and stereos. If so, that may have been because of their discouragement about the difficulty of accumulating enough for a down payment, given the uncertainty of their jobs and the rising costs of such essentials as health insurance. In any event, the pattern of young couples buying "starter" homes and moving to something more commodious a few years later as their family and incomes grew was being broken.

Savings and loan associations (S&Ls) began losing money in 1979 when they had to finance old mort- **Savings and Loan** gages made at rates below 10 percent with money **Associations** borrowed at substantially higher rates. Soon they were unable to stop the hemorrhaging this caused, and by 1981 many were failing or being merged by the Federal Savings and Loan Insurance Corporation (FSLIC) with healthier counterparts. To avoid losses by depositors, the FSLIC began to draw money from its reserves. To prevent being trapped by further interest-rate squeezes, S&Ls and banks made variable-rate or adjustable-rate mortgages, with rates determined periodically by what the lender had to pay for the funds borrowed by homebuyers. Consequently monthly payments rose significantly, out of the reach of borrowers and contributing to high default rates. Even as these things occurred, deregulation of financial institutions continued.

Measures taken by the government to strengthen the surviving S&Ls seemed to work, and by the end of 1982 the worst appeared to be over—

but it was not. As savings and loan associations failed, the insurance corporations that protected depositors endured the losses. By February 1987 the FSLIC's assets, derived from premiums paid by the S&Ls, amounted to about $2 billion, only half enough to cover the claims against it. An act of Congress enabled it to raise funds by issuing long-term bonds, with the revenue being used to bail out failed institutions. Estimates in 1988 of likely costs of cleaning up the mess by closing failed S&Ls and returning investments to their depositors ranged between $50 and $100 billion. With such numbers in sight, everyone looked for villains. They found them in S&L officials who were guilty of mismanagement and fraud, politicians who allowed big contributions by S&L officials to cloud their judgment, and regulators of the Federal Home Loan Bank Board who allowed lax accounting rules to hide financial problems. By the time the government got on top of the problem, the projected cost of the bailout by taxpayers had reached $200 billion. Financing it through thirty- and forty-year government bonds would result in interest costs of an additional $200 to $300 million.

Crime   According to the Federal Bureau of Justice Statistics, major crime dropped by 2 percent in 1981 and by another 5 percent during the first six months of 1982, compared with the same period in 1981. The unanticipated downward trend continued in 1983, but by the mid-1980s figures reported by the FBI showed the trend to have reversed again, suggesting that crime figures are cyclical. Most likely they are related to other cycles, such as those involving drug use. Between 1985 and 1990 the rate of crimes committed per 10,000 population again approached the level it had reached in 1980. In 1990 the overall crime rate was triple what it had been in 1960, and the rate of violent crimes had increased fivefold. Statistics gathered by the Federal Bureau of Justice Statistics support the inference of criminologists that the increases were partly due to a greater willingness by victims to report crimes.

Statistics tell only part of the story concerning crime in the United States. Events such as the attempted assassination of President Reagan in 1981 and the mass murders that occurred in Pennsylvania, Texas, Florida, and California in 1982, sensationalized by the mass media, heightened the nation's awareness of criminal occurrences. Incidents like the one in 1988 in which a man armed with an "assault rifle" killed five children and wounded the teacher and twenty-nine others in a California schoolyard prompted local and state efforts to ban the sale and possession of such weapons. The federal government's ban on importation of semiautomatic assault weapons was largely a symbolic gesture, since— according to the U.S. Bureau of Alcohol, Tobacco, and Firearms—imports represented only about 25 percent of such weapons available in the United States. The federal ban and actions taken at state and local levels opened intense debates over the rights of individuals to own fire-arms and of government to limit their sale and possession.

On September 29, 1982, four persons living in the Chicago area, three of them in the same family, died after taking Extra-Strength Tylenol capsules that had been laced with cyanide. The next day three more Chicagoans were poi-soned in the same way, and a man in California suffered convulsions after taking Tylenol capsules. The manufacturer of this pain-relief med-ication immediately recalled Tylenol from counters across the United States, and law enforcement officials had a new kind of crime to deal with. In subsequent weeks there were more than ninety reports of "copy-cat" crimes involving tampering with foods and other consumer prod-ucts. The Food and Drug Administration then required over-the-counter medicines to be carried in tamper-proof packages, a practice that soon spread to food products as well.

Product Tampering

Another kind of crime, sexual abuse of children, be-came an urgent social issue in the mid-1980s. In October 1984, officials in the U.S. Department of Justice stated that as many as one out of four girls and one out of ten boys might be sexually molested before the age of 18 and that perhaps only one-tenth of such molestations were being reported to law enforcement authorities. The year before, reports of hundreds of alleged incidents in a preschool in California led to indictments of seven persons on 115 counts of child molestation, with 93 more counts added later. The case resulted in the longest criminal trial in U.S. history and ended with the preschool director and her adult son found not guilty on 52 counts of child abuse and molestation. The director spent two years in prison as the case moved forward; her son was held for five years before being released on bail; and the state spent $15 million on the thirty-month trial.

Sexual Abuse of Children

Although authorities did not know how extensive actual occurrences of molestation were, awareness of the potential for incidents increased. This was largely a result of accounts by persons claiming to have been the victims of sexual abuse in day-care programs and other places, in-cluding their own homes. They reported experiencing psychological pain and bewilderment, leading to shame and fear, and they seemed to speak for many more who were afraid or unwilling to reveal what had hap-pened to them.

Parents naturally wondered whether their own children might have been the victims of sexual abuse, and they were urged to watch for signs of it. In addition to physical symptoms, there might be sleeplessness, fear of being in the presence of certain persons, or sexual conduct not appropriate for a given age. Parents warned their children against allow-ing anyone, including family members, to touch them in ways that made them feel uncomfortable. Warnings against getting into cars or going into rooms with persons they did not know or even speaking to such persons became common.

NOTE

1. Quoted in *Time*, August 17, 1981, 16.

29

Diversions

Although Americans in the 1980s enjoyed a cafeteria of entertainment possibilities, the main fare for most remained   **Television**
television. Thanks to the Federal Communications Commis-
sion (FCC), what they watched on TV underwent certain changes. Mark
Fowler, appointed by President Reagan to head the FCC, regarded television as just another appliance, "a toaster with pictures," that should
be treated like a business, nothing more or less. Under Fowler's leadership, the FCC in 1981 discontinued rules limiting the number of minutes
per hour that could be devoted to advertising and stopped requiring
television stations to play a public service role.

A 1990 Gallup poll showed that the percentage of persons who considered watching television as their favorite way to spend an evening
declined from 46 percent in 1974 to 24 percent in 1990, no doubt reflecting their complaints about the quality of programming. During these
years, dining out, going to movies or the theater, playing cards and other
games, dancing, and listening to music showed comparably sharp declines in popularity. Taking their places were activities not included in
the 1974 survey, such as jogging, working in crafts, and gardening. Reading and spending time at home with the family showed slight increases.
Nonetheless, the average American spent some twenty-eight hours in
front of a television set each week. Many of those were daytime hours,
as soap operas and talk shows remained popular.

TV Violence   From the perspective of later years, television programs of the 1960s, 1970s, and even the 1980s seem rather tame.

Nonetheless, concern over their content mounted. By the mid-1980s, depictions of violence led the American Psychological Association (APA) to recommend that parents monitor their children's viewing. Although acknowledging that it was impossible to cite specific harm done by watching violent scenes, the APA reported research findings that showed a relationship between televised violence and children's aggressive behavior. The APA also urged the television industry to reduce the violence in its programs, including cartoons, and asked Congress to take action that would decrease televised violence.

Cable Television   The continued diversification and extension of programming through cable channels meant that television did even less to pull families together than it had done in the past. Sometimes it had the opposite effect. For example, when MTV, a thoroughly postmodern cable channel, was launched in 1981 and aimed particularly at teenagers by bringing twenty-four hours of rock videos and commercials daily into millions of homes, adults expected their children to watch it in their own rooms with doors closed. Within two years of its arrival, MTV claimed to have viewers in 14 million homes daily.

As MTV evolved, it brought greater variety and creativity to its programming, responding to initial criticisms that it favored established groups of white artists and presented objectionable anti-female images. Being featured on MTV boosted sales of the performers' records by some 15 to 20 percent. MTV appearances also made stars, among the most notable being Michael Jackson and Madonna. Experimentation by MTV with postmodern cultural styles paved the way for comparable experiments in programs like *Miami Vice*.

Another cable channel, ESPN, established in 1978, initially showed mainly college football games. Two years later it offered 24-hour programming of games and contests in many different sports. By 1990, however, the network's variety had diminished, returning to the old standbys of football, basketball, baseball, boxing, golf, and tennis.

By the end of the 1980s, with service reaching into nearly 60 percent of American homes, cable television seemed to be approaching a saturation point. Households without it probably could not afford it or simply did not want it. Nonetheless, its existence in more than 50 million households meant a further diffusion of viewing audiences and a decline in the influence of the old, established networks. Indeed, by 1990 ABC, CBS, and NBC claimed less than 60 percent of viewing time. Remote-control units no doubt weakened the grip of the major networks and fragmented viewing audiences further. Before it became standard equipment in most homes, TV watchers tuned in to a single channel and stayed with it for a whole show, enduring or ignoring commercials. Remote control changed all that, as viewers hit "mute" buttons during commercials or "grazed" up and down the spectrum of channels to see what else was playing. Viewers' starting point might have been a network station, but their landing place may have been a cable channel.

What cable channels offered frequently made the programming of the networks attractive. On some cable channels viewers saw reruns of programs like *I Love Lucy* and *Leave It to Beaver*. On the premium channels, such as HBO and Showtime, they could watch a mix of made-for-TV movies and reruns available elsewhere on videocassettes. Two of the most popular new network shows of the early 1980s, *The Cosby Show* and *Family Ties*, reworked the themes of 1950s sitcoms, the former featuring a middle-class black family. Before the end of the decade *Roseanne*, starring Roseanne Barr as a factory worker and joke-telling wife and mother, replaced *The Cosby Show* at the top of the sitcom ratings. Some regarded these programs as a contest between blue-collar chic and black-family chic. Also popular at the decade's end was a prime-time animated cartoon, *The Simpsons*. The fact that this satiric family comedy ran on the new Fox network and challenged *The Cosby Show* in head-to-head competition was another indication of the loss of dominance by the big-three networks, ABC, CBS, and NBC.

Network Programs

The consistently popular sitcom *M*A*S*H*, inspired by a 1970 movie by the same name that poked fun at war, drew an audience of more than 121 million for its 251st and last show in 1983. In the same year, a made-for-TV movie, *The Day After*, caused considerable controversy by depicting the effects of nuclear war on Kansas City, Missouri, and Lawrence, Kansas. Presented by ABC, it attracted an estimated 100 million viewers. Topping that was the eighteen-hour miniseries, *The Winds of War*, another ABC presentation. Its audience, estimated at 140 million, was the largest in history. *The Civil War*, an eleven-hour documentary produced by Ken Burns and broadcast in 1990 on PBS, showed that there remained audiences for the good and serious documentaries television was capable of presenting.

As alternatives to commercial and public television, viewers increasingly turned to rental of videotapes. By the end of the 1980s homes equipped with videocassette players rented, on average, two to three videos each month. In homes that included persons ages 18 to 29 the rentals were more numerous, and they were much lower in those with persons age 60 and older. Rental of videos represented a $13 billion market. In 1987, the film industry's revenue from rentals, along with that from films shown on cable television, surpassed its income from ticket sales. Many owners, surveys showed, never learned how to program their VCRs for taping shows to be replayed

VCRs

later and used them only for rented tapes. As VCRs grew in popularity, so did camcorders for recording instant versions of home movies—especially in 1990 when they became much smaller and offered longer playback times.

Newspapers   Newspapers had difficulty competing with television for readers' time. The *Washington Star* shut down in 1981 and the *Philadelphia Bulletin* in 1982; also in 1982 nine newspapers located in all parts of the country merged their morning and evening papers into single morning or all-day publications, resulting in the loss of one kind of coverage or another. In 1985 the 131-year-old *St. Louis Globe-Democrat* folded when a new owner could not rescue it from bankruptcy. At the end of the decade the *Los Angeles Herald Examiner* and the *Raleigh Times* (North Carolina) ceased publication, and the evening *Kansas City Star* was absorbed by the morning *Kansas City Times*.

Perhaps the biggest change in the newspaper business occurred in 1982 when the Gannett Company, owner of a chain of dailies, launched *USA Today*. This national newspaper made explicit attempts to compete with television as a primary source of news. Boxes dispensing it on street corners displayed the front page in windows that looked like television screens. News reports and features were brief and crisply written, and pictures, often in color, were more plentiful than in other newspapers. The fast-glimpse qualities of *USA Today* inspired critics to compare its fare with that offered in fast-food restaurants. McNews, they called it. Within the next several years Gannett also acquired a number of major newspapers, including the *Detroit News*, the *Des Moines Register*, and the *Louisville Courier-Journal* and *Louisville Times*. Although Gannett-owned newspapers maintained individual identities, they also reflected traits displayed most prominently by *USA Today*, such as the shortened news reports, and readers detected a loss of local flavor in the papers' coverage.

Following *USA Today*'s lead, other newspapers printed more pictures in color and abbreviated their reporting. Perhaps this enabled them to remain a staple in the life of the two-thirds of American adults who read them daily. Only one in five of the readers spent more than 30 minutes with the daily paper, and they tended to be older and better-educated. Meanwhile television continued to grow as the main source of news for the American people, partly because the network anchors seemed like authoritative guests in many homes, and partly because of the news coverage of CNN.

Magazines   Big-circulation magazines intended for general audiences saw their sales slump as their traditional readership was aging and dying. Smaller, more precisely targeted magazines fared better, as did some fashion magazines. The wide range of choices, symbolic of postmodern conditions, no doubt encouraged browsing rather than selecting one magazine and staying with it. Reflecting the get-rich climate of the times, *Forbes*, one of the nation's leading business magazines, saw its circulation grow and the median age of its readers move downward.

By the end of the 1980s total book sales approached $15 billion, double the amount recorded at the beginning of the decade.   **Books** Much of publishers' revenue came from the works of bestselling authors. Stephen King landed ten horror novels on bestseller lists during the decade, and Danielle Steele eight romances. Sometimes outstanding works like Umberto Eco's *The Name of the Rose* and Toni Morrison's *Beloved* also became bestsellers, promising to become classics.

In 1982, readers of established classics by American writers welcomed the appearance of eight handsome, sturdy, meant-to-last volumes in the new "Library of America" series. Published in the first year were works by Walt Whitman, Herman Melville, Harriet Beecher Stowe, Nathaniel Hawthorne, Jack London, Mark Twain, and William Dean Howells. Admirers of such bestsellers as Robert Fulghum's *All I Really Need to Know I Learned in Kindergarten* (1988) would contend that these were classics too. The very fact that there were such best-sellers alleviated fears that books would be crowded out of people's lives by television and computers. So did the continued popularity of children's books—long-time favorite writer Theodore Geisel published two more Dr. Seuss bestsellers—since children who grow up with books are more likely to be serious readers as adults.

The diverse tastes of producers and audiences were evident in the variety of films winning honors each year. In 1982, for   **Movies** example, *Gandhi*, the story of the man who led India's struggle for independence, won an Oscar for Best Picture. Several years later the Oscar went to *Amadeus*, which treated the life of the great composer Wolfgang Amadeus Mozart. Then came *Out of Africa* and *The Last Emperor*, the latter being the story of a bygone China. Named Best Picture in 1988 was *Rain Man*, starring Dustin Hoffman who was named Best Actor for his performance; this film introduced audiences to autism, a baffling mental disorder. It was followed by *Driving Miss Daisy*, with Jessica Tandy playing the role of an eccentric but lovable elderly woman and winning Best Actress for it. Then came *Dances with Wolves* directed by and featuring Kevin Costner (Best Director) in a romanticized story of the Lakota Sioux nation.

Award-winning films were often bested at the box office by those featuring daring themes or techniques. That explains the success of the 1981 blockbuster *Raiders of the Lost Ark*, and another in 1982, *E.T.—The Extra-Terrestrial*, the story of love between an Earth boy, lonely in suburbia, and a stranded alien from space. Both were directed by Steven Spielberg. *E.T.* grossed $228 million at the box office and demonstrated the commercial success that lay in embedding a film's vocabulary ("Elliot,"

"Ouch," and "Phone Home") into the language of everyday life and in marketing a film's images on such things as lunch boxes, bicycles, and even underwear. Another blockbuster success was Tim Burton's *Batman* in 1989. Although it did not match the revenue produced by *E.T.*, the "Batmania" it inspired paid dividends to marketers of products bearing the image or logo of the Batman.

Sylvester Stallone's *Rambo: First Blood, Part II* is a good example of a popular film featuring violence. Stallone played the role of a Vietnam veteran who freed prisoners of war, thereby exposing the alleged indifference of the U.S. government. The film's pro-war perspective drew complaints by those who thought it tried to revise truths about the war, but the complaints did not keep Rambo from becoming a folk hero or Rambo guns and knives from becoming popular children's toys.

Movie Ratings   In 1984 the Motion Picture Association of America (MPAA) added a new rating, PG-13, the first change since the introduction of the rating system sixteen years earlier. The new rating placed films between PG (parental guidance suggested) and R (restricted). It was "advisory" in that it did not exclude viewers under age 14, but it informed parents that violence or other content in the film might not be suitable for their children. In 1990 the MPAA replaced the controversial X rating, which had come to be regarded as synonymous with pornography, with NC-17. The new rating was intended for movies that despite depictions of explicit sex or extreme violence, such as *Henry & June*, were regarded as serious artistic efforts.

Radio   As it had done with television, the Federal Communications Commission in 1981 discontinued rules limiting the number of minutes per hour devoted to advertising on radio and requiring stations to commit 6 to 8 percent of their programming time to news and public affairs. The FCC also attempted to deal with "shock radio" by ruling that stations were free to air "indecent material" between midnight and 6 A.M., when children would be least likely to hear it. This 1987 action did not define indecent, however, and broadcasters felt free to fill their programs with whatever listeners were willing to tolerate. To the satisfaction of broadcasters, the FCC in the same year abolished what was called the fairness doctrine, which required radio and television stations to broadcast all sides of controversial issues.

FM stations' ability to broadcast in stereophonic sound increased their popularity and resulted in a proliferation of such stations. During the 1980s, FM's share of listening audiences rose from one-half to three-fourths.

Lake Wobegon   Occasionally radio programming met with unpredictable success, as a program featuring writer and radio personality Garrison Keillor demonstrates very well. Introduced in 1974 by Minnesota Public Radio and heard by 4 million listeners over public radio stations, Keillor's *Prairie Home Companion* presented a variety of music and imaginative skits. Most popular was Keillor's news from Lake Wobegon, his mythical hometown, a place where ordinary people's ordinary ways were always quite extraordinary. Keillor's monologues, usually about 15–20 minutes long, began with "It's been a quiet week in Lake Wobegon, my hometown," and ended with "Lake Wobegon . . . Where all the women are strong, all the men are good looking, and all the children are above average." Keillor's book, *Lake Wobegon Days*, became a bestseller and his monologues were distributed widely in sets of cassette tapes. In 1987 Keillor announced that he was discontinuing the show, but before long he brought it back in a modified form from New York City. In 1992, however, he returned with it to St. Paul, Minnesota, the show's natural home.

By the 1980s, the rock music young people had found so appealing and their elders so appalling in earlier de- **Popular Music** cades enjoyed a large measure of acceptance in mainstream America. Indeed, it became a standard feature of mainstream advertising. One reason is that the teenagers of the 1960s did not forsake their earlier tastes in music when they reached their thirties. Another reason is that rock music lost much of its shock quality. A third is that the varieties of rock music were so plentiful that persons who did not like one variety had plenty of other choices. The same was true of performing groups. Fans could love one and detest another. Consequently, variations of rock music thrived alongside of country music, surf music, jazz, disco, and a new arrival, Jamaican reggae.

Music continued to be big business. Bruce Springsteen's *Born in the U.S.A.* sold more than 13 million copies within eighteen months of its 1984 production, and his concert tour, lasting from July 1984 to October 1985, attracted some 5 million fans. Respondents to a *Rolling Stone* poll placed him first in six categories, and one of his singles, "Dancing in the Dark," earned him American Music Awards and Grammys. He was not alone among rock stars, as many others also enjoyed large followings.

On occasion, rock music became more than big business. Or, rather, it joined the big business of fund raising. In the mid-1980s, Live Aid concerts featuring many of the most prominent stars and bands were broadcast by satellite to raise money through "telethons" in some thirty nations. People in need around the world benefited from millions of dollars raised by these events. In the United States, some Live Aid concerts were held for the benefit of farmers facing hard times.

Rock music's lyrics, with themes of sex and violence, worried many. The National PTA and the Parents' Mu- **Worries about** sic Resource Center (a group based in Washington, D.C.) **Popular Music** urged the Recording Industry Association of America to rate its records in a system similar to the one used for motion pictures. The Association refused to do so, but it recommended that its members label some of their records "Explicit Lyrics—Parental Advisory." Such

Performers at this Live Aid concert at Philadelphia's JFK Stadium included Bob Dylan, Mick Jagger, and Tina Turner. *UPI/CORBIS-BETTMANN.*

measures did not appease rock music's harshest critics. Allan Bloom, a professor at the University of Chicago, seemed to reflect their sentiments in his attack on rock music in his bestselling *The Closing of the American Mind*. He contended that rock music "has one appeal only, a barbaric appeal, to sexual desire—not love, not *eros*, but sexual desire undeveloped and untutored. . . . Rock gives children, on a silver platter, with all the public authority of the entertainment industry, everything parents always used to tell them they had to wait for until they grew up and would understand later."[1]

Those who worried about rock music had more to worry about when rap became popular in the late 1980s. Initially rappers mixed bits of songs, repeated passages, and added rhythmic scratching sounds as background for recited lyrics, or raps. At first rap was a street phenomenon accompanied by acrobatic displays in break dancing and a hip-hop look featuring, among other things, fancy sneakers, caps turned backward, and heavy gold jewelry. Soon it made its way into recording studios, and by the 1980s it gained considerable popularity for its protests (typically as insults) against poverty, violence, and racism. Sales surveys found that the biggest market for rap was among suburban white youth.   **Rap Music**

Before the end of the decade the lyrics of several rap groups, such as Slick Rick and 2 Live Crew, drew sharp criticism for their explicit description of sexual organs and activities and for seeming to encourage violence against women. To many, the lyrics were offensive or unintelligible. When a sheriff in Florida brought an obscenity complaint against a store owner for selling records of 2 Live Crew, a U.S. District judge convicted the owner after months of hearings. The leader of 2 Live Crew and two band members were arrested and brought to trial, too, but a jury found them not guilty of obscenity charges. The jury foreman acknowledged that members of the jury found it difficult to understand the key piece of evidence, a tape recording of the performance that had led to the defendants' arrest.

The difficulties faced by symphony orchestras, opera companies, and composers suggested that classical music was no longer a central feature of American culture. Operating deficits were common. Listening audiences had never been diverse, but in the words of an anonymous administrator quoted by the *New York Times*, they were now "white, rich, and almost dead." Portions of their audiences were tired of the standby classical pieces by great composers of the past; other portions had no use for the avant-garde works of contemporary composers. Imitations of classical forms by contemporary composers did not work either.   **Classical Music**

Moreover, as younger generations matured they generally failed to replace their popular tastes, which were so different from those of previous generations of youth, with classical ones. Linda Sanders explained it this way in *Civilization*: "It was one thing for educated adults to tell hormone-crazed teenagers back in the 1950s that 'Blue Suede Shoes' was worthless trash. It was quite another for educated adults to try to tell other educated adults in the 1980s that blues, reggae, and minimalism (or, for that matter, the Beatles, Bruce Springsteen and Prince) were either musically or spiritually inferior to Bach and Beethoven."[2] Add to this the sense maturing generations' opinion that classical music was for the intellectual and social elite, and it is easy to see why classical music was losing its appeal and its audiences.

Technology also caused problems for performers of classical music. The intensity and spontaneity of live performances were unmatched, but if precision and purity were what mattered, they could be found by listening to compact disks through high-quality sound systems. For the price of a ticket, one could purchase a couple of choice compact discs, to be listened to repeatedly and without the hassle of attending a concert.

Performing groups therefore had to change their programming, the staging of performances, promotion methods, and general understandings of themselves. They had to find the balance between being perpetuators of a sacred classical canon and a community center for the enjoyment of music and advancement of musical knowledge.

Board games have long been a popular diversion for children.
Games Monopoly, for example, a Parker Brothers game, has been around since 1935. To celebrate its golden anniversary in 1985, it held championship matches in Atlantic City, New Jersey, with the winner receiving $15,140—the equivalent of the total play money in the Monopoly game. Scrabble, a word game invented by James Brunot in 1948, remained popular. Game players were ready for something new, however, when Trivial Pursuit arrived from Canada in 1983. Sales figures are a good way of measuring the impact of a new arrival. At one point there were back orders for a million games, and in its first year sales of Trivial Pursuit totaled $777 million. (What kind of questions did Trivial Pursuit ask? Ones like this: "Who invented Trivial Pursuit?") In Pictionary, another board game, players advanced by deciphering their teammates' pencil drawings. Introduced in Seattle in 1985, its sales reached $3 million in 1987 and continued upward.

Sales of board games were no match for the electronic games that became increasingly popular after the introduction of Atari in the mid-1970s and Pac-Man in 1981. The first ones were played as attachments to television sets, but before long they were separate gadgets in a variety of shapes and sizes. When Nintendo came along in 1985 it started running up big numbers: Sales amounted to $830 million in 1987 and exceeded $3 billion in 1990. Electronic toys, unlike board games, could be played alone and therefore required no communication and interaction among children.

Electronic games and toys were not the only ones to enjoy popularity. The Teenage Mutant Ninja Turtles, comic-book characters created by cartoonists Peter Laird and Kevin Eastman in 1983, spawned a multi-billion dollar industry that produced toys, films and videos, a stage show, and logos on children's wearing apparel—licensed, of course.

Major-league baseball tested its place in the hearts of many Americans when a seven-week players' strike interrupted the   **Sports** 1981 season. The strike caused the middle third of the schedule to be canceled, resulting in the major leagues' first split season. The origins of the discord between players and management lay in legal actions taken by players in the mid-seventies to gain the right for veteran players to sign with other teams as free agents. When the owners' absolute power over players was broken, they established a system that required the loss of a free agent to be compensated in the form of a player from the team with which the free agent had signed. In the impasse that followed, fans were caught in the middle and left with a gameless midsummer.

In 1982 the National Football League (NFL) faced a similar situation. No games were played during a 57–day strike. In 1987, though, when the season was interrupted by a 24-day strike by players over rules surrounding the free agency of players, management canceled games on the first weekend but then fielded teams made up of replacement players and regulars who drifted back. When the players decided to go back to work, the owners told them they could not play immediately and would not be paid. The National Labor Relations Board ruled in the players' favor and ordered the NFL to pay striking players more than $20 million in lost wages and incentive bonuses for the game they had missed. As with baseball, the fans were on the sidelines—mostly disgusted with both players and management.

The United States hosted the 1984 Summer Olympics in Los Angeles. Broadcast by ABC, the event's 168 hours on the   **Olympics** air drew ratings higher than expected, and it produced several heroes: Carl Lewis won gold medals in the 100-meter dash, the 200-meter dash, the 400-meter relay, and the long jump, duplicating what Jesse Owens had done in 1936 in Berlin. In contrast to earlier times, the rules of the Olympics allowed Lewis to earn about $1 million yearly and still compete as an amateur. Another hero was the Olympics' real crowd pleaser, Mary Lou Retton, a 16-year-old whose five medals included a gold in all-around gymnastics. Her feat gained her many commercial endorsements.

By 1988 the Olympics were greeted as welcome television fare by millions of viewers. To accommodate their interests, the Winter Games, held in Calgary, Canada, were extended to sixteen days. But ratings were disappointing, partly because the United States won only two of the forty-six gold medals, in addition to a silver and three bronzes. The Summer Games, held in Seoul, Korea, also lasted sixteen days. Although the competition provided enjoyable viewing, much of the attention went to

Bicycle riders travel the rolling hills of western Iowa in their six-day ride across the state in an annual event that attracts thousands of cyclists from across the nation (1988). © *Ann Karras. Used by permission.*

controversies concerning the use of drugs that had been banned—particularly anabolic steroids. This drug makes athletes stronger and enables them to train harder, putting them at a competitive advantage, but it also has harmful side-effects. Altogether, eighteen athletes were disqualified before or during the games, including Canada's Ben Johnson, who had defeated Carl Lewis in the 100-meter dash.

Fitness   Physical fitness participants in this decade wanted to look good, feel good, lose weight, have fun, make friends, develop personal discipline, and, above all, stay well. Avid runners claimed that running gave them more daily energy, sharpened their mental edge, kept them in good physical condition, and increased their resistance to illness. Tennis players were just as avid about their sport, although they made fewer claims for its benefits. Bowlers, golfers, skiers, bikers, and participants in other sports were avid, too, but their fitness claims were less audible. Many of them considered their participation as recreational rather than fitness-driven.

Private health clubs eagerly exploited the fitness interests of many

Americans. The number of clubs increased from 7,500 in 1980 (not including YMCAs or golf, tennis, and other sports-specific clubs) to more than 20,000 by the end of the decade. Membership in health and fitness clubs reached about 40 million before the end of the decade. The quest for fitness could be satisfied in one's home, too, as the popularity of *Jane Fonda's Workout Book* (1981) bears witness. In addition to providing an exercise regimen, this book by an actress-turned-political-activist and now fitness promoter included dietary advice and musings on ways for women to maintain good health. A bestseller, it opened the way to Fonda's further commercial ventures—exercise studios, cassette tapes with music to accompany workouts, and an exercise video. Other exercise promoters, such as Richard Simmons, also produced videos for use at home, and sales of home exercise equipment by Nordic Track, Nautilus, and other companies boomed. So did sales of improved equipment for outdoor sports.

Household pets, particularly dogs and cats, played increasingly larger parts in the daily lives of Americans. The pet census taken **Pets** by the Gallup Poll in 1990 estimated that there were 57.9 million dogs in American homes, and 48.9 million cats. Nearly 60 percent of Americans had pets—not just cats and dogs but rabbits, hamsters, snakes, and birds, and even pot-bellied pigs. According to the pet census, half again as many people would like to have had one. Personal preference and living arrangements deterred some from owning pets, but cost was no doubt another deterrent. Owners said they spent an estimated $1,500 annually on pet care, for such things as food, medical treatment, toys, and grooming. Expenditures on dog and cat food alone passed $6 million in 1990.

NOTES

1. Allan Bloom, *The Closing of the American Mind* (New York: Simon & Schuster, 1987), 73, 80–81.

2. Linda Sanders, "Facing the Music," *Civilization*, May/June 1996, 38–39.

30

Concerns of Daily Life

Eating and drinking practices frequently did not match the
heightened awareness of the need for healthful foods. Ad-   **Nutrition**
vertising for such foods abounded, and labels became more
honest and explicit in reporting the contents of food packages, especially
after a law passed in 1990 required it. But even with accurately labeled
food products and repeated warnings concerning the health hazards
posed by cholesterol, fats, salt, and sugar, junk-food consumption increased. Reports that poultry was more healthful than pork and beef led
to increased poultry consumption, but not enough to catch up with either
of its competitors. Nutritional concerns led to other healthful changes,
including increased consumption of fruits and vegetables and reduced
intake of fats and oils. The food industry encouraged the trend. In 1988
it spent more than $1 billion on advertising that included some type of
health message, although critics contended that the messages were both
confusing and misleading.

Health and drunk-driving concerns contributed to a slight
decline in consumption of alcoholic beverages in the later   **Drinking**
1980s. At the same time, the consumption of soft drinks increased by almost 20 percent. Diet drinks got a boost in 1983 when the
Food and Drug Administration approved the use of aspartame, an artificial sweetener. Although critics warned that aspartame's effects on
certain chemicals in the brain could cause behavioral changes, diet-
conscious consumers ignored the warnings and the sweetener quickly
became popular. Much sweeter than sugar, aspartame has the advantage

of not causing tooth decay. Consumption of bottled water doubled in the latter half of the 1980s.

Coca-Cola Consumers of soft drinks were ready for a new sweetener, but millions let the Coca-Cola Company know they were not ready for a new taste. In 1985, a year before its 100th birthday, Coca-Cola decided to change its formula for Coke, the world's most popular soft drink, by making it sweeter. A $100 million advertising campaign promoting the new Coke attracted unbelievable attention. A survey by the company claimed that 81 percent of Americans heard about the change within twenty-four hours of its announcement—higher than the percentage who were aware in the same length of time of the 1969 moon landing. But the campaign failed to persuade angry protesters that the new formula was better than the old, so within three months the company brought back the original formula, now labeled Coca-Cola Classic. Some preferred the new taste, however, so the company produced both the old and the new. The controversy gave the Coca-Cola Company valuable free publicity, boosting sales of both the old Coke and the new and arousing suspicions (which the company denied) that creating controversy had been the plan all along. The episode provided a dramatic demonstration of corporate America's responsiveness to consumers.

Fashion In the fashion world, the transition from the homier times of Jimmy and Rosalyn Carter to the show-business style of Ronald and Nancy Reagan meant that fashionable women wore more elaborate and expensive clothes. Elsewhere, though, permissiveness in fashions continued. Casual sportswear remained popular, and sweatshirts—sometimes with fancy touches, including hand-painted decorations—became a standard part of wardrobes. So did androgynous fashions, the result of blurred distinctions between appropriate clothing for women and men. Women increasingly wore garments formerly worn exclusively by men, most of them conspicuously over-sized. Men's clothing adopted some of the softer, loose-fitting features and colorfulness of clothes worn by women.

For both women and men, the casual attire was welcome, but some regretted the absence of standards that had guided decisions on what to wear. Women now had to choose between a dress, a mix-and-match outfit, a pants suit, and other possibilities. For men, was a jacket required? A tie? Or would a sweater and an open collar do? Not everything was casual, of course. The more "sober styles," as one observer called them, suited those who were among the increasing numbers of women entering professions or positions in the business world. Men in the business world, too, found traditional attire appropriate.

Wrinkles and baldness are the bane of many adults, just as acne is for young people. In 1988 came indications of possible answers to all three conditions. Doctors reported in the *Journal of the American Medical Association* (*JAMA*) that

Personal Appearance

tretinoin, marketed as Retin-A, could reduce wrinkles and age spots resulting from exposure to the sun. Within days of the *JAMA* report, patients swamped physicians with requests for prescriptions. Although the Food and Drug Administration warned against indiscriminate use of this medication and emphasized that there was limited scientific evidence of its effectiveness, the manufacturer and retailers could not keep up with the demand for it.

At about the same time, the FDA approved Rogaine (minoxidil) as a prescription drug to treat hair loss. Although studies showed that Rogaine stimulated hair growth in only a small number of men who tried it and that only after being taken for several years, there was no shortage of men willing to give it a try. For acne, the prescription drug Accutane (isotretinoin), introduced in 1982 and proven to be effective, was later identified as a cause of birth defects if taken by pregnant women. The manufacturer agreed to include a picture of a baby deformed by Accutane in the information sheet packaged with the drug.

The retail world responded to new economic patterns and lifestyles, leading to new shopping practices. With so many women holding full-time jobs, their best time for shopping was Sunday. To make that possible, the remnants of the once-

Sunday Shopping

common "blue laws" that had kept stores closed on Sundays were repealed or not enforced.

The Home Shopping Network, a cable television channel that arrived in 1986, invited viewers to call in orders for items featured by the host or hostess—such things as neck-

Television Shopping

laces, small appliances for the kitchen, housewares, toys, gadgets for automobiles, and tools. Before the end of the year the Home Shopping Network supplemented its cable television outlets by purchasing conventional channels in ten cities and reached as many as 36 million homes. New competitors in the home shopping field would soon appear and sales would soar.

Large national chains of discount stores also continued to fare well, with sales showing year-to-year increases and the number of discount outlets expanding. Three big discounters (Target, Kmart, and Wal-Mart) reported sales in 1990 of $8.2

Discount Shopping

billion, $24.9 billion, and $25.7 billion, respectively. T.J. Maxx is an example of one of many successful specialty-store chains. Calling itself an "off-price retailer" and dealing mainly in clothes, it began with two stores in Massachusetts in 1977. By the mid-1990s it had 550 stores in 47 states. Warehouse clubs—no-frills operations featuring bulk purchases along with standard merchandise—showed the largest increases, with sales growing about tenfold between 1984 and 1990.

Shopping Malls   None of this was good news for shopping malls. Although malls remained popular for shopping and as social outlets, by the end of the decade as many as 20 percent showed signs of being in trouble. As the department stores that anchored them—Sears, for example—struggled, so did they. They were also hurt by the popularity of specialty shops that fared well in strip malls, where parking was more convenient. A new kind of competition began to emerge in the 1980s—the outlet mall. By the end of the decade there were nearly 200 such malls, with more than 6,000 shops. Typically situated in open areas outside cities, they came to be tourist attractions. Chartered buses brought dedicated shoppers to spend the day there.

Gambling   Another opportunity for people wanting to spend money spread across the nation, almost like an epidemic. State governments' quests for nontax revenues meshed well with citizens' desires to try their luck in state-sponsored lotteries. Before long, other forms of gambling—called gaming by those who made big money from them and the politicians who encouraged them—became popular in many places.

Lotteries typically came first, not necessarily in response to citizens' demands but as a way for states to raise funds without raising taxes. New Hampshire's, begun in 1963, showed how lotteries worked. Eventually other states started their own and formed networks to increase the size of the jackpots. Seeing more prospects for revenue, states began to allow slot machines in bars. Montana was first. South Dakota's lottery agency placed video lottery terminals (VLTs)—in effect, electronic slot machines—in bars and convenience stores. Until 1988, only Nevada and New Jersey allowed gambling casinos, but six years later twenty-three states were operating or had authorized casinos, some on riverboats, and more were proposed.

Between 1982 and 1988, legal wagering rose from $126 billion to $240 billion, on its way to nearly $330 billion in 1992; money lost by bettors reached nearly $30 billion in 1992. The implications of spending so much on gambling become significant when one considers who spent it and the needs and pleasures of daily life that were neglected when gambling got to a family's budget first. Robert Goodman, in *The Luck Business* (1995) presents research showing that the higher one's income, the more one tends to see gambling as entertainment, a social activity. The lower one's income, the more gambling is considered a form of investment. Being unable to invest in real estate or the stock market, the poor see gambling less as play and more as a serious chance to improve their lives. They do not spend more money on gambling than middle-income people, but they do spend a substantially higher percentage of their income on it. If gambling is, in effect, an alternative form of taxation, it imposes its highest rates on those who are least able to afford it. When gambling becomes compulsive, it presents social problems that states were only beginning to deal with at the end of the decade.

Gambling also affects the communities in which it occurs. Promoters of gambling claim that it provides jobs, as indeed it does. Nonetheless, according to Goodman, there are few economic benefits for communities and real economic costs. He cites, for example, a business survey of Natchez, Mississippi. A few months after the first riverboat casino opened there, 70 percent of the local businesses recorded declines in sales of 10 to 20 percent. A year later, restaurants and bars in the neighborhood of the riverboat closed and house tours and evening entertainment during tourist season were down by more than 20 percent.[1]

In the 1980s the portion of the gross national product devoted to health care increased from 9.1 percent to 12.2 **Health Care** percent, on its way to more than 14 percent by the mid-1990s. The rate of increase in the total health bill for the nation was double the inflation rate. Not only did the annual increases have implications for state and federal budgets, but they also had significant effects on family budgets. Insurance premiums and payments made directly to doctors and hospitals multiplied several times between the late 1970s and 1990. Employers felt the squeeze, too, as the cost of providing health-care insurance for their employees skyrocketed.

In the absence of a national plan guaranteeing health insurance for all Americans, some simply accepted the spiraling costs of individual and group coverage, some did without coverage and hoped that hospitals' emergency rooms or charity policies would meet their needs, and some tried to control costs by joining health maintenance organizations (HMOs). Although the relatively lower costs of HMO coverage made them popular, to compete with other forms of coverage they had to relax their initial limits on patients' rights to choose their doctors. Even so, the less-restricted choices left many of their members unsatisfied.

That no doubt reflected a cynicism about providers of health care in general. One survey reported that only 29 percent of its respondents believed that physicians performed important services. Another 27 percent said that few physicians perform such services. In another survey, respondents expressed much greater confidence in pharmacists than in physicians and were more satisfied with their services. The changing health-care scene prompted changes in the education of pharmacists, who were taught to counsel persons about their prescriptions. Their pill-counting role was being taken over by more accurate and efficient technological devices.

Health and Diseases Despite the high costs of medical care, the superior training of doctors, and the breakthroughs in research, health problems were far from solved. The National Cancer Institute reported that cancer deaths continued to rise. Between 1973 and 1987, for example, occurrences of cancer increased by 14 percent. Melanoma (skin cancer) showed the greatest increase (83%), followed by prostate cancer (46%), lung cancer (31%), breast cancer in women over age 50 (30%) and under age 50 (20%). Incidents of stomach, uterine, and cervical cancer declined. Heart disease also remained a major cause of death, with coronary disease or heart attacks accounting for more than 25 percent of the deaths occurring annually.

Mental Health People in the 1980s complained frequently about pressures of time, family responsibilities, earning a living, and adjusting to change, among other things. The fact that many were indeed affected by stressful conditions could be documented by psychologists and psychiatrists. Moreover, a survey conducted by the National Institute of Mental Health in 1984 concluded that almost 20 percent of adults in the United States suffer mental disorders. Women were shown to be more prone to depression and phobias, and men to drug and alcohol abuse and antisocial behavior.

Decades earlier the quest for relief from mental conditions often involved psychoanalysis. Patients poured out tales of their past to persons trained to listen and, by asking questions, help them understand themselves and deal with their problems. By the 1980s neither the pace of life nor the terms of medical insurance allowed for protracted psychoanalytical treatment, and psychoanalysts had few patients. Nonetheless, counseling—both individual and in group therapy sessions—remained important in dealing with mental and emotional problems.

At the same time, the growing belief that mental disorders were often caused by such physical problems as chemical imbalances led psychiatrists increasingly to prescribe medications. This may explain the popularity of Prozac, introduced in 1988 as an apparently effective treatment for depression. Before long it was also used to treat problems associated with obesity, gambling, and anxiety over public speaking. Although many benefited from it and its side effects were few, some physicians and psychologists were concerned that Prozac and similar drugs were substitutes for dealing directly with what was wrong in the lives of their users. There were reasons to wonder, too, whether medications might inhibit creative powers in those who were dependent on them.

One condition that received considerable attention
in the 1980s is attention deficit disorder (ADD); some-　　**Attention Deficit**
times the term *hyperactive* also describes an aspect of　　　　**Disorder**
the condition known as ADHD. Although physicians
and psychologists made many of the diagnoses of ADD and ADHD,
many other cases were self-diagnosed. In fact, most people could see in
themselves varying degrees of ADD's most common symptoms: a tendency to be easily distracted from tasks at hand, a low tolerance for
frustration or boredom, an inclination to act impulsively, and a fondness
for situations of high intensity. When diagnoses were made by professionals, they were followed by counseling and sometimes by medication,
such as Ritalin. Indeed, overuse of Ritalin for children suffering from
attention deficit and hyperactive disorder worried parents and teachers.
Persons who diagnosed their own condition apparently compensated for
it by doing such things as establishing demanding schedules or setting
goals that required them to work obsessively.

If there was in fact an ADD epidemic in the United States, it was
probably related to the hyperactive nature of society. Edward Hallowell
and John J. Ratey, both psychiatrists, wrote in *Driven to Distraction* that
"American society tends to create ADD-like symptoms in us all. We live
in an ADD-ogenic culture." They identified some of the hallmarks of
American culture that are typical of ADD as well as of postmodern times:

> The fast pace. The sound bite. The bottom line. Short takes, quick
> cuts. The TV remote-control clicker. High stimulation. Restlessness.
> Violence. Anxiety. Ingenuity. Creativity. Speed. Present-centered,
> no future, no past. Disorganization. Mavericks. A mistrust of au-
> thority. Video. Going for the gusto. Making it on the run. The fast
> track. Whatever works. Hollywood. The stock exchange. Fads. High
> stim.
> It is important to keep this in mind or you may start thinking
> that everybody you know has ADD. The disorder is culturally syn-
> tonic—that is to say, it fits right in.[2]

Painful visits to the dentist's office for teeth to be filled
or extracted, one of the dreads of childhood, had begun　　**Dental Health**
to disappear in the United States by the 1980s. Not only
had dentists' tools and treatments improved, but in the decade preceding
1981 tooth decay in schoolchildren declined by more than one-third,
partly as a result of the fluoridation of water in most communities and
the presence of fluorides in 90 percent of the tooth cleansers used at
home. Changes in diet and better dental care practices also played a part.

Even though dental caries declined, dental care for other problems increased. Orthodontists treated children and adults who were concerned about uneven teeth and malocclusions, and periodontic (gum) treatment, endodontic (root canal) therapy, and bridgework enabled more adults to retain their natural teeth.

In March 1981 the Centers for Disease Control determined that
Herpes cases of the sexually transmitted disease known as genital herpes had reached epidemic proportions in the United States. Victims suffered painful, recurring sores on their genital organs. Between unpredictable outbreaks the virus withdraws into nerve cells, where it remains out of the reach of the body's immune system. A medication existed to relieve the symptoms when initial outbreaks occurred, but there was no means as yet to prevent or relieve the symptoms in subsequent recurrences, making this the first incurable sexually transmitted disease since the introduction of antibiotics. Research continued for medications to prevent outbreaks for those afflicted with the disease and for vaccines to protect others from contracting it.

At the same time a more deadly disease, usually transmitted
AIDS sexually, leaped into the nation's consciousness. In June 1981 the Centers for Disease Control reported five cases of a strain of pneumonia among previously healthy homosexual men in Los Angeles hospitals. This strain, *pneumocystis carinii,* usually occurs in infants or in adults receiving immunosuppressive drugs, as in the chemotherapy treatment of cancer patients. Reports of other cases of strange illnesses appeared elsewhere, most commonly among homosexual men. Initially labeled GRID (for gay-related immunodeficiency), the name was changed when the victims included recipients of blood transfusions, female prostitutes, intravenous drug users, and heterosexual Africans and Haitians. The disease was then named AIDS (acquired immunodeficiency syndrome).

By the end of 1982, 750 AIDS cases had been reported in the United States and almost 1,600 worldwide. A year later the number of reported cases reached about 3,000. With the number of cases growing daily, the AIDS crisis became one of the big stories of the decade. Other factors also made it so, such as movie star Rock Hudson's revelation in 1985 that he was battling AIDS and his death later that year. The dedication of an AIDS hospice in New York by Mother Teresa, a nun renowned for her work with the poor and suffering, also increased public awareness. Close-to-home reminders of the dangers posed by AIDS came in 1987 and 1988, when patients began to see their doctors and dentists slip their hands into latex gloves before treating them.

The trends toward openness in sexual relationships established in prior decades continued. So did candor in depicting sexual ex- **Sex** periences in films, television programs, books, and magazines. Practices that not many years earlier would have been regarded as promiscuous, if not sinful, came to be accepted with few raised eyebrows. The new themes made no reference to controlling sexual urges. At least not until the arrival of AIDS. Fear of AIDS and other sexually transmitted diseases persuaded many who might not have thought casual sex to be wrong to become practitioners of "safe sex." In both heterosexual and homosexual relationships "safe sex" became a code phrase for "use condoms." The rising incidence of sexually transmitted diseases, particularly AIDS, led U.S. Surgeon General C. Everett Koop, a conservative Christian, to call for the use of condoms as a preventative measure. At around the same time, television stations and magazines abandoned their restrictions on advertising condoms.

Those seeking new restrictions on smoking found ammunition in the 1982 report by the surgeon general of the **Smoking and** United States that cigarette smoke "is clearly identified **Health** as the chief preventable cause of death in our society and the most important public health issue of our day." The report identified smoking as the major cause of cancer of the larynx, oral cavity, and esophagus and a contributing factor in cancer of the bladder, pancreas, and kidney. Association of cigarette smoking with lung cancer had long been established, but now it was linked also with cancer of the stomach and cervix. Even though more than 30 million Americans had quit smoking since 1964, smoking-related health-care costs were estimated to be about $13 billion annually.

In 1984, Surgeon General Koop released a 515-page report on smoking and health that said the federal government had evidence showing that nonsmokers exposed to cigarette smoke can suffer lung diseases as a result. Congress then approved legislation to make warning labels on cigarettes more explicit, requiring them to cite relationships between cigarette smoking and heart disease, lung cancer, and emphysema. The labels were also required to warn pregnant women that cigarette smoking could damage the fetus they were carrying and possibly cause premature birth. This was an important warning, since by the 1980s women smokers outnumbered men who smoked.

The Environmental Protection Agency declared in 1990 that secondhand smoke was a human carcinogen—that is, a cancer-causing substance—and that passive smoking caused 2,500 deaths from lung cancer annually among nonsmokers. This fact did not necessarily cause smokers to quit, but it provided more reasons to continue the trend toward limiting smoking in public places and offices.

Alcohol
Despite alarming reports of marijuana and cocaine use among teenagers, alcohol was the drug most commonly used. Incidents involving drunk driving had terrible consequences for teens. In 1985 alone, automobile accidents involving alcohol killed 6,063 boys and girls between the ages of 15 and 19 (and 7,772 men and women aged 20–24). Why teenagers drank, many of them heavily, is not easy to explain. Studies by the Research Triangle Institute (RTI) and the National Institute on Alcohol Abuse and Alcoholism (NIAAA) found that peer pressure, sometimes subtle, sometimes overt, played a leading role. One study showed that 59 percent of students who were moderate or heavy drinkers had at least one parent who drank, but some students who drank were rebelling against anti-drinking parents. Some characteristics associated with students who drank, such as low grades and poor self-respect, may have been a cause as well as a consequence of their drinking.

Drug Abuse
Alcohol abuse was the main drug problem for teenagers, but not the only one. In the mid-1980s cocaine gained in popularity, and the gradual trends toward reduced use of other drugs ended. Cocaine in the smokable form known as crack was both more potent and more addictive than sniffed powder, and crack caught on with some groups of high school students. Marijuana and amphetamines, or "uppers," were the drugs more commonly used by teenagers. Less common, but present, were various hallucinogens, especially LSD (lysergic acid diethylamide—often referred to as acid) and PCP (phencyclidine). The practice of inhaling legal but toxic substances, such as spray paint and glue, became increasingly popular. Parents in the 1980s were not only slow to catch on to drug use by their offspring, but they did not even know or understand the lingo that was familiar even to non-using children.

Throughout the 1980s, drug and alcohol abuse seemed to be an insoluble problem. Reports on the abuse varied from year to year. In 1983, for example, federal agencies reported that heroin use was increasing in middle and upper classes of U.S. society. Hospital admissions for injuries and deaths related to heroin abuse were also going up. Cocaine had become more widely available, with somewhere between 200,000 and a million persons dependent on it. In other years the numbers might be slightly different and the drugs of choice might change, but the drug problem remained. Addiction by uncertain numbers of Americans to medication prescribed by doctors was a parallel but less publicized problem.

Legalization of Drugs
Critics of drug policies, such as the National Organization for the Reform of Marijuana Laws (NORML), contended that the drug problem lay in the fact that the drugs people wanted to use were illegal. That made them expensive; in turn, drug dealing became both highly profitable and highly dangerous. In the critics' view, the large sums the federal gov-

ernment was spending to enforce drug laws—the budget increased from $800 million in 1981 to $2.5 billion in 1988, much of it in vain efforts to cut off drug supplies from Latin America and Asia—were wasted. Making possession and use of drugs legal, particularly marijuana, they contended, would take the profit out of drug dealing and reduce drug-related crimes. They failed to generate widespread support for their views, however, and translating them into laws proved to be impossible. Instead, Congress authorized even larger sums for fighting drug problems—$8.8 billion in a bill enacted in 1989.

If legalization of drugs was not an acceptable answer to problems caused by substance abuse—the term covering both alcohol and drug abuse—what was? Organizations looking for answers learned that **Combating Substance Abuse** messages intended to scare teenagers about the dangers of drugs were ineffective. Teenagers in particular closed their ears to seemingly constant anti-drug admonitions, like Nancy Reagan's "Just Say No."

What seemed to be effective was peer pressure against drinking and drugs, exerted most convincingly by testimonials by those who had paid the price as users, perhaps by being involved in an accident or being arrested. Students Against Drunk Driving (SADD), founded in 1981, used this approach. SADD also asked students to sign a Contract for Life, in which they promised to call their parents for a ride home if they or the driver they were with had been drinking.

Under pressure from MADD (Mothers Against Drunk Driving) Congress enacted a law, signed by President Reagan, requiring states to raise the minimum drinking **Minimum Drinking Age** age to 21 by October 1, 1987, or lose 5 percent of some federal highway funds. A year later the penalty would rise to 10 percent per year. All but eight states met the deadline. Some states had raised the minimum drinking age earlier, and traffic fatalities dropped in those states. However, teenagers who wanted to drink had little trouble buying alcoholic beverages, even where sales were prohibited. In locations where young would-be buyers were "carded," that is, required to show identification bearing their age, they found others to buy it for them or made fraudulent IDs for their own use.

Employers, as well as administrators and coaches in schools, colleges, and universities, wanted to know who in their workforce or on their team was a sub- **Testing for Substance Abuse** stance abuser. Testing of urine samples was one way to find out, and in 1986 President Reagan called for mandatory testing for all government employees in sensitive positions. Perhaps as many as one-third of the nation's businesses had already established testing practices. Testing, however, was controversial, and court challenges by those who opposed it as a violation of privacy rights were common.

Medicare Changes   In 1983 Medicare, the federal health insurance program for the elderly and disabled, began to phase in
a three-year plan applying predetermined rates for
paying hospitals for treatment. Until these 467 treatment categories
(known as diagnosis-related groups, or DRGs) were established, Medicare simply based its reimbursements on hospitals' costs. The intent of
the new plan was obvious: to compel hospitals to reduce their costs. As
an incentive, hospitals were allowed to keep money they saved when
they held costs below the fixed rate. Initially the rates varied by region
and according to the location of the hospital, urban or rural, but the
regional variations were to be discontinued in 1986. The new arrangement affected both doctors and patients: Doctors felt they were losing
control of decision-making responsibilities, and patients wondered
whether hospitals were placing too much emphasis on holding costs
down and not enough on maintaining essential services.

NOTES

1. Robert Goodman, *The Luck Business: The Devastating Consequences and Broken
Promises of America's Gambling Explosion* (New York: Free Press, 1995).

2. Edward M. Hallowell and John J. Ratey, *Driven to Distraction* (New York:
Pantheon Books, 1994), 191.

31

Technology

Personal computers (PCs) had been manufactured since 1977, but the market for them did not come of age until 1981, when IBM produced its first one. IBM's size enabled **Personal Computers** it to market its PCs aggressively, and sales climbed in three years from 25,000 to 3 million, although its experiment with a low-cost model, the PCjr., failed. The Apple Corporation, famous for development of the Apple II, introduced the Macintosh in 1984. By 1987 its Macintosh II and SE models were the most powerful personal computers on the market. The Mac was also regarded as more user-friendly than personal computers with "disk operating systems," and debates over Mac versus DOS continued for years. The Mac's "mouse" for moving the cursor on the screen made it even more user-friendly, and eventually other lines of computers also made the mouse a standard feature.

Sales of personal computers stood at 1.4 million in 1981. Sales doubled in 1982, on their way to 10 million in 1988, at a cost then of $22 billion. A number of other computer developments made news that year. One was the "virus," a mischievous small program planted in an operating system with the intent of altering or deleting data throughout the network as the virus spreads. Another was the expanded capacity and speed of laptop computers, with sales exceeding $1 million. A third concerned possible health hazards posed by computer monitors, known as video display terminals. Studies showed that many people who worked at monitors for six hours or more each day developed difficulties in focusing their eyes. Long hours spent at keyboards also caused injuries to hands and arms, sometimes to a disabling extent.

Genetic Engineering   Advances in biotechnology in the 1980s began to affect the lives of many Americans, mostly in unseen ways and in terms not well understood by nonscientists. Because biotechnology in the form of genetic engineering is certain to play increasingly important roles in medicine, as well as in plant and animal science, it is important to understand what it involves.

That requires an understanding of certain terms. *Genetic engineering* is defined by William S. Klug and Michael R. Cummings as "the technique of altering the genetic constitution of cells or individuals by the selective insertion, removal, or modification of individual genes or gene sets."[1] *Chromosomes* are structures in the cell nucleus that carry an organism's genes. All living species have a consistent number of chromosomes in each cell. In human beings there are twenty-three pairs of chromosomes, or forty-six in all. *Genes* are the basic units of heredity, with all genes containing coded information for producing proteins. *Proteins*, in turn, are complicated, three-dimensional molecules composed of amino acids that are important components in an organism's tissues. Proteins carry out many life processes that determine structural and functional characteristics in an organism. They may act as regulatory chemicals known as *hormones* (but not all hormones are proteins) and *enzymes*, which are molecules that serve as catalysts in chemical reactions.

DNA (deoxyribonucleic acid) is the central component of chromosomes. The DNA molecules have the shape of a long, twisted ladder, with each gene being a section of the ladder. The information carried in an organism's genes, determined by the order of the DNA ladder's "rungs," gives each organism specific physical characteristics. *Recombinant DNA*, also called gene splicing, refers to the splicing of DNA from one organism into the living cells of another organism. Work in genetic engineering in the 1970s was done on viruses and bacteria and demonstrated great potential for understanding life processes. The wide use in recombinant DNA work of the bacterium known as *E. coli* gave rise to concern that it could escape from laboratories and pose dangers to animal and plant life. Scientists therefore voluntarily agreed to restrict certain kinds of research with this organism. By the 1980s, however, they had developed better understandings of the nature of genetic engineering, and the restrictions were eased.

Throughout the 1980s, research continued on uses of genetic engineering. Among the leading uses was changing the "genetic blueprint" of farm animals to make them larger or healthier and of crop plants to make them hardier, more nutritious, or more resistant to disease and insects. As far as humans are concerned, there was hope that genetic engineering could correct hereditary physical deficiencies or deformities and treat hereditary diseases through "gene therapy." In the final months of 1990, researchers began their first federally authorized case of gene therapy and were successful in treating a 4-year-old girl who had a rare genetic disorder of the immune system. Further use of gene therapy was at that time largely in research and development stages, but researchers had begun to identify genes associated with tendencies toward certain illnesses, such as lung cancer, arthritis, and possibly even alcoholism.

Genetic engineering stirred controversy, particularly because it holds potential for going beyond therapeutic use in the treatment of inherited disorders. Critics **Ethical Concerns** worried that it would be used to alter human germ cells and create new forms of life. In response, President Carter appointed the President's Commission for the Study of Ethical Problems in Medicine and Biomedical and Behavioral Research, and President Reagan authorized its continuation. In 1982 the Commission's report, *Splicing Life,* stated, "Human beings have not merely the right but the duty to employ their God-given powers to harness nature for human benefit. To turn away from gene-splicing, which may provide a means of curing hereditary diseases, would raise serious ethical problems."

The Commission acknowledged, however, that genetic engineering might in time tempt humanity to "play God" and try to create "perfect human beings." It therefore recommended the establishment of a government-sponsored council to oversee the development and application of gene splicing and to guard against misuses of technology. In 1984, Congress approved legislation that established a Biomedical Ethics Advisory Commission to be made up of professionals from the sciences and the humanities, as well as two members from the general public.[2]

Meanwhile, scientists laid plans for "mapping" the human "genome." The genome consists of about 60,000 to 100,000 human genes and their 3 billion units of DNA. Mapping enables researchers to identify the molecular basis of inherited diseases and find ways to prevent or treat them. The Human Genome Project, funded in 1988 by the National Institutes of Health and the Department of Energy and carried out by scientists working in different locations, was expected to cost as much as $3 billion and last for at least fifteen years. Since its founding, the Project has devoted about 5 percent of its budget to research designed to anticipate ethical, legal, and social issues. Worldwide interest meant that this project would be part of an international network of gene researchers.

The decade began on a promising note for the space program when the *Columbia,* the first reusable space- **Space Research** craft, touched down at Edwards Air Force Base in April 1981. Its landing in the Mojave Desert concluded a flight begun more than 54 hours earlier when the spaceship launched as a rocket. In 36 orbits of the earth it operated like a typical spacecraft, and it landed like an airplane on a runway. An amazingly successful mission, it gave Americans a renewed sense of pride and raised the prestige of the nation worldwide.

The goals of the space program, though, went beyond pride and prestige. The National Aeronautics and Space Administration (NASA) hoped to make orbiting in space a profitable venture. The communications industry was its early client, but NASA wanted to encourage advancements in medicine and other technologies. It faced competition from other nations, as well as from private companies trying to break into space travel.

Tragedy The American people took success in space exploration for granted until January 28, 1986. On that day the space shuttle *Challenger* exploded 73 seconds after liftoff from Cape Canaveral, Florida. Six astronauts died, along with a teacher on board, Christa McAuliffe. Her presence had attracted special attention to the flight, and millions of schoolchildren saw the explosion on television. Newsmen could say nothing to set the children at ease, and the entire nation was stunned.

Failures of other spacecraft occurred in subsequent months, but none so dramatically as the *Challenger*. Almost three years passed before the launching of *Discovery* again put a shuttle in space. Things went well for a while, but an event in 1990 that should have been a spectacular achievement turned out to be tarnished. The space shuttle *Discovery* launched the $1.5 billion Hubble Space Telescope into orbit, only to find very soon thereafter that an incorrectly made mirror blurred the images it was to transmit back to earth.

Compact Discs Most changes in technology were less spectacular than those displayed in space ventures, but they were important to those who used them. The clear, uncluttered sound of compact discs is an example. Recording processes translate sounds received by microphones into what is called digital data. This data is pressed into the molded plastic surface of a disc. Using a laser beam, the CD player reads the digits off the spinning disc, and a processor translates the digits into electric signals, which are fed through an amplifier into a speaker. Because CDs are touched only by a light beam, they should never wear out. Their introduction gave the music industry a needed boost. Sales of music records and tapes had dropped from a high of 683 million in 1979 to 577.4 million in 1982. Thereafter sales climbed steadily to 865.7 million in 1990. Although compact discs were initially popular for the quality of their recordings, they were also used for storing huge quantities of data, such as the contents of an encyclopedia, on a single disk. Before long such CDs played an important part in the operation of many businesses, and CD-ROM units were built into personal computers.

New technological devices, such as cellular phones, are typically quite costly. At the end of 1982, motorists **Cellular Phones** in Chicago could have cellular phones in their cars for an installation fee of $3,000 and a service fee of $150 per month. The placement of low-power transmitters around the city, used in conjunction with a computer system, enabled the use of such phones to spread and the cost to come down.

NOTES

1. William S. Klug and Michael R. Cummings, *Concepts of Genetics*, 4th ed. (New York: Macmillan, 1994), Appendix B-8.

2. Cited in Thomas H. Maugh II, "Changing Life's Blueprint," *The 1985 World Book Year Book* (Chicago: World Book, 1985), 73.

32

More Discord

In April 1983, Secretary of Education Terrel H. Bell released
a report entitled *A Nation at Risk*. It was the work of an eigh-   **Education**
teen-member National Commission on Excellence in Educa-
tion appointed to "make practical recommendations for action." The
appointment had been inspired in part by concern over the nationwide
decline in scores on the Scholastic Aptitude Tests that had begun in 1963
and continued in 17 of the next 20 years. Coincidentally, a slight improvement in the scores occurred in 1982, as well as in 1983 and 1984,
but that did not alleviate concerns about the quality of the nation's
schools.

A 1981 Gallup poll and a study by the Charles F. Kettering Foundation
had shown that the majority of Americans wanted more demanding curricula, more control over student behavior, and more attention to ethical
concerns. But the surveys also detected a growing feeling that parents
were more deficient than schools in the upbringing of their children.
Polls also showed a continued decline in the public's willingness to support schools financially. Rejection of proposed tax increases to support
school improvements was common.

A Nation at Risk presented a comprehensive indictment of American
education, citing high rates of adult illiteracy, declining SAT scores, and
poor performance on nineteen international academic achievement tests.
On none of these tests had American children ranked first or second.
The "educational foundations of our society," the report contended, "are
presently being eroded by a rising tide of mediocrity that threatens our
very future as a Nation and a people." The tragedy, it continued, was

that no unfriendly power was responsible for what had happened to the nation's schools, but rather, "we have allowed this to happen to ourselves."

The report made five recommendations. First, that all students seeking a high school diploma be required to have four years of study in English, three years in mathematics, three in science, and three in social studies, as well as half a year in computer science—fields identified as "the New Basics." Second, that all educational institutions expect more of their students and that requirements for admission to four-year colleges and universities be raised. Third, that significantly more time be devoted to learning the New Basics through more effective use of the existing school day or that the school day or year be lengthened. Fourth, that the preparation of teachers be strengthened and that teaching be made a more rewarding and respected profession. Fifth, that citizens require elected officials to support these reforms and provide funds necessary to accomplish them. The report concluded by urging parents to expect much from their children and for students to put forth their best efforts in learning.[1]

Although critics of *A Nation at Risk* insisted that many schools were doing a good job, the report struck a responsive chord in the general public. So did a flurry of other reports appearing immediately after its release, each with a different theme, each reflecting the interests of a specific constituency.[2]

Responses to the Reports
Responding to the reports, many critics of the schools, including some in Congress and the Reagan administration, insisted that "throwing money at the schools" would not improve them. Critics could point to the fact that expenditures for elementary and secondary education had nearly tripled (in 1989 dollars) between 1960 and 1990 and could claim that there was little to show for it. In reply, defenders of the schools could cite not only increased enrollment from 46 million students in 1960 to almost 52 million in 1990, but the high costs of many of the schools' new responsibilities, such as mainstreaming of disabled children. Dealing with children from troubled or impoverished homes placed extra demands on schools' resources. Costly instructional technology was just being introduced in 1960; by 1990 computers and other communication technologies, as well as scientific equipment for school laboratories, required large sums of money.

More money was needed, not less, according to the American Association of School Administrators (AASA). The AASA estimated that public school funding would have to be increased by at least 25 percent to reverse the "rising tide of mediocrity" cited by *A Nation at Risk.* State legislatures and local school boards across the country debated a variety of proposals for increasing funding.

Astute observers identified glaring omissions in the reports. For example, the president of Teachers College, **Omissions and** Columbia University, Lawrence A. Cremin, noted that **Misplaced** the reports had little to say about the development of **Emphases** moral character in students. Moreover, the reports "did not fully reckon with the prodigious tasks of curriculum development, innovation in the art of teaching, and teacher training and retraining that would be required to enable every American high school student to try seriously to master trigonometry, or biology, or a foreign language." Cremin noted, too, that by seeming to suggest that schools alone could solve the nation's problems in education, the reports ignored the dramatic changes in American homes that made the challenges of schools more awesome. The reports also paid insufficient attention to television's influence on children's learning and to the potential for contributions by churches, synagogues, libraries, museums, and business organizations.[3]

Criticisms of schools continued through the decade, long after the impact of the initial reports had faded. School ad- **Continuing** ministrators and teachers answered charges, among others, **Criticisms** that children's intellectual abilities were not being developed; that loss of industrial leadership worldwide and the lack of productivity of American workers were the fault of schools; that teachers were not qualified to teach and did not work hard enough; that textbooks promoted immorality; that parental dissatisfaction with schools was widespread; that because private schools responded to market forces— in other words, they provided what the consumers wanted—they were inherently better than public schools. Many criticisms came from conservatives with political agendas, and their growing influence in political circles gave them influence, though not necessarily validity. Three issues—school choice, textbooks, and declining Federal support—demonstrate the discord surrounding the schools.

School desegregation plans requiring children to attend schools in neighborhoods other than their own of- **School Choice** ten drew criticism as threats to a seemingly sacred neighborhood-school concept. By the 1980s, however, some parents wanted to choose their children's school with less regard for its location. *School choice* became a popular phrase. For some, this meant giving parents tax monies to send their children to private schools. Others simply wanted to send their children to schools across district boundaries. The practice of allowing students to attend out-of-district schools gained acceptance, but using tax funds for sending children to private schools was tried on a very limited basis and almost always challenged in the courts.

Textbooks   In a number of school districts, particularly in southern states, parents identifying themselves as Christian and conservative found certain textbooks objectionable. In Hawkins County, Tennessee, for example, a number of parents removed their children from public school reading classes because the textbooks offended their religious beliefs. A lower court ruled in their favor, but an appeals court asserted in 1987 that neither the books nor the classes violated religious freedom guaranteed by the First Amendment. A district court in Alabama allowed the banning of forty-four history, social studies, and home economics textbooks on the grounds that they promoted "the religion of secular humanism." Promoting moral behavior without reference to God, claimed the lower-court judge, made humanism a religion, and using books that lacked information on Christianity and other religions advanced godless principles that also amounted to a religion. The judge's rulings were reversed by a court of appeals, also in 1987, but that did not change the sentiments of the 600 fundamentalist parents, students, and teachers (or that of Alabama's former governor, George Wallace) who had initiated or supported the lawsuit that brought the case to trial.

Declining Federal Support   Traditionally, public school funding has depended primarily on revenue from local and state taxes. Private schools depend on tuition and support from churches or other sponsoring institutions. Public colleges and universities have always relied principally on funds provided by the state and on student tuition. Private colleges depend on higher tuitions and income from endowments.

Since the mid-1960s, as these resources proved inadequate for meeting the needs of schools, colleges, and universities, modest measures of federal support came into play. Federal funding, for example, provided support for educating students considered to be "at risk." Mental, physical, social, or other handicaps made meeting the higher academic standards sought by school reformers unlikely. Educators at all levels worried about the effects of substantial reductions in federal funding in the 1980s. For academic year 1981–1982, budgets for elementary and secondary schools, colleges, and universities totaled approximately $200 billion. About $20 billion of this amount was federal money. Although this was a substantial sum, it represented a reduction of $4 billion from the previous year. The reduction affected many aspects of education budgets, from support for disabled and disadvantaged children to grants and loans for college students.

Throughout the decade, local communities and state legislators looked for ways to improve schools, and several leading business groups encouraged and supported school reform efforts. In 1989, President George Bush **School Reform Efforts** attempted to revive the momentum of the early 1980s by assembling the nation's governors in an "education summit." The agenda addressed such things as recruitment of teachers, school reorganization, reducing the number of dropouts, and establishment of national performance goals. The summit attempted to address the problem of federal involvement in local institutions by exploring ways to relax federal and state regulation of local districts. Following the summit, a number of states led by their governors, such as Bill Clinton in Arkansas, launched their own school reform initiatives.

The National Endowment for the Arts, the National Endowment for the Humanities, and the Institute for Museum Services were all targets of budget cuts in the 1980s. Already strapped symphony orchestras, opera companies, **Arts and Humanities** and museums scrambled to find ways to make up for the loss of federal support. One way was to tap corporations for support and, in turn, recognize their sponsorship in the programs. Sometimes corporations or individuals underwrote specific chairs in an orchestra or the appearance of guest artists. Museum exhibitions also came to depend on corporate sponsorship for guest exhibitions and ongoing support.

Political conservatives had never been enthusiastic about the National Endowment for the Arts (NEA), but several controversial exhibits funded in part by the NEA in 1989 gave the most extreme among them an opportunity to attack the agency. One was a photograph by Andres Serrano showing a crucifix lying in the artist's urine; another was an exhibition of photographs by Robert Mapplethorpe that included images of men engaged in homosexual acts. As the attacks continued and were joined by criticisms from religious conservatives, the NEA came up for renewed funding. Debates in Congress became heated. John Frohnmayer, the agency's chairman, already the object of criticism from the political right, antagonized artists by requiring recipients of grants to sign oaths pledging not to use NEA funds in the creation of obscene works of art. When Congress approved reauthorization of the agency, it required that grants be made for work that was "sensitive to the general standards of decency." In the twenty-four years of the NEA's existence only about 20 of its 85,000 grants had caused controversy, so this standard would affect a very small number of the applications, but its imposition stirred a controversy pitting artists against conservative politicians that lasted for years.

Environment James G. Watt, the Reagan administration's secretary of the interior, began promptly in 1981 to initiate pro-development policies on federal lands in the West. This pleased western gas and oil operators and other developers, but environmental organizations like the Wilderness Society, the National Wildlife Federation, and the Sierra Club were outraged. More than a million people signed a petition calling for Watt's ouster. President Reagan came to his support, saying that the country had been victimized by "environmental extremists." Watt, he said, did not want to destroy the environment. "He just wants to recognize that people are ecology, too."[4] Watt's actions were no surprise, since he had fought environmental groups while serving as president of the Mountain States Legal Foundation.

Reagan proposed reducing the budget of the Environmental Protection Agency by 50 percent by the end of 1984. This caused worries that enforcement of rules and implementation of legislation calling for the safe disposal of tons of hazardous waste would be jeopardized. Debates over the Clean Air Act dealt with President Reagan's desire to weaken it, but measures toward that end were blocked by the Congress controlled by Democrats. Debates over air quality recurred throughout the decade, stirred by concerns over acid rain and the thinning of the ozone layer in the upper atmosphere. (Acid rain occurs when sulfur dioxide and nitrogen oxide gases—the product of fossil fuels—become sulfuric and nitric acids in the atmosphere and fall to the earth in rain or dust, contaminating water and harming plant and animal life.) Finally in 1990 the Congress enacted and President Bush signed a new comprehensive Clean Air Act that was expected to have many beneficial effects.

Endangered Species In 1982, President Reagan approved a three-year extension (with minor revisions) of the Endangered Species Act of 1973. More than 1,000 leading scientists had urged the extension, reflecting their concern for the preservation of the 763 species listed by the U.S. Fish and Wildlife Service as endangered. When the bill expired in 1985 it was extended annually by special appropriations, and the original act was reinstated in 1988. Most Americans regarded protection of endangered species as desirable but distant from their lives. Those whose jobs stood to be threatened by such protection saw things differently. For example, when the U.S. Fish and Wildlife Service determined in 1990 that the northern spotted owl was a threatened species—that is, not yet endangered but likely to be—as many as 28,000 jobs in the timber industry were in danger. The roughly 2,000 pairs of spotted owls known to exist lived in old-growth forests of Oregon and Washington, and protecting them would mean an end to harvesting this valuable timber. Environmentalists claimed that because 90 percent of the old-growth forests had already been harvested, cutting down what was left in the next decade would cost the same number of jobs. The timber industry and its supporters wanted the law to provide that an endangered species would be allowed to decline if protecting it would cause severe economic disruption.

Many environmental issues in the late 1980s affected people's lives every day. They had reasons to ask such **Concerns Close** questions as: What should be done about high indoor **to Home** levels of radon, a naturally occurring radioactive gas that seeps out of soils, building materials, and water that is found in one-third to one-fifth of the homes tested? How credible were the tests that link radon to lung cancer? Was polluted air causing increases in respiratory allergies and asthma? What should be done about the dangers resulting from disposal of medical waste products—hypodermic syringes and vials of blood like those that washed ashore on some beaches, for example? Were threats to the health of those who lived or worked in buildings where cancer-causing fibers from asbestos insulation were regularly shed into the air serious enough to require corrective actions? To these questions the easy answers were "Yes," or "Do Something," or "Fix the Problem," but taking the next steps, usually expensive ones, was never easy.

Consumer advocates in the 1980s could point to laws and regulations that had moved them toward their goal of mak- **Consumer** ing the daily lives of the American people safer and more **Protection** healthful. Protesting that government rules were too many and too complex, President Reagan began to neutralize or eliminate some of them. First, he froze all pending rules for sixty days and set up a task force on "regulatory relief" to screen out those judged unnecessary. The task force headed by Vice President George Bush soon announced that more than 100 pending regulations—most of them concerning safety, the environment, or consumer matters—were being held up for review, revision, or postponement. The main criterion in the review, Bush said, would be whether the benefits from the regulation would exceed the cost.

The Reagan administration also persuaded Congress to reduce funds needed by regulatory agencies to maintain their current levels of operation. The budget of the Consumer Product Safety Board was cut by 30 percent for 1982; that of the National Highway Traffic Safety Administration by 33 percent. The Federal Trade Commission was spared such sharp reductions only because it had been hit earlier. Pressure from both Congress and the White House, however, caused the FTC to relax a number of consumer-protection rules and regulations. Reversing earlier practices, the Reagan administration discontinued publications by the Departments of Transportation and Energy and the Occupational Safety and Health Administration that were designed to benefit consumers.

Eventually a coalition of public-interest groups protested what it called the administration's sledge-hammer approach to regulation—a sign that consumer protection would remain an issue.

Nuclear Energy Although the commercial U.S. nuclear power industry marked its twenty-fifth anniversary in 1982, it was not a happy occasion. Demand for electricity was down, the economy was weak, and most important, safety concerns were abundant. Even if accidents could be averted, disposal of highly radioactive waste products posed difficult challenges. Utility companies ordered no new nuclear power plants, and some orders for new reactors under construction were canceled. At the same time, the companies were only a decade or two away from decommissioning their older reactors, with no plans as to how to do it.

To stimulate construction of new nuclear power plants, the Department of Energy, at President Reagan's request, proposed a plan in 1982 for streamlining nuclear licensing and regulations and cutting the time and costs required to build new plants, but not much happened as a result. By 1985 about 15 percent of the nation's energy came from nuclear power plants. Although new reactors went into operation, increasing the share to about 20 percent in 1990, not a single new nuclear plant was ordered after 1978. In fact, 112 plants ordered before 1985 were canceled, some even after construction had begun.

Those who believed the dangers posed by nuclear energy were exaggerated had reason for second thoughts on April 26, 1986. On that day the name of a power station in the Soviet Union became a part of the American vocabulary: Chernobyl. A hydrogen explosion there ripped the reactor apart, sent the roof flying, set more than thirty fires, and scattered radioactive debris and extremely radioactive fuel into a 32,000-square-mile area. After two weeks of fighting deadly threats in the disaster, crews were able to begin to shut the reactor down. But much damage had already been done, and further damage resulting from radiation would continue for years. The death toll of more than thirty persons was thought to be only the beginning. Estimates of the number of deaths likely to be attributed to radioactive exposure from Chernobyl over the next three decades ranged as high as 40,000.

A decade later those estimates appear to have been too high; however, we must wait for another decade or two before an authoritative casualty count can be made. Whatever the actual toll, *Chernobyl* joined *Three Mile Island* as a code word for the potential of nuclear disaster. The need for more energy did not go away, however, and where to get it remained a dilemma.

A cover story in *Time* magazine in 1991 said of nuclear energy, "The public is afraid of it. Wall Street doesn't even want to hear about it. Most environmental groups are still vigorously antinuclear. Yet, here, there, in more places every day, support is building. The National Academy of Sciences called this month for the swift development of a new generation of nuclear plants to help fight the greenhouse effect [caused by the diminishing ozone layer]."[5] But could the industry convince the public that the new technology would be safe? And even if safe nuclear plants could be built, could their waste products be disposed of safely?

Polls showed that the religious involvement of the American people remained relatively constant throughout the decade. About 92 percent of the American people had a religious **Religion** preference, 68 percent said they were members of a church or synagogue, 40 percent said they attended church or synagogue in a given week, and 56 percent claimed religion to be very important in their lives. Mainstream denominations suffered general declines in membership, however, whereas more conservative ones held their own or gained.

Alongside traditional religious commitments, something described loosely as *New Age* gave expression to spiritual sentiments. Its basic doctrine, according to *Time* magazine, was, **New Age** "you can be whatever you want to be." Defining *New Age*, though, is difficult. It includes, says *Time*, "a whole cornucopia of beliefs, fads, rituals; some subscribe to some parts, some to others. . . . All in all, the New Age does express a cloudy sort of religion, claiming vague connections with both Christianity and the major faiths of the East, plus an occasional dab of pantheism and sorcery. The underlying faith is a lack of faith in the orthodoxies of rationalism, high technology, routine living, spiritual law and order."[6] It is not surprising that in the postmodern 1980s there were organizations, publications, radio stations, and some 2,500 bookstores to serve the growing number of persons attracted to the sort of spirituality New Age offered.

Conflict was common within religious denominations. In some instances, as in the Southern Bap- **Intradenominational** tist Convention, conservatives faced off with **Conflict** moderates over interpretation of the Bible. Year after year the conservatives consolidated their power and began to place limits on what seminary professors could teach. Some whose teaching did not meet their standards were removed. Here and there, and from time to time, moderates made modest gains in efforts to keep the conservatives from controlling everything in the church body, but before the decade ended it was apparent that moderates would soon have no power.

In other denominations—the United Presbyterian Church in the U.S.A., for example, and the Episcopal Church—differences over policies and practices created discord. As earlier, ordination of women and the churches' positions on homosexuality were at the center of prominent

The Reverend Connie A. Miller with Bishop Reginald Holle following her ordination into the ministry of the Evangelical Lutheran Church in America, July 1984. © *Connie Miller. Used by permission.*

disputes. Ordination of women as rabbis was a troubling question in Judaism. The Church of Jesus Christ of Latter-day Saints (LDS), whose members are known as Mormons, found itself at sharper-than-usual odds with the Reorganized Church of Jesus Christ of Latter Day Saints (RLDS) over a document purporting to show that Joseph Smith, founder of the LDS, had wanted his son to be his successor. Joseph Smith III had led his followers to Missouri and formed the RLDS, whereas Brigham Young had persuaded many Mormons to go with him to Utah and establish a new kingdom there. The document, "discovered" by an accomplished forger, did nothing to keep the LDS from being the fastest-growing denomination in the United States.

Catholicism   Despite longstanding opposition by Protestant denominations to diplomatic recognition of the Vatican, President Reagan appointed an ambassador to that political state and ecclesiastical entity in 1984. A coalition of Protestant groups responded by filing a lawsuit to nullify the new relationship, claiming it violated guarantees of separation of church and state.

Discord existed within the Roman Catholic Church, too, providing further evidence that the Church once run with unquestioned authority now had to cope with dissent and disobedience. In 1986 the Vatican ordered Father Charles E. Curran, who taught moral theology at the Catholic University of America, to retract his statements on the moral authority of the Church on such matters as birth control, abortion, homosexuality, premarital sex, and divorce. When Curran said that "for reasons of conscience" he could not change his positions, the Vatican withdrew his credentials for teaching as a Catholic theologian. Around the same time, the Vatican reassigned some of the authority of Seattle's Archbishop Raymond G. Hunthausen. It considered his teachings on birth control, homosexuality, and nuclear arms to be too liberal.

While the discord in these instances involved a scholar and an archbishop, there is little doubt that the views of Curran and Hunthausen were shared widely among Catholic laity. Perhaps that is why the Vatican felt it necessary to crack down on them, hoping its action would keep discord from spreading. To reinforce the Church's position on its authority—as well as on such matters as birth control, medical procedures using artificial means in human reproduction (in vitro fertilization, described earlier), and abortion—Pope John Paul II undertook a highly publicized tour of the United States in September 1987. His reception was favorable in the nine cities he visited.

Around the same time, charges of sexual misconduct made against prominent members of the clergy brought Catholicism unfavorable attention. Most prominent among those charged was the archbishop of Atlanta; revelations of his "intimate relationship" with a woman led him to resign. Accusations against parish priests known well in their own communities caused greater concern. Accusations of misconduct gained credibility by reports of a 25-year celibacy study done by a former priest, now a psychotherapist, that reported significant degrees of sexual and homosexual involvements among priests. Church officials claimed that because the study was based on interviews with persons who were in treatment for sexual misconduct or who had been touched by such misconduct, it was distorted.

For television evangelists, 1987 was a bad year. It started when Oral Roberts, one of the best known **Televangelism's** among them, announced that God would call him **Scandals** "home" unless his followers contributed $8 million to a medical fund he had started. The money came in, but Roberts's fellow evangelists thought his announcement had tarnished fund-raising practices for all of them. They all depended on contributions from viewers and could not afford to have their lifelines jeopardized.

The more widely publicized scandal occurred in 1987 when other televangelists accused Jim Bakker, the leading public figure in an organization known as PTL (Praise the Lord, or People That Love), of an extramarital sexual encounter. In addition, they claimed, Bakker had paid more than $250,000 to silence the person with whom it occurred. One of the accusers, the Reverend Jimmy Swaggart, remarked that "the gospel of Jesus Christ has never sunk to such a level as it has today."[7] When the scandal forced Bakker to resign, PTL leaders asked televangelist Jerry Falwell to rescue the organization. Despite strenuous fundraising efforts, PTL soon declared bankruptcy. The entire scandal placed under further scrutiny the practices used by televangelists to raise funds and called into question their high incomes and lavish lifestyles. Eventually Bakker was convicted of 24 counts of fraud, sentenced to a prison term of 45 years, and fined $500,000. In the next year, Jimmy Swaggart himself was forced to confess to his Baton Rouge, Louisiana, congregation that he had committed a "sin," later reported as involving sexual misconduct. His denomination, the Assemblies of God, suspended him from preaching for a year, and when he refused to comply, it removed him from the ministry. Before long he was preaching again as an independent minister.

New Christian Right
          Attempts continued by what came to be known as the New Christian Right to change American institutions. For example, it sought to have public schools teach theories concerning the origins of the universe and humankind based on a literal interpretation of the Bible. Advocating what it called scientific creationism, the New Christian Right argued that schools taught theories of evolution as though they were a religion and that their own theories merited equal time. Laws in Arkansas and Louisiana requiring schools to teach "creation science" were ruled unconstitutional in both instances, but that did not deter leaders of the New Christian Right from trying to find new ways to accomplish their goals—ways that usually met the same fate in the courts.

The New Christian Right also pushed for a constitutional amendment that would have allowed voluntary individual or group prayer in public schools, overturning the 1962 Supreme Court decision it judged to be so objectionable. President Reagan sent a proposed amendment to Congress in 1982, but it died in committee. The intensity of the Christian Right's commitment to an amendment increased when a Supreme Court ruling in 1985 seemed to put more mortar in the wall of separation between church and state by invalidating an Alabama law that permitted a one-minute period of silence daily "for meditation or voluntary prayer" in public schools.

When the Centers for Disease Control (CDC) reported the first
cases of AIDS in June 1981, it opened one of the decade's big　**AIDS**
stories. At first awareness of AIDS spread slowly, but within five
years just about everyone knew that scientists, physicians, hospitals, and
the victims and their friends and families faced dreadful challenges. In
1986 the Department of Health and Human Services (HHS) estimated
that the number of cases and deaths would increase tenfold in the next
five years. In 1991, predicted HHS, some 50,000 Americans would die of
AIDS—more than the number killed in most years in automobile accidents. That prediction may have been too grim. In 1990 there were 29,781
deaths, bringing the total since the Center began keeping records in 1981
to 98,350. With about 140,000 cases known, however, the CDC made
another grim prediction: that the AIDS death total could reach 340,000
by 1993.

Reporting on the spread of AIDS in 1986, the Department of Health
and Human Services noted that about 70 percent of the victims of AIDS
were homosexual or bisexual men. This prompted those who regarded
homosexuality and bisexuality as sinful to call AIDS God's punishment.
They judged the 25 percent of the victims who were intravenous drug
users infected by contaminated needles in much the same way. The fact
that more than one-third of the known cases were in New York and San
Francisco gave those hostile to homosexuality an opportunity to con-
demn these cities as centers of wickedness.

Wherever cases appeared, AIDS victims were kept at arms' length,
even though it was well established that the virus that caused AIDS
could not be spread by casual contact. In well-publicized instances that
caused controversy across the nation, even children who had been infected through blood transfusions were kept out of the schools they had
been attending. The gravity of the AIDS epidemic, lack of information
about the disease, and attitudes about it compelled the federal government to educate the American public about its nature and consequences.
In May 1988 the government took the unprecedented step of mailing an
explicit eight-page booklet, *Understanding AIDS*, to 106 million households.

An often-controversial search continued for vaccines
to prevent the further spread of AIDS and cure existing　　　**Quest for**
cases. In 1989, two studies showed that the drug AZT　**Treatment and**
offered hope as a treatment for AIDS. Initially AZT had　　**Prevention**
been used to treat severely ill patients, but the studies
indicated that it could delay the onset of symptoms if it was administered when early signs of damage to the immune system appeared. But
AZT was not without side effects. The National Cancer Institute reported
in 1990 that persons with AIDS who received it stood a nearly 50

Understanding AIDS

A Message From The Surgeon General

This brochure has been sent to you by the Government of the United States. In preparing it, we have consulted with the top health experts in the country.

I feel it is important that you have the best information now available for fighting the AIDS virus, a health problem that the President has called "Public Enemy Number One."

Stopping AIDS is up to you, your family and your loved ones.

Some of the issues involved in this brochure may not be things you are used to discussing openly. I can easily understand that. But now you must discuss them. We all must know about AIDS. Read this brochure and talk about it with those you love. Get involved. Many schools, churches, synagogues, and community groups offer AIDS education activities.

I encourage you to practice responsible behavior based on understanding and strong personal values. This is what you can do to stop AIDS.

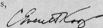

C. Everett Koop, M.D., Sc.D.
Surgeon General

Este folleto sobre el SIDA se publica en Español.
Para solicitar una copia, llame al 1-800-344-SIDA.

U.S. Department of Health
& Human Services
Public Health Service
Centers for Disease Control
P.O. Box 6003
Rockville, MD 20850

Official Business

BULK RATE
CARRIER ROUTE PRESORT
POSTAGE & FEES PAID
PHS/CDC
Permit No. G-284

POSTAL CUSTOMER

HHS Publication No. (CDC) HHS-88-8404. Reproduction of the contents of this brochure is encouraged.

This eight-page brochure, printed so that it could be posted on bulletin boards, was mailed by Surgeon General C. Everett Koop to 106 million households.

percent chance of developing lymphoma after three years on the drug. The cost of $7,000–$8,000 per year for those being treated with AZT also inhibited its widespread use. Although other therapies were beginning to be developed, it was too early to determine their effectiveness.

Understandably, the slow progress in AIDS research coupled with homosexuality as a culturally divisive issue made this a hot political subject.

The fact that discord in cultural standoffs over abortion would continue at the national level was certain. The same **Abortion** was true in states and localities. The fact that political solutions to differences over abortion would be elusive was also certain. But would Supreme Court decisions effectively overturn *Roe v. Wade*, thereby placing responsibilities for abortion law in the hands of state legislatures? Would there be an amendment to the Constitution of the United Sates outlawing most abortions—or all of them? If nothing changed at the federal level, how would state legislatures respond to pressures from all sides on abortion issues? How would men and women with no strong feelings on abortion issues respond to ongoing debates about it?

Seeking one kind of answer to these questions were those who called themselves pro-choice. Some on this side con- **Pro-Choice** tended that the Supreme Court's ruling in *Roe v. Wade* meant that decisions concerning abortions should be made exclusively by pregnant women in consultation with their physicians. The circumstances that led to the pregnancy, the marital status of the woman, the health of the woman and child and the economic prospects facing them, the size of the family a new baby would enter, the convenience or inconvenience of bearing a child at a given time—all these were matters to be taken into account. But they believed that to have or not have an abortion ultimately should be the woman's choice alone. There should be no interference from the government or parties not directly affected by her decision.

Others on the pro-choice side took a less expansive view. Believing that abortions should be legal and safe, they also believed that they should occur only rarely. They considered the reasons for seeking an abortion to be relevant. If the health of the woman was in jeopardy, or if the pregnancy resulted from a rape or incest, or if there were critically important personal considerations, they regarded abortions as regrettable but permissible. They saw the need for pregnant women to be counseled, for involvement of other family members in abortion decisions, and for measures that would discourage what some called abortion on demand. Despite personal differences over abortion practices, pro-choice encompassed all who approved of *Roe v. Wade*.

On the other side were those who described their position as pro-life. Some contended that abortions should not be per- **Pro-Life** mitted under any circumstances. Some were willing to take into account the health of the mother in extreme circumstances. Some agreed reluctantly that it might be permissible in some cases to terminate pregnancies caused by rape or incest. The more unyielding the position

Pro-choice and pro-life demonstrators confront each other at the Preterm Clinic in Boston in 1989. © *Ellen Shub. Used by permission.*

taken by pro-lifers, the harsher the language they used. The most ex-treme pro-lifers referred to persons who performed abortions as baby-killers, condemned women who had abortions and the doctors who performed them, and berated those who supported a woman's right to choose whether or not to have an abortion. The more unyielding their stands, the more aggressive they became in their actions. Under the lead-ership of organizations like Operation Rescue, some picketed clinics where abortions were performed, marched outside the homes of physi-cians who performed abortions, distributed gruesome pictures of aborted fetuses, and judged political candidates solely on their stand on abortion. Some foes of abortion rights considered such radical methods of protest to be counterproductive, but they could not persuade those who used them to act otherwise.

Churches and Abortion
Abortion was a topic of debate within religious denom-inations. Many churches took an official position, either favoring abortion rights or opposing them. The Roman Catholic Church took a rigid position in opposition, which put it at odds with prominent members of the church, including

the 1984 vice presidential candidate, Geraldine Ferraro, New York Governor Mario Cuomo, and Massachusetts senator Edward Kennedy. Also at odds with the Church's teaching were the many Catholic women who had abortions. According to some surveys, Catholic women had abortions in proportions as high as non-Catholic women, if not higher, possibly because of the pregnancies resulting from honoring the Church's opposition to the use of artificial methods of contraception.[8]

In the midst of the debates, how many lives were touched directly by decisions on abortion? A statistical summary compiled by the Park Ridge Center for the Study of Faith, Health, and Ethics in 1990 provides an-   **Lives Touched by Abortions**

swers. Noting that there is some variation in the numbers provided by the Centers for Disease Control, the Alan Guttmacher Institute, national polling agencies, and other independent sources, the Center found agreement that approximately 1.6 million American women had abortions each year. About 80 percent of these women were unmarried, 26 percent were teenagers, 33 percent were 20–24 years of age, and the rest were 25 years old or older. For 57 percent of the women, the abortion was their first; for 27 percent, their second; for 11 percent, their third; and for 5 percent, their fourth. Ninety-one percent of all abortions were performed within the first twelve weeks of pregnancy and only 1 percent after twenty-one weeks of pregnancy. Nationally, about one in four pregnancies ends by abortion. As far as economic factors are concerned, low-income women were approximately three times more likely to have abortions than those with higher incomes. Also, women in minority groups were more likely to have abortions than were white women.[9]

At the national level, proposals for constitutional amendments outlawing abortions made no progress despite President Reagan's endorsement. The most   **Abortion Politics**

that opponents of abortion could accomplish was to deny federal funding for abortions for poor women who had become pregnant because of rape or incest. For eight years the denial survived challenges, but in 1989 Congress reversed itself. However, it failed to override President Bush's veto and the denial of funding continued.

State legislatures dealt with abortion issues in various ways. Some states passed laws prohibiting the spending of public funds for abortions. Some required parents or spouses of women seeking abortions to give their consent. On occasion, these laws faced legal challenges. In 1981, in what hinted at a chipping away of *Roe v. Wade*, the Supreme Court upheld a Utah law requiring physicians to notify parents of minors seeking abortions. Two years later, however, the Court reaffirmed a woman's constitutional right to an abortion by disallowing local ordinances that attempted to curtail it. Addressing a challenge to *Roe v. Wade* that was supported by the Reagan administration, the Court in 1986 struck down a Pennsylvania abortion law, asserting its belief that the law would in-timidate women seeking an end to an unwanted pregnancy.

The chipping away met with success, however, in 1989, when the Su-preme Court (in *Webster v. Reproductive Health Services,* while upholding a woman's constitutional right to an abortion) let stand a Missouri law that prohibited publicly employed medical personnel from performing or assisting in abortion procedures unless the mother's life was in dan-ger. It also barred the use of public buildings for performing abortions. In cases involving women who had been pregnant for twenty weeks or longer, the law required doctors to conduct tests to see if the fetus could live outside the womb. Those opposed to abortions applauded the de-cision and vowed to work for similar legislation in other states. In 1990 the Supreme Court upheld several state laws requiring parental notifi-cation before an abortion could be performed on an unmarried minor.

Continuing Discord over Abortion For all the debates, laws, and court decisions concerning abortion, the standoff over abortion issues persisted. Quests for middle ground proved fruitless. James Davison Hunter, author of *The Culture Wars,* aptly summarized the standoff in an article entitled "What Americans Really Think about Abortion." The disagreement over abortion is not a legal problem, he wrote, nor are laws the solution. It would be dreaming for abortion rights advocates to think that their opposition will tire and go away. Similarly, foes of abortion rights should not imagine that all would be well if *Roe v. Wade* were to be overturned. Legal outcomes that might develop would not settle the dispute or ease tensions, since "the abortion controversy is in its nature a culture controversy. No matter what hap-pens in courts and legislatures, the abortion issue will not disappear until we somehow reach a greater consensus with respect to the standards of justice and goodness our communities will abide by. If there is to be an abortion law that is politically sustainable over the long haul, then, the fundamental task must be one of moral suasion."[10] At the end of the decade there was little reason for optimism that moral suasion could diminish the discord, but conscientious men and women had not given up on trying.

Homosexuality As already noted, the AIDS crisis and disputes in churches over ordination of homosexuals brought in-creased attention to homosexuality. While the attention was often unfavorable in tone and substance, it also broke taboos against speaking about homosexuality. Some consider the wider acceptability of homosexuality resulting from discussions about the AIDS crisis as one of the few silver linings of AIDS. Gay men and lesbians, many of whom had come "out of the closet" reluctantly, fearing social and employment discrimination, worked toward greater acceptance, if not approval, of their lifestyles. Small steps in that direction came with such things as the sympathetic, nonjudgmental depiction of homosexuals in movies, most notably in *Victor/Victoria*. Several decades earlier, homosexuals had been portrayed in movies as being driven to suicide by disorders from which they suffered.

Efforts to gain protection through political processes proved difficult, as an experience in Houston revealed. In 1984, Houston's City Council approved amendments to existing laws to prohibit employment discrimination on the basis of sexual orientation. A group of conservative political and religious leaders, however, conducted a petition drive that succeeded in forcing a public vote on these amendments. Early in the following year, as a sign of what was to come in other cities and states, voters overturned the amendments by a margin of 4 to 1. For example, several years later voters in Oregon repealed an order by the governor banning state government discrimination against homosexuals. Not all news concerning civil rights for gay men and lesbians was adverse. In 1989 voters in Massachusetts approved a measure that prohibited discrimination in employment, housing, public accommodations, credit, and insurance on the basis of one's sexual orientation. Wisconsin was the only other state with such a law, but by 1995 similar laws had been enacted in seven additional states.

A 1986 ruling by the Supreme Court was a setback for homosexuals. By a 5-to-4 decision, the Court said that a Georgia sodomy law making certain sexual practices illegal, even when performed in private by consenting adults, was constitutional. Writing for the majority, Justice Byron R. White asserted that the idea that "any kind of private sexual conduct between consenting adults is constitutionally insulated from state prosecution is unsupportable."[11]

Homosexuality and the Law

On one side in the controversies were those who condemned homosexuality because, as they saw it, the Bible condemned it. Citing selected texts in the books of Leviticus (18:22 and 20:13), Romans (1:26–27), and I Corinthians (6:9), they claimed that they had no choice but to regard homosexuality as contrary to God's plan and therefore as sinful. Fear of differences (in particular, fear that homosexuals might influence their children to choose to be homosexual) no doubt caused them to strongly uphold these texts.

Choosing Sides

Homosexuals and those who shared their concerns over discrimination generally believed that homosexuality was not a conscious, individual choice. Rather, they believed, its origins are uncertain. Some attributed it to genetic make-up; others to such factors as hormonal influences in the womb and prenatal and early infant environmental factors. Nature, in their view, not nurture or choice, determined who would be homosexual. Scientific studies increasingly supported these interpretations of homosexuality, but not everyone accepted their validity. Indeed, for those who took the most rigid positions against the rights of homosexuals to be protected against discrimination, it seemed that no study could convince them to change their minds.

Gun Control   The attempted assassination of President Reagan on March 30, 1981, along with concern over the use of handguns in crimes, led to standoffs between those who believed that government should impose controls on the ownership and use of firearms and those who opposed such controls. Individuals who sought controls found a persuasive symbol in Jim Brady, President Reagan's press secretary who had suffered permanent physical and mental damage in the assassination attempt. His wife, Sarah, became a lobbyist for gun control. The National Rifle Association (NRA), with its large membership and the money it used to influence elections, rallied opponents around the claim that the Second Amendment guaranteed "the right of the people to keep and bear arms." The NRA argued that any restriction at all would compromise its position, so it opposed even the most modest measures. Opponents argued that the NRA's position ignored the conditional clause in the Second Amendment: *"A well regulated militia being necessary to the security of a free State,* the right of the people to keep and bear arms shall not be infringed."

How big an issue was gun control? If figures on deaths by handguns matter, it was a big one. In 1990 there were 10,657 deaths by handguns, compared with virtually insignificant numbers in countries where gun ownership is not so widespread—87 in Japan, 68 in Canada, and 22 in the United Kingdom. In any case, passions on both sides of gun control issues run deep and strong. As the 1980s ended, a desire to find common ground did not exist.

NOTES

1. National Commission on Excellence in Education, USA Research, ed., *A Nation at Risk: The Full Account* (Cambridge, Mass.: USA Research, 1984), 5, 69–79.

2. The following reports are cited in Lawrence A. Cremin, "Grading America's Public Schools," *The 1984 World Book Year Book* (Chicago: World Book, Inc., 1984), 66–83; Twentieth Century Fund's Task Force on Federal Elementary and Secondary Education Policy, *Making the Grade*; College Board's Educational Equality Project, *Academic Preparation for College: What Students Need to Know and Be Able to Do*; Education Commission of the States' Task Force on Education for Economic Growth, *Action for Excellence*; Joint Center for Political Studies, *A Policy Framework for Racial Justice*; National Science Board's Commission on Precollege Education in Mathematics, Science, and Technology, *Educating Americans for the 21st Century: A Plan of Action for Improving Mathematics, Science and Technology Education for All American Elementary and Secondary Schools so That Their Achievement Is the Best in the World by 1995.*

3. Ibid.

4. *The 1982 World Book Year Book*, s.v. "Congress of the United States," 259.

5. *Time*, April 29, 1991, 54.

6. *Time*, December 7, 1987, 64.

7. Quoted in Sean Wilentz, "The Trials of Televangelism," in *Culture in an Age of Money: The Legacy of the 1980s in America*, ed. Nicolaus Mills (Chicago: Ivan R. Dee, 1990), 142.

8. *Abortion, Religion, and the State Legislature after Webster: A Guide for the 1990s* (Chicago: Park Ridge Center for the Study of Health, Faith, and Ethics, 1990).

9. James R. Kelly, "Catholic Abortion Rates and the Abortion Controversy," *America*, February 4, 1989, 82–83, 85.

10. James Davison Hunter, "What Americans Really Think about Abortion," *First Things: A Monthly Journal of Religion and Public Life*, July 1992, 13.

11. *Bowers v. Hardwick*, 478 U.S. 186, 204 (1986). *Newsweek*, 14 July 1986, described the controversy surrounding the decision.

33

Prospects

When the 1980s drew to a close, there were few signs that
sources of discord would soon fade away. Moreover, **Latent Events**
what historians call the latent events of the 1960s through
the 1980s meant that discord was likely to broaden and deepen. Latent
events—in contrast to events that are seen as they occur and have immediate, observable consequences—are generally unnoticed, partly because their consequences are postponed. Latent events of the decades
treated in this book, particularly the 1980s, carry prospects of consequences awaiting future generations of Americans.

Some latent events merit mention here. Interpretations of their meaning, speculation on the nature of their consequences, and ideas on how
they should be dealt with are left to the book's readers.

The 1970s and 1980s were decades of stagnation or income loss for the poor and the American middle class. The **Income**
wealthy and very wealthy, on the other hand, fared very **Disparities**
well. Robert J. Samuelson reports in *The Good Life and Its
Discontents* that the income of Americans in the poorest fifth of the population increased 2.9 percent (computed in 1993 dollars) between 1970
and 1990. The increase for the second fifth amounted to 7 percent. In the
highest fifth, the increase was 31.3 percent, and in the richest 5 percent
of the population it was 35.3 percent.[1] Figures produced by the Congressional Budget Office indicate that when income groups are shown
by tenths, the bottom four groups suffered income declines between
1977 and 1988 (measured in 1987 dollars). In the next five groups the

increases ranged from 0.2 percent to 7.9 percent. The top tenth showed an increase of 27.4 percent.[2]

Children in Poverty
The widening gap between rich and poor Americans hit children particularly hard. In 1989, 20 percent of the nation's children lived in poverty, compared with 14 percent in 1973. The fact that 36 percent of the girls from welfare families found themselves on welfare as adults at the end of the 1980s, compared with only 9 percent from nonwelfare families, is evidence of poverty's self-perpetuating nature.

Aging Population
Each year there were more elderly persons in the United States than ever before, and the proportion of elderly grew steadily. When the baby boomers begin to reach age 65 in 2011, the growth in numbers and proportions will be dramatic. Furthermore, the elderly are living longer. Census figures show that in 1960 there were 900,000 persons 85 years old and older. By 1990 that number had more than tripled. Projections indicate that in the next three decades it will more than double, and by the year 2050 it will reach almost 18 million.

The economic status of the elderly improved dramatically between 1960 and the 1990s. In 1960, according to Lester Thurow, an economics professor at the Massachusetts Institute of Technology, the average 70-year-old spent only 60 percent as much as a 30-year-old. By the mid-1990s, "that 70-year-old was spending 30 percent more." Social Security and Medicare, supplemented by private pension plans and savings, made that possible. By then, however, sustaining Social Security, Medicare, and other entitlement programs benefiting the elderly consumed about half the federal budget, excluding interest on the national debt. Even though children living in poverty outnumber senior citizens who are poor, says Thurow, "the government spends nine times as much per person on the elderly (who vote) as it does on the young (who don't)." Because benefits derived from Social Security by most persons exceeded their working-years contributions, those benefits were funded by persons currently paying Social Security taxes. When baby boomers reach retirement age, the beneficiaries will substantially outnumber the payers.[3]

The Changing Population Mix
Between 1980 and 1990 the African American population increased by 13 percent, compared with a 6 percent increase in the white population. The 30 million African Americans represented 12.1 percent of the nation's population in 1990. Projections based on Census Bureau data indicate that that percentage will increase to 16.2 by 2050. The Hispanic population grew at five times the national average, reaching the 20 million mark in 1989. More than 60 percent had Mexican roots, although the fastest-growing segment came from South and Central America. Hispanics (of any race) made up more than 9 percent of the total population in 1990.

They are expected to account for 21.1 percent of the population by 2050. Asian American immigration in the 1980s helped that segment of the population grow from 1.5 percent to 3 percent of the U.S. total, pointing toward an Asian and Pacific Islander representation of 10.7 percent in 2050. By then, the percentage of the population counted as "non-Hispanic white" will decline to 52.7 percent, from 75.7 in 1990.

Shifts in political power accompanied the growing in-equality of income. The Democratic Party once repre-   **Power Shifts** sented the interests of Americans at the lower end of the income scale. Party organizations at the ward and precinct level spread the word about the party's candidates and goals and made sure that voters got to the polls on election days. For a number of reasons, some of them noted in this book, this party lost much of its former strength, resulting in a loss of influence by poorer citizens. Accompanying this decline, as described by Thomas Byrne Edsall, was "the growing dominance over politics of a new fund-raising, polling, consulting, and electioneering elite" who run "technology-based campaigns dependent on television and on vast sums of money."[4] Increasing amounts of money for political campaigns came through political-action committees (PACs), and increasing amounts of power were wielded by lobbyists. The sense of powerlessness experienced by persons in lower income groups probably accounts for their lower turnout at elections.

Robert Samuelson's book, subtitled *The American Dream in the Age of Entitlement, 1945–1995*, treats what   **Disenchantment** he calls "the paradox of our time." Americans, he says,   **with Institutions** "are feeling bad about doing well." Compared with their forebears, they were more prosperous, enjoyed better health, lived longer, faced fewer discriminatory practices, and experienced more personal freedom. In addition, the government's safety net for the poor, disabled, and elderly was something never before provided. Yet, Samuelson says, "Americans are routinely glum," living in "an almost permanent state of grumpiness." The reason for this paradox "is *entitlement*," that is, "the belief that certain things are (or ought to be) guaranteed to us." Those "certain things" include everything that would make life ideal.[5] (Samuelson might have called attention, too, to forces that nourish grumpiness, such as negative political advertising, the negative tone and content of radio talk shows, and the negative perspective in many journalists' reporting.)

Entitlements lead to demands. When responses to demands fall short of expectations, disillusionment sets in. That, in turn, leads to loss of confidence in those expected to deliver on the demands. Opinion surveys recorded sharp declines in confidence in a number of institutions between 1966 and 1985. Samuelson reports the following such declines: Congress, 42 to 16 percent; the executive branch, 41 to 15 percent; major companies, 55 to 19 percent; the press, 29 to 16 percent; colleges and universities, 61 to 35 percent; and medicine, 73 to 35 percent. For all except major companies, the decline continued. Ranking lowest in 1994 was Congress, at 8 percent; next came the executive branch, at 12 percent.[6]

Nonetheless, demands on Congress and the president, as well as on state governments, had produced results. Citing a survey of the Congressional Research Service, Samuelson shows that in 1992 almost 52 percent of the nation's families received at least one form of government payment. More than one-fourth received Social Security benefits, and almost that many were served by Medicare. Other payments were for food stamps, unemployment compensation, school lunches, government retirement, Aid to Families with Dependent Children, energy assistance, and education assistance. According to Samuelson, 30 percent of the families in the richest fifth of the population received at least one benefit, and 37 percent of those in the next fifth did so as well.[7]

Conclusion   Given the decades of discord leading into the 1990s, are there reasons to hope that harmony can *ever* be reached on critical issues in American society? Does the diffusion of interests resulting from postmodern behaviors and the power of technologies allow room for the American people to pull together in common cause toward that end?

The nation's resources seem to be sufficient to allow a "Yes" to both questions. Among those resources, surprisingly, is discord itself. As noted earlier, discord can be constructive as well as destructive. We find a good reminder of this in the lives of John Adams and Thomas Jefferson. After collaborating in the founding of the United States, they became bitter rivals. The sting of Adams's loss of the presidency to his vice president, Thomas Jefferson, in 1800 lingered for more than a decade. Correspondence between Mrs. (Abigail) Adams and Mr. Jefferson eventually opened the way to reconciliation.

In 1813, John Adams wrote to Jefferson: "You and I ought not to die, before We have explained ourselves to each other."[8] In response, Jefferson stated his opinion "on a point on which we differ, not with a view to controversy, for we are both too old to change opinions which are the result of a long life of inquiry and reflection." Then he recalled that the two of them had "acted in perfect harmony thro' a long and perilous contest for our liberty and independence." Although the nation acquired a constitution neither of them thought perfect, both considered it "as competent to render our fellow-citizens the happiest and the securest on whom the sun has ever shone." (Adams served as ambassador to England and Jefferson to France during the Constitutional Convention, so neither had a hand in writing it.) "If we do not think exactly alike as to its imperfections," Jefferson continued, "it matters little to our country which, after devoting to it long lives of disinterested labor, we have delivered over to our successors in life, who will be able to take care of it, and of themselves."

Jefferson, with Adams's assistance, stated the ideals of the United States eloquently in the Declaration of Independence, including equality and certain unalienable rights, among them life, liberty, and the pursuit of happiness. The Constitution, drafted by others during months of discord—only 39 of the 55 men in attendance signed it—states further ideals in its preamble: a more perfect union, justice, domestic tranquility, a common defense, the general welfare, and liberty. Reiterated frequently through the decades, the ideals of the Declaration and the Constitution provide the American people with common ground on which to stand. Now we face the challenge of finding the will, individually and collectively, to use the resources available for addressing problems of discord and using discord itself constructively.

Never have there been three decades in the history of the United States that could be called "decades of *accord*," nor will there be in the future. A *perfect* society, embodying all the nation's professed ideals, is beyond human reach. A *better* society is not, especially when it is built by people who take the time to explain themselves to one another. The phrase is trite but true: Where there is a will, there is a way. Even in discordant times.

NOTES

1. Robert Samuelson, *The Good Life and Its Discontents: The American Dream in the Age of Entitlement, 1945–1955* (New York: Random House, 1995), 72.

2. Cited in Thomas Byrne Edsall, "The Return of Inequality," *Atlantic Monthly*, June 1988, 89.

3. Lester Thurow, "The Birth of a Revolutionary Class," *New York Times Magazine*, May 19, 1996, 46–47.

4. Thomas Byrne Edsall, "The Return of Inequality," *Atlantic Monthly*, June 1988, 87–94.

5. Samuelson, *The Good Life and Its Discontents*, 3–4.

6. Ibid., 51.

7. Ibid., 158.

8. John Adams [July 15, 1813], *The Adams-Jefferson Letters: The Complete Correspondence between Thomas Jefferson and Abigail and John Adams*, ed. Lester J. Cappon (Chapel Hill: University of North Carolina Press, 1959, 1988), 358; Thomas Jefferson [October 28, 1813], *Thomas Jefferson: Writings*, ed. Merrill D. Peterson (New York: Library of America, 1984), 1310.

•

Selected Bibliography

Many sources used in writing this volume are identified in the chapter notes. The more significant among them are listed also here, as are other sources that were consulted but not cited in chapter notes. They are organized here by category or general topic as representative of works that will be useful to readers seeking further information.

GENERAL

These works provide overviews, chronologies, and specific information:

Glennon, Lorraine, ed. *Our Times: The Illustrated History of the 20th Century.* Atlanta: Turner Publishing, 1995.

Gordon, Lois, and Alan Gordon. *The Columbia Chronicle of American Life, 1910–1992.* New York: Columbia University Press, 1995.

Jonas, Susan, and Marilyn Nissenson. *Going Going Gone: Vanishing Americana.* San Francisco: Chronicle Books, 1994.

Trager, James. *The People's Chronology: A Year-by-Year Record of Human Events from Prehistory to the Present.* New York: Henry Holt, 1994.

World Book Year Books. Chicago: World Book, 1961–1991.

Two multi-volume encyclopedias are particularly valuable for identifying themes, placing events in historical context, amplifying facts and judgments, and finding leads to additional sources:

Cayton, Mary Kupec, Elliott J. Gorn, and Peter W. Williams, eds. *Encyclopedia of American Social History,* 3 vols. New York: Charles Scribner's Sons, 1993.

Stanley I. Kutler, ed. *Encyclopedia of the United States in the Twentieth Century,* 4 vols. New York: Charles Scribner's Sons, 1996.

MAGAZINES

The following magazines provide contemporary accounts of events in the decades treated:

Business Week

Life

Newsweek

Smithsonian

Time

U.S. News & World Report

STATISTICS

Most of the statistics in this book can be traced to:

U.S. Department of Commerce, Bureau of the Census. *Historical Statistics of the United States, Colonial Times to 1970*, 2 vols. Washington, D.C.: U.S. Department of Commerce, Bureau of the Census, 1970.
———. *Statistical Abstract of the United States.* Washington, D.C.: U.S. Department of Commerce, Bureau of the Census, published annually.

Statistical information is also found in:

Chadwick, Bruce A., and Tim B. Heaton, eds. *Statistical Handbook on the American Family.* Phoenix, Ariz.: Oryx Press, 1992.
Hacker, Andrew. *U/S: A Statistical Portrait of the American People.* New York: Viking Press, 1983.
Roberts, Sam. *Who We Are: A Statistical Portrait of America Based on the Latest U.S. Census.* New York: Times Books, 1993.
Wattenberg, Ben J. *The First Universal Nation: Leading Indicators and Ideas about the Surge of America in the 1990s.* New York: Free Press, 1991.
———. *The Real America: A Surprising Examination of the State of the Union.* Garden City, N.Y.: Doubleday, 1974.
Wattenberg, Ben J., with Richard H. Scammon. *This USA: An Unexpected Family Portrait of 194,067,296 Americans Drawn from the Census.* Garden City, N.Y.: Doubleday, 1965.

Two volumes edited by Eric Miller for Research Alert provide statistics and point readers to additional sources:

Miller, Eric. *Future Vision: The 189 Most Important Trends of the 1990s.* Naperville, Ill.: Sourcebooks Trade, 1991.
———. *The Lifestyle Odyssey.* Naperville, Ill.: Sourcebooks Trade, 1992.

PUBLIC OPINION

Public opinion data can be found in various Gallup publications—*Gallup Opinion Index* (1965–1981), *Gallup Poll Report* (1982–1989), and *Gallup Poll Monthly*. (1990–), published by the Gallup Poll, Princeton, N.J. Other works cited throughout this bibliography also provide statistical information relevant to daily life.

Gallup, George H. *The Gallup Poll: Public Opinion, 1935–1971*, 3 vols. New York: Random House, 1972.
———. *The Gallup Poll: Public Opinion, 1972–1977*, 2 vols. Wilmington, Del.: Scholarly Resources, 1978.

CONTEXTUAL WORKS

A number of books describe the larger political, economic, and diplomatic-military context in which daily life occurs. Although they are cited in chapter notes, their comprehensiveness warrants mentioning them here:

Boyer, Paul. *Promises to Keep: The United States since World War II*. Lexington, Mass.: D.C. Heath, 1995.
Chafe, William H. *The Unfinished Journey: America since World War II*, 3d ed. New York: Oxford University Press, 1995.
Rosenberg, Norman L., and Emily S. Rosenberg. *In Our Times: America Since World War II*, 5th ed. Englewood Cliffs, N.J.: Prentice-Hall, 1995.

1960S AND 1970S

Works on the 1960s, some of which carry their accounts into the 1970s, are plentiful. The most useful for information and insight on daily life and for extensive bibliographic information are among those listed here. Interpretative accounts of the 1970s and 1980s remain to be written.

Anderson, Terry. *The Movement and the 1960s*. New York: Oxford University Press, 1995.
Blum, John Morton. *Years of Discord: American Politics and Society, 1961–1974*. New York: W.W. Norton, 1991.
Burner, David. *Making Peace with the 60s*. Princeton, N.J.: Princeton University Press, 1996.
Caute, David. *The Year of the Barricades: A Journey through 1968*. New York: Harper & Row, 1988.
Collier, Peter, and David Horowitz. *Destructive Generation: Second Thoughts about the 1960s*. New York: Summit Books, 1989.
Gitlin, Todd. *The Sixties: Years of Hope, Days of Rage*, rev. ed. New York: Bantam Books, 1993.
Jackson, Rebecca. *The 1960s: An Annotated Bibliography of Social and Political Movements in the United States*. Westport, Conn.: Greenwood Press, 1992.

Kaiser, Charles A. *1968 in America: Music, Politics, Chaos, Counterculture, and the Shaping of a Generation.* New York: Weidenfeld & Nicolson, 1988.

Matusow, Allen J. *The Unraveling of America: A History of Liberalism in the 1960s.* New York: Harper & Row, 1984.

Miller, Douglas T. *On Our Own: Americans in the 1960s.* Lexington, Mass.: D.C. Heath, 1996.

Miller, James. *Democracy Is in the Streets: From Port Huron to the Siege of Chicago.* New York: Simon & Schuster, 1987.

O'Neill, William L. *Coming Apart: An Informal History of America in the 1960's.* Chicago: Quadrangle Books, 1971.

Schachtman, Tom. *Decade of Shocks: Dallas to Watergate, 1963–1974.* New York: Poseidon Press, 1983.

Steigerwald, David. *The 1960s and the End of the Modern Era.* New York: St. Martin's Press, 1995.

Stern, Jane, and Michael Stern. *Sixties People.* New York: Knopf, 1990.

Unger, Irwin. *Turning Point, 1968.* New York: Scribner's Sons, 1988.

Viorst, Milton. *Fire in the Streets: America in the 1960s.* New York: Simon & Schuster, 1979.

ABORTION

Ginsburg, Faye D. *Contested Lives: The Abortion Debate in an American Community.* Berkeley: University of California Press, 1989.

Rosenblatt, Roger. *Life Itself: Abortion in the American Mind.* New York: Random House, 1992.

Staggenborg, Suzanne. *The Pro-Choice Movement: Organization and Activism in the Abortion Conflict.* New York: Oxford University Press, 1991.

Tribe, Laurence H. *Abortion: The Clash of Absolutes.* New York: Norton, 1990.

AFRICAN AMERICANS AND CIVIL RIGHTS

Carson, Clayborne. *In Struggle: SNCC and the Black Awakening of the 1960s.* Cambridge, Mass.: Harvard University Press, 1981.

Carter, Dan T. *The Politics of Rage: George Wallace, the Origins of the New Conservatism, and the Transformation of American Politics.* New York: Simon & Schuster, 1995.

Conot, Robert E. *Rivers of Blood: Years of Darkness.* New York: Bantam Books, 1967.

Dittmer, John. *Local People: The Struggle for Civil Rights in Mississippi.* Urbana: University of Illinois Press, 1994.

Fairclough, Adam. *To Redeem the Soul of America: The Southern Christian Leadership Conference and Martin Luther King, Jr.* Athens: University of Georgia Press, 1987.

Lemann, Nicholas. *The Promised Land: The Great Black Migration and How It Changed America.* New York: Knopf, 1991.

Mills, Kay. *This Little Light of Mine: The Life of Fanny Lou Hamer.* New York: Dutton, 1993.

Morris, Aldon D. *The Origins of the Civil Rights Movement: Black Communities Organizing for Change.* New York: Free Press, 1984.

Powledge, Fred. *Free at Last? The Civil Rights Movement and the People Who Made It.* Boston: Little, Brown, 1991.

Sikora, Frank. *Until Justice Rolls Down: The Birmingham Church Bombing Case.* Tuscaloosa: University of Alabama Press, 1991.

Sitkoff, Harvard. *The Struggle for Black Equality, 1954–1992.* New York: Hill and Wang, 1993.

Whalen, Charles, and Barbara Whalen. *The Longest Debate: A Legislative History of the 1964 Civil Rights Act.* Washington, D.C.: Seven Locks Press, 1985.

AGING AND SENIOR CITIZENS

Achenbaum, W. Andrew. *Old Age in the New Land: The American Experience since 1790.* Baltimore: Johns Hopkins University Press, 1978.

Fischer, David Hackett. *Growing Old in America.* New York: Oxford University Press, 1977.

Haber, Carolyn. *Old Age and the Search for Security: An American Social History.* Bloomington: Indiana University Press, 1993.

Mendelson, Mary Adelaide. *Tender Loving Greed: How the Incredibly Lucrative Nursing Home "Industry" Is Exploiting America's Old People and Defrauding Us All.* New York: Knopf, 1974.

Shield, Renee Rose. *Uneasy Endings: Daily Life in an American Nursing Home.* Ithaca, N.Y.: Cornell University Press, 1988.

AIDS

Altman, Dennis. *AIDS in the Mind of America.* Garden City, N.Y.: Anchor Press/Doubleday, 1986.

Bayer, Ronald. *Private Acts, Social Consequences: AIDS and the Politics of Public Health.* New York: Free Press, 1989.

ARTS AND HUMANITIES

Biddle, Livingston. *Our Government and the Arts: A Perspective from the Inside.* New York: ACA Books, 1988.

ASIAN AMERICANS AND CIVIL RIGHTS

Gall, Susan, and Irene Natividad, eds. *The Asian-American Almanac: A Reference Work on Asians in the United States.* Detroit, Mich.: Gale Research, 1995.

Kitano, Harry H.L., and Roger Daniels. *Asian Americans: Emerging Minorities.* Englewood Cliffs, N.J.: Prentice-Hall, 1988.

O'Hare, William P., and Judy C. Felt. *Asian Americans: American's Fastest Growing Minority Group.* Washington, D.C.: Population Reference Bureau, 1991.

CITIES AND SUBURBIA

Herbers, John. *The New Heartland: American's Flight beyond the Suburbs and How It Is Changing Our Future.* New York: Times Books, 1986.

CONSUMERS

Berman, Ronald. *Advertising and Social Change.* Beverly Hills, Calif.: Sage Publications, 1981.

Boorstin, Daniel J. *Democracy and Its Discontents: Reflections on Everyday America.* New York: Random House, 1974.

Gruen, Victor, and Larry Smith. *Shopping Towns USA: The Planning of Shopping Centers.* New York: Reinhold Publishing, 1960.

Lebergott, Stanley. *Pursuing Happiness: American Consumers in the Twentieth Century.* Princeton, N.J.: Princeton University Press, 1993.

Mandell, Lewis. *The Credit Card Industry: A History.* Boston: Twayne Publishers, 1990.

McCarry, Charles. *Citizen Nader.* New York: Saturday Review Press, 1972.

Redstone, Louis G. *New Dimensions in Shopping Centers and Stores.* New York: McGraw-Hill, 1973.

Savan, Leslie. *The Sponsored Life: Ads, TV, and American Culture.* Philadelphia: Temple University Press, 1994.

Shields, Rob, ed. *Lifestyle Shopping: The Subject of Consumption.* New York: Routledge, 1992.

Vance, Sandra S., and Roy V. Scott. *Wal-Mart: A History of Sam Walton's Retail Phenomenon, 1962–1992.* New York: Twayne Publishers, 1994.

Walton, Sam, with John Huey. *Sam Walton, Made in America.* New York: Doubleday, 1992.

COUNTERCULTURE

Fairfield, Richard. *Communes USA: A Personal Tour.* Baltimore: Penguin Books, 1972.

Hedgepeth, William. *The Alternative: Communal Life in New America.* New York: Macmillan, 1970.

Melville, Keith. *Communes in the Counter Culture: Origins, Theories, Styles of Life.* New York: Morrow, 1972.

Miller, Timothy. *The Hippies and American Values.* Knoxville: University of Tennessee Press, 1991.

Roberts, Ron E. *The New Communes.* Englewood Cliffs, N.J.: Prentice-Hall, 1971.

CRIME AND VIOLENCE

Davey, Joseph Dillon. *The New Social Contract: American's Journey from Welfare State to Police State.* Westport, Conn.: Praeger, 1995.

Oatman, Eric F., ed. *Crime and Society.* New York: H.W. Wilson Company, 1979.

CULTURAL CONFLICT

Hunter, James Davison. *Culture Wars: The Struggle to Define America.* New York: Basic Books, 1991.

EATING AND DRINKING

Clark, Walter B., and Michael E. Hilton, eds. *Alcohol in America: Drinking Practices and Problems.* Albany: State University of New York Press, 1991.

Cross, Jennifer. *The Supermarket Trap: The Consumer and the Food Industry,* rev. and enl. ed. Bloomington: Indiana University Press, 1976.

Farb, Peter, and George Armelagos. *Consuming Passions: The Anthropology of Eating.* Boston: Houghton-Mifflin, 1980.

Lender, Mark E., and James Kirby Martin. *Drinking in America: A History.* New York: Free Press, 1982.

Levenstein, Harvey. *Paradox of Plenty: A Social History of Eating in Modern America.* New York: Oxford University Press, 1993.

Packard, Vernal S., Jr. *Processed Foods and the Consumer: Additives, Labeling, Standards, and Nutrition.* Minneapolis: University of Minnesota Press, 1976.

ECONOMIC CONDITIONS

Boris, Eileen. *Home to Work: Motherhood and the Politics of Industrial Homework in the United States.* New York: Cambridge University Press, 1994.

Davidson, Osha Gray. *Broken Heartland: The Rise of American's Rural Ghetto.* New York: Free Press, 1990.

Ehrenreich, Barbara. *The Worst Years of Our Lives: Irreverent Notes from a Decade of Greed.* New York: Pantheon Books, 1990.

Evans, Sara, and Barbara J. Nelson. *Wage Justice: Comparable Worth and the Paradox of Technocratic Reform.* Chicago, Ill.: University of Chicago Press, 1989.

Newman, Katherine. *Declining Fortunes: The Withering of the American Dream.* New York: Basic Books, 1993.

———. *Falling from Grace: The Experience of Downward Mobility in the American Middle Class.* New York: Free Press, 1988.

Phillips, Kevin. *The Politics of Rich and Poor: Wealth and the American Electorate in the Reagan Aftermath.* New York: Random House, 1990.

Rae, John Bell. *The American Automobile Industry.* Boston: Twayne Publishers, 1984.

Sale, Kirkpatrick. *Human Scale.* New York: Coward, McCann & Geoghegan, 1980.

Shostak, Arthur B., and William Gomberg, eds. *Blue-Collar World: Studies of the American Workers.* Englewood Cliffs, N.J.: Prentice-Hall, 1964.

Sorenson, Elaine. *Comparable Worth: Is It a Worthy Policy?* Princeton, N.J.: Princeton University Press, 1994.

EDUCATION

American Association of School Administrators, Commission on School Administration in Newly Reorganized Districts. *School Administration in Newly*

Reorganized Districts. Washington, D.C.: American Association of School Administrators, 1965.

Cohen, Arthur M., and Florence B. Brawer. *The American Community College.* San Francisco: Jossey-Bass, 1982.

Dennison, George. *The Lives of Children: The Story of the First Street School.* New York: Random House, 1969.

Diener, Thomas. *Growth of an American Invention: A Documentary History of the Junior and Community College Movement.* Westport, Conn.: Greenwood Press, 1986.

Gearhart, Bill R., and Mel W. Weishahn. *The Handicapped Child in the Regular Classroom.* St. Louis: Mosby, 1976.

Kohl, Herbert R. *The Open Classroom: A Practical Guide to a New Way of Teaching.* New York: Vintage Books, 1970.

Lipset, Seymour Martin, and Sheldon S. Wolin. *The Berkeley Student Revolt: Facts and Interpretations.* Garden City, N.Y.: Anchor Books, 1965.

Madaus, George F., Thomas Kellaghan, and Richard L. Schwab. *Teach Them Well: An Introduction to Education.* New York: Harper & Row, 1989.

Peshkin, Alan. *God's Choice: The Total World of a Fundamentalist Christian School.* Chicago: University of Chicago Press, 1986.

———. *Growing Up American: Schooling and the Survival of Community.* Chicago: University of Chicago Press, 1978.

———. *The Imperfect Union: School Consolidation and Community Conflict.* Chicago: University of Chicago Press, 1982.

Sigman, S.B., ed. *Critical Voices on Special Education.* Albany: State University of New York Press, 1990.

Silberman, Charles. *Crisis in the Classroom: The Remaking of American Education.* New York: Random House, 1970.

Tyack, David B., and Elisabeth Hansot. *Managers of Virtue: Public School Leadership in America, 1920–1980.* New York: Basic Books, 1982.

Winzer, Margaret A. *The History of Special Education: From Isolation to Integration.* Washington, D.C.: Gallaudet University Press, 1993.

ENVIRONMENT

Bailey, Ronald, ed. *The True State of the Planet.* New York: Free Press, 1995.

Blumberg, Louis, and Robert Gottlieb. *War on Waste: Can America Win Its Battle with Garbage?* Washington, D.C.: Island Press, 1989.

Commoner, Barry. *Making Peace with the Planet.* New York: Pantheon Books, 1990.

Ehrlich, Paul. *The Population Bomb.* New York: Ballantine Books, 1968.

Gottlieb, Robert. *Forcing the Spring: The Transformation of the American Environmental Movement.* Washington, D.C.: Island Press, 1993.

Rathje, William L. *Rubbish! The Archaeology of Garbage.* New York: HarperCollins, 1992.

Rubin, Charles T. *The Green Crusade: Rethinking the Roots of Environmentalism.* New York: Free Press, 1994.

Shabecoff, Philip. *A Fierce Green Fire: The American Environmental Movement.* New York: Hill and Wang, 1993.

FAMILY-RELATED MATTERS

Bane, Mary Jo. *Here to Stay: American Families in the Twentieth Century.* New York: Basic Books, 1976.

Blankenhorn, David, Steven Bayme, and Jean Bethke Elshtain, eds. *Rebuilding the Nest: A New Commitment to the American Family.* Milwaukee: Family Service America, 1990.

Buunk, Bram, and Barry van Driel. *Variant Lifestyles and Relationships.* Newbury Park, Calif.: Sage Publications, 1989.

Cherlin, Andrew J. *Marriage, Divorce, Remarriage,* rev. and enl. ed. Cambridge, Mass.: Harvard University Press, 1992.

———, ed. *The Changing American Family and Public Policy.* Washington, D.C.: Urban Institute Press, 1988.

Coontz, Stephanie. *The Way We Never Were: American Families and the Nostalgia Trap.* New York: Basic Books, 1992.

Degler, Carl. *At Odds: Women and the Family in America from the Revolution to the Present.* New York: Oxford University Press, 1980.

Goldscheider, Frances K., and Linda J. Waite. *New Families, No Families? The Transformation of the American Home.* Berkeley: University of California Press, 1991.

Hayes, Cheryl D., and Sheila Kamerman, eds. *Children of Working Parents: Experiences and Outcomes.* Washington, D.C.: National Academy Press, 1983.

Hayes, Cheryl D., John L. Palmer, and Martha J. Zaslow, eds. *Who Cares for American's Children: Child Care Policy for the 1990s.* Washington, D.C.: National Academy Press, 1990.

Hewlett, Sylvia. *When the Bough Breaks: The Cost of Neglecting Our Children.* New York: Basic Books, 1991.

Jacobs, Herbert. *Silent Revolution: The Transformation of Divorce Law in the United States.* Chicago: University of Chicago Press, 1988.

Kamerman, Sheila, and Cheryl Hayes, eds. *Families That Work: Children in a Changing World.* Washington, D.C.: National Academy Press, 1982.

Levitan, Sar A., Richard S. Belous, and Frank Gallo. *What's Happening to the American Family? Tensions, Hopes, Realities,* rev. ed. Baltimore: Johns Hopkins University Press, 1988.

Masnick, George, and Mary Jo Bane. *The Nation's Families, 1960–1990.* Boston: Auburn House, 1980.

Polakow, Valerie. *Lives on the Edge: Single Mothers and Their Children in the Other America.* Chicago: University of Chicago Press, 1993.

Popenoe, David. *Disturbing the Nest: Family Change and Decline in Modern Societies.* New York: A. de Gruyter, 1988.

Riley, Glenda. *Divorce: An American Tradition.* New York: Oxford University Press, 1991.

Skolnick, Arlene S. *Embattled Paradise: The American Family in an Age of Uncertainty.* New York: Basic Books, 1991.

Stacey, Judith. *Brave New Families: Stories of Domestic Upheaval in Late Twentieth Century America.* New York: Basic Books, 1990.

FASHION

Lister, Margot. *Costumes of Everyday Life: An Illustrated History of Working Clothes.* Boston: Plays, Inc., 1972.
O'Hara, Georgina. *The Encyclopedia of Fashion.* New York: H.N. Abrams, 1986.
Wilson, Elizabeth. *Adorned in Dreams: Fashion and Modernity.* Berkeley: University of California Press, 1987.

HEALTH AND HEALTH INSURANCE

Bruch, Hilde. *The Golden Cage: The Enigma of Anorexia Nervosa.* New York: Vintage Books, 1979.
Brumberg, Joan Jacobs. *Fasting Girls: The Emergence of Anorexia Nervosa as a Modern Disease.* Cambridge, Mass.: Harvard University Press, 1988.
Hsu, L.K. George. *Eating Disorders.* New York: Guilford Press, 1990.
Marmor, Theodore R. *The Politics of Medicare.* Chicago: Aldine, 1973.
Oster, Gerry, Graham A. Colditz, and Nancy L. Kelly. *The Economic Costs of Smoking and Benefits of Quitting.* Lexington, Mass.: Lexington Books, 1984.

HISPANICS AND CIVIL RIGHTS

Dunne, John Gregory. *Delano, the Story of the California Grape Strike.* New York: Farrar, Straus & Giroux, 1967.
Jiménez, Alfredo. *Handbook of Hispanic Cultures in the United States: History.* Houston: Arte Publico Press, 1993.
Kanellos, Nicolás. *The Hispanic-American Almanac: A Reference Work on Hispanics in the United States.* Detroit: Gale Research, 1993.
Reddy, Marlita A., ed. *Statistical Record of Hispanic Americans.* Detroit: Gale Research, 1993.
Steiner, Stan. *LaRaza: The Mexican Americans.* New York: Harper & Row, 1970.

LEISURE AND SPORTS

Roberts, Randy.*Winning Is the Only Thing: Sports in America since 1945.* Baltimore: Johns Hopkins University Press, 1989.
Rybczynski, Witold. *Waiting for the Weekend.* New York: Viking, 1991.

MOVIES

Jowett, Garth, and James M. Linton. *Movies as Mass Communication.* Beverly Hills, Calif.: Sage Publications, 1980.

NATIVE AMERICANS AND CIVIL RIGHTS

Cornell, Stephen E. *The Return of the Native: American Indian Political Resurgence.* New York: Oxford University Press, 1988.

Deloria, Vine, Jr. *Custer Died for Your Sins: An Indian Manifesto*. New York: Macmillan, 1969; Norman: University of Oklahoma Press, 1988.

Josephy, Alvin, Jr. *Now That the Buffalo's Gone: A Study of Today's American Indians*. New York: Knopf, 1982.

Reddy, Marlita A., ed. *Statistical Record of Native North Americans*. Detroit, Mich.: Gale Research, 1993.

Steiner, Stan. *The New Indians*. New York: Harper & Row, 1969.

POSTMODERNISM

Gergen, Kenneth. *The Saturated Self: Dilemmas of Identity in Contemporary Life*. New York: Basic Books, 1991.

Harvey, David. *The Condition of Postmodernity: An Enquiry into the Origins of Cultural Change*. Oxford, England: Blackwell, 1989.

Jencks, Charles. *What Is Post-modernism?* 3rd rev., enl. ed. New York: St. Martin's Press, 1989.

McGowan, John. *Postmodernism and Its Critics*. Ithaca, NY: Cornell University Press, 1991.

Pangle, Thomas. *The Ennobling of Democracy: The Challenge of the Postmodern Era*. Baltimore: Johns Hopkins University Press, 1992.

Rosenau, Pauline Marie. *Post-Modernism and the Social Sciences: Insights, Inroads, and Intrusions*. Princeton, N.J.: Princeton University Press, 1992.

RELIGION

Ammerman, Nancy Tatom. *Bible Believers: Fundamentalists in the Modern World*. New Brunswick, N.J.: Rutgers University Press, 1987.

Balmer, Randall. *Mine Eyes Have Seen the Glory: A Journey into the Evangelical Subculture in America*. New York: Oxford University Press, 1989.

Carroll, Jackson W., Douglas W. Johnson, and Martin E. Marty. *Religion in America, 1950 to the Present*. San Francisco: Harper & Row, 1979.

Flowers, Ronald B. *Religion in Strange Times: The 1960s and 1970s*. Macon, GA: Mercer University Press, 1984.

Lienesch, Michael. *Redeeming America: Piety and Politics in the New Christian Right*. Chapel Hill: University of North Carolina Press, 1993.

Marty, Martin E. *A Nation of Behavers*. Chicago: University of Chicago Press, 1976.

———. *Pilgrims in Their Own Land: 500 Years of Religion in America*. Boston: Little, Brown, 1984.

———. *Righteous Empire: The Protestant Experience in America*. New York: Harper & Row, 1970, 1977.

Marty, Martin E., and R. Scott Appleby. *The Glory and the Power: The Fundamentalist Challenge to the Modern World*. Boston: Beacon Press, 1992.

ROCK MUSIC

Chapple, Steve, and Reebee Garofalo. *Rock 'n' Roll Is Here to Pay: The History and Politics of the Music Industry*. Chicago: Nelson-Hall, 1977.

DeCurtis, Anthony, and James Henke, eds. *The Rolling Stone Illustrated History of Rock & Roll: The Definitive History of the Most Important Artists and Their Music*. New York: Random House, 1992.

Frith, Simon. *Sound Effects: Youth, Leisure, and the Politics of Rock 'n' Roll*. New York: Pantheon Books, 1981.

Hardy, Phil, and Dave Laing. *Encyclopedia of Rock*, rev. ed. New York: Schirmer, 1988.

Pattison, Robert. *The Triumph of Vulgarity: Rock Music in the Mirror of Romanticism*. New York: Oxford University Press, 1987.

Podell, Janet. *Rock Music in America*. New York: H.W. Wilson, 1987.

Romanowski, Patricia, and Holly George-Warren, eds. *The New Rolling Stone Encyclopedia of Rock & Roll*. New York: Fireside Press, 1995.

SCIENCE AND TECHNOLOGY

Boorstin, Daniel J. *The Republic of Technology: Reflections on Our Future Community*. New York: Harper & Row, 1978.

Kennan, Erlend. *Mission to the Moon: A Critical Examination of NASA and the Space Program*. New York: Morrow, 1969.

Norman, Colin. *The God That Limps: Science and Technology in the 1980s*. New York: W.W. Norton, 1981.

Ordway, Frederick I., III, Carabie C. Adams, and Mitchell R. Sharpe. *Dividends from Space*. New York: Crowell, 1972.

Postman, Neil. *Technopoly: The Surrender of Culture to Technology*. New York: Knopf, 1992.

Rae, John Bell. *The American Automobile Industry*. Boston: Twayne Publishers, 1984.

Segal, Howard P. *Future Imperfect: The Mixed Blessings of Technology in America*. Amherst: University of Massachusetts Press, 1994.

Tenner, Edward. *Why Things Bite Back: Technology and the Revenge of Unintended Consequences*. New York: Knopf, 1996.

Watkins, Bruce O. *Technology and Human Values: Collision and Solution*. Ann Arbor, Mich.: Ann Arbor Science Publishers, 1977.

Williams, Trevor I., ed. *Science: A History of Discovery in the Twentieth Century*. New York: Oxford University Press, 1990.

SEX AND HOMOSEXUALITY

Adam, Barry D. *The Rise of a Gay and Lesbian Movement*. Boston: Twayne Publishers, 1987.

D'Emilio, John. *Sexual Politics, Sexual Communities: The Making of a Homosexual Minority in the United States, 1940–1970*. Chicago: University of Chicago Press, 1983.

D'Emilio, John, and Estelle B. Freedman. *Intimate Matters: A History of Sexuality in America*. New York: Harper & Row, 1988.

Duberman, Martin. *Stonewall*. New York: Dutton, 1993.

Greenberg, David. *The Construction of Homosexuality.* Chicago: University of Chicago Press, 1988.

Katz, Jonathan. *Gay American History: Lesbians and Gay Men in the U.S.A.: A Documentary.* New York: Harper & Row, 1976, 1985.

Mohr, Richard. *Gays/Justice: A Study of Ethics, Society, and Law.* New York: Columbia University Press, 1988.

SOCIAL POLICY

Berkowitz, Edward D. *America's Welfare State: From Roosevelt to Reagan.* Baltimore, Md.: Johns Hopkins University Press, 1991.

Berkowitz, Edward D., and Kim McQuaid. *Creating the Welfare State: The Political Economy of Twentieth-Century Reform.* Lawrence: University of Kansas Press, 1992.

TELEVISION

Adler, Richard, ed. *Understanding Television: Essays on TV as a Social and Cultural Force.* New York: Praeger, 1981.

Altschuler, Glenn C., and David I. Grossvogel. *Changing Channels: America in TV Guide.* Urbana: University of Illinois Press, 1992.

Barnouw, Erik. *Tube of Plenty: The Evolution of American Television*, 2d ed. New York: Oxford University Press, 1990.

Bower, Robert T. *The Changing Television Audience in America.* New York: Columbia University Press, 1985.

———. *Television and the Public.* New York: Holt, Rinehart and Winston, 1973.

Cantor, Muriel. *Prime Time Television: Content and Control.* Beverly Hills, Calif.: Sage Publications, 1980.

Comstock, George A. *Television and Human Behavior: The Key Studies.* Santa Monica, Calif.: Rand, 1975.

Kaplan, E. Ann. *Rocking around the Clock: Music Television, Postmodernism, and Consumer Cultures.* New York: Methuen, 1987.

MacDonald, J. Fred. *One Nation under Television: The Rise and Decline of Network TV.* New York: Pantheon Books, 1990.

Postman, Neil. *How to Watch TV News.* New York: Penguin Books, 1992.

Rader, Benjamin G. *In Its Own Image: How Television Has Transformed Sports.* New York: Free Press, 1984.

Sklar, Robert. *Prime-time America: Life on and behind the Television Screen.* New York: Oxford University Press, 1980.

Spigel, Lynn. *Make Room for TV: Television and the Family Ideal in Postwar America.* Chicago: University of Chicago Press, 1992.

UNDERCLASS

Auletta, Ken. *The Underclass.* New York: Random House, 1982.

Wilson, William Julius. *The Truly Disadvantaged: The Inner City, the Underclass, and Public Policy.* Chicago: University of Chicago Press, 1987.

VIETNAM WAR AND ANTIWAR PROTEST

Arlen, Michael J. *Living-Room War*. New York: Viking Press, 1969.
Baritz, Loren. *Backfire: A History of How American Culture Led Us into Vietnam and Made Us Fight the Way We Did*. New York: W. Morrow, 1985.
Berman, Larry. *Planning a Tragedy: The Americanization of the War in Vietnam*. New York: Norton, 1982.
DeBenedetti, Charles. *An American Ordeal: The Antiwar Movement of the Vietnam Era*. Syracuse, N.Y.: Syracuse University Press, 1990.
Dougan, Clark, Stephen Weiss, and the editors of Boston Publishing Company. *The American Experience in Vietnam*. New York: Norton, 1988.
Emerson, Gloria. *Winners and Losers: Battles, Retreats, Gains, Losses, and Ruins from a Long War*. New York: Random House, 1976.
Lifton, Robert J. *Home from War: Vietnam Veterans: Neither Victims nor Executioners*. New York: Simon & Schuster, 1973.
McQuaid, Kim. *The Anxious Years: America in the Vietnam-Watergate Era*. New York: Basic Books, 1989.
Michener, James A. *Kent State: What Happened and Why*. New York: Random House, 1971.
Olson, James S., and Randy Roberts. *Where the Domino Fell: America and Vietnam, 1945–1990*. New York: St. Martin's Press, 1991.
Powers, Thomas. *The War at Home: Vietnam and the American People, 1964–1968*. New York: Grossman Publishers, 1973.
Timberg, Robert. *The Nightingale's Song*. New York: Simon & Schuster, 1995.
Young, Marilyn. *The Vietnam Wars, 1945–1990*. New York: HarperCollins, 1991.

WHITE ETHNICS AND CIVIL RIGHTS

Novak, Michael. *The Rise of the Unmeltable Ethnics: Politics and Culture in the 1970s*. New York: Macmillan, 1972.

WOMEN AND WOMEN'S RIGHTS

Aaron, Henry J., and Cameran Lougy. *The Comparable Worth Controversy*. Washington, D.C.: Brookings Institute, 1986.
Chafe, William H. *The Paradox of Change: American Women in the 20th Century*. New York: Oxford University Press, 1991.
Cowan, Ruth Schwartz. *More Work for Mother: The Ironies of Household Technology from the Open Hearth to the Microwave*. New York: Basic Books, 1983.
Evans, Sara. *Personal Politics: The Roots of Women's Liberation in the Civil Rights Movement and the New Left*. New York: Vintage Books, 1980.
Faludi, Susan. *Backlash: The Undeclared War against Women*. New York: Crown, 1991.
Gilligan, Carol. *In a Different Voice: Psychological Theory and Women's Development*. Cambridge, Mass.: Harvard University Press, 1982.
Hewlett, Sylvia. *A Lesser Life: The Myth of Women's Liberation in America*. New York: Morrow, 1986.

Olson, Kristin. *Chronology of Women's History*. Westport, Conn.: Greenwood Press, 1994.

Wandersee, Winifred. *On the Move: American Women in the 1970s*. Boston: Twayne Publishers, 1988.

Index

tion, 315; environment, 203, 314; fashions, 292; Federal Communication Commission (FCC), 277; illegal aliens, 259–60; inaugural address, 268; mandatory drug testing, 301; nuclear power, 316–17; President's Commission for the Study of Ethical Problems in Medicine and Biomedical and Behavioral Research, 305; recognition of Vatican, 318; school desegregation, 256; school prayer, 320; underclass, 257–58

Recording Industry Association of America, 211, 283

Redistricting, 256

Red Skelton, 6, 116

Reich, Charles, xvi–xvii

Religion, 52–56, 74, 169–73, 230–33, 317. *See also* Polls, Gallup; Polls, Harris; *individual church bodies and persons*

Reorganized Church of Jesus Christ of Latter Day Saints (RLDS), 318

Republican Party, 13–14; Republicans, 19, 110, 257

Research Triangle Institute (RIT), 300

Reservists, military, 265

Retin-A (tetrinoin), 293

Retton, Mary Lou, 288

Reuther, Walter, 90

"Revenue sharing," 104

Rh factor, 62

Richmond, Julius B., 217

Ride, Sally, 260

Riesman, David, 70

Ripon Society, 110

The Rise of the Unmeltable Ethnics, 92

Ritalin, 297

Roberts, John, 121

Roberts, Oral, 232, 319

Robertson, Pat, 232

Rock music. *See* Music, rock

Roe v. Wade, 85, 235–36, 323, 325

Rogaine (minoxidil), 293

Rollerblade, Inc., 213

Rolling Stone, 283

Rolling Stones, 69, 123, 211

Roman Catholic Church: abortion, 231, 324–25; birth control, 54, 67, 319; changes, 230–31; church practices, 54; discord, 319; Vatican, 318; Vatican Council, Second, 53–55, 173, 230–31. *See also individual popes*

Romper Room, 6

Roosevelt, Franklin Delano, 46

Root, Waverly, 37

Roots, 207–8

Roseanne, 279

Rosenman, Joel, 121

Roszak, Theodore, 125

Rowan and Martin's Laugh-In, 116

Running, 38, 123–24, 213, 288; running shoes, 38

Safe Drinking Water Act (1974), 144

"Safe sex," 299

St. Louis Globe-Democrat, 280

Sale, Kirkpatrick, 144

Samuelson, Robert J., 331, 333–34

Sanders, Linda, 285

Sanford and Son, 206

San Francisco State University, 165

Saturday Evening Post, 167

Saturday Night Fever, 211

Saturday Night Live, 207

Savings and loan associations (S&Ls), 273–74

Savio, Mario, 22

Sayre, Francis B., 111

Schirra, Walter, 60–61

Schlafly, Phyllis, 234, 262

Scholastic Aptitude Tests (SAT), 228–29, 309

Schools, elementary and secondary, 159–65, 226–29; controversies and criticisms, 159, 163–64, 226, 311; desegregation, 11, 89, 160–62, 188, 311; district reorganization, 162–63; Elementary and Secondary Education Act (1965), 45–46, 164; *Engel v. Vitale* (1962), 55; enrollment, 228; federal funding of, 312; federal involvement in, 164–65, 228; funding problems, 160, 226, 310–12; mainstreaming, 194; *A Nation at Risk*, 309–11; "New Basics," 310;

About the Author

MYRON A. MARTY is the Ann G. and Sigurd E. Anderson University Professor and Professor of History at Drake University. His other works include *Nearby History: Exploring the Past Around You* (1982); *Your Family History: A Handbook for Research and Writing* (1978); *Retracing Our Steps: Studies in Documents from the American Past* (1972); and *Lutherans and Roman Catholicism: The Changing Conflict: 1917–1963* (1968).